PLANTING HEALTHY CHURCHES

Gary Teja & John Wagenveld

EDITORS

multiplication
network

more churches, stronger churches

Published by:
MULTIPLICATION NETWORK MINISTRIES (MNM)
22515 Torrence Ave., Sauk Village, IL 60411, USA
www.multiplicationnetwork.org
708-414-1050

PLANTING HEALTHY CHURCHES

© 2015 Gary Teja and John Wagenveld

PRINTED IN THE UNITED STATES OF AMERICA

Cover artwork by Rachel Fontaine Morris
Cover and layout design by Libby Dykstra

TABLE OF CONTENTS

INTRODUCTION

Planting Healthy Churches is both an academic textbook and a course. It is provided by Multiplication Network Ministries (MNM) as a free resource for Bible colleges and seminaries. The textbook, prepared by nine contributors from different denominations and written at an introductory level, is the center-piece of a church planting course. The authors write with church planting experience in different countries and with a background in training and teaching thousands of students and church planters. Together with the textbook, MNM is also providing PowerPoints, and a whole suite of practical training manuals for those desiring to move from the academic to the practical. These resources are downloadable at no cost from www.multiplicationnetwork.org.

This free digital textbook has been a labor of love intended to bless the Church at large. It took two years to produce. About half the book includes some expanded and revised material from a similar book in Spanish, *Sembremos Iglesias Saludables (Let's Plant Healthy Churches: FLET, Miami, ed. John Wagenveld)* that has been used and tested for a decade in Latin America and Spain. Suggestions for improving any future editions of this textbook or accompanying helps can be sent to the editors or www.multiplicationnetwork. org. All suggestions will be gratefully received.

A foundational premise of this work is that the world needs more churches and stronger churches that bear witness to the coming Kingdom of God. Planting churches is not only a biblical task, but also a very strategic one as the Church participates with the Holy Spirit in God's work of renewing all things in Jesus Christ for the Glory of God. In Isaiah 65 and Revelation 21 we note that God's end vision is nothing less than a new heaven and a new earth. Through church planting the new communities of faith become an instrument, sign and foretaste of the Kingdom of God as a demonstration plot of faith, hope, and love of Christ's sovereign and redemptive reign over all creation. Its mission is to faithfully participate with God as ambassadors of the Kingdom to promote the kind of transformation that only He can bring and the world so desperately needs.

For the edification of the Church.
For the sake of the world.
For the Glory of God!

Editors:
Gary Teja, Ph.D.
John Wagenveld, D.Min.
©Multiplication Network Ministries, 2014

WHAT IS CHURCH PLANTING?
DEFINITION, JUSTIFICATION, AND OBJECTIONS

Daniel Sánchez

A Great Commission Perspective

More churches are being planted around the world today than at any other time in the history of Christianity. In his book *Church Planting Movements*, Dr. David Garrison was already sharing surprising statistics about the expansion of the gospel and the success of church planting in countries like China and India and even in Muslim areas.[1] Since then even more church planting has been taken place. We thank God for what is happening, but we are also aware that the world's population is growing quickly and there are many groups throughout the world who have not heard the gospel. Even in countries where the gospel has been preached for years, there are many communities that do not have evangelical churches.

Despite these facts, there are people who are not convinced that we need to plant churches. One of the reasons for the lack of enthusiasm about planting churches is that many people, including church leaders, do not have a clear concept of what the church is and its mission in the world. To address this problem, we begin this chapter by defining what we consider church planting to be. Then we focus our attention on the reasons we should plant churches.

1   David Garrison, *Church Planting Movements: How God is Redeeming a Lost World.*

Finally, we present a number of objections that we may hear when we attempt to plant churches, and how we can answer them.

I. Description of the Church

The meaning of the phrase "church planting" seems so clear that it shouldn't need to be defined. Planting churches means simply establishing new congregations of believers in Christ. Most people do not have a problem in understanding this concept. What is needed is an explanation of the type of churches to be planted and how they are going to be established.

When talking about the type of church to be established, we first need to define the word church. One of the reasons that some people do not understand the expression "church planting" is that they do not understand the biblical concept of the church. For many people, the word church refers to a building. When they say, "We're going to church," they are referring to the building where the congregation meets. If church planting is mentioned, they think, "We don't have money to build more buildings; we're still trying to pay for the building we have now."

We need to see what the Bible says about the church. It doesn't give a clear and concise definition of the church: instead, we find a series of metaphors and a few models from which we can identify principles that are important in the life and ministry of a Christian church. In the New Testament the church is presented as the body of Christ (1 Cor. 10:16-17; Eph. 1:22-23), the congregation of saints (1 Cor. 1:9), the people of God (1 Pet. 2:9; Rom. 9:25), the priests of God (1 Pet. 2:9), and a living organism (1 Cor. 12:12-31), among other metaphors.

The New Testament also provides examples or models of churches. When studying the nature and the activities of the church in Jerusalem, we learn a lot about the functions of a Christian church. From Acts 2:40-47, we can conclude that a church is a group of believers who have responded to the message of the gospel (v. 41), have been baptized (v. 41), remain firm in the doctrine of the apostles (v. 42), share with others (v. 42), pray (v. 42), celebrate the Lord's Supper (v. 42), maintain unity (v. 44), minister to the needy (v. 45), meet together to praise God (v. 47), and share the message of salvation (v. 47). Note that this group of people who were converted after hearing the message preached by Peter was called the church from the beginning, even though they did not have their own building. They met in the temple in Jerusalem, while this was permitted, as well as in their homes (v. 47; also Rom. 16:5), in meeting rooms (Acts 20:8), and in schools (Acts 19:9).

The church in Antioch was formed by a group of refugee Christians who had fled from persecution in Jerusalem (Acts 11:19-26). This church should be admired because they not only reached their own cultural group, the Jews (v. 19), but also extended their ministry to reach another cultural group, the Greeks (v. 20); sent missionaries to reach the world (Acts 13:1-3); helped their sister churches (Acts 11:27-30); and cooperated with their sister churches (Acts 15). The model of the Antioch church challenges today's churches. This church understood Jesus' deep desire to reach all cultural groups and subcultures with the gospel. First, they did all they could to reach their own cultural group; then they reached the Greeks that lived in the city; then they sent missionaries to proclaim the message of salvation throughout the known world at that time. In Antioch we find the model of a church that strives to fulfill the Great Commission.

From the church of Jerusalem we can learn the essential functions of a New Testament church; from the Antioch church we can learn what is required for a church to fulfill the Great Commission. From their examples and the metaphors mentioned above, we conclude that a church is a congregation of believers in Christ that proclaims and lives the gospel, disciples believers, follows the teachings of the Bible, shares with their brothers and sisters, ministers to others, prays, worships, maintains unity, and strives to fulfill the Great Commission. In light of this description, we can say that a church can be a large or small group of believers, with or without a building, with leaders who have formal education or who do not, with very elaborate organizational structures or very simple ones. In other words, there are many types of churches, and we should not allow requirements that are not mentioned in the Bible to hinder the process of starting thousands of churches among the multitudes that do not know Christ. Church planting can be defined as the effort to bring together groups of people who believe in Christ so that they can be and function as the body of Christ in their community and can fulfill the Great Commission.

II. Reasons We Should Plant Churches

There are many reasons we should plant churches, some biblical and others practical or strategic. The biblical reasons are based on the purposes of the kingdom of God, on the Great Commission of our Lord Jesus Christ, and on Jesus' teachings about the people of God. The practical reasons are really an extension of the biblical reasons, because they are primarily applications of biblical principles. So, first, we will focus our attention on the biblical reasons for planting churches.

A. Biblical Reasons

New churches are more effective at making disciples.

One of the main reasons we should begin new churches is that this is the best way to fulfill the Great Commission. Jesus said, "All authority in heaven and on earth has been given to me. Therefore go and make disciples of all nations, baptizing them in the name of the Father and of the Son and of the Holy Spirit, and teaching them to obey everything I have commanded you. And surely I am with you always, to the very end of the age" (Matt. 28: 18-20). In the Greek text this passage has three gerunds: going, teaching, and baptizing. These are action words. The verb mathetusate, translated as "make disciples," is the imperative of this commission: Jesus commanded us to make disciples of the people of all nations. It is important to go where people are, to teach them the Word of God, and to baptize them. But the final goal is for people to become disciples dedicated to Jesus Christ. The most effective way to fulfill this command is to win people for Christ and to bring them together in churches where they can grow spiritually and obey all that Christ has commanded. We should plant churches because this is the most effective way of fulfilling the Great Commission.

New churches contribute to testifying to the kingdom of God.

A second reason to plant churches is that planting churches contributes to the extension of the mission of proclaiming God's kingdom. Jesus said, "The time has come. The kingdom of God is near. Repent and believe the good news!" (Mark 1:15). Jesus proclaimed the kingdom of God with his words and his actions. Although the incarnation of Jesus fulfilled the prophecies of the Old Testament, and in this sense the kingdom had come, nevertheless the consummation of the kingdom of God has not yet happened. During the present era, believers live out the kingdom of God (the dominion of God in their lives) in submission to the lordship of Christ.

How is the kingdom of God related to establishing new churches? These new churches are created through God's dynamic rule, which took shape with the coming of Jesus. New congregations participate in God's mission (missio dei) when they announce through word and deed God's sovereignty over all his creation. These new congregations have the opportunity to demonstrate the kingdom of God by living as a unique culture that questions the values and lifestyles of the society that surrounds it. We need many churches in many communities, churches that practice the teachings of the kingdom and that point others to it. New congregations contribute to testifying to the divine rule of God over the earth.

New churches contribute to the expansion of God's people.
A third reason we should plant more churches is that new churches contribute to the expansion of God's people. When new congregations are begun, there is an opportunity to include individuals and groups of people that have not previously identified with the gospel of Jesus Christ. When Paul mentions that the gospel is for both Jews and Greeks (Rom. 1:16), he is declaring that the gospel is universal. New congregations have the opportunity to include people who have been excluded in the past, whether intentionally or through neglect. When congregations are begun in new cultural and linguistic groups, there are opportunities to cross geographic and cultural barriers as mentioned in the Great Commission: "You will receive power when the Holy Spirit comes on you; and you will be my witnesses in Jerusalem, and in all Judea and Samaria, and to the ends of the earth" (Acts 1:8). When new congregations are established, groups that were once excluded or ignored can be reached with the gospel of Jesus Christ.

New churches proclaim a relevant message.
A fourth reason we should plant new churches is that new churches proclaim a message that is relevant to the culture surrounding them. The apostle Paul's missionary strategy took into account the great cultural, linguistic, philosophical, and religious diversity of the groups that he wanted to reach with the gospel. In the synagogue of Antioch, for example, Paul spoke to his Jewish audience about the patriarchs, prophets, and prophecies and presented Christ as the fulfillment of prophecy (Acts 13). In Athens, on the other hand,

Paul did not mention the Jewish patriarchs but rather talked about God as the creator of all humanity. There Paul used the example of the Athenians' "unknown god" to talk to the people about the true God (Acts 17). In 1 Corinthians 9:22b Paul says, "I have become all things to all men so that by all possible means I might save some." We can call Paul's missionary strategy the contextualization of the gospel. Given the great diversity of languages, cultures, lifestyles, and socioeconomic levels, it is not surprising that different groups of people may prefer very different styles of worship, communication, leadership, and preaching. When church planting takes into account the apostle Paul's strategy of contextualization, there is a greater response to the gospel and many people are won for Christ.

B. Practical Reasons

Besides the biblical reasons for planting churches, there are also practical reasons. These agree with the biblical principles related to the fulfillment of the Great Commission. Since we are commanded to preach the gospel to every creature and to make disciples of every cultural group, we should look for the most practical ways to fulfill this mandate.

The population is growing rapidly.
One practical reason that we should plant churches, even if there already are many churches in an area, is that the population continues to grow rapidly. There are communities in which the population has doubled or even tripled, but the number of churches has not grown. This means that if we do not begin new congregations, we will have fewer churches in proportion to the population than in the past. In time, the witness of the churches in our communities will become weaker rather than stronger.

New churches bring in more people than established churches.
A second reason we should plant new churches is that, in general, new churches bring more people to Christ and baptize more people than do churches that have been in existence for many years. Studies carried out by many denominations show that a large percentage of conversions and baptisms are due to the efforts of new churches. Professor Peter Wagner, an expert in church growth, affirms these results when he points out that without ex-

ception, the denominations that are growing are those that emphasize church planting.[2]

Established churches tend to become stagnant.

A third reason for planting new churches is that established churches tend to stagnate when they reach about ten years of age. This is due in part to the fact that over time they begin paying more attention to activities within the church building—meeting the members' needs—than to the task of winning the lost for Christ. Pastors may dedicate more time to preparing sermons and visiting church members than to training and guiding members in community evangelism efforts. The church's leaders and its organizations (Sunday school, the music program, women's and men's ministries) spend so much time in their activities that they do not have time for visiting people who do not belong to the church. As a result, the church becomes inward-focused and stops growing. In contrast, the leaders and members of new congregations are excited and motivated to win lost people for Christ and to involve them in the life of the church.

New churches can inspire established churches.

A fourth reason for establishing new churches is that they can inspire established churches. Many churches that have begun new congregations have experienced renewal. After watching their daughter churches grow, established churches have been filled with new enthusiasm and have broadened their vision for fulfilling the Great Commission. They have felt led to evangelize with more passion and have remembered their priorities with respect to discipleship. Like a family with a new baby, an established church feels new enthusiasm when they watch a daughter congregation begin and grow. When they hear the testimonies of new believers, the established church is filled with joy for being a part of an effort that has had an impact on the lives of many people.

Churches are needed where the lost people live.

A fifth reason we should plant new churches is that it is easier to win people if we begin a congregation where they live. There are many communities—sometimes entire populations—that do not have churches. The closer the churches are to people, the easier it will be to reach them with the gospel and disciple them.

---

2   Peter Wagner, *Church Planting for a Greater Harvest.*

Some time ago I heard the testimony of a young man. His father had been murdered because he was involved in drug trafficking. His mother and two brothers were in prison for the same reason. But one day a small church began meeting close to where this young man lived. There he heard the message of salvation, and his life changed completely. Today he is the director of the student missionary program at an evangelical university. It is painful to think about what could have happened in this man's life if that church had not begun meeting near his house. Because transportation can be so difficult and expensive in many cities, our goal should be to plant a church in every neighborhood so that people can walk to church if necessary.

New churches are more flexible.

A sixth reason to plant new churches is that they are more flexible and can adapt more rapidly to the needs of their communities. In general, established churches are satisfied with their worship style, education, evangelism, and leadership. This means that often they are not willing to change in order to attract new people or to make adjustments to reach new generations.

New churches develop leaders quickly.

Another reason to plant new churches is that new churches develop new leaders more quickly than established churches do. Established churches often have only a few of their members serving in leadership positions. In many cases it can take years for people to become Sunday school teachers or deacons or to take on other positions of responsibility. There are not enough positions for members to exercise their gifts. Members can grow accustomed to this situation and not develop their spiritual gifts or leadership abilities. When people have the opportunity to help start a new congregation, they can develop their gifts as leaders, and the number of responsible leaders grows.

Geographic proximity aids discipleship.

An eighth reason to begin new churches is that members participate more fully in a church's activities if they do not live far from the church's gathering place. In other words, the church's discipleship of members is affected by how far away they live. In general, those who live further away may attend only one service during the week, usually on Sunday morning or evening. These members often do not participate in other activities that would help them to grow spiritually, such as prayer meetings, social activities, or church ministries.

The closer the members live to the church, the greater their opportunity to participate in these activities.

While there are may be other reasons to plant new churches, these strong reasons motivate us to fulfill the Great Commission by starting new churches. They will help us as we start conversations with our own church leaders about planting churches, and as we spend time praying for the Lord's guidance in our decision to begin a new congregation.

III. Objections to Planting Churches and Responses

Although there are many biblical and practical reasons to begin new congregations, many people are not convinced that more churches need to be planted, or at least they do not feel compelled to participate in these efforts. Here are some common objections and our responses.

Starting new churches weakens established churches.

Some pastors, leaders, and members of established churches believe that helping to start a new congregation will weaken the existing congregation. They believe the result will be fewer members, fewer financial resources, fewer leaders, and less influence in the community for the established church.

Perhaps these people have forgotten the principle that Christ taught: he who sows generously will harvest generously. They believe that by concentrating on strengthening their congregation, they will be able to do more for the kingdom of God. What is certain is that a selfish attitude will produce a church with a limited vision and a ministry that never reaches its potential. On the other hand, a church with a broad vision (like that of the church in Antioch) will have a global impact and will contribute to the fulfillment of the Great Commission. Many pastors have testified that their churches have been refreshed as a result of establishing new congregations.

Some people argue that a congregation that isn't strong will be a poor or sickly mother church and therefore isn't ready for planting churches. However, planting churches may be just the cure for a weak church or a church that isn't getting enough exercise. Planting a church can strengthen the mother church.

Beginning new churches requires a large amount of resources.

It's likely that people who believe this statement think that starting a new church requires a building, a full-time pastor, all the equipment and materials, and a substantial budget. One question we must ask these people is, "Where do we find these requirements in the Bible?" As we mentioned in the introduction, the early church did not have buildings, professional leaders, or substantial financial resources. The first Christians simply proclaimed the gospel, met where they could find space (homes, schools, meeting rooms), and fulfilled the functions of a church. Today, churches are following this pattern in a marvelous way in China, India, Muslim countries, and many other parts of the world. People who think that it costs a lot to start new churches need to return to the New Testament model, concentrate on what is essential, and trust Christ—who promised to be with us until the end of the world—to provide the necessary means for the kingdom to expand through the planting of thousands of churches.

We will lose a lot of people.

Some pastors and church leaders believe that if they start new churches, they will lose a lot of members. Although it is true that some church planting models use a group of members to start a new congregation, we can make several observations. First, this is not the only church planting model. There are many strategies that do not require many members to leave. Second, even if this model is used, God can raise up new members for churches who "tithe" their members to begin another congregation. Many pastors have told how their churches have grown as a result of this investment. Their church planting efforts have resulted in a surge of new leaders and a renewed dedication to win people for Christ. Third, as we have said, it is impossible for a church to reach and retain all of the people in its community. Due to the great diversity of styles of leadership, worship, preaching, and decision making, there will be people who prefer a style different from the established church's style. If the members do not have a choice, they will look for alternatives. Sometimes when a church breaks up, it is an indication that members did not feel they had another option. Starting new churches gives people more options.

We already have a lot of needs.

"Our ministry already has many needs that take the pastor's time; we don't need more responsibilities." We should congratulate members for wanting to protect their pastor, but at the same time we need to challenge them: Who said that starting a church is only the pastor's job? This attitude reflects a philosophy that does not agree with the doctrine of the priesthood of all believers. Many lay people can and should be involved in the task of beginning new churches. We need to examine our priorities in the light of Scripture. Christ did not give the Great Commission only to the apostles, nor just to those who witnessed his ascension; he gave it to all who would become his disciples. Our priority should be the proclamation of the gospel and the discipling of new believers in congregations where they can grow and reproduce. Christ will always provide the means if we trust him and strive to fulfill his command.

We shouldn't force church planting.

There are people who believe that we shouldn't force the planting of a church in a new community. They believe that we should wait for the people of the community to tell us that they want a church there. Although it is true that we should treat people with respect and love, the most effective way to show our love is to guide people to know Christ as their Savior. When they come to know Christ, they will want to meet with other brothers and sisters in the faith to worship God, to encourage each other, and to share with their families and neighbors what they have received. Many missionaries in countries like China and India have testified that the first thing new believers want to do is to share their faith with their families and to meet with others who have had the same experience. We shouldn't worry that people may reject the idea of a church.

We won't be able to protect our doctrine.

Some well-intentioned religious leaders have expressed concern that if many new churches are established quickly, we won't be able to make sure that these new congregations teach the right things. This is an important concern. Nevertheless, establishing a large number of churches does not mean that new converts will fall into doctrinal error. Leaders who have witnessed the founding of thousands of house churches in China state that an effective discipleship program can prevent new believers from falling into doctrinal error. These church planters follow the example of the apostles, described in Acts: "Day after day, in the temple courts and from house to house, they never stopped teaching and proclaiming the good news that Jesus is the Christ" (Acts 5:42). The missionaries emphasize a discipleship that focuses on obeying the teachings of Jesus, and they say that the new believers are so focused on practicing what they learn and sharing what they learn with others that they don't have time to fall into doctrinal error.

Beginning new churches creates denominational competition.
Some people are against planting new churches because they believe it creates competition among churches of different denominations. They say that planting a church of another denomination in a community will weaken the established churches.

Others are concerned about competition among churches of the same denomination. They argue that it is better stewardship for denominations to plant churches in new communities rather than to have multiple churches in the same community. It is obvious that churches that are trying to reach the same groups of people using similar methods will be competing. However, church growth specialist Lyle E. Schaller, in his book *44 Questions for Church Planters*, explains that congregations benefit from denominational competition and that having two or more churches of the same denomination brings greater health and vitality to the congregations than if there were only one church of that denomination in the community.[3]

Another argument in favor of having several churches in a community is that many cities have people from different language, cultural, and socioeconomic groups. If it is clear that some of these groups are not being reached, new congregations that can adapt better to the cultures and lifestyles of these unreached groups may be more effective at reaching these groups than established churches can be.

One church for each city is the New Testament pattern.
A similar objection is based on the argument that there should only be one church in each city. People who believe this point out that the New Testament mentions only one church per city, such as the church in Jerusalem, the church in Corinth, the church in Ephesus, etc. Those who use this argument are often the pastors of the first church that their denomination established in their city, and they believe that planting more churches there will weaken the church that they pastor.

---

3   Lyle E. Schaller, *44 Questions for Church Planters*.

This argument is incorrect for two reasons. First, the New Testament doesn't teach that there should be only one church in each city. What is true is that the epistles were written when the churches were just beginning—there hadn't yet been enough time for multiple churches to be established in each of these cities. Also, the churches mentioned in the New Testament were not large institutions with big buildings and large budgets; most of them were house churches. This argument is not based on what we observe in the Bible, and it shows a lack of the type of vision that the missionaries of the New Testament, like the apostle Paul, had.

Beginning churches will not help me in my ministerial career.

Although most pastors would not say it in public, some may believe that focusing on starting many churches will not bring them much recognition from their denomination. They think that only pastors of large churches are recognized, are named to important positions, and are invited to speak at national meetings. Although it is true that many pastors from large churches do receive this type of attention, pastors with this attitude have a very limited vision and are not focused on pleasing God as their greatest goal.

We need to remember that studies have shown that new churches and smaller churches reach more people for Christ, proportionately. Two pastors advised Ralph Moore not to plant more churches until the mother church he led was stronger. Twenty years later, the churches of those two pastors had grown by about 200 people, while Moore's church had planted dozens of daughter churches and reached thousands of people with the gospel, while the mother church continued to grow.

CONCLUSION

There may be other reasons for planting new churches and other objections that need to be answered. However, the biblical and practical reasons for planting churches that we have discussed here should motivate all Christians and all established churches to fulfill the Great Commission by planting new churches. Being prepared to respond to these objections can help church planters motivate others to get involved in such a worthy task. Let's remember what Dr. C. Peter Wagner stated: "The single most effective evangelistic methodology under heaven is planting new churches."[4]

---

4   Wagner, *Church Planting for a Greater Harvest*, 12.

Questions

1. How would you define the term "church planting" in your own words?

2. Are buildings a requirement for a group to be considered a church? Explain

3. What is the imperative (mandate) of the Great Commission and what is the implication of this for church planting?

4. How many of the functions of the Jerusalem church (Acts 2:40-47) are being carried out in your church and to what extent are they being carried out in a biblical manner?

5. Based on our discussion on "Biblical Reasons for Church Planting," how would you try to convince a group that there are strong reasons for us to be involved in church planting today?

6. What practical reasons would you give a group to establish a case for church planting in your area?

7. What objections to church planting are you encountering in your area and how would you respond to these objections?

8. What is your response to Peter Wagner's statement: "The single most effective evangelistic methodology under heaven is church planting"? In light of that are you motivated to plant churches?

2 WHY MULTIPLY HEALTHY CHURCHES?
BIBLICAL AND MISSIOLOGICAL FOUNDATIONS

Charles Van Engen

Over a decade ago, in the foreword of David Martin's book *Tongues of Fire: The Explosion of Protestantism in Latin America*, Peter Berger, well-known sociologist of religion, commented on the situation today:

> This book deals with one of the most extraordinary developments in the world today—the rapid spread of Evangelical Protestantism in vast areas of the underdeveloped societies, notably in Latin America. . . . If one looks at today's religious scene in an international perspective, there are two truly global movements of enormous vitality. One is conservative Islam, the other conservative Protestantism. . . . The potential impact of (the growth of conservative Protestantism) is likely to be very powerful indeed. . . . The growth of Evangelical Protestantism in Latin America . . . is the most dramatic case.[1]

---

1   Peter Berger, foreword in *Tongues of Fire: The Explosion of Protestantism in Latin America*, vii.

*NOTE: This chapter was originally published in Spanish as "¿Por Qué Sembrar Iglesias Saludables? Bases Bíblibas y Misiológicas" in *Sembremos Iglesias Saludables: Un Aceramiento Bíblico y Práctico al Estudio de la Plantación de Iglesias* by John Wagenveld, 43-94.

In the 21st century, it is essential that our thinking on multiplying new churches come from clear motives. Today we are confronted by a complicated and almost contradictory reality regarding this topic. For example, the religiosity of Latin American people is a two-sided coin. On one side, 95 percent of the Latin American population considers themselves "Christian" in some way. There is a radical difference between the religion of the people and that of the official and formal churches; a small percentage of the population attends church regularly, and secularization and nominalism grow every day. And although there is a marked difference from country to country, there is, nonetheless, in almost all of the republics, a general feeling among the people of disillusionment with the institutional church.

Nevertheless, there is another side to this coin. In this new century in Latin America, we find an atmosphere of profound spiritual hunger, in which it seems everyone is open to any religious subject, open to try it out and believe all of it. We live in a time of phenomenal changes regarding religious loyalty. We are faced with changes so large and profound that the Reformation of the 16th century in Europe seems to pale in comparison, even though those Reformers, such as Luther, Calvin, Zwingli, Bucer, and others remain prominent in our minds. As Peter Berger mentioned above, we are navigating a time of great religious revolution in the creation of new religious forms, new church structures, and new spiritual expressions.

Both sides of this religious reality contribute to the creation of an atmosphere of competition and suspicion, which has a profound impact on multiplying new churches. In a place where there has been only one recognized church for centuries, a church that still dominates the religious reality for many republics, what does it mean to multiply new churches? In an atmosphere of such radical religious change and competition for new followers, it is of greatest importance to examine our motives. What will be our motives for multiplying new, healthy churches?

This chapter has to do with the biblical basis and values that motivate us to spend our time and energy in multiplying new, healthy churches, to look for creative ways to do so, and to pay the necessary price. We want to glorify God not only in our actions but also in our motives. The reasoning behind multiplying churches is as important as the methods we use in multiplying them. And this is especially true in the religious atmosphere we find today in much of the world where church multiplication is being carried out. In the end, as we will see later, the task of multiplying churches is not our own: it is God's. It is because of this that our motives must bring glory to our God.

Knowing this, it is perhaps important to examine ourselves and highlight some of our motives that might not be in line with the heart of God. In order to save space, these motives are presented in list-form. The reader is invited to reflect on the following motives that are not consistent with the love of Christ. Why multiply healthy churches?

- NOT to extend the small kingdom, domain, or influence of our own denomination, mission organization, church, or pastor. In all such cases, we are only establishing new branches of a religious corporation— not multiplying the church of Jesus Christ.
- NOT because all the other churches in our city or nation are not truly Christ's churches. In this case we see ourselves as forced to prove that only we have the truth and that all others are wrong before God. This kind of thinking means that our negative motivation focuses on other churches in place of positively pointing to Christ, the head of the church. On the contrary, Jesus invites us to examine the plank in our own eye before we try to remove the speck from our neighbor's eye (Matt. 7:3-5).
- NOT because we want to forcefully impose one way of religiosity for all people. This type of church "multiplying" has already been tried in Latin America in the Colonial era, with disastrous results. On the contrary, the Bible calls us to extend an open, loving, tender, and gentle invitation to all who, by the power of the Holy Spirit, would come to confess their faith in Jesus Christ and, based on this faith, become members of Christ's church.[2]

---

2   With regard to this wrong motive, I am beginning to see that in Latin America especially we might avoid using the word "plant" to refer to starting new churches. Latin American evangelicals have borrowed this word from English-language terminology where it has been used for the past forty years in reference to starting new congregations and churches in North America. However, in the context of Latin America, the word "plant" has certain historical roots and makes one think of the Spanish and Portuguese conquests during which churches were "planted" in a mostly brusque, forced, conquering, and destructive manner. I was born in Mexico City and raised in San Cristobal de Las Casas in the state of Chiapas in Southern Mexico. In both of these places the history of the Spanish conquest includes the killing of thousands and thousands of people from pre-Columbian cultures, all in the name of "planting" churches. This is a sad and disheartening history of the imposition of forms of "Christianity" in ways not consistent with a biblical

- NOT because we are in a competition for more converts over against other churches, as if multiplying churches were a soccer championship. If our motivation is competition, what we would be doing is a "recycling of the saints" or "stealing sheep." This is not God's mission.
- NOT because we want to manipulate the people of God in such a way that they would follow us and we could gain a lot of money and prestige in our community and nation.
- NOT because multiplying churches gives us pride or recognition, making us great or famous. Although we do know that some church leaders have psychological leanings in this direction, it is imperative that we acknowledge this predisposition and "offer [our] bodies as a living sacrifice, holy and pleasing to God" so that our activities in multiplying new, healthy churches can be our "true and proper worship," our offering to God (Rom. 12:1).

If we reject these motives that honor neither our Savior Jesus Christ nor the Holy Spirit, we then must focus on finding true and biblical motives that will lead us to multiply new, healthy churches. Biblical motivations for multiplying new, healthy churches need to be based on a trinitarian missiology.[3] Because of this, I submit that the Bible presents us with at least the following five reasons why we should multiply new churches:

A. Because God the Father seeks and finds the lost.
B. Because the love of Christ obligates us.
C. Because the Holy Spirit has been sent for all human beings (all flesh).
D. Because the local congregation is the primary locus of the kingdom of God, the rule of the King.
E. Because multiplying churches is for praise of the glory of God.

---

understanding of mission. This same story was repeated in many parts of Latin America and the Caribbean. There have also been situations in some aspects of Protestant missionary work of the 19th and 20th centuries in which the imposition of foreign religious practices is alarmingly similar to the European conquest of the 16th century. Perhaps, in reference to our evangelization and mission in Latin America and other places in the world that were the result of forced colonization, we should use the word "multiply" with more of a sense of humility and hope. Or, if we use the word "plant," perhaps we need to conceptualize that as one who places a small seed in the ground in the hope that the seed will die and God will bring it to new life so that, with time, it may yield a harvest. (For example, see Mark 4:26-29; John 4:36-37; 1 Cor. 3:6; 15:36-37).

3 See Ajith Fernando, "Grounding Our Reflections in Scripture: Biblical Trinitarianism and Mission," 189-256.

Thesis

This chapter's main idea is that the biblical motivation for multiplying healthy churches resides in the loving and compassionate mission of the triune God (missio Dei), who desires that all men and women be disciples of Jesus Christ and be responsible members of a church, the body of Christ. As such, these congregations are witnesses to the coming reign of God for the honor and glory of God.

Main Points

In this chapter there is only enough space to present the biblical foundation in a rather broad outline. This is presented here with the hope that this review will challenge the reader to study his/her Bible in a new way, allowing it to answer the question "Why does God want us to multiply new, healthy churches in Latin America and around the world?" The first reason is found in the nature and will of God.

I. Because God the Father Seeks and Finds the Lost

The first biblical foundation for multiplying new, healthy churches is the most basic of all of them. It stems from the nature of God. Every effort within missions, including multiplying new churches, comes from and flows out of the will of God (missio Dei), who loved the world so much "he gave his one and only Son, that whoever believes in him should not perish but have eternal life" (John 3:16).

Hendrikus Berkhof affirms that the most basic attribute of God is that he is a God who reveals himself to us.[4] In 1 John 4:8, we read that God is agape, love that is self-giving. God is always the one who initiates the search to reach humans, looking to draw them in and receive them within a covenant relationship. "I will be your God, you will be my people, and I will dwell in your midst" is the fundamental biblical affirmation of the will of God.[5]

The God of the Bible is neither the Unmovable Mover nor the Original Cause of the European Enlightenment of the 15th, 16th, and 17th centuries.

---

4 Hendrikus Berkhof, *Christian Faith,* 41-65.
5 Charles Van Engen, *Mission on the Way: Issues in Mission Theology,* 71-89.

The God of the Bible is not the god of the deists, a god who supposedly put the "laws of nature" into place and then removed himself in order to let "nature" govern the world. The God of the Bible is not merely the God of the "omni's" (omnipresent, omniscient, omnipotent, etc.) as, for example, he is described in the Westminster Confession, although these are included in God's characteristics. The God of the Bible is not just the creation of our own subjective experience, as Schleiermacher presented; nor is God only a part of categories of the mind, as Emmanuel Kant expressed. The God of the Bible is neither an immanent God, a product of cultural world-and-life-views, nor the product of a psychological hunger for meaning. He is also not the pure object of human religious searching.

On the contrary, the God of the Bible is loving, compassionate, slow to anger, benevolent, and full of mercy, who constantly and always desires to share his grace and love with humans and to enter into covenant with them. The Bible presents us with a God who is actively involved in his creation, who reveals himself to humanity, who responds, even emotionally to the human rejection of his love, and who—in Jesus Christ—preserves and sustains his creation, as Paul says in the high Christology of Colossians 1. What follows will be an outline of the biblical texts that speak to the missionary nature of the God of the Bible.

A. God created and cares for all human beings, even in spite of the fact that humanity rejects God.

- All human beings share the same origin in their creation by the God of the universe. (Gen. 1-3; Job 38-42; Isa. 41-46; Jonah; John 1; Acts 17:16-31; Rom. 1; Ps. 64:9; 65; 66:1, 4, 8; 67:3-5; 2 Pet. 3:8-13; Rev. 21:1). As such, all people have common ancestors in Adam and Eve (Gen. 1-5).
- All humanity is judged in the flood. Noah and his family are the ancestors of all people, and God established a covenant with all people, as evidenced by the rainbow (Gen. 6:10).
- The "Table of Nations" presents the idea that all people are descendants of the same race (Gen. 10:5, 6, 20, 31, 32).
- The tower of Babel affirms that all human beings have common ancestry in terms of language (Gen. 11:1-9). Here we see different people

groups within the universal love of God, a concept that is reaffirmed in the genealogy of Shem and Terah.

- God is the King of all the earth, creator, ruler, the "King of glory" (2 Sam. 15:10; 2 Kings 9:13; Isa. 52:7; Ps. 24; 47:8; see, for example, Jer. 17:12 and the Christology of Eph. 1, Col. 1; Phil. 2; Rev. 4:9, 10; 5:1, 7, 13; 6:16; 7:10, 15; 19:4).

The God of the Bible always takes the first step. He initiates the search and invites all humanity into a new relationship with him through reconciliation. This God has created and continues creating human beings with the intent that they will be in constant communion with him. With his own hands, the God of creation formed human beings out of mud. Having breathed life into that lump of clay (Gen. 2:7), he took it and lovingly, joyfully, and carefully formed humanity in the image of God—imago Dei (Gen. 2:20-25). This is the God of the Bible who, after Adam and Eve sinned against him and hid themselves from his face, cried out in pain and anguish, "Where are you?" (Gen. 3:9). This God of the Bible is the God who saved Noah and his family and promised to never destroy all people again (Gen. 6-9).

As children of this creating and sustaining God, we must also learn to care for the creation over which we have been given dominion. We must make the effort to affirm the value of human life and to safeguard it as much as possible. In regard to multiplying healthy churches, this first truth suggests that we work so that every human being might come to know their creator. We invite all human beings, by faith in Jesus Christ, to join with us in praising and glorifying our creator. In this way members of our congregations can participate in God's work of caring for creation and the life of each human being, thus transforming the reality in which they live.[6]

B. God is a God of love and mercy.

Time after time the Bible affirms that God is loving and merciful. This triune God of the Bible, as mentioned earlier is love (agape), the one who reveals himself to his people. Moses found himself in the presence of God after the delivery from slavery in Egypt. About that encounter, the Bible tells us the following: "And he passed in front of Moses, proclaiming, 'The LORD,

---

6 Ray Bakke, *Misión Integral en la Ciudad* and C. René Padilla and Tetsunao Yamamori, eds, *La Iglesia Local Como Agente de Transformación: Una Eclesiología para la Misión Integral.*

the LORD, the compassionate and gracious God, slow to anger, abounding in love and faithfulness, maintaining love to thousands, and forgiving wickedness, rebellion and sin. Yet he does not leave the guilty unpunished; he punishes the children and their children for the sin of the parents . . .'" (Ex. 34:6-7). This description of God's being is repeated innumerable times in the Bible (see, for example, Ex. 22:27; Num. 14:18; Deut. 5:9-10; 7:9-10; 2 Chron. 30:9; Neh. 9:17; Ps. 51:1; 86:5, 15; 103:8, 11:4; 112:4; 116:5; 145:8; Joel 2:13; Jon. 4:2; Mic. 7:18; James 5:11).

The God of the Bible is the God of love from the Psalms. There are a multitude of psalms that speak of God's love, mercy, and care. For example, Psalm 23 says, "The Lord is my shepherd, I lack nothing. . . ."

In Isaiah 6, one finds the call of the prophet Isaiah. He is in the temple and encounters the missionary God, the God of Abraham, Isaac, and Jacob. In this encounter with the presence of God, Isaiah shows that all five of his senses were engaged: he saw God high and lifted up, he heard the seraphim praising God, he felt the building shake, he smelled the smoke filling the temple, and he tasted the coal of God's forgiveness with which the seraphim touched his lips. The primary importance of this encounter is not limited to the relationship between Isaiah and his God. Additionally, there is a missionary element to it. The God of love and mercy cries out, "Whom shall I send? And who will go for us?" (Isa. 6:8). This calling, Isaiah's vocation, is centered on this missionary God's desire to send his messenger to Israel and all the nations. The moment will come when Isaiah will declare the following about Israel and the coming Messiah, words that Jesus of Nazareth will speak much later in the Gospel of Luke concerning his mission.

> This is what God the LORD says—the Creator of the heavens ... "I, the LORD, have called you in righteousness; I will take hold of your hand. I will keep you and will make you to be a covenant for the people and a light for the Gentiles, to open eyes that are blind, to free captives from prison and to release from the dungeon those who sit in darkness." (Isa. 42:5-7; compare with Isa. 49:6; 61:1-3; Luke 2:32; 4:18-19).

The messianic and missional prophecies in Isaiah form part of the background for the words of Mary, the mother of Jesus. The main emphasis of

Mary's Magnificat in Luke 1:46-55 is God's loving and merciful nature toward Israel and all other nations.

Jesus stresses that this love is an attribute of his heavenly Father as well, who because of love, seeks to be in relationship with his people. Jesus said to Nicodemus the Pharisee, a member of the Sanhedrin (a council of 70 people who governed the people of Israel during Jesus' time) and a leader of the Jews, "God so loved the world he gave his one and only Son, that whoever believes in him shall not perish but have eternal life" (John 3:16). In his teaching Jesus again stressed God's loving nature. Another example of this is in the parable of the tenants in Luke 20:9-18. God, represented as the owner of the vineyard, constantly tries to enter into a relationship with his workers (compare with Isa. 5). Additionally, in the parable of the great banquet, God, who is characterized by the host of the dinner, sends his servant, "Go out quickly into the streets and alleys of the town and bring in the poor, the crippled, the blind and the lame. . . . Go out to the roads and country lanes and compel them to come in, so that my house will be full" (Luke 14:15-24; Matt. 22:1-ff). Luke 15 combines three parables that show us how this God loves, seeks, and finds the lost. This God, as a shepherd does, looks for and finds his lost sheep. He is like a woman who looks for and finds her lost coin. He is also like a father who anxiously waits for the day when his lost son will return home. Upon finding the lost, the God of the Bible throws a party with his angels and joyfully celebrates that the lost has been found. Concerning this point, the reader should note that in these parables the idea of being "lost" has to do with a break in a close relationship with God: with the shepherd on behalf of the sheep, with the woman on behalf of the coin, and with the father on behalf of the prodigal son.

In regard to this God of love, Paul asks, "He who did not spare his own Son, but gave him up for us all—how will he not also, along with him, graciously give us all things?" (Rom. 8:32). Peter also affirms that God is a God of love and mercy and "he is patient with you, not wanting anyone to perish, but everyone to come to repentance" (2 Pet. 3:9). In his first letter, John affirms this most basic characteristic of God as well: "God is love" (1 John 4:8). Additionally, in Revelation we see that this God of love will bring people from every tribe, language, people, and nation together, around the Lamb in the new Jerusalem (Rev. 5:9; 7:9; 15:4; 21:24; 22:1-2).

In Christ we have become children of this loving and merciful Father (John 1:12). Therefore, as his children, we must be involved and challenged to participate with our loving Father in the search and rescue of the lost. It is not possible to be sons and daughters of this loving God and refuse to participate in this search for the lost. Additionally, when we as sons and daughters of God come together to worship this God of love, we are incomplete because we are missing those who have not yet come to know our loving and merciful Father. Each time we come together to worship God is a challenge and a call to invite others to join with us in praise to our God, who loves all humanity.

C. God chooses his people to be his instruments of love in the search among the nations.

God is the God of particular people and at the same time is the God of all nations. In the Bible the word for "nations" does not refer to a modern political entity like Mexico, for example. It refers to a particular group of people connected by language, culture, ancestry, and history. In the Old Testament the term "nations" speaks to the ethnic entities, people, and cultural groups of Israel's immediate environment. Israel is the "am," the people of God, and "the nations" are the "goyim," all the other people groups who are not part of God's "am." Beginning with the call of Abraham, the Bible is clear that Abraham and Sarah's descendants, the people of God, exist in order to be God's instrument of love among the nations.

The God of Abraham, Isaac, and Jacob heard the cry of his people in Egypt and used Moses and his creation to bring about their deliverance from slavery in Egypt. This deliverance had two interrelated purposes. The first purpose was so that the people of Israel would come to know God in a new way and would worship the God of Abraham, Isaac, and Jacob and of Mount Sinai (Ex. 6:2-7; 7:16; 8:1, 20; 9:1, 13; 10:3, 8; 14:31; 20:2). However, this was only part of what God wanted to teach his people through their deliverance from Egypt. His plan is much bigger, deeper, and more profound. Through the exodus from Egypt, God wanted all of Egypt and the surrounding "nations" to come to know that the God of Abraham, Isaac, and Jacob is the only true God who created and sustains all of life of earth (Ex. 5:2; 7:5; 17; 8:10; 9:14, 16; 10:2; 14:4, 18, 31). God's use of his people as his instruments among the nations is so important that, centuries later, Paul cites one of these passages in his own description of the mission of God's love. During the exodus, God used Moses to say to Pharaoh, "But I have raised you up for this very purpose, that I might show you my power and that my name might be proclaimed in all the earth" (Ex. 9:16; Rom. 9:17).

What follows is an outline of some of the texts that show the love of God and his desire to bring this love to "the nations."

1. God gives specific commandments regarding the special care that Israel must offer to "the stranger that is among you" (Gen. 12:10; 20:1; 21:34; 47:4; Ex. 20:10; 22:21; Lev. 18:26; 20:2; 25:40; Num. 15:14-16; Deut. 10:18-19; 26:5-11; 1 Kings 8:27, 41-43; 2 Chron. 6:18, 32—the dedication of Solomon's temple).

2. The "nations" play an important role in God's activity (Deut. 26:19; 1 Chron. 16:8, 31; Ps. 9:1, 19-20; 47:1, 7-9; 64:9; 65; 66:1, 4, 8; 67:1-5; 72:17-18; 96:1-3, 7, 10, 13; 97:5-6; 98:2-3, 9; 102:13-15; 108:3; 113:4; Isa. 2:2-4; 40:5, 17; 49:5-6; 52:15; 55:4-5; 56:6-7; 60:3, 11; 62:2; 66:2, 19-20; Jer. 4:2; Zeph. 2:11-13; Amos; Jonah; Mic. 1:1-7; 4:1-5).

3. In the Old Testament and in the words of Jesus, the "house of prayer for all the nations." Solomon's temple was a special place for prayer for the "stranger" (2 Chron. 6:32-33; Mic. 4:1-2; Isa. 56:7; Jer. 7:11; Matt. 21:13; Mark 11:17; Luke 19:46; Matt. 25:32. Compare with Acts 14:15-17).

4. God chose Israel to "be among the nations" as his instrument of love for all people (Ex. 6:6-8; 19:5-6; Deut. 4:20; 7:6; 14:2; 26:1; Titus 2:14; 1 Pet. 2:9-10). In his conversation with Nicodemus (John 3) and in the declaration of his messianic mission (Luke 4:18-19), Jesus mentions God's intention for his people. See also the following related passages: Isaiah 35:4-8; 61:1; Hebrews 1:9; Psalm 45:7: Matthew 11:1-6; Psalm 145:14ff.; Luke 1:46-55; 1 Sam. 2:1-10; Matt. 25:31ff.; Acts 2:42-47.

5. Paul understood the universal mission of God in such a way that he considered himself to be a debtor to all people (Rom. 1:14) and was committed to participating in the "mystery of Christ" (Eph. 2:11-3:21).

6. The people of God are a sign of the universal love of God that he has for all nations (Isa. 11:12; 49:22; 62:10; Matt. 5; John 3:14-15; 12:32; Rom. 1:14).

7. The covenant that God makes with his people has within it the purpose of reaching out to the nations who do not already know their Creator. Emilio Nuñez, focusing on the covenant with Noah, helps us understand this missionary element of God's covenant. Nuñez explains the following:

> For the purpose of our missiological reflection, what we want to emphasize the most from God's covenant with Noah and other unconditional covenants that Yahweh establishes with humans is the divine interest in the salvation of all human beings. This salvation is not limited to the forgiveness of sins and the gift of eternal life. It also had to do with the spiritual (shalom) and physical well-being of human beings. The promise covers everything from the animal kingdom (Gen. 9:8-17) to the plant world (Gen. 8:22-9:3). God has made a covenant with "the earth" (Gen. 9:13). This blessing is also ecological. "As long as the earth endures, seedtime and harvest, cold and heat, summer and winter, day and night will never cease" (Gen. 8:22). The effects of the covenant are cosmic, as a blessing for all humanity. . . .
>
> The rainbow is mentioned in Ezekiel 1:28 and Revelation 4:3 as a symbol of God's majesty. The rainbow becomes an apocalyptic sign and symbol for humanity. Judgment day is coming. . . .
>
> God does not want "anyone to perish, but everyone to come to repentance" (2 Pet. 3:9). He "wants all people to be saved and to come to a knowledge of the truth" (1 Tim. 2:4). He wants the biblical stories of the flood with the rainbow in the clouds to be a powerful incentive for all human beings to repent and believe in Christ for their salvation. . . .
>
> Every time we participate in the Lord's Supper, in communion with our brothers and sisters in Christ, we remember the blood that was shed as a seal of this new covenant (Matt. 26:26-29), taking on the

sins of the world (1 John 2:2), as a ransom for many (Matt. 20:28; 1 Pet. 1:18-19), in order to reconcile the world with God (2 Cor. 5:18-21; Eph. 2:16; Col. 1:20-21). We should remember that the blood of the Lamb was poured out to "take away the sin of the world!" (John 1:29). We must also remember that, in obedience to God, the church must continue to come around the table of communion "until he comes again." In other words, until the Son of David returns to reign over all the earth. . . .

God's covenant with Noah and those established with the people of Israel attest to the divine interest in the salvation of all people. The covenants in the Old Testament provide a solid base to the universal Christian mission. They also serve as a foundation for the concept of holistic missions because the promises of the covenants include the spiritual as well as the material. They offer blessings for all human beings.[7]

The reality of God's love for all people, as noted above, shows us that all believers in Christ must by definition be involved in the search for the lost because of God's nature. In other words, to be children of God means that we must multiply new, healthy churches. Our heavenly Father seeks out the lost, and as his children we must do the same.

Those of us who have known Christ for some time and are members of an evangelical church probably know the above truths in our heads but too often fail to live them out. The fundamental basis for multiplying new, healthy churches lies in the nature of God, a loving, merciful God who reveals God's self to humans and looks to be in covenant relationship with them. Because of this, multiplying churches is not optional. On the contrary, it is part of the essential nature of our faith. If we are children of this God, we must then do all that is possible in seeking out, finding, receiving, and incorporating all human beings into the community of faith so that they can be reconciled with God (2 Cor. 5). A biblical missiology recognizes that ultimately our motivation for multiplying new, healthy churches does not merely stem from the nature of the church but flows from the will of God.

---

7 Emilio Nuñez, *Hacia una Misionlogía Evangélica Latinoamericana,* 181-82, 214. Translated by the editors of this volume.

In the footnote below, the reader will find a short list of supporting works that emphasize a similar perspective of the God who, because of his love and mercy, seeks and finds the lost.[8]

II. Because the Love of Christ Compels Us

The way God shows his love and mercy (through seeking and saving the lost) is the foundation for the mission of Jesus Christ, for the sending of the Holy Spirit, and for the church's call to announce the good news of God's reign to the whole world, bringing honor and glory to God. Therefore, in this section we will briefly examine the mission of Jesus Christ as the second main motivation for multiplying new, healthy churches.

A. The Incarnation

"God so loved the world that he gave his one and only Son, that whoever believes in him shall not perish but have eternal life" (John 3:16). "The Word became flesh and made his dwelling among us. We have seen his glory, the glory of the one and only Son, who came from the Father, full of grace and truth" (John 1:14). The love of God does not remain in theory or in speculation. On the contrary, God, because of his great love, became flesh. "He came to that which was his own" (John 1:11). In Jesus, the Christ (the Messiah), God became human, flesh and bone, culturally a Jew, a man who lived in Palestine during the first century A.D., under the rule of Caesar Augustus, while "Quirinius was governor of Syria" (Luke 2:2). God did not come in an

---

8 Karl Barth, "An Exegetical Study of Matt. 28:16-20," 55-71; Johannes Blauw, *The Missionary Nature of the Church*; Richard de Ridder, *Discipling the Nations*; John Fuellenback, *The Kingdom of God*; Arthur Glasser et al., *Announcing the Kingdom*; Ken Gnanakan, *Kingdom Concerns*; Roger Hedlund, *The Mission of the Church in the World*; Walter Kaiser, *Mission in the Old Testament;* George Ladd, *The Gospel of the Kingdom*; Helen Montgomery, *The Bible and Mission*; Johannes Nissen, *New Testament and Mission*; Nuñez, *Hacia una Misionlogía Evangélica Latinoamericana*; Padilla, *Bases Bíblicas de la Misión*; Donald Senior and Carroll Stuhlmueller, *The Biblical Foundations for Mission*; Norman Snaith, *The Distinctive Ideas of the Old Testament;* John Stott, "The Living God is a Missionary God," 10-18; Valdir Steuernagel, *Al Servicio del Reino en América Latina*; Mark Strom, *The Symphony of the Scripture*; Gerhard Kittel and Gerhard Friedrich, eds, *Theological Dictionary of the New Testament;* Charles Van Engen, Dean Gilliland, and Paul Pierson, eds, *The Good News of the Kingdom*; Gailyn Van Rheenen, *Biblical Anchored Missions;* Gerhard von Rad, *Old Testament Theology Vol. 1*; and George Wright, *The Old Testament Against its Environment.*

abstract or purely mystical way. He came to be in relationship with human beings in concrete situations, in a visible and identifiable reality.

As with Jesus and his disciples, "Christ's love compels us" to make the love of God visible through our interactions with all people. For "if anyone is in Christ, the new creation has come: The old has gone, the new is here! All this is from God, who reconciled us to himself through Christ and gave us the ministry of reconciliation that God was reconciling the world to himself in Christ, not counting people's sins against them. And he has committed to us the message of reconciliation." Therefore, as a new creation, we cry out to all people throughout the world: "Be reconciled to God" (2 Cor. 5:14-20).

Just as God became flesh to dwell among humanity, Christ's disciples are part of communities, towns, and cities. Because of this, multiplying new, healthy churches guarantees that the good news is born out of and grows in concrete places, particular cultures, and among specific people. And in reality these new, healthy congregations are the ambassadors of the presence and grace of God. Through these groups of Christ's followers, God invites everyone who comes to them to be reconciled with God.

During his ministry, Jesus had a number of followers (maybe even up to 120) who walked with him during the three years of his ministry. They walked together, ate together, prayed together, laughed together, cried together. That group of disciples was the first congregation of the New Testament. And just as the first group of Jesus' followers were the first congregation of the New Testament, Jesus' followers today make up a new congregation. As people become disciples of Jesus Christ, new congregations are born. The people who make up these groups are made of flesh and bone, influenced by their culture and context.

Multiplying new, healthy churches is the fruit of missionary activity that flows out of the nature of the church. Christ's love compels us to proclaim the salvation that he offers. And when people decide to follow Christ and come together in his name, a new congregation is born. Even more, Jesus promises that "where two or three gather in my name, there am I with them" (Matt. 18:20). Jesus promises to be present (through the Holy Spirit) in those moments and places wherever his followers come together in his name. Even more, "Anyone who loves me will obey my teaching. My Father will love them, and we will come to them and make our home with them" (John 14:23). In other words, when Jesus' disciples come together in his name and when they love each other, Jesus and God the Father are present through the Holy Spirit.

Why must we multiply new, healthy churches? Because Christ's love always is shown in a concrete way when his disciples come together in his name, in an atmosphere of love. This occurs in specific places: the countryside, a village, between people of flesh and bone, who have their own particular language and culture. And in these places "Christ's love compels us" to invite those around us to become disciples of the King of kings and the Lord of lords.

B. Contextualization

When Jesus' disciples come together, they gather in an atmosphere where he is present. In this atmosphere the gospel of Jesus Christ becomes natural to the cultural context of the church. The genius behind multiplying new, healthy churches is that they come from people who reflect the culture in which they have been multiplied. In his ministry, Jesus responded differently to each person with whom he interacted. He offered living water to the Samaritan woman. He gave food to hungry crowds. For Mary and Martha, he gave them life in bringing back Lazarus, their brother, from the dead. In Jesus' ministry his gifts were tailored for those who were receiving them. As such, each congregation should not just reflect its denomination, mission organization, or mother church. It must also reflect the culture in which it has been multiplied in terms of economy, language, and world-and-life view. Healthy congregations must reflect the culture of their surrounding contexts. In other words they must not be like a foreign bush, planted among native shrubs. Instead they must be planted in their native soil where they can grow well. For more than 100 years, missiologists have followed this concept, drawing from the thinking of Roland Allen, John Nevius, Mel Hodges, John A. Mackay, Orlando Costas, Rubén Tito Paredes, and others. The local congregation is where the gospel becomes contextualized.

C. The Calling into Mission

A healthy congregation is not only made up of followers of Christ who come together to think only about themselves. A congregation will not be healthy and mature if it does not reach outside of its surrounding culture. True followers of Jesus try to make new followers of Christ. One can clearly see this call in chapters 9 and 10 of Luke, in addition to the five Great Commission passages (Matt. 28:18-20—compare with Matt. 10:5-15; Mark 16:15-16; Luke 24:46-49 through Acts 1:8; and John 15:12-17 with 21:15-17). [9]

Biblically speaking, making new disciples has never been a merely individual pursuit but is rather a collective activity. Since the birth of the church in Acts, one can see that the disciples of Christ, by the fact of being his followers, came together with other disciples in collective congregations. As we saw before, Jesus says, "Wherever two or three are gathered in my name . . ." Exercising one's Christian faith always happens collectively.

A missionary Christology does not separate Christ's personhood from his actions or his humanity from his divinity; nor does it separate the "Jesus of history" from the "Christ of faith." On the contrary, it emphasizes Jesus' missionary ministry as one who was sent from the Father to save the world. This holistic ministry includes his offices (Prophet, Priest, King) and his ministry as Savior, Liberator, and Sage. Jesus transfers his mission to his disciples: "As the Father has sent me, I am sending you" (John 20:21). Jesus' mission and ministry are the basis for the calling and commitment of Christ's followers.

In his first sermon in Acts, Paul says, "This is what the Lord has commanded us: 'I have made you a light for the Gentiles, that you may bring salvation to the ends of the earth'" (Acts 13:47—compare with Luke 2:32, with reference to Jesus). Jesus transfers his offices, his ministry, and his mission to his disciples who together make up the body of Christ, the physical presence of Christ in the world. It is in this way that we, as Christ's disciples, come to be prophets, priests, kings, healers, liberators, and sages in mission. The local congregation as the body of Christ exists to put into action the mission and ministry of Jesus in the world. Fundamentally speaking, the local congrega-

---

9 Most missiologists write about a biblical basis for starting new churches by drawing from the Great Commission. In many of these cases, the authors pay little attention or put little effort into examining the hermeneutics behind, and the significance of, the Great Commission as it relates to the mission of God throughout the entire Bible. See, for example, Robert Logan, *Beyond Church Growth*, 190-92 and "Church Reproduction," 159; Aubrey Malphurs, *Planting Growing Churches for the 21st Century*, 119-23; Marlin Nelson, *Principles of Church Growth*, 39-47; Elmer Towns and Douglas Porter, *Churches That Multiply*, 11-25; and C. Peter Wagner, *Church Multiplying for a Greater Harvest*, 19 and *Your Church Can Grow*, 44-46.

tion exists to invite other people—all human beings—to be disciples of Jesus Christ, just as it is seen in the message of the book of Acts.[10]

Missiologists with a missionary mindset recognize that salvation is neither found in participating in church activities nor in simply being a member of a church. In this sense, our calling is not to simply "multiply" churches. At its most basic, our calling is to make disciples of Jesus Christ. In other words, multiplying new, healthy churches is making new groups of people who participate in Christ's mission by being his disciples.

Our message is not the superiority of our church or its creeds and confessions. Additionally, we do not exist to simply be instruments of socioeconomic or political change. Our message is simple: that Jesus Christ lived, was crucified, "rose again from the dead . . . is seated at the right hand of God the Father almighty," and from there "will come to judge the living and the dead," as the Apostles' Creed states.

In Revelation, John sees the future: "After this I looked, and there before me was a great multitude that no one could count, from every nation, tribe, people and language, standing before the throne and before the Lamb. They were wearing white robes and were holding palm branches in their hands. And they cried out in a loud voice: 'Salvation belongs to our God, who sits on the throne, and to the Lamb'" (Rev. 7:9-10; see also 5:9; 10:11; 11:9; 13:7; 14:6; 17:15). This vision fulfills the promise that John had previously heard from Jesus when the Savior said, "And I, when I am lifted up from the earth, will draw all people to myself" (John 12:32). The local congregation is a sign and a symbol, a representation of that multitude around the throne of God, the Lamb. As we wait for the fulfillment of this time, during this time-between-the-times of his first and second comings, Jesus and our heavenly Father have sent us the Holy Spirit to build his church.

III. Because the Holy Spirit Has Been Sent for All People and to Build the Church

The third fundamental reason for multiplying healthy churches is because this action is the work of the Holy Spirit. Ultimately, we are not the ones who

---

10   Van Engen, *God's Missionary People: Rethinking the Purpose of the Local Congregation,*119-30.

multiply churches. You and I do not grow the church. The church exists only because of the work of the Holy Spirit. There are three aspects to this truth.

A. The Holy Spirit was given for all people.

God the Father and his Son, Jesus Christ, sent the Holy Spirit out of their desire that no one be lost and that all might be saved. In Acts 2, Luke narrates the events of Pentecost, when the Holy Spirit came to Jesus' disciples who were "all together in one place" (Acts 2:1). They formed a new local congregation. The Holy Spirit was sent in the form of fire and with the sound of wind, and the disciples "began to speak in other tongues" (Acts 2:4). Peter explains, using the words of the prophet Joel, that "in the last days, God says, I will pour out my Spirit on all people" (Acts 2:17). Luke also offers us a list of peoples from many places who were able to hear, in their own language, Peter's sermon, in order to emphasize the fact that the Holy Spirit was sent for all people (Acts 2:8). In the map below, the reader can appreciate Luke's genius in providing us a list of the main cultures and nations surrounding Jerusalem during this time. People from these places heard the gospel of Jesus Christ in their own language. This was a miracle of the ear and was through the special work of the Holy Spirit.

The "Table of Nations" in Acts

In Acts 2:9-11, Luke mentions 15 places of origin for those who heard Peter's sermon on Pentecost. This "Table of Nations" in Acts echoes that of Genesis 10. In Acts 2, Luke seems to indicate that the confusion of tongues from Babel has been transformed and healed at Pentecost. The people present at Pentecost came mainly from the provinces of Asia (of the Roman Empire) and from the empire of the Medes and Persians, as well as from Crete and Rome (see the map below). All of these people heard the gospel in their own language.

The New Testament "Table of Nations" at Pentecost

Provinces of the Roman Empire		Cities of the Roman Empire	Provinces of the Parthian Empire
5. Judea	10. Pamphylia	Jerusalem	1. Parthia
6. Cappadocia	11. Egypt	13. Rome	2. Medla
7. Pontus	12. Cyrene		3. Elam
8. Asia	14. Crete		4. Mesopotamia
9. Phrygia			

Why multiply new, healthy churches? Because through new congregations the Holy Spirit wants to continue transforming the lives of all people. It is interesting that in Acts, Luke tells us four more times, in four different places, representing four different cultures, when the Holy Spirit comes in a form identical to that of Pentecost in Acts 2 (see chap. 4 [Judea]; chap. 8 [Samaria]; chap. 10 [Cornelius, a God-fearing Gentile in Caesarea]; and chap. 19 [Gentile disciples in Ephesus], all showing the spread of the gospel outward "to the ends of the earth"—Acts 1:8). The Holy Spirit wants to multiply new, healthy, local congregations made up of women and men who represent "all people." It is clear from Acts that in order to reach this goal, the Holy Spirit uses Christ followers from local churches to multiply new, healthy churches. This process is the norm of the New Testament.

B. The Holy Spirit builds new healthy congregations.

In the end, we need to recognize that, as humans, we are not the ones who build the church. In reality we are also not the ones who multiply new, local congregations. This work begins with the Holy Spirit. The book of Acts clearly teaches that the Holy Spirit is responsible for the growth, health, and development of a church. In Acts, we see that the Holy Spirit does all of these things—and more:

The Holy Spirit . . .

Builds the church.
Reforms and transforms the church.
Gives power to the church.
Unifies the church.
Gives new knowledge and illumination to the words of Jesus.
Sends the church out.
Creates within the church a desire to grow.
Accompanies the church on its mission.
Guides the church.
Prays through the church and intercedes for the church.
Gives the church the words for testimony and proclamation.
Facilitates communication.
Develops and facilitates the receptivity of the listeners.
Convinces people of their sin, of justice, and of judgment.
Converts people to faith in Jesus Christ.
Brings together and unifies Christians so that together they can be the church.
Receives new believers.
Sends the church out into the world that God loves so much.

One of the Holy Spirit's most profound desires is to grow the church. Even the best strategies cannot make the church grow. The church is the "mysterious creation of God" (in the words of Karl Barth) and exists through the work of the Holy Spirit. Ultimately we know this truth, but often we forget it. Perhaps we forget the Holy Spirit's role because the Holy Spirit rarely works alone. The Holy Spirit enjoys using human instruments, Jesus' disciples, to accomplish the work of creating new, healthy churches.

This desire of the Holy Spirit is evident throughout Acts and the New Testament. It is emphasized in a notable way in Acts 13. After giving us a list of the church leaders in Antioch, Luke tells us that it was the Holy Spirit who said, "Set apart for me Barnabas and Saul for the work to which I have called them" (Acts 13:2). The rest of the book is the story of how the Holy Spirit used Paul, Barnabas, and many others in multiplying new, healthy churches in the different places Luke mentions in Acts 2. Accordingly, every congregation throughout the world must listen to the call of the Holy Spirit to be agents of the triune God in multiplying new, healthy churches. All healthy churches should be concerned about, and actively involved in, multiplying new churches through the power of the Holy Spirit.

C. The Holy Spirit gives gifts to and sends out the members of the church so that they will multiply new congregations.

In order to carry out this multiplying, the Holy Spirit gives gifts to believers of Christ as a means of special grace. Surely the reader is familiar with New Testament passages that mention the different gifts the Holy Spirit gives to members of the body of Christ. (See Rom. 12; 1 Cor. 12; Eph. 4; 1 Pet. 4:10-11.) One could say that the Holy Spirit is like the central nervous system of the body. Just as one cable produces electricity and one nerve produces an electrical impulse to the brain, so the Holy Spirit carries the commands from the Head of the church (Christ) to the members of the body and moves the muscles to action. That is, the Holy Spirit moves the members of the body of Christ in their mission in the world. It is not possible to multiply new, healthy churches without the careful and efficient use of the gifts of the Holy Spirit.

A careful study of Ephesians 4 shows that the gifts of the Spirit are given with two complementary purposes. On the one hand, the gifts are used for the development and maturity of the members of the church. But the work of the Holy Spirit does not stop here. The members' development and maturity has a purpose beyond the confines of the church. They are given for mission in the world. In Ephesians 4:12 Paul says that the gifts have been given "to equip his people for works of service, so that the body of Christ may be built up." The word Paul uses here, translated into English as "service," is diakonia. This word, from which we get our word "deacon," is a key word that Paul frequently uses as a synonym for the mission of God. For example, see Ephesians 3:1-7, where Paul says that he became a "servant" [deacon] of the "mystery" that the Gentiles are "heirs together with Israel, members together of one body, and sharers together in the promise in Christ Jesus" (Eph. 3:3-4, 6-7). The gifts are activities of ministry that are practiced as much outside as inside the church-in-the-world in order to bring to Christ those who do not yet know him as their Savior. When these gifts are carried out in this way, the church is "built up"—that is, it grows in a holistic way: organically, spiritually, socially, and numerically.[11] The gifts of the Spirit are missionary gifts that the Spirit wants to use to touch the lives of all who are not yet disciples of Christ, in order to transform them and bring them into the church of Christ, creating new, healthy congregations.

Because these gifts are given directly from the Holy Spirit, they must only be used in an atmosphere drenched in the fruit of the Spirit: love, joy, peace, patience, kindness, gentleness, etc. (Gal. 5:22-23; Eph. 4:1-6). When these gifts are used biblically, the anticipated result is that new people will come to Christ and new, healthy churches will develop. The Holy Spirit does not give these gifts just to grow already established churches. Biblical growth results in the multiplication of believers and of new, healthy, congregations. Biblical growth should also result in the transformation of the society and culture of the neighborhoods surrounding these new congregations.

Currently, there are too many megachurches around the world that have not given birth to new congregations. It seems as if they want to hoard God's grace all for themselves and not share it with "all people." A healthy church looks to reproduce itself, multiplying new congregations—locally, regionally, and globally. A healthy church participates in the mission of Jesus Christ through the power of the Holy Spirit as "witnesses in Jerusalem, and in all Judea and Samaria, and to the ends of the earth" (Acts 1:8). In this missionary activity, by the work of the Holy Spirit, a healthy church will multiply other new, healthy churches.

---

11   See the following three works from Orlando Costas: *The Church and Its Mission: A Shattering Critique from the Third World; El Protestantismo en América Latina Hoy;* and *The Integrity of Mission: The Inner Life and Outreach of the Church.*

IV. Because the Local Congregation Is the Primary Agent of the Kingdom of God

The exposition above on the work of the Holy Spirit drives us to consider the fourth fundamental reason why new and healthy churches should be multiplied. This has much to do with the nature of the church and its relationship with the kingdom of God. I want to suggest here that it is a natural and essential aspect of the very nature of the church for it to reproduce itself into new congregations.[12] This is something that may be expected of every healthy congregation. We could also say it negatively: something is wrong with a local congregation that does not reproduce itself. We can think about this from three points of view:

A. The description of healthy congregations in Acts 2 and 1 Thessalonians 1

We first must consider what the Bible teaches us about the nature of a healthy congregation. When we multiply new and healthy churches, what are we multiplying? That answer may be found in Acts 2 and in 1 Thessalonians 1. In each passage we find a description of a new congregation less than a year old. Luke explains the characteristics of the congregation in Acts 2:43-47 with the purpose of proving that it is made up of messianic Jews who faithfully follow the Old Testament commandments and are also faithful followers of the Messiah, Jesus of Nazareth. In the case of the believers at Thessalonica, Paul mentions the characteristics of that church in order to prove that "he has chosen you" (1 Thess. 1.4). How can one know that the believers at Thessalonica are chosen? It is known because they manifest the following characteristics.

Given the biblical context in which these characteristics appear, I believe that Luke, like Paul, offers us not only a description of a particular group of believers (written only in descriptive form), but he also gives us a summary of what he believes constitutes a true and authentic local church (written in nor-

---

12 One of the best resources I have encountered concerning the development of the biblical basis for multiplying healthy churches is the work of Fernando Mora, a pastor and biochemical engineer in Caracas, Venezuela. See chapter 3 of Mora's *Manual de Líderes de Células*. This book is self-published and may be found by contacting Fernando at fmorac@cantv.net. Also consider the work of Stuart Murray, *Church Multiplying: Laying Foundations*, 36-65.

mative form). In other words, our congregations and new, healthy churches should demonstrate the following characteristics:

Characteristics of a Healthy Church Revealed in Acts 2:43-47
- There are miracles and extraordinary signs.
- The congregation has an impact in its surrounding context.
- The members of the congregation have everything in common. They care for one another.
- They eat together and celebrate Communion and special unity.
- They praise and worship God.
- The Lord adds to their number each day those who have been chosen for salvation.

Characteristics of a Healthy Church Revealed in 1 Thessalonians 1:2-10
- They confess Jesus as their Savior.
- The gospel arrives with power. There are miracles and special signs.
- The Word is preached.
- They experience a communion of love.
- They express an exemplary form of living.
- They suffer on behalf of the gospel.
- They show a spiritual joy.
- They show radical conversion.
- Their witness is known throughout the world.
- They demonstrate a new hope.

There is much that could be said concerning these descriptions of healthy churches. However, here I only want to mention one thing. Both of these new churches are committed to evangelization, to mission, and to the numerical growth of believers and congregations. There are occasions when we wish to emphasize one or two of these characteristics mentioned in the two passages. However, these characteristics describe a reality understood when all are considered together. It is not possible to accept or emphasize one or two of these characteristics and pass over the rest. To do so would be to ignore the form in which Luke and Paul describe these two congregations. The description of each one is a complete package: organic and holistic. To emphasize unity, or worship, or signs and wonders means that one must also stress the missionary work of these congregations in announcing the gospel, the way they bring forth the numerical growth of believers and their attempts to multiply new and healthy churches.[13]

B. The relationship between the church and the kingdom of God[14]

The local congregation, as the missionary people of God, is an instrument of the kingdom of God, the principal agent of the kingdom of God, a sign of the kingdom, and the principal environment in which the kingdom is made known.[15] A mission-minded congregation is the local manifestation of the covenant community of the King. As was discussed in the first part of this chapter, from the time of Abraham the people of God are seen as a covenant community. Later Israel understood that she was a unique people, as described in Deuteronomy 10:15 (see also Ex. 19:5-6; Deut. 26:18-19; 1 Pet. 2.9). We can see in the Old Testament that Israel saw herself as a special nation created by the direct action of God. The Israelites understood that God the creator of all that exists had chosen them to be a special people with a specific inheritance, with a defined mission and a special hope. To be the people of God meant commitment as an instrument for the good of all the nations. In addition, it meant being within the sphere of the universal action of the sovereignty of God over all the world.[16]

The election of the church as the new Israel has a similar purpose. God the Father, Son, and Holy Spirit set up the church so that pagans might see the church's "good deeds and glorify God on the day he visits us" (1 Pet. 2:12). Light to the Gentiles, a priesthood for all nations—here is the specific calling and the essential nature of a missionary-minded congregation. She is the

13 Van Engen, *The Growth of the True Church: An Analysis of the Ecclesiology of Church Growth Theory*, 178-90.

14 This section has been adapted from chapter 7 of Van Engen, *God's Missionary People*.

15 There are several missiologists who connect the mission of the church, and, in some cases specifically, the multiplying of new churches, with the theme of preaching the good news of the kingdom of God. See, for example, Juan Driver, *Imágenes de una Iglesia en Misión: Hacia una Eclesiología Transformadora*, 61-69; Darrell L. Guder, *The Continuing Conversion of the Church*, 28-48; Fred Herron, *Expanding God's Kingdom Through Church Multiplying*, 3-30; Padilla, *Mission Between the Times*, 180-193; Daniel Sánchez et al., *Starting Reproducing Congregations*, 9-14; Howard Snyder and Daniel Runyon, *Decoding the Church*, 161; Valdir R. Steuernagel, *Obediencia Misionera y Práctica Histórica*, 154-56; Van Engen, Dean Gilliland and Paul Pierson, eds. *The Good News of the Kingdom*, 69-106; and Johannes Verkuyl, *Contemporary Missiology*, 89-204.

16 For more on the universal sovereignty of Christ, see Blauw, *The Missionary Nature of the Church* and de Ridder, *Discipling the Nations*.

missionary nation of God whose reason for being is derived directly from the purposes of God for the world. The specially chosen people of God, for the purpose of their calling, emerges in human history as the covenant community of the King, an arm of the kingdom of God. Whoever grasps the importance of this local congregation in the mission of God should also carefully consider the special nature of the church and its purpose in the world as the covenant community of followers of Jesus Christ.

As the Body of Christ, we are the community through which Christ is present in and reaching out to the world. The witnessing role of the church is the representation to the world (and to each other in the church) of the fact and opportunity of the gospel. To be the body of Christ, then, means to be the channels through which the work of Christ continues to be done. Christ has committed to his church the proclamation of the great event of reconciliation that he accomplished on the cross, and, in that sense, the completion of the work he both began and did: the declaration of the "wonderful deeds of him who called you out of darkness into his marvelous light" (1 Pet. 2:9). As his body, we are to incorporate ("embody") that message as we proclaim it.[17]

Although the church and the kingdom of God are intimately interrelated, they are not identical. Some years ago, Philip Schaff pointed out that in many passages of the Bible, one may not substitute the church for the kingdom of God as if they were synonymous.[18] The kingdom of God, in its action, time, and state is far deeper, wider, and purer than the church. However, the "already but not yet" aspect of the kingdom is also true for the church. Herman N. Ridderbos, George Eldon Ladd, Oscar Cullman, John Bright, and others stressed that the kingdom, the active rule of Jesus Christ, is already present

---

17 Guder, *Ser Testigos de Jesucristo: La Misión de la Iglesia, Su Mensaje y Sus Mensajeros*, 28.
18 Phillip Schaff, *History of the Christian Church Vol. 1*, 509. Schaff mentions as examples Matt. 6:9; Mark 10:14; Luke 17:21; 1 Cor. 6:10; Rom. 15:17 where substituting the word *church* for *kingdom* would not make any sense. There is general agreement among many theologians that the concepts of church and kingdom are not synonymous, even though they are intimately related. See, for example, Herman Ridderbos, *The Coming of the Kingdom*, 347; David Bosch, *Witness to the World*, 219; Blauw, *The Missionary Nature of the Church*, 79; and Hans Küng, *The Church*, 94.

though it still awaits its fulfillment.[19] It has come, but it has not yet arrived.[20] Herman Ridderbos says the following:

> On the basis of what has been said above it is possible in our opinion to summarize our view of the relation between the basileia and the ekklesía. There can be no uncertainty about either the connection or the difference between these two fundamental notions: The basileia is the great divine work of salvation in its fulfillment and consummation in Christ; the ekklesía is the people elected and called by God and sharing in the bliss of the basileia. Logically, the basileia ranks first, not the ekklesía. . . .
>
> Insofar as the basileia is already a present reality, the ekklesía is also the place where the gifts and powers of the basileia are granted and received. It is, further, the gathering of those who, as the instruments of the basileia, are called upon to make profession of Jesus as the Christ, to obey his commandments, to perform the missionary task of the preaching of the gospel throughout the world. In every respect the church is surrounded and impelled by the revelation, the progress, the future of the kingdom of God without, however, itself being the basileia, and without ever being identified with it.[21]

The kingdom of God and the church are related through the person of Jesus Christ, the King of the kingdom and the Head of the church. The believer becomes a member of the kingdom of God through the redemption found in Jesus Christ the Head of the body, the church. The Father whose fullness dwells in Christ makes this transference possible (Col. 1:13, 19). The church and the mission of the kingdom of God are connected. They are not identical, but they are inextricably intertwined in the mission of God through the people of God sent to the world that God loves. What is more, it should be understood that the church is the missionary community of the disciples of the King.[22]

---

19 Ridderbos, *The Coming of the Kingdom*, 342-45; George Ladd, *The Presence of the Future*; Jürgen Moltmann, *The Church in the Power of the Spirit*, 98-196.

20 Van Engen, *God's Missionary People*, 101-18.

21 Ridderbos, *The Coming of the Kingdom*, 354-56.

22 This is the main theme found in the writings of Arthur Glasser. It is very clearly found in his book, *Announcing the Kingdom*.

This perspective has far-reaching consequences for how we perceive missionary communities whose nature and calling are not derived from an affiliation with a certain denomination or any structured institution. Missionary communities exist because they are covenant communities of the King, called to be instruments in the hands of God for the transformation of its environment and to be a blessing to the nations. In the words of René Padilla:

> All churches are called to collaborate with God in the transformation of the world, starting with a gospel centered in Jesus Christ as the Lord of the universe, whose dominion provides the basis for a holistic ecclesiology and mission.[23]

The church and the kingdom are neither identical nor completely distinct. A new consensus has arisen with respect to the nature of the kingdom.[24] This new consensus defines the kingdom as present, inaugurated, and beginning, while also being eschatological, coming, and future. This kingdom cannot be seen physically or institutionally. It is the dynamic and active rule of God through Jesus Christ by the means of the Holy Spirit. And so the gospel consists of the good news of the kingdom that has already come and is yet coming. God comes to humanity (Emmanuel), and God reigns over all humanity. Jesus speaks of future signs of the kingdom of God as he unveils his messianic credentials to the disciples of John the Baptist (consider Matt. 11:4-6; Isa. 61:1-3; Luke 4:18-19). The kingdom is already at hand but still is not completely manifest. Even though the church is not what it should be, it is still the primary locus of the rule of the King amid the King's loyal subjects, and where the kingdom is manifest during the time between the times, between the Ascension and the Second Coming. The kingdom is at hand, and local churches are the signs that direct the world's attention to the King who comes.

The church is the community ruled by the King.

In every cultural context, missionary congregations need to see themselves as the unique community of those who recognize the authority of Jesus Christ as their Lord and King. These followers of Jesus the Christ are different from other men and women they encounter within the larger sphere of the king-

---

23 Padilla and Yamamori, eds, *La Iglesia Local Como Agente de Transformación,* 13-45. Translated by the editors of this volume.
24 Ridderbos, *The Coming of the Kingdom,* 342.

dom of Christ. They freely and voluntarily commit to Jesus Christ as their Lord.[25]

The church is the central locus[26] of the rule of the King.

In whatever country or culture they are found, missionary congregations have a central place in the rule of the King because Christ reigns in them in a special way, as the Head of the body which is the church. The only place where Christ can reign in this way as the Head of the body of Christ is in the church. Therefore, when each new missionary church emerges, God's reign grows. The proclamation of the gospel results in the conversion of those who were previously in the realm of darkness to enter into the kingdom of light (Rom. 6:15-22; Col. 1:9-14). In these missionary congregations one can see this change of those who were once rebels transformed into followers of the King: obedient and ready to do his will. This conversion is at the heart, the essence, of the nature of the local congregation as the covenant community of the King. Therefore, the holistic growth of missionary congregations is a sign of the coming of God's kingdom.

The church is the anticipatory sign of the rule of the King.

Missionary congregations are made up of those who live out their lives and function in society under God's reign. These people are the "first fruit" of those who wait for the kingdom of God in the world.[27] The church is not the kingdom in its fullness. It is only a sign of the coming kingdom of God that is already here but is yet to come. As a result, Christians live in anxious expectation. In the words of Paul, missionary congregations know that "our present sufferings are not worth comparing with the glory that will be revealed in us. For the creation waits in eager expectation for the children of God to be revealed" (Rom. 8:18-19). Missionary congregations spring forth to the extent in which they practice, announce, show, and serve as heralds of the coming of God's kingdom, which is already present. Local congregations experience the lordship of the King as eschatological heralds of the One who is to come. The "already" gradually moves toward the anticipated "not yet" while the church announces the coming of the kingdom.

---

25   Van Engen, *The Growth of the True Church*, 282-83.

26   Barth, *Credo: A Presentation of the Chief Problems of Dogmatics with Reference to the Apostles' Creed*, 140-41.

27   Barth, *Church Dogmatics*.

The church's mission is to spread the knowledge of the rule of the King.

As the principle aspect of the coming kingdom of Christ, the missionary congregations are called to spread the knowledge of this reign throughout the world. This means that the local church is not an end in itself. It is also not the end goal of this mission. Local churches are instruments of something greater than themselves; they are instruments of the kingdom of God.

The church cannot create, bring about, or expand the kingdom. It can and should only be a witness to it.

Clearly, we see that the witness is carried out in word and deed,[28] in miracles, signs, and wonders. It is also seen in the transformation of people's lives, in the presence of the Holy Spirit, and in the radical work of creating a new humanity. When the local congregation testifies to the rule of King Jesus, this act becomes part of Christ's reign which is proclaimed. The kingdom comes when men and women come to know Christ. Consequently, local churches expand the church when they preach, proclaim, and live out their lives in faithfulness and obedience to the King. Congregations participate in the coming of the kingdom when they live in covenant community, as disciples of the King, as branch offices—satellites—of the kingdom of God. As the numbers of those who know and recognize the sovereignty of the King grow, the church becomes the instrument that anticipates the "already but not yet" kingdom of God.

The church cannot bring about the kingdom—only the King can do this. What the church can do is proclaim, come together, and grow in the expectation of the day when every knee will bow and all will confess that Jesus is Lord (Phil. 2:10). The New Testament uses the rhetorical device of parables to illustrate the growth and coming of the kingdom: for example, the parables of the sower, the mustard seed, the wedding feast, and the ten virgins (with the lamps with oil) in Matthew 13, 22, and 25. Jesus illustrates these truths further through his teachings on the day of judgment in Matthew 24-25.

The holistic development of the missionary church goes along with the fulfillment of the kingdom through Christ's dominion—the local missionary churches, embodied in one particular time, place, and culture. The church, not the kingdom, is the new Jerusalem (Rev. 21). The church, not the kingdom, is made up of those who have washed their clothes in the blood of the

---

28   Harvie Conn, *Evangelism: Doing Justice and Preaching Grace.*

Lamb (Rev. 7:14) and to whom Christ will present himself without stain or blemish (Eph. 5:27; Jude 24). Therefore, in this "time between times," we concentrate on the church because we understand that when we build up the missionary congregations, we are already participating in our final goal, the coming of the kingdom (consider Col. 1:13-20).

C. Multiplying new churches: the penultimate goal of God's mission

As the body of Christ, the church is the physical presence of God in this world for the blessing and transformation of the world (Rom. 12; 1 Cor. 12; Eph. 4; 1 Pet. 2 and 4). This truth obligates us to emphasize the ultimate importance of the church. The universal church, the church in the world, of all times and cultures is an idea, nothing more. Actually, this church does not exist in concrete, visible form. What exists is a multitude of local congregations, local churches who are each a local manifestation of the church universal. You and I and all the believers of Jesus Christ will never experience the universal church. The base from which we are sent into the world is the local congregation, in which we experience the communion of saints and grow spiritually. As such, it is impossible to overestimate the importance of the local congregation of men and women who love Christ and worship God through the power of the Holy Spirit.

Nevertheless, the final goal of our mission cannot only be the local congregation. Multiplying, growing, and watching over the development of the local church is the penultimate goal of our mission, as Orlando Costas helps us see.[29] The final goal of our missionary labor is the glory of God, as we will see in the last part of this chapter.

Needless to say, the penultimate goal of multiplying healthy churches is essential work. God has chosen the local congregation as his main instrument for his mission in the world. As such, in order to reach the final goal, it is of utmost importance to build thousands of new missionary congregations around the world. God is glorified when people's lives are changed and the family, socioeconomic, and political structures of a city or nation experience a radical transformation—all because the Holy Spirit uses the local churches to announce the coming of the kingdom of God in Jesus Christ in a holistic

---

29 See Costas' works: *The Church and Its Mission*, 90; *The Integrity of Mission*, 37-59; and *Christ Outside the Gate*, 46-48.

way, through word and deed, and in a contextually appropriate and biblically sound manner.

V. Because Multiplying New Churches Gives Glory to God

Why multiply new, healthy churches? The fifth reason overarches all the others. Multiplying new churches brings glory to God. At the end of the story, building new, healthy churches is not for the glory of a denomination or a missionary organization. It is not for the glory of a pastor or an evangelist. It is not for the glory of the mother church. Our fundamental motivation for multiplying new, healthy churches always must be from a profound desire to give glory to God.

A. "The Ten Blessings" of Ephesians 1

All that has been said previously in this chapter can be summed up in the words of Paul in the first chapter of Ephesians. Upon beginning his letter to the Ephesians, his main letter regarding the church and its mission, Paul uses the words of one of the oldest hymns of the primitive church. Although the music is not known, the words have been preserved because Paul used them to begin his letter. The hymn contains ten words that grammatically are verbs: ten action words. These ten actions are divided into three verses, one for each of the three people of the Trinity. Because of this I have called this passage "The Ten Blessings." Each verse emphasizes the work and special role of each person of the Trinity. This review of what God has done for us is beautiful, profound, and moving. Nevertheless, the most outstanding part of the hymn is a phrase that is repeated three times and serves as a chorus interwoven throughout the hymn. The phrase is "For the praise of his glory." See the words of the hymn below.

Ephesians 1:1-14: "The Ten Blessings"
Through the Father
    1. Chosen
    2. Made saints
    3. Predestined
    4. Adopted
Chorus: For the praise of his glory.

Through the Son
>   5. Redeemed
>   6. Pardoned
>   7. Made participants of the mystery
>   8. United with Christ
>   9. Co-heirs with him
>   *Chorus: For the praise of his glory.*

Through the Holy Spirit
>   10. Marked with the seal of the promise through the Holy Spirit,
>   who is the deposit (first payment) of our inheritance until the
>   redemption of God's possession
>   *Chorus: For the praise of his glory.*

Centuries later we find an echo of Paul's emphasis in Ephesians in the writings of Gisbertus Voetius (1589-1676). A Dutch theology professor, Voetius was one of the first protestant missiologists. Writing during the beginning of the 17th century, he affirmed that biblically, the mission of the church has a three-part goal. He declared that the goal of God's mission in the Bible was *conversio gentili; plantatio ecclesiae; gloria Dei*: (a) the conversion of people to faith in Jesus Christ; (b) the multiplying of churches; and (c) the glory of God.[30] During the past five centuries, this perspective has been the most fundamental basis for missionary work among evangelical churches, descendants of the Protestant Reformation. In its most basic expression, these evangelical churches' motivation for church expansion was derived from this visionary goal: God wants men and women to become followers of Christ, responsible members of the church, and agents of the transformation of their contexts, to the glory of God.[31] Notice that all three parts of Matthew's articulation of the Great Commission (Matt. 28:18-20) are found here: "disciple, baptize, and teach."

B. The vision in Revelation

The new, healthy church that stands out the most in the Bible is the congregation that comes together around the throne of Jesus Christ, the Shepherd of God in the new Jerusalem. What an amazing vision John describes in the

---

30   See John H. Bavinck, *An Introduction to the Science of Missions*, 155ff.
31   This phrase is an adaptation of the definition of mission from Donald McGavran, *Understanding Church Growth*, 35.

last few chapters of Revelation! The angel tells John that he will show him "the bride, the wife of the Lamb" (Rev. 21:9). This rhetorical figure, this verbal picture, is one of the main representations of the church of Jesus Christ, which Paul also describes as a bride ready to go to Jesus, her husband (Eph. 5:23-27). How marvelous! The angel is presenting the church as the new Jerusalem. The church has become a city with twelve gates that will never close, made from the twelve stones from Aaron's vestments in the tabernacle from the desert. The angel also makes him see that the "kings of the earth will bring their splendor into it." This vision is truly remarkable. The "kings of the earth" bring the splendor of their language, culture, history, civilization—bringing all of this to the new Jerusalem, which is the church, whose temple is Jesus Christ, whose sun and light is Christ, whose doors never close so that they can constantly and eternally invite all people to wash in the blood of Christ. Then they can come together with all the saints around the throne of the Shepherd. Together, all the members of this new, healthy church, sing in a thousand languages, as if in answer to the miracle of Pentecost in Acts 2. All the nations, families, tongues, and tribes of the world praise God with the hymn of eternity:

> "You are worthy, our Lord and God to receive glory and honor and power, for you created all things, and by your will they were created and have their being. . . . To him who sits on the throne and to the Lamb be praise and honor and glory and power, for ever and ever! . . . Salvation belongs to our God, who sits on the throne, and to the Lamb. . . . Amen! Praise and glory and wisdom and thanks and honor and power and strength be to our God for ever and ever. . . . Great and marvelous are your deeds, Lord God Almighty. Just and true are your ways, King of the nations. . . . Let us rejoice and be glad and give him glory! For the wedding of the Lamb has come, and his bride has made herself ready." (Rev. 4:11; 5:13b; 7:10b, 12; 15:3b; 19:7)

In this city that represents the church, there is a very special tree: the tree of life whose leaves are "for the healing of the nations" (Rev. 22:2). To multiply healthy churches is to participate in this vision, to be conduits, through the power of the Holy Spirit, in moving toward this new reality, the new heaven and the new earth—for the praise of the glory of our God. One of the ways in which we represent, signal, prepare the way for, invite others to join in, and participate in this vision is by multiplying new, healthy churches for the glory of God. The Bible teaches us that the people of God, the church, journeys from a garden to a new city, the new Jerusalem.

C. The final goal: for the praise of his glory

Why should we devote all the money, time, energy, and personnel resources to multiply healthy churches? In this essay I have suggested that fundamentally such an endeavor flows from God's nature and mission: "for God so loved the world." Love, God's initiative, his missionary action, forms the foundation, the basis for all efforts in multiplying new, healthy churches. God's love, then, forms the fountain from which flow the five reasons we have examined as to why we should multiply new congregations:

- Because God the Father seeks and finds the lost
- Because the love of Christ compels us
- Because the Holy Spirit has been sent for all people and to build the church
- Because the local congregation is the primary agent of the kingdom of God
- Because multiplying churches gives glory to God

We could then express the mission of the church in the following way:

> *It is the will of God that men and women of all peoples of the earth be invited to become followers of Jesus Christ, responsible members of Christ's church, joined together in faith communities, in the power of the Holy Spirit. These groups of believers, as the agents of the kingdom of God, seek to transform the reality of their context in order to give praise to God.*

The church of Jesus Christ is therefore called to creative missionary action in the world as it seeks to proclaim the good news of the kingdom of God in ways that are biblically faithful, contextually appropriate, and globally transformative. The Head of the church is Jesus Christ, the Lord. From this point of view, the church's existence has only one purpose: it exists for the praise and the glory of God.

What will be our motives for multiplying new, healthy churches? Will we choose human, sinful, selfish, and oppressive motives? Or will we choose the motives—and the goals—that the Bible gives us? Will we multiply churches for our own glory? Or will we commit ourselves to participate in God's mission for the praise of his glory?

CONCLUSION

The hope of the world and the possibility to transform the reality that we face today resides in multiplying thousands of new, healthy churches in every city, town, and village throughout the world. These congregations are to be made up of sons and daughters of God, followers of Jesus Christ, blessed with the presence and gifts of the Holy Spirit, who intentionally and carefully look to be signs of the coming of the kingdom of God, for the praise of the glory of God.

Questions

1. What are three of the five wrong motives for multiplying new, healthy churches?

2. List five biblical reasons for multiplying new churches.

3. Explain the term "missio Dei" in relation to church multiplication.

4. What do you think the author means when he writes, "God chooses his people to be his instruments of love in the search of the nations"?

5. What is the main purpose of God's covenants with his people and how does this go beyond the mere forgiveness of sins and the gift of eternal life?

6. Why is the multiplying of new, healthy churches not optional for the people of God?

7. In understanding the incarnation, how does the fact that "God became flesh among humanity" speak of how we, as his disciples, should live?

8. Explain the role of the Holy Spirit in the multiplying of new, healthy churches.

9. Why does the author refer to the Holy Spirit as being like the central nervous system of the body and how does this affect believers and their task in multiplying new churches?

10. Describe how the local congregation is the primary agent of the Kingdom of God, that the church and the kingdom are not synonymous.

11. Explain what the author means by "Multiplying new churches" is "the penultimate goal of God's mission."

3 CHURCH PLANTING IN THE NEW TESTAMENT

Todd Benkert

Introduction

If you look for the term "church planting" in the Bible, you will not find it, and yet you see churches planted throughout the history of the early church as it unfolds in the New Testament. Evangelism, discipleship, church planting, and church health are all aspects of the ministry of the gospel as followers of Christ take his message to the world. The New Testament is not a church planting manual, yet you see church planting strategy and methodology played out on the pages of Scripture as the first Christians evangelized their world. In the New Testament, evangelization includes church planting, and church planting does not exist apart from evangelism. Further, the New Testament church planters were concerned that these new churches functioned as healthy churches and that the believers in those churches grew to maturity and Christlikeness. Thus it is clear from the New Testament that the church can only fulfill its mission through evangelism that leads to the planting of healthy churches. In this chapter we will explore the concept of church planting as it intersects the ministries of Jesus, his disciples, and the apostle Paul.

I. Jesus Prepares His Followers for Evangelistic Work

Our study of church planting in the New Testament begins with the ministry of Jesus as he chose, trained, and sent out his disciples. While church planting itself did not begin until after Jesus' resurrection and ascension, Jesus laid the theological and preparatory groundwork for evangelistic work as he prepared his disciples for ministry. From the beginning of his public ministry, Jesus prepared his disciples to spread the message of his kingdom to the peoples of the world.

A. The Calling and Instruction of Jesus' Disciples

When Jesus initially called his disciples, he indicated that he would send them out as messengers of the good news. Jesus appointed twelve disciples "that he might send them out to preach" (Mark 3:14). Among them, Jesus called Matthew to "follow me" (Matt. 9:9) and issued a similar call to Phillip (John 1:43) and the other disciples. In his call of Simon and Andrew (Mark 1:16-20; Matt. 4:18-22; Luke 5:11), we clearly see the implications of becoming a disciple of Jesus. Jesus called to them, "Follow me, and I will make you fishers of men." This call to follow Jesus meant not only allowing Jesus to be their teacher but also following in his example and work—to become apprentices who would learn and carry out the same work as Jesus did.[1] These men would change from being fishermen to become "fishers of men," carrying on Jesus' work of reaching people with the good news of the kingdom. Thus, in the gospels, the call to discipleship was a call not only to be with Jesus and learn from him but also to join him in his mission and in his redemptive purpose as his messengers, sent out in his name.

As Jesus instructed his new disciples, he did not delay in including them in his mission work. In the midst of their training, Jesus sent out the Twelve (Matt. 10:5; Mark 6:7; Luke 9:2) and later seventy- two (Luke 10:1) disciples on an evangelistic campaign. Both Matthew and Luke identify the content of the message Jesus gave them. They were to "proclaim the kingdom of God" (Luke 9:2); "the kingdom of heaven is at hand" (Matt. 10:7). In their procla-

---

1   Donald A. Hagner, *World Biblical Commentary Volume 33A: Matthew1-13,* 76-77; W.D. Davies and Dale C. Allison Jr., *A Critical and Exegetical Commentary on the Gospel According to Saint Matthew, ICC,* 1:398; R.T. France, *The Gospel of Matthew,* 96, 147; John Nolland, *The Gospel of Matthew,* 179.

mation, the disciples preached essentially the same message that John the Baptist and Jesus had already been preaching (Matt. 3:2; 4:17; 9:35; Mark 1:4, 15). Now Jesus sent out his disciples as messengers of the kingdom. This sending during Jesus' earthly ministry prepared the disciples for the evangelistic and church planting work that was to come after his death and resurrection.

As he prepared to send out the Twelve (Matt. 10:1) and the seventy-two (Luke 10:1), Jesus instructed his disciples using a metaphor of "harvest." Jesus told them, "The harvest is plentiful, but the laborers are few. Therefore, pray earnestly to the Lord of the harvest to send out laborers into his harvest" (Matt. 9:37-38; Luke 10:2, ESV). Here Jesus used Old Testament imagery to explain that the salvation that had been promised in the past (e.g., Isa. 27:12; Hos. 6:11; Ps. 126:6) was being accomplished in the present and many were ready to be gathered into his kingdom.[2] Jesus used "harvest" imagery again in John 4:35-38. As many Samaritans gathered to see Jesus, he declared to his disciples, "Look, I tell you, lift up your eyes, and see that the fields are white for harvest" (John 4:35, ESV). Jesus was indicating that the time of spiritual harvest had now come and the disciples were to be a part of it. The church planting activity that would occur following Jesus' ascension was a part of the spiritual harvesting of those who would respond to the good news.

B. The Commissioning of Jesus' Disciples

After his death and resurrection, in the final days before his ascension, Jesus explicitly commissioned his disciples for evangelistic ministry. If the disciples had not yet understood their calling to take the gospel to the peoples of the world, that calling was now made clear. All four gospels and the book of Acts record commissioning statements of Jesus in which he explicitly sends them out as missionaries (Matt. 28:18-20; Mark 16:15; Luke 24:46-49; John 20:21; Acts 1:8). The foundation of church planting work rests on this Great Commission of Jesus to his disciples.

---

2 Nolland, *World Biblical Commentary Volume 35B: Luke 9:21-18:34*. 551; Davies and Allison, *A Critical and Exegetical Commentary*, 2:149; Joseph A. Fitzmyer, *The Gospel According to Luke I-IX Volume 28*, 2:846.

John 20:21.

As part of the harvest teaching in the Gospel of John, Jesus had explained to his disciples, "I sent you" (John 4:38) to reap a harvest. Now, at the end of his gospel, John records a similar commissioning statement. Here, Jesus compares his own ministry to that of the disciples: Just as the Father had sent Jesus, he states, "I also send you" (John 20:21; cf. 17:18, NASB).[3] The ministry of the disciples would be a continuation of the ongoing ministry of Jesus as he himself had been sent by the Father. John's gospel records several aspects of this ministry for which Jesus was sent. The Father sent the Son to speak the words of the Father (7:16; 8:26, 28; 12:49-50; 14:24; 17:8; cf. 3:34), to accomplish his works (5:36; 9:4), to do the Father's will (4:34; 5:30; 6:38; 8:28-29) to follow his commands (10:18; 14:31), and ultimately to seek his glory (7:18). Because Jesus sent his disciples just as the Father sent him, his disciples were to follow this same pattern. Jesus did not merely send his disciples on a mission. He sent them to carry on his mission, and that mission concerned bringing people to faith in him.

The later planting of churches by these disciples was a result of their being sent out in this way. When the disciples spoke the words of Jesus, like him, they spoke words that led to eternal life (5:24; 6:63; 12:50). When the disciples were sent out by Jesus, they were sent to reap a harvest for eternal life (4:36, 39a; cf. 6:39-40) by one whose will is to save (3:17). As Jesus laid down his life (10:18; 3:16), his disciples were sent out with the message of eternal life. Thus the church planting of these disciples was part of the sending activity of God. When we too are sent with the gospel message, new believers and new communities of faith are the necessary outcome. Church planting results when God sends us to take his message to the world.

Luke 24:46-49.

The Gospel of Luke also records a commissioning statement of Jesus. In this gospel, Jesus commissions his disciples during his final post-resurrection appearance. Here Jesus links the proclamation of repentance and forgiveness of sins to the eternal purposes of God. The primary verb phrase, "it is written" to which the other verbs refer, is an indication that the death and resurrection and the evangelistic activity that would follow were all part of God's plan.

---

3   Note, the word πέμπω in John 20:21 carries essentially the same meaning as ἀποστέλλω in John 4:38. Andreas J. Köstenberger, *The Missions of Jesus and the Disciples According to the Fourth Gospel*, 97-106.

Fred Craddock notes, "To say that 'It is written' is the equivalent of saying, 'It has been God's plan all along.' . . . The mission to the world was God's plan from the beginning."[4] Thus, not only did the Scripture speak to what had just occurred, "that the Christ should suffer and on the third day rise from the dead," but also it declared what would come next. It was God's plan from the beginning that the gospel of repentance and forgiveness "would be proclaimed in his name to all nations." Just as the death and resurrection fulfill the prophecy of the Old Testament and of Jesus himself, so the evangelistic mission of the disciples would fulfill such prophecy as well.[5] Taken with other Scriptures, we can rightly conclude that church planting, the gathering of new believers into churches, is a fulfillment of the redemptive purpose of God and has been God's intention from the beginning.

Acts 1:8.

In the first chapter of Acts, Luke records a second commission statement from the final post-resurrection appearance of Christ. Jesus begins by stating, "You will receive power when the Holy Spirit has come upon you" (NASB). Jesus had already promised the Holy Spirit (1:5), and now he promised that with the Spirit they would receive "power" (δύναμιν). Power, here, refers to spiritual enabling for witness as the disciples proclaim the message of Christ (2:14ff.; 4:31, 33; 14:3; cf. 6:10; Rom. 1:16-17).[6] As the book of Acts unfolds, we see this promise of the Spirit fulfilled, and this enabling power is not only for the Twelve but for other believers as well.[7] Modern day church planters should likewise depend on and expect the enabling power of the Holy Spirit as his witnesses.

The phrase "you shall be my witnesses" (NASB) indicates the role the disciples will play in the Lord's plan. The concept of "witness" in Acts refers to "witnesses who bear a divine message."[8] For the Twelve, the most obvious aspect of their role was as eyewitnesses of the resurrection and of the earthly

---

4   Fred B. Craddock, *Luke: Interpretation: A Bible Commentary for Teaching and Preaching*, 291; cf Acts 10:43; 26:22-23.

5   John T. Squires, *The Plan of God in Luke-Acts*, 139-47.

6   Darrell L. Bock, *Acts: Baker Exegetical Commentary on the New Testament*, 63; Fitzmyer, *The Acts of the Apostles: A New Translation with Introduction and Commentary*, 205.

7   Eckhard J. Schnabel, *Early Christian Mission*, 1:392-93. Schnabel notes the following texts here: Acts 6:3, 5; 9:31; 11:24, 28; 13:52; 15:28; 21:4, 11.

8   BAGD, *Greek-English Lexicon of the New Testament and Other Early Christian Literature*, 2nd ed., 494 and BDAG, *Greek-English Lexicon*, 3rd ed., 619.

ministry of Jesus. Thus, in one sense, the ministry of the apostles was unique as they were not only eyewitnesses of Jesus but divinely chosen by him as official representatives of that witness. In that sense, the role of the Twelve includes "a once-for-all unrepeatable witness."[9] The Twelve, however, are not the only witnesses of Christ. Luke uses the noun "witness" also of Stephen (22:20) and Paul (22:15; 26:16). Additionally, the Old Testament prophets (10:43; cf. 26:22), the Holy Spirit (5:32), and God the Father himself (14:3; 15:8; cf. 14:17) all "bear witness" of Christ. While at times Luke employs the word "witness" to signify the special role of the Twelve, Luke does not limit the concept of witness to these men.

Thus, while the Twelve had a unique role, Jesus' call to be witnesses extends to all believers. We too are witnesses when we testify to our own experience with Christ the significance of the gospel message. Likewise, church planters are those who have themselves had an experience with the risen Christ and who bear witness to the significance of the gospel message and call others to turn in faith to Christ.

Further, "witness" in the book of Acts is not merely a recollection of events. Rather, the messengers bear witness of something they believe and seek to convince others to believe as well. They give witness of something so significant that they cannot stop speaking about what they have seen and heard (4:20). Allison Trites notes, "Witnesses are passionately involved in the case they seek to represent. They have been apprehended by it, and so they have an inner compulsion to plead its merits with others."[10] Witnesses desire to persuade others to accept the truth and the significance of their message. Church planting in the New Testament was a result of the ministry of these witnesses as they went out to persuade others to believe the good news of Jesus that they themselves believed and experienced.

Matthew 28:18-20.

Of the commissioning passages of Jesus, none is more often cited among evangelicals than the Great Commission text of Matthew 28:18-20. The commission in Matthew has three parts in which Jesus gives the disciples a word of authority, a word of commission, and a word of promise.[11] Jesus begins by

---

9   Andrew C. Clark, *Parallel Lives: The Relation of Paul to the Apostles in the Lucan Perspective*, 45.
10   Lothar Coenen and Allison A. Trites, "Testimony, Witness," 1,049.
11   Schnabel, *Early Christian Mission*, 1:353.

stating that "all authority" has been given to him. Many scholars see here an allusion to the "Son of Man" in Daniel 7:13-14.[12] W. D. Davies and Dale Allison describe this allusion as "an overwhelming depiction of the Son of Man's triumphant victory and consequent authority (both given to him by God the Father)."[13] Jesus commissions the disciples on the basis of that authority. Further, a significant element of the passage is the fourfold use of the word "all," of which this is the first. The use of "all" signals a "universal perspective" in which "the exalted Son of Man is Lord over all people and over all things, over heaven and earth and therefore over all nations."[14] Jesus has authority not only over the disciples but also over "all nations" to whom they are to go. The church planting activity that would result was under this authority. Jesus not only has the right to send us, but we go out as emissaries of his divine authority.

Having established his authority, Jesus then commissioned his disciples. The disciples were to intentionally "go and make disciples."[15] The primary verb is "make disciples" (μαθητεύσατε). Jesus essentially instructed his disciples "to make more of what they were themselves."[16] That is, as disciples, they were to make more disciples. This final commission by Jesus was a shift from his previous sending out of the disciples to "preach" (Matt. 10:7). David Bosch notes, "The task of the disciples is no longer merely that of 'preaching,' but of enlisting people into their fellowship."[17] The fact that the passage uses the verb "make disciples" rather than "preach the gospel," combined with the following participles, "baptizing" and "teaching," indicates that more than merely preaching the gospel is in mind here. As the gospel is preached, persons will become disciples of Jesus Christ. Church planting is the natural result of this "disciple-making" ministry.

---

12   See especially Davies and Allison, *A Critical and Exegetical Commentary on the Gospel According to Saint Matthew*, *ICC*, 3:682-83; also Schnabel, *Early Christian Mission*, 1:353-54; and Köstenberger and Peter O'Brien, *Salvation to the Ends of the Earth*, 102.

13   Davies and Allison, *The Gospel According to Saint Matthew*, 3:688.

14   Schnabel, *Early Christian Mission*, 1:354.

15   While the verb "πορευθέντες" is not imperative in form, Cleon Rogers makes a convincing case that the verb is imperative in force and thus the command includes that the disciples must intentionally go. Cleon L. Rogers, "The Great Commission," 258-67. See also Daniel B. Wallace, *Greek Grammar Beyond the Basics*, 642, 645.

16   Michael J. Wilkins, *Discipleship in the Ancient World and Matthew's Gospel*, 162.

17   David J. Bosch, "The Scope of Mission," 24.

The remaining verbs follow naturally. "Make disciples" includes both "baptizing" and "teaching." These supporting verbs indicate that "make disciples" goes beyond mere preaching, but refers to a preaching that results in new disciples who are then baptized into the church and are trained in the teachings of the Word of God. As the gospel goes out to "all nations," new believers and new churches will be the expected result. In the New Testament, church planting is first and foremost about making disciples—obedience to the Great Commission.

A final section of the commission provides a word of promise: "and behold, I am with you always, to the end of the age" (ESV). This final phrase of Matthew's gospel is emphatic, including both an introductory clause, "and behold," and the use of the personal pronoun "I". Jesus promises to be with his disciples "even to the end of the age" (NASB). Thus, Jesus promises his presence with the disciples as they do their evangelistic and church planting work. Jesus does not send out the disciples to complete this mission on their own. "He will be in their midst, though unseen, and will empower them to fulfill the commission he has given them."[18] Those who choose to follow the Lord in church planting work can be assured of his presence as they go about the work.

II. The Church Planting Ministry of the Twelve

The book of Acts reveals that the disciples took Jesus' commission seriously. As a result of their obedience, the Twelve firmly established the church in Jerusalem and its many house congregations. Beginning in Jerusalem, the book of Acts charts the progress of the Word from these initial churches planted by the disciples in Jerusalem to the establishment of the church among the peoples and cities of the Roman Empire.

A. The Twelve as Church Planting Missionaries

The book of Acts was not written as a history of church planting nor as a handbook for church planting strategy. As Luke describes the ministry of the Twelve, he gives very little explicit information about their church planting strategy and little data from which to discern one. Rather, Luke's purpose is to show the advance of the gospel as it spreads from Jerusalem to the ends of

18 Hagner, *Matthew 14-28*, 889.

the earth and from the Jewish people to the Gentiles. Thus, rather than a full accounting of the church planting activities of the Twelve—and much less an explanation of a specific strategy—Luke only follows Peter and John, with most of the focus on Peter. Despite this small amount of biblical data, however, we see evidence that the Twelve were obedient to the Great Commission and were intentional in their evangelistic practice as they sought to establish churches throughout Jerusalem and later "to the ends of the earth" (Acts 1:8).

Following the empowering by the Spirit at Pentecost (Acts 2), the disciples began their preaching ministry. Primarily focusing on Peter, Luke portrays the disciples boldly proclaiming the gospel in Jerusalem. The Jerusalem church grew quickly as the gospel spread. The primary role of the disciples in Acts was to witness to the Christ event and its significance, calling people to repentance and faith in Jesus. Thus the primary "method" of the apostles in Acts is proclamation,[19] and through that proclamation the Twelve established the church and its house congregations throughout Jerusalem.

Beyond the initial proclamation of the gospel and establishing of the church in Jerusalem, however, Luke provides little information. A few stories of Peter remain that take place outside Jerusalem, but there is no narrative record in Acts of a broad evangelistic campaign by the Twelve outside the holy city. In the New Testament there is very little available information about the early apostolic mission. Luke writes for his own unique purposes and is very selective in his use of materials. Thus our knowledge of the early activity of the apostles is limited. Nevertheless, Luke emphasizes the positive effects of the Twelve's ministry.[20]

Luke shows the disciples as bold proclaimers of the gospel who fill Jerusalem with the teaching about Jesus and win many to faith in him. In Acts the disciples begin with a centralized mission and work outward. Michael Green explains,

> They seem consistently to have *worked outwards from a warm centre.* . . . They gave attention to their own unity and prayerfulness, obedience and expectancy. And they were able to move out from that hot

---

19 For a discussion of the primary terminology for Christian proclamation in the New Testament, see Michael Green, *Evangelism in the Early Church*, 48-77.

20 Schnabel, *Early Christian Mission*, 1:522-23.

centre on to the streets with enormous effect on the day of Pentecost and in the months that followed. In obedience to Jesus they began to be his witnesses in Jerusalem first, then Judaea, then Samaria, and then to the uttermost ends of the earth. It was an effective strategy. . . . God added daily to the church those who were being saved.[21]

Luke seems to focus on Jerusalem as the center from which the gospel will go forth, and on the Twelve as the leaders of an Israel that God has restored. Andreas Köstenberger and Peter O'Brien explain:

> Although we might have expected to be given an account of the missionary travels of the twelve apostles, generally this does not appear in Acts. . . . Instead, Luke sees them as closely linked with the city of Jerusalem, a connection that persists throughout the narrative. As the nucleus of the restored Israel, they are preeminently witnesses to Israel 'in Jerusalem', from which centre the word of the Lord will sound forth, as the Old Testament prophecies had anticipated (*e.g.,* Isa. 2:1-4; Mic. 4:1-5).[22]

Luke thus focuses on the beginnings of the mission in Jerusalem. He highlights the tremendous success in Jerusalem (Acts 2:41, 47; 4:4; 5:14; 6:7) both in evangelism and in the establishing of the church. Up until the martyrdom of Stephen and the persecution by Saul, Luke records, "The word of God kept on spreading; and the number of the disciples continued to increase greatly in Jerusalem" (Acts 6:7, NASB). Jerusalem becomes the center from which the surrounding areas are reached with the gospel.

While it is not Luke's focus, we do see evidence of evangelistic ministry outside Jerusalem. For example, Peter and John confirmed the mission of Philip to the Samaritans (8:14-17) and, in the process, undertook a preaching tour of Samaritan villages (8:25). Likewise, after the conversion of Paul, because of peace in the region and rest from persecution, Peter began a traveling evangelistic ministry (9:31-32a).[23] The fact that he preached in Lydda, Joppa,

---

21 Green, *Thirty Years That Changed the World: The Book of Acts for Today,* 47-48.
22 Köstenberger and O'Brien, *Salvation to the Ends of the Earth,* 139. See also Schnabel, *Early Christian Mission,* 1:524.
23 This fact is contrary to the popular conception that the disciples began their traveling ministry only as a result of the persecution and only after martyrdom of James in Acts 12. The "all" (πάντων) of 9:32 refers back to "Judea, Galilee, and Samaria" in 9:31.

and Caesarea is evidence that his mission activity extended well beyond Jerusalem.[24] In Caesarea, Peter led the Gentile Cornelius and his family to faith in Christ (10:34-48). Returning to Jerusalem, Peter explained what had happened and how repentance and new life had now come to the Gentiles (11:1-18). After persecution broke out in Jerusalem, James, the brother of John, was martyred, and Herod had Peter arrested (12:1-3). Upon his miraculous release (12:4-17), Peter "departed and went to a different place" (12:17, ESV).

Outside of Acts, we see further indications of a church planting ministry of the disciples beyond Judea. In the longer ending of Mark, the disciples received their commission from Jesus, "went out and preached everywhere" (Mark 16:20).[25] In 1 Corinthians 9:5, as Paul defends his rights as an apostle, he notes the practice of Peter and the other apostles to take along their believing spouses. The context refers to the accompanying of their wives as they traveled on mission.[26] Eckhard Schnabel also argues, from circumstantial evidence in the New Testament, that the apostles were engaged in missionary activity beyond Jerusalem. He suggests that Paul's reference to the apostles taking along their wives (1 Cor. 9:5), Paul's unwillingness to build on another's foundation (Rom. 15:20), and his insistence that he worked harder than the other apostles (1 Cor. 15:10), implies that the Twelve were engaged in church planting activity. Further, Schnabel argues persuasively for at least the general authenticity of later traditions that the apostles, after twelve years in Jerusalem, engaged in a planned mission to the regions of the known world.[27] Thus, the earliest church planting activity occurred as the Twelve planted the Jerusalem church and later began to take the gospel to the Gentile regions beyond.

---

24 Oscar Cullmann, *Peter: Disciple, Apostle, Martyr*, 36.
25 Whether one recognizes the ending of Mark to be authentic to the gospel or not, the phrase here does reflect the viewpoint of the early church of the activity of the apostles. On this text George Peters comments, "The exact locations and geographical areas we are unable to establish with certainty. From the course of history of Christianity in apostolic times, we are justified to conclude that all of them were effective evangelists and missionaries. According to tradition, most of them laid down their lives as martyrs in the mission fields of the world. The rapid and far-flung spread of Christianity within a few decades is our best commentary on the zeal and labors of the apostles." Peters, *A Biblical Theology of Missions*, 134.
26 Hans Conzelmann, *1 Corinthians, A Commentary on the First Epistle to the Corinthians*, 153; Ferdinand Hahn, *Mission in the New Testament*, 49 n. 2; C. K. Barrett, *A Commentary on the First Epistle to the Corinthians*, 203-04.
27 Schnabel, *Early Christian Mission*, 1:527-32.

B. The Strategy and Methodology of the Twelve

Piecing together a "strategy of the Twelve" from the accounts in Acts is somewhat tenuous. Those who seek to discern the particulars of such a strategy will be frustrated by a lack of biblical material from which to do so. Nevertheless, given the limited material, one can surmise that in terms of method, the disciples preached the gospel liberally and responded to receptive people. In terms of strategy, the apostles sought to saturate Jerusalem and Judea with the gospel and establish the church there before moving on to other areas.

Not enough evidence exists to say with confidence that the apostles had a strategy for fulfilling the Great Commission to the "uttermost part of the earth" (Acts 1:8, KJV). The New Testament does provide at least enough evidence to show that such a strategy was possible if not probable.[28] Ample evidence exists, however, to discern the practice of the Twelve, at least as it pertained to their mission to Jerusalem and Judea. While the evidence in Acts is minimal, Schnabel summarizes the missionary tactics of the disciples this way: "Proclamation of the good news of God's redemptive action in Jesus Christ to as many people as possible, to Jews and to Gentiles, in all regions and among all peoples, at every opportunity."[29]

They preached the gospel abundantly.

If their primary method was the clear proclamation of the gospel, their primary local strategy was to preach at every opportunity. In Acts the apostles make a continual practice of teaching and preaching the good news (Acts 2:42, 46; 5:42). Further, the disciples take advantage of every opportunity they have to spread the gospel message. Luke records that Peter preached to crowds gathered after the miracle at Pentecost (Acts 2:6, 14) and again after the healing of a lame man (Acts 3:11-26). When he was brought before the Sanhedrin, he used the opportunity to proclaim the gospel to the Jewish leaders (Acts 4:8-12; 5:29-32; cf. Stephen before the synagogue leaders in Acts 7:1-53). When the apostles traveled to validate the Samaritan mission, they used the occasion to preach to the surrounding villages (8:25). They preached in the temple (Acts 2:46; 3:11; 5:20-21, 42; cf. 5:12), in homes (Acts 2:46; 5:42; 10:27), and before the Jewish council (5:27-32) in Jerusalem and in the

---

28 For a detailed analysis of the possibility of an extensive apostolic strategy and mission, see Schnabel, *Early Christian Mission*, 1:436-551.

29 Ibid, 1:512.

surrounding villages and cities of Judea, Galilee, and Samaria (8:25; 9:31-32).[30]

The result of this abundant sowing of the gospel was that the area became saturated with the gospel message. The number of Christian disciples continued to grow (Acts 2:47; 4:4; 5:14; 6:7; 9:31, 35, 42). The Jewish leaders, in opposition to the gospel, recognized that the apostles had "filled Jerusalem" with the teaching of the resurrection of Christ (Acts 5:28). The persecution in Acts 8:1-4 is further evidence that the gospel had spread in Jerusalem and was effectively taking hold. Ironically, the purpose of the persecution was to stop the message of the gospel, but by scattering many of the church leaders, the persecution ended up multiplying the influence of the Jerusalem church and thus contributed to the continuing spread of the gospel to the surrounding region.[31]

Further evidence of the liberal preaching of the gospel and its subsequent success is the establishment of the church in the region. By chapter nine of Acts, Luke refers to "the church throughout all Judea and Galilee and Samaria" (ESV). Later Paul would refer in his letters to "the churches of Judea" (Gal. 1:22)[32] and "the churches of God in Christ Jesus that are in Judea" (1 Thess. 2:14, ESV). The continued teaching ministry in the church (Acts 2:42-47; 5:42; cf. 9:31-32) is evidence that the apostles are committed to the

---

30 In Acts 9:32, Luke records that Peter traveled "among them all" (διά πάντων), a phrase that likely refers to the church in the regions of Judea and Galilee and Samaria mentioned in 9:31. Howard Marshall notes, "Peter is represented as traveling among the churches outside Jerusalem in order to give them apostolic teaching (2:42); his activity, however, is not confined to teaching the Christians, but also includes evangelism" in *The Acts of the Apostles: An Introduction and Commentary*, 178. For further discussion of the phrase διά πάντων, see Barrett, *Acts of the Apostles*, 1:479.

31 Bock, *Acts*, 320. The persecution was not God's way of getting them to obey the Great Commission. Rather, the disciples were so effective that persecution came. Those who were scattered made the most of the opportunity. The Twelve stayed in Jerusalem, continuing the work there. Schnabel further notes, "The comment in Acts 8:3 that Saul entered 'house after house' in order to drag off both men and women whom he arrested and committed to prison may plausibly be taken as an indication of house churches that actively proclaimed the gospel and attracted new converts." Schnabel, *Early Christian Mission*, 1:420. Additionally, Luke's recording of the seventy-two who were trained by Jesus in mission work is an indication that gospel proclaimers likely included more than the Twelve from the first days of the church. If so, the fact that those scattered proclaimed the gospel wherever they went would be expected rather than coming as a surprise.

32 Interestingly, J. Gresham Machen suggests that the reason Paul was unknown to the apostles other than Peter and James in Gal. 1:19-22 is that "the others were out of the city, engaged in missionary work in Judea" in *The Origin of Paul's Religion*, 76.

discipleship of these new believers and the establishment of the church. Those who would engage in the task of church planting today should not miss that the primary means of that first church planting movement was the abundant preaching of the gospel message at every opportunity. Church planting in the New Testament begins and depends on the abundant preaching of the message of the resurrected Christ.

They responded to the receptive.

Another key factor of the church planting activity of the apostles is their pattern of responding to receptive peoples. At least on one occasion, the disciples recognized the work of God in making people receptive to the gospel. While the apostles continued in Jerusalem, those who were dispersed because of persecution began to evangelize other areas (Acts 8:4). When the Samaritans were receptive to the preaching of Philip, the apostles sent Peter and John to them (Acts 8:14).[33] There the disciples responded to the receptivity of the Samaritans. During their mission, they engaged in a preaching and teaching ministry among them (8:25). The text does not reveal how long this ministry took place. However, Peter and John spoke not only to the Samaritans in that particular location but also to "many villages" of the Samaritans.[34] Thus, while the Twelve were not the initial carriers of the gospel message there, they affirmed and expanded the evangelistic ministry to the Samaritans and responded to their receptivity by multiplying the spread of the gospel message among them. As a result, the response in Samaria was significant enough that Luke later describes the church as extending "throughout all . . . Samaria" (9:31). Church planting among the people of Samaria was a result of fervent evangelistic work among these people who were receptive to the gospel message.

III. The Church Planting Ministry of Paul

The central church planting figure in the New Testament is the apostle Paul, and we rightly focus much of our attention on his ministry activity. More than any other person in the apostolic era, the apostle Paul took the gospel to the Gentile world and established churches wherever he went. The

---

33 The term ἀπέστειλαν implies an official mission. Fitzmyer, *Acts of the Apostles*, 405.
34 Barrett notes that the phrase πολλὰς κώμας indicates "an extensive evangelistic tour among Samaritan villages" in *Acts of the Apostles*, 1:418. John Polhill further notes, "The reference to the apostles evangelizing the Samaritan villages is significant. Not only did they endorse the Samaritan mission, but they also enthusiastically participated in it." Polhill, *Acts: An Exegetical and Theological Exposition of Holy Scripture: Acts*, 221.

book of Acts focuses the latter half of the book on the missionary activity of Paul as the word of God spread from Judea and Samaria to the uttermost parts of the earth.

A. Paul as Church Planting Missionary

Acts records three missionary journeys of Paul and his companions. In his epistles to churches and individuals, we see further evidence of Paul's church planting missionary activity and continued concern for those churches he planted. Paul saw it as his mission to win people to faith in Christ and to establish churches in places where there were none. Paul's calling and purpose was to preach the gospel where it had not been named (Rom. 15:20), and we can learn much from him as we explore his activity, strategy, and methods outlined in the New Testament.

In Romans 15:14-33, Paul gives his own summary of his church planting ministry. Here Paul speaks about his specific church planting goals. In his own words, we can discern the goals that Paul sought to reach in his missionary activity and his method of church planting activity. The aim of Paul in the evangelistic task was both the initial conversion and the spiritual growth of believers in Christ. In verses 14-18, Paul speaks in terms of the result of his ministry, that is, the conversion and growth of the Gentiles. In verse 19 and following, Paul continues to speak of the results of his ministry, but now he speaks in geographic terms. As a result of the power of God working through him, Paul states that he has "fulfilled" (ESV, πεπληρωκέναι; cf. Col. 1:25) the gospel "from Jerusalem all the way around to Illyricum" (Rom. 15:19). The statement that he has "fulfilled the ministry of the gospel" refers neither to his manner of preaching, nor to the idea that every person in the region has heard the gospel. Rather, Paul has completed the pioneering task assigned to him and has strategically planted churches in the region extending from "Jerusalem all the way around to Illyricum."[35] The following chart (see next pages) from Craig Ott shows the church planting activity of Paul as it has been described in the New Testament.[36]

---

35 C.E.B. Cranfield, *A Critical and Exegetical Commentary on the Epistle to the Romans*, 2:762; Thomas R. Schreiner, *Romans*, 770; Douglas J. Moo, *The Epistle to the Romans*, 896.
36 Craig Ott, "Churches Planted by the Apostle Paul in the Book of Acts."

Churches Planted by the Apostle Paul in the Book of Acts

City/Text	Location	Coworkers	Method	Factors	Results	Misc.
			The First Missionary Journey – 46-48 A.D.			
Cyprus (Salmis & Paphos) 13.4-12	Perhaps previously evangelized (11:20). Barnabas & several disciples come from Cyprus (4:36; 21:16).	Barnabas, John-Mark	Teaching in the synagogue [2] Meeting the proconsul Sergius	Power encounter with magician Bar-Jesus und Eymas.	Sergius becomes a Christian.	Cyprus later served by Barnabas &. John-Mark (15.39)
Pisidian Antioch 13.13-52	Commercial center; many Jews. Roman colony. Ethnically mixed. (Attalia & Perga are passed over.)	Barnabas	Teaching in the synagogue. On 2nd Sabbath "nearly the whole city came.	Paul possibly sick (Gal 4.13).	Many Jews, God-fearers and other Gentiles believed. Persecution from the Jews (cf. 2Tim 3.11)	**The Word of the Lord spread through the whole region.** (13.49).
Iconium 14.1-7	Wealthy and fruitful. In a different region than Lystra and Derbe		Teaching in the synagogue	Signs and wonders.	Many Jews and Greeks believe. Persecution from the Jews.	They remained "a long time" there preaching and teaching.
Lystra 14.6-20a	Away from the primary trade route, a safe place.		Begins with a healing.	Healing.	P & B are mistaken for gods. Some become disciples. Persecution from the Jews. P. is stoned	Timothy comes from this church (16.1)
Derbe 14.20-21	On the eastern border of the Roman Province.		Preaching		Many became disciples.	Gaius comes from Derbe (20.4)
Perga 14.25	Leading city of Pamphylia. Strong Artemis cult.		Preaching		No church is reported in Acts, but a 4th century basilica is witness of an early church there.	
					Believers were "commended to the Lord", 14.21b-23.	

Paul visited, strengthened, exhorted and installed elders in these churches on the return trip of the first missionary journey, 15.40-16.5. The HS forbids Paul to preach in Asia & Bithynia. 16.6-7

Most churches were visited and strengthened again at the start of Paul's second missionary journey.

City/Text	Location	Coworkers	Method	Factors	Results	Misc.
			The Second Missionary Journey – 49-52 A.D.			
Philippi 16.11-40	Leading city of the region on the Via Egnatia. Roman colony and military settlement. Few Jews. A medical school. (Troas, Samothrace & Neapolis[3] are passed over)	Silas (=Silvanus), Timothy, Luke.	Jewish women's prayer meeting.	Guidance through a vision. Power encounter with the fortune-teller leads to imprisonment. Miraculous prison release.	Lydia and her household, and the jailer and his household believe and are baptized. Due to arrest and opposition Paul leaves the city.	Paul receives financial support from Philippi (Phil. 4.10,15-17). Luke perhaps comes from Philippi (Ramsay). Tim & Erastus minister here later? (19.22)
Thessalonica 17.1-9	Capitol of Macedonia. With 50,000 to 100,000 residents the largest city of the region. A port city at the crossing of two trade routes. (Amphipolis & Apollonia[3] are passed over.)	Silas, Timothy	Teaching in the synagogue on three Sabbaths.	Preaching was "in the power of the Holy Spirit and full conviction" (1Th 1.5). Housed by Jason.	Several Jews, many God-fearers believe, a number of "leading women". Opposition from the Jews and from "countrymen" (1Th 1.16, 14). Gentiles repent "turning to serve a living and true God" (1Th 1.9).	Coworkers remain after P. Tim. returns later (1Th 3.2). **An example in the region; the Word spread from Thess to "every place" beyond Macedonia & Achaia** (1Th 1.7-8). Aristarchus & Secundus from Thess. (20.4, 27.2)

City/Text	Location	Coworkers	Method	Factors	Results	Misc.
Berea 17:10-15	No particular historical or political importance. Many residents, not on the trade route (A refuge? cf. Cicero).	Silas. Tim comes later. Silas & Tim remain after Paul departs.	Teaching in the synagogue.		Jews receive the Word eagerly and daily examined the teaching. Many Jews and prominent Greek women and men believe. Opposition from the Jews from Thess.	Sopater from Berea (20:4)
Athens 17:16-34	500 years prior the center of classical philosophy. Its cultural glory had now passed.	Paul alone?	Reasoning in the synagogue & daily at the market place. Areopagus speech.	Reference to an "unknown god" and quotes Greek poets.	Some sneered, others wanted to hear more. Some men believed.	No mention of a church being founded
Corinth 18:1-17	Capital of Achaia, pop. between 250,000 and 500,000. The largest city of Greece. Center of trade & religion. Prosperous & infamous for immorality. A militarily and commercially strategic port city. Ethnically mixed.	Aquila & Prcilla become coworkers. Silas & Tim join Paul later.	Each Sabbath teaching in the synagogue until opposition arises. P. then continues teaching in the house of Titus Justus next to the synagogue.	P works as tentmaker until Silas & Tim bring money from Phil. (18:5; 2Cor 11:9; Phil 4:14-15). Preaching is not in human wisdom, but "in demonstration of the Spirit and power" (1Cor 2:4)	Many believe & are baptized incl. Crispus, ruler of the synagogue, & his household; Stephanas' household (1Cor 1:16; 16:15). Gaius, in who's house a church meets (1Cor 1:14, Rom 16:23), & Erastus, city treasurer (Rom 16:23). Jews bring P to the "judgment seat" before Galileo.	P remains 18 months, during which he perhaps visits other locations in Achaia (2Cor 1:1; 11:10). Later Apollos ministers here (18:27-28, 1Cor 1:12), as do Titus (2Cor 8; 12:18) & Erastus (2Tim 4:20). The church has many problems and conflicts. Erastus from Corinth, Ro 16:23

P visits these churches again on his 3rd missionary journey (19:21; 20:1-4) with various coworkers (e.g. Apollos in Achaia 18:27; Tim & Erastus in Macedonia 19:22). The churches are visited by P's other coworkers (e.g. Apollos in Achaia 18:27; Tim & Erastus in Macedonia 19:22).

The Third Missionary Journey — 53-58 A.D.

City/Text	Location	Coworkers	Method	Factors	Results	Misc.
Ephesus 18:19-20,1	Asia Minor's most famous and largest city, pop. ca. 300,000; capital of the province Asia; port city on the crossroads of important trade routes. Lost its importance as a trade center through the sanding of the harbor. Remained a relig. center with the Artemis Temple (one of the 7 wonders of the world) & as a center of the imperial cult.	Aquila & Priscilla. Apollos is added. Tim & Erastus? (19:22) Gaius & Aristarchus (19:29)	P leaves Priscila & Aquila in Eph to minister in the synagogue. P returns later & teaches 3 months in the synagogue, then 2 years in the hall of Tyranus. Elders are installed.	Some had already heard of Jesus and Joh. the Baptist. Reception of the H.S. with signs, miracles, healings, exorcism. Magic books destroyed.	On first visit P asked to stay/return. Upon his return many become believers. Opposition from the Jews and craftsmen, P thus leaves Eph. Church in the house of Priscilla and Aquila (1Cor 16:19). Church in the house of Onesiphorus? (2Tim 1:16; 4:19)	P ministers ca. 3 years in Eph. **The Word of the Lord grew mightily and prevailed** (19:20; vg V 26). A "wide door of effective service" was opened to P (1Cor 16:9). P during this time active in other parts of Asia, e.g. churches in Kol & in towns of the Lycos valley? (19:26) Trophimus from Eph (21:29). Later Tim (1Tim 1:3), Tychicus & Trophimus (20:4; 2Tim 4:12), Pr.u.A. (2Tim 4,10,19) & John.
Troas? 2Cor 2:12	Important port city connecting Europe and Asia.		Preaching	A door was opened up for Paul.		Visited by P at the end of the 3rd miss. journey (Ac 20:5-12).
Illyricum? Rom 15:19	Region of Yugoslavia. Latin speaking.					2Tim4:10 Dalmatia in Illyricum.

1 Attalia: an important trade center. As P. was sick, Perga was perhaps passed over due to its unfavorable climate. 2 Wherever a synagogue was present, P began there.
3 Samothrace & Neapolis were port cities. 4 Amphipolis: A commercial center in a strategic military location. Apollonia was at the end of the Via Egnatia.

C. Ott

B. The Overarching Strategy of Paul

Because of his importance in the New Testament in establishing the church in the Gentile world, many modern theologians and practitioners have attempted to outline the elements of Pauline strategy and methodology.[37] When reading the biblical record from a missiological point of view, a pattern emerges as Paul embarks on his missionary journeys. Paul followed the same or nearly the same pattern throughout his itinerant ministry. The following are some general observations about the overall strategy of Paul as he intentionally took the gospel to unreached peoples and places.

Paul proceeded from a home base.

Paul saw his mission as part of the overarching plan of God. To fulfill his role in that mission, Paul needed a strong "home base."[38] In different respects, both Antioch and Jerusalem served as a home base for his church planting ministry. Both remained important to Paul as he went out as a missionary to the surrounding areas and the world. Antioch was the sending church, having set apart Paul and others and sent them out as missionaries (Acts 13:1-3). After his first missionary journey, Paul returned to Antioch and remained there for a time (15:30-33). After his second missionary journey, Paul returned to Antioch again and spent time there before leaving a third time (Acts 18:22-23). Thus, each of his three missionary journeys began at Antioch (13:3-4; 15:35-36; 18:22-23).

Paul had a home connection with the Jerusalem church as well. Kane suggests that Jerusalem was the "mother" church, being the starting place for the new faith and the original home of the Twelve. Paul later returned to Jerusalem to counsel with the leaders there, especially concerning the Gentiles (Acts 15:2).[39] Donald Senior and Carroll Stuhlmueller suggest that, theologically, Paul kept continued ties to Jerusalem, rather than Antioch, as the basis for his mission. "He was always aware that his starting point to the Gentiles re-

---

37 See, for example, Roland Allen, *Missionary Methods, St. Paul's or Ours*, viii; J. Herbert Kane, *Christian Missions in Biblical Perspective*, 74-85; David Hesselgrave, *Planting Churches Cross-Culturally*, 47-48; Dean Gilliland, *Pauline Theology and Mission Practice*, 284-91; Paul Bowers, "Fulfilling the Gospel: The Scope of the Pauline Mission," 185-88; Ed Stetzer, *Planting New Churches in a Postmodern Age*, 46-47.

38 Kane, *Christian Missions in Biblical Perspective*, 75.

39 Ibid.

mained 'from Jerusalem' (Rom. 15:19)."[40] Paul saw himself as sent physically by Antioch, and theologically by Jerusalem. The significance of a home base for Paul is demonstrated both practically and theologically in the final stage of his rhetorical progression in Romans 10:15, "How will they preach unless they are sent?"

Paul sought to reach provinces.

From these home bases, Paul commenced his mission tours. In examining his mission travels, one can see a clear pattern in the location of his evangelistic activity. Paul narrowed his focus to work in a smaller area than the entire world. In Romans 15, Paul describes the broad area from Jerusalem to Illyricum. Later he desired to go to Spain. Part of the reason for his success was that Paul did not see the ultimate mission of whole-world evangelization as his alone. Instead, he concentrated his efforts on a confined area. Kane has observed from the biblical texts that Paul worked primarily in four provinces: Galatia, Asia, Macedonia, and Achaia.[41] Kane attributes the success of Paul to his focus on planting churches in these provinces: "His aim was not simply to cover territory but to plant churches. To accomplish this it was necessary not only to sow the seed but also to reap a harvest. This could best be done by confining his efforts to a fairly restricted area."[42] Roland Allen also observes this focus on provinces. He argues,

> The object that he [Paul] set before himself was the establishment of the Church in the province rather than in the city or town or village in which he preached. . . . Both St. Paul and St. Luke constantly speak of the provinces. . . . This principle is worthy of notice not only because it witnesses to the largeness of his vision and of his faith, but because . . . it greatly influenced him both in his choice of cities in which he would preach, and in his method of preaching the gospel.[43]

---

40 Donald Senior and Carroll Stuhlmueller, *The Biblical Foundations for Mission*, 184.

41 Kane, *Christian Missions in Biblical Perspective*, 75. For evidence of Kane's assertion, see Acts 16:6-7, 9-12; 18:5, 23, 27; 19:10, 21, 22, 26, 29; 20:18; 1 Cor. 16:1, 5, 15, 19; 2 Cor. 1:1, 8, 16; 2:13; 7:5; 8:1; 9:2; 11:10; Gal. 1:2; Rom. 15:26; Phil. 4:15; 1 Thess. 1:7-8; 4:10; 1 Tim. 1:3; 2 Tim. 1:15.

42 Kane, *Christian Missions in Biblical Perspective,* 75.

43 Allen, *Missionary Methods*, 17-18. Note the subtitle of his book: *A Study of the Church in the Four Provinces.*

The focus of Paul on the province, then, was narrow enough to be a manageable and reachable goal but large enough to be one worthy of his God. Paul's ministry to the provinces served in advancing him toward his larger missiological goal. What, then, were the criteria Paul used in selecting the provinces on which he would focus his efforts? Paul looked for those provinces in which Christ had not been named and the church had not yet been established (Rom. 15:20).

Paul focused on cities and urban centers.

To reach the provinces, Paul narrowed his focus even further. He chose particular cities that would help him reach his goal of spreading the gospel quickly to the world.[44] In fulfilling his call to Macedonia (Acts 16:10), Paul focused on Philippi, "a leading city of that district" (Acts 16:12), and Thessalonica, "where there was a Jewish synagogue" (Acts 17:1). Similarly, Paul focused on Ephesus for Asia, and on Corinth for Achaia. It also appears that Paul had some criteria by which he selected the cities on which he would focus his ministry. These criteria would explain why he did not spend time in every city and hurried through some in favor of others.

What was the reason Paul chose the cities he did? Allen notes four characteristics of the cities Paul chose. (1) They were centers of Roman administration. (2) They were centers of Greek civilization. (3) They were centers of Jewish influence. (4) They were centers of trade.[45] Dean Gilliland makes similar observations, adding that Paul went to cities because the masses of people were there. Because of the Roman highway system, these cities were places where the diversity of the empire could be found. They were centers of travel and commerce.[46] I. Howard Marshall sees the selection of cities by Paul as evidence of his strategic choice. He notes that of the five major cities in the Roman Empire in his day, Paul visited four of them, stopping also in other major towns. This fact suggests to Marshall that Paul saw in the cities their importance for achieving his goals.[47] In order to reach the region, he must first reach these strategic cities.

---

44   Kane, *Christian Missions in Biblical Perspective*, 77.
45   Allen, *Missionary Methods*, xii, 19-27.
46   Gilliland, *Pauline Theology*, 287; cf. Kane, *Christian Missions in Biblical Perspective*, 76-77; Senior and Stuhlmueller, *Biblical Foundations for Mission*, 184; and Bosch, *Transforming Mission: Paradigm Shifts in Theology of Mission*, 131.
47   Marshall, "Luke's Portrait of the Pauline Mission," 103.

What about the other cities? How would they be reached? During his time of ministry, Paul sent his companions and other ministers to evangelize the surrounding areas (see, for example, Col. 1:6-8; Acts 19:10; 2 Cor. 1:1).[48] The thrust of Paul's strategy to reach key cities, however, was that from these centers, the surrounding areas would receive the good news. These strategic cities served as a springboard for the message of the gospel.[49] Kane explains:

> It was never Paul's intention to preach in *every* city. That was neither possible nor desirable. He established missionary churches in the major centers of population and they in turn engaged in "saturation evangelism" in their own areas.[50]

Paul left the work of reaching these surrounding areas to those whom he had reached, or perhaps to other missionaries.[51] David Bosch summarizes Paul's strategy in this way:

> He chooses cities that have a representative character. In each of these he lays the foundations for a Christian community, clearly in the hope that, from these strategic centers, the gospel will be carried into the surrounding countryside and towns.[52]

The hope Paul had for reaching specific regions was in his reaching of these strategic centers. By planting churches in these strategic centers, as each church was established, the surrounding areas would be reached as well.[53]

C. The Church Planting Methodology of Paul

In addition to what we can observe about Paul's overall strategy for reaching unreached regions, an examination of the materials in Acts also shows a pattern of activity that Paul followed in each location where he ministered. The following are elements of Paul's methodology in each location.

---

48   Schreiner, *Romans*, 770.
49   Kane, *Christian Missions in Biblical Perspective*, 76; Gilliland, *Pauline Theology*, 233.
50   Kane, *Christian Missions in Biblical Perspective*, 82.
51   Senior and Stuhlmueller, *Biblical Foundations for Mission*, 184.
52   Bosch, *Transforming Mission*, 130.
53   Schreiner, *Paul, Apostle of God's Glory in Christ: A Pauline Theology,* 60-61.

Paul sought open forums for the message.

While there is little doubt that Paul engaged in personal (Acts 16:14, 31) and "house to house" (Acts 20:20) evangelism, his primary strategy for evangelism was in finding an open forum in which to preach. Apart from the proclamation of the gospel, there was no other means of salvation.[54] Therefore, Paul looked for every opportunity and forum for preaching. We see one example of this practice in his preaching at the Areopagus (Acts 17:18-34). There Paul used the opportunity offered by the Epicurean and Stoic philosophers to proclaim and defend the faith in a public presentation. At other times, Paul used his arrests and trials as forums to proclaim the gospel. As Peter (Acts 4) and Stephen (Acts 7) had done previously, Paul boldly used the opportunity of his trials to preach Christ (Acts 24:10-21; 25:26:1-23). Paul even attempted—unsuccessfully at Ephesus but successfully at Jerusalem—to use the occasions of mass riots as opportunities for preaching to the people (Acts 19:30-31; 21:39-40).

His most common forum—which was most readily available and from which Paul most always began—was the synagogue. Robert Garrett comments,

> We have already noted that one of the characteristics of the cities Paul chose was that they were of Jewish influence. In each of these cities, Paul began at the synagogue (Acts 13:5, 14; 14:1; 17:1-3; 18:4, 19). Paul had theological reasons for starting at the synagogue (Rom. 11:13), but a strategic one as well. Paul saw in the synagogue, a ready preaching point; one that was open to him because of his rabbinic background and status in the synagogue.[55]

The synagogue gave Paul an open forum from which to preach to Jews, proselytes, and God-fearing Gentiles.[56] Many of them responded to the gospel (Acts 13:42-43; 14:1; 17:4; 18:4).

---

54   Joseph A. Grassi, *A World to Win: The Missionary Methods of Paul the Apostle*, 53-62.
55   Robert Garrett, "The Gospels and Acts: Jesus the Missionary and His Missionary Followers," 81; Kane, *Christian Missions in Biblical Perspective*, 78-79.
56   Johannes Blauw, *The Missionary Nature of the Church: A Survey of the Biblical Theology of Mission*, 95-96; Kane, *Christian Missions in Biblical Perspective*, 78.

Paul preached to receptive people.

At least one reason Paul started in the synagogue was that it provided an audience for his message. Another reason may be that the synagogue attendees would be most likely to be responsive to the gospel. The added benefit to this forum was that the groups present at the synagogue had a prior awareness of the one true God, were familiar with the Hebrew Scriptures, and were awaiting a Messiah. The synagogue provided a "unique opportunity" and the greatest chance for Paul to spread the gospel in his context. He had a ready audience among the Jews; and when they rejected his message, the proselytes and God-fearers were responsive.[57] Thus, while it does not appear that Paul chose his locations based on receptivity, it is likely that within a locality, Paul sought out and responded to those he thought would be receptive people.

On several occasions, when the Jews opposed his gospel, Paul turned to the Gentiles (Acts 13:45-48; 18:6-7; 19:9; 28:23-29). That is, Paul responded to the unreceptive by turning to those who *were* receptive. Paul made it clear that he would not continue to preach to a people who rejected his message. Kane describes Paul's reasoning:

> He believed that every ethnic group has the right to hear the gospel and he would gladly preach it to them; but if they adamantly and consistently refused the message, no further purpose could be served by continuing to preach to them. Better far to move on to another group who would respond.[58]

Paul expected a response on the part of his hearers, and when one group rejected the gospel, he turned to another.[59]

Paul established churches.

For Paul, however, his mission of evangelism was not complete until churches were established. Paul called people not merely to an individual re-

---

57 Kane, *Christian Missions in Biblical Perspective*, 78-79; cf. Gilliland, *Pauline Theology*, 286-87.

58 Kane, *Christian Missions in Biblical Perspective*, 80.

59 One should note that this rejection of the Jews was never a final rejection. Paul would begin in the synagogue whenever he entered a new city and maintained his theological priority of "for the Jew first" (see Rom. 1:16). Nevertheless, Paul turned to the Gentiles in each location where the Jews rejected the gospel. In this sense, then, we may agree with Donald McGavran in *Understanding Church Growth* that Paul focused on the receptive.

sponse to Christ but to a relationship with his body, the Church. Gilliland defines this kind of evangelism as "the presenting of Christ in a way that will lead people to make decisions to accept him as Lord and to seek the nurture of the new faith within the company of believers."[60] Paul did not think his task of preaching the gospel was finished until there was an established church.[61] Paul Bowers comments, "Paul saw his mission as more than gospel proclamation and conversion of individuals; through and beyond these endeavors he understood his missionary role to concern the establishment of settled, believing communities."[62] Bowers sees Paul's definition of "proclaiming the gospel" as not only preaching but also including the "full sequence of activities resulting in settled churches."[63] The appointment of leaders for the new church completed the process.[64]

D. The Importance of Church Health in Paul's Church Planting Strategy

A brief word should be included here on the importance of church health for Paul's church planting ministry. One can see from the New Testament record that Paul established churches wherever he took the gospel and that he left these churches after they had been established. At this point, the churches were no longer dependent on Paul. Paul left the churches to govern and support themselves. He entrusted them to the Holy Spirit.[65] Paul continued his ministry to these churches, however, through a nurturing ministry. Paul saw this continued ministry as necessary in his overall evangelistic strategy of making disciples.[66]

His primary nurturing method was through his letters. The letters demonstrate the heart of Paul for the spiritual health of these congregations and his desire that they endure in their faith and grow to spiritual maturity. Thomas Schreiner explains the importance of the epistles in this regard: "Paul did not conceive of his mission as successful if his converts initially believed the gospel and then lapsed. His work was in vain unless his converts persisted in the faith

---

60   Gilliland, *Pauline Theology*, 289-90.
61   Schreiner, *Paul*, 67.
62   Bowers, "Paul and Mission," 732.
63   Bowers, "Fulfilling the Gospel," 198.
64   Gilliland, *Pauline Theology*, 290.
65   Allen, *Missionary Methods*, 198.
66   David F. Detwiler, "Paul's Approach to the Great Commission in Acts 14:21-23," 36.

(1 Thess. 3:1-10). Thus his letters were part of his missionary work, written to encourage believers to continue in their newfound faith."[67]

In addition to his letters, Paul nurtured his churches by returning to visit them when possible, and by sending others to minister to them.[68] Paul was concerned not merely with the initial conversion of believers or of merely planting a church. Paul wanted to be sure his converts grew to maturity in Christ and that his churches remained healthy. Just as the task of evangelization was not complete until new believers were gathered into new churches, the task of church planting was not complete until those churches grew to health and spiritual maturity. In the New Testament, church health goes hand in hand with church planting.

IV. The Remaining Task

The New Testament is a missionary book and demonstrates the missionary activity of the apostles and the early church. In the first century after the resurrection of Christ, the gospel spread throughout Jerusalem, Judea, and Samaria, and churches began to be planted among the uttermost places on the earth. At the same time, the New Testament presents us not with a task completed but with a task begun. There is work that remains and will remain until the gospel is proclaimed throughout the entire world (Matt. 24:14). The New Testament reveals that the task of church planting is not yet complete and that believers must continue the task of proclaiming the gospel and planting new, healthy churches wherever we are and among the unreached peoples of the world.

CONCLUSION

The book of Acts ends with the story unfinished. Luke records that God is still at work and the word continues to go forth, but he leaves the story open-ended (Acts 28:31).[69] Luke's point seems to be that God will indeed em-

---

67 Schreiner, *Paul*, 39.
68 Bosch, *Transforming Mission*, 131.
69 Bock, *Acts*, 759.

power the spread of the gospel and establish his church, but the task remains incomplete. Acts 29 remains to be written as other disciples take up the evangelistic task as Christ's witnesses to the uttermost parts of the earth.

Indeed, Paul did not see his task as complete. As the book of Acts ends, he is in Rome—and his letter to the Romans reveals his intent to continue on to Spain (Rom. 15:24, 28). Even as Paul saw completion in the task behind him, he was looking on to the task that remained—to preach Christ where he has not been named (15:20). Paul recognized that even as he had "fully preached the gospel" (15:19, NASB), the work was not done in those areas. Even as Paul was called to further pioneer missions—others would complete the work as he planted, others watered, and God gave the increase (1 Cor. 3:6). Though Paul saw his own work as complete, he knew that there was still work to do. Others would take up the mantle of church planting until all had been reached with the gospel.

The harvest teachings of Jesus (Matt. 9:37-38; Luke 10:2) remind us as well of the remaining task. In addition to bringing in the harvest, the role of harvesters includes praying to the Lord of the harvest to recruit more workers and send them to the field.[70] Today there is still work to be done. As God continues to ripen harvest fields and make people receptive to the gospel, he calls us to be laborers in his harvest field and to pray for still more laborers. The remaining task of planting more, healthy churches requires that we pray for more church planters and then join in the effort ourselves.

The Great Commission also reminds us that the command to take the gospel to the nations is not yet complete. There remain peoples who have no gospel witness and persons whom God desires to save (Matt. 24:14; 2 Pet. 3:9; John 10:16). Until the Lord returns, his people must continue to be obedient to the command to be witnesses to the uttermost parts of the world (Acts 1:8) and preach the gospel of repentance and remission of sin (Luke 24:14). God sends us out (John 20:21) so that we might make disciples of all peoples (Matt. 28:19). A review of church planting in the New Testament is not complete until we recognize that God still desires us to go with the gospel and plant new healthy churches. As long as there are people who do not know the name of Christ, our task remains.

---

70 See Robert H. Gundry, *Matthew: A Commentary on His Literary and Theological Art*, 181 and Leon Morris, *The Gospel According to Matthew*, 240.

Questions

1. Describe how Jesus prepared his disciples for missionary work.

2. Which books of the Bible contain a commissioning statement from Jesus to his disciples? What are the key texts?

3. What is significant about the "sending" of the disciples by Jesus in the Gospel of John?

4. Describe the concept of "witness" in the book of Acts.

5. Did the Twelve disciples have a mission strategy? Explain.

6. List several elements of Paul's overall mission strategy.

7. Roland Allen lists several characteristics of the cities Paul chose for ministry. What are they?

8. Identify and explain several elements of Paul's church planting strategy.

9. Describe how the Twelve and Paul sought out "receptive" people.

10. What are some indications in the New Testament that there is a remaining missions task for the church today?

4 HISTORICAL HIGHLIGHTS OF CHURCH PLANTING: INSTRUCTION & INFORMATION FOR TODAY

Blayne Waltrip

Introduction

This chapter explores the historical highlights of church planting. Since the ascension of Christ, the church has been participating in the mission of God by proclaiming the gospel and making disciples of all nations as mandated in the Great Commission. As Jesus affirmed in the Gospel of John (20:21), he sends his church for mission as the Father sent him. Jesus never said, "Go start a church!" However, as the church has proclaimed Christ and made disciples, local congregations for disciples to live out the kingdom of God in community has always been a natural result.

As the church was dispersed in the book of Acts, they started local communities of faith in Judea and Samaria. The church in Antioch became a missional church that eventually sent out Paul and Barnabas on mission voyages.[1]

---

1   I use the term "missional church" often in this chapter. There is a body of literature by church leaders who advocate that the Western Church return to its missional roots. Exact definitions of "missional church" are challenging. Though the "missional conversation," led by authors such as Alan Hirsch, Michael Frost, Alan Roxburgh, Darrell Guder, Neil Cole, Leonard Sweet, Craig Van Gelder and many others, is targeted toward the Western Church, the call to participate in God's mission is for the global church. It is about who the church is, not only what it does. Because God is love, mission is God's. Mission is the vocation of the church. As the church, we are called

Through their ministry, local churches were planted throughout Asia Minor and Greece. Eventually Paul arrived in Rome. As a consequence, communities of the kingdom were established in the capital of the empire. Since the time and the events of Acts 28, the church has expanded to the ends of the earth. This chapter attempts to chart the "29th chapter" of Acts.

As the church multiplied throughout history, local communities of the kingdom were planted. What those churches looked like varied from culture to culture and from one historical period to another. When organized churches became stagnant and lost sight of God's mission, God would raise up fresh missional movements to proliferate life-giving churches anew. Here is how it worked: Christianity began as a Jewish sect, became a Gentile faith, and eventually became the religion of the Roman Empire. After the break-up of the empire, Christianity evolved into a Western (Roman Catholic) and Eastern (Orthodox) European faith. With colonial expansion, Christianity took root in the New World. In the past thirty years, Christianity has increasingly evolved from a mainly Western faith into a faith predominantly of the global South—Africa, Asia and Latin America.[2] It is safe to say that we are reaching the ends of the earth. The local expressions of the global church are diverse but are united in their faith in Christ. However, our missional task is not yet finished. Because there are still thousands of unreached people groups, especially in the 10/40 Window (North Africa, the Middle East, Central Asia, and East Asia), and because Western nations have become post-Christian, the church needs to continue the mandate to evangelize in word and deed and to make disciples by teaching and baptizing. In order to continue the missional task, we must continue to plant churches.

This chapter is a historical survey of church planting. It is impossible to look at the details of how churches were planted in every period of history, in every context, and by every tradition. The historical information is vast, and detail is beyond the scope of this book and course. Instead, we will look at highlights. As we survey the broad strokes of history, I will point out how the

---

and sent by God to participate in his mission. We are a missional people. The very nature of the church is missional.

2   In the book *The Next Christendom*, Philip Jenkins traces these developments and the continued explosive growth of Christianity in the global South. He describes the global diversity of the church and explains the various reasons for the surging growth, including the economic circumstances in the global South, radical community, and population growth. See Jenkins, *The Next Christendom: The Coming of Global Christianity*, 55-89.

church grew in certain periods to consider the role of church planting so that we can learn and reflect on where our current task stands in light of the great narrative of the church. Where have we been, where are we going, and what can we learn to participate in the missional mandate to advance the kingdom of God in every context by multiplying churches?

In response, we will begin by looking at the nature of church planting in the early church up to Constantine's legalization of Christianity. Next, we will observe church planting from Constantine to the Reformation. The historical contours of church planting after the Reformation will then be explored, followed by church planting during the period of the Great Awakenings and the Great Century of Missions (the 18th and 19th centuries). In the subsequent section, we will explore church planting in the 20th century. Finally, this chapter will discuss where church planting seems to be going in the 21st century and we will explore what we can learn from the historical evidence.

I.   Church Planting in the Early Church

The period of the early church is a period of persecution and great growth. In the book *The Forgotten Ways*, Alan Hirsch gives some interesting statistics. Around the year 100 A.D., there were approximately 25,000 Christians. By the year 310 A.D., there were as many as 20,000,000 Christians.[3] During the first three hundred years, churches were normally planted very organically. In other words, churches were planted among people groups and villages wherever possible. Like organic life (plants, grass, bushes, flowers, etc.), house churches were planted in places wherever Christians went. The early Christians did not have church buildings as we know them today. As Hirsch points out, while "archaeologists have discovered chapels dating from this period, they were definitely exceptions to the rule, and they tended to be very small converted houses."[4] Their worship included celebrating the Eucharist (the Eu-

---

3   Alan Hirsch obtained the information from Rodney Stark in his book, *The Rise of Christianity: Reactivating the Missional Church*, 18.

4   Hirsch is correct, at least regarding the first two centuries A.D. Most of the churches were house churches, but many of the houses were designed to be a house church. In the book *The Story of Christianity* by Michael Collins and Matthew A. Price, the authors provide pictures of the earliest surviving church building found by archaeologists. The building was a middle-class house with a room designated as a worship room "with space for an altar and chair and some sixty people." The book further describes the house as having a smaller room decorated as a baptistery chapel with scenes of the resurrection and miracles of healings. Christians in this period would meet in the houses of richer members of the congregation. Collins and Price, *The Story of Christi-*

charist was the center piece of the service), baptizing, studying the Scriptures, praying, and singing hymns. Christians in the early church likely continued the same way of church life that is described in Acts 2:42-47:

> They devoted themselves to the apostles' teaching and to fellowship, to the breaking of bread and to prayer. Everyone was filled with awe at the many wonders and signs performed by the apostles. All the believers were together and had everything in common. They sold property and possessions to give to anyone who had need. Every day they continued to meet together in the temple courts. They broke bread in their homes and ate together with glad and sincere hearts, praising God and enjoying the favor of all the people. And the Lord added to their number daily those who were being saved.

The Christians were especially known for their faith and their love for others. Tertullian quotes a pagan in *Apologeticum* describing the early Christians: "'Look,' they say, 'how they love one another' (for they themselves hate one another); 'and how they are ready to die for each other' (for they themselves are readier to kill each other)."[5]

As the church grew throughout the Roman Empire, Christians were persecuted, as in many parts of the world today. Of course, the first martyr was Stephen in the book of Acts. In its first four hundred years, Christianity was an outlaw religion in the Roman Empire. As a result, they could not organize legal church bodies or have designated church buildings. In fact, many early Christians were slaves. At times, persecution was severe. Many of the early church fathers gave their lives for their faith, such as Ignatius, Polycarp, and Justin Martyr.[6] Christians were often killed by lions in the Roman Coliseum. In the year 64, the Roman Emperor Nero persecuted Christians after blaming them for starting a destructive fire in Rome. He was especially brutal as

---

anity: 2,000 Years of Faith, 49. By the year 325, since Constantine returned church property back to Christians, we can conclude that they did have buildings of some sort.

5   Usually quoted as "See how [these Christians] love one another." Tertullian, *Apologeticum*, chap. 39, 7.

6   Polycarp was the Bishop of Symrna (Asia Minor) and was burned on a stake in the second century. The story of his martyrdom is one of the earliest recorded. As the magistrate encouraged him to reject Christ so that he could be released, Polycarp responded: "For 86 years I have been his servant, and he has done me no wrong. How can I blaspheme my King who saved me?" As told in Collins and Price, *The Story of Christianity*, 44.

Christians were torn to death by dogs, crucified, or burned to death as torches. *The Story of the Church* tells the story of forty-eight Christians who were slain in 177 in amphitheaters throughout Gaul (France). One slave woman was actually gored by a bull.[7] Most of the persecutions were local and temporary until efforts by the Emperor Decius to systemize persecution in the year 250.

In addition to suffering persecution, the church faced internal challenges during this period. As Christianity expanded, heresies began to emerge, including Gnosticism, Montanism, Monarcianism, Marcionism, Apollinarianism, Arianism, and Nestorianism. Gnosticism was especially challenging for the growing church. Gnostics promoted a dualistic teaching that the material world was evil and the spiritual world was good. True enlightenment, or what the Gnostics called the realization of Gnosis, was the way to salvation of the soul from the material world. They saw the material world as created by the "demiurge" (an intermediary being) rather than by God. According to Gnosticism, the God of the Old Testament is not the same as Jesus, the God of the New Testament. Their ideas were accepted by many of the churches. As a result, many of the writings by the early church leaders and Christian apologists addressed heretical Gnostic teaching.

Marcionism was another major heresy in the second century. It was founded by Marcion, who taught an anti-Jewish Christianity. He organized a movement that threatened the "true faith."[8] Another perceived heretical group during this period was Montanus and his followers. The Montanists encouraged Christians to live a Spirit-filled and ascetic lifestyle that included the gifts of the Spirit (especially prophecy), abandoning marital relations and separation from the world. They developed holy communities that strove for lives of "perfection" (sanctification). Though they were considered by some in the church as heretics, others, including a few bishops at the time and many historians today, recognized them as fanatics, not heretics. The most prominent Montanist was Tertullian of Carthage, a Christian apologist and an Ante-Nicene father of the church.[9]

---

7   Robert G. Clouse, Richard V. Pierard and Edwin M. Yamaugh, *The Story of the Church*, 30.
8   Tim Dowley, *Eerdmans Handbook to the History of Christianity*, 75.
9   Ibid, 74. Ante-Nicene fathers were the prominent church leaders before the Nicene Council of 325 A.D.

Despite persecutions and multiple heresies, the church grew exponentially. Churches started wherever people could gather and worship together. According to the *Eerdmans Handbook to the History of Christianity*, Christians had two primary approaches to spreading the gospel at this time: (1) various methods of direct communication of the gospel and (2) apologetics—the careful, intelligent explanation of the faith to counter heresies and attacks by critics.[10] One method of communication was public open-air preaching, which was mentioned often in the book of Acts. Incidentally, that practice apparently declined after Nero's persecution of Christians. Modeled after Paul, preaching in the Jewish synagogues was also common. However, after the destruction of Jerusalem in 70 A.D., there was a strong anti-Christian reaction by Jews. Evangelism in the synagogues was no longer available. Another method of evangelism was preaching in the Christians' own places of worship. The *Handbook* explains that Sunday services were divided into one part that was open to anyone and another part for communion that was restricted to baptized believers. When persecution was minimal in the third century, there were many interested outsiders who attended the first part of the Sunday worship. Many of these visitors would hear the presentation of the gospel and convert to Christianity.

Personal witness through relationships was the most common method of evangelism. For example, Justin Martyr became a Christian after speaking with an old man in Ephesus, and Cyprian accepted Christ by talking to a church elder.[11] When Christians did evangelize through friendships and personal interactions with people, they supported their witness through acts of lovingkindness. In addition, the witness of martyrdom was unsurprisingly very effective. By the late third century, the church also began to absorb features of paganism into Christianity. For example, churches took over temples, worship of martyrs replaced old gods, and festivals of the Christian year took the place of pagan celebrations and holy days.[12]

The challenge of exponential and organic growth, however, was keeping unity. The apostolic fathers and subsequent church leaders strove to keep unity and establish orthodox doctrine. Because of church divisions, heresies, and theological debates in the church, early church fathers defended the faith by

10   Ibid, 85.
11   Ibid, 86.
12   Ibid, 88.

writing books to the church. They were known as the "Apologists." They included people like Origen, Justin Martyr, and Tertullian. However, it was in the local churches where proper doctrine was taught and people were discipled. Despite persecution, divisions, and heresies, Christianity continued to spread across most of the Roman Empire. In the year 311, Christians were finally given permission by the Emperor Constantine to worship in public for the first time. Constantine is known as the first Christian emperor. Legalization of Christianity and Constantine's influence changed the way of doing church. The empire would influence the church as much as the church would influence the empire.

II. Church Planting from Constantine to the Reformation

Christianity had grown throughout the Roman Empire. As the church spread throughout the empire, the structure of the local church began to form along the Roman governmental patterns of the second and third centuries. "Constantine the Great," as he came to be known, was the son of a tolerant emperor by the name of Constantius Chlorus, and he married a Christian woman by the name of Helena. Constantine succeeded his father as co-emperor of the western part of the Roman Empire in the year 306 A.D.[13] In the year 312, Constantine gained power over the entire Roman Empire by winning the "Battle of Milvian Bridge" against another co-emperor, Maxintus. According to tradition, Constantine had a vision the night before the battle. In the vision, a cross of light was emblazoned against the sun, and he saw Latin words spell out "through this sign you will win." Because of the vision, he prayed to the "Christian God" and placed the cross, the sign of Christ, on the shields of his soldiers.

After winning the battle, Constantine gave credit to the Christian God for the victory and became the first emperor to convert to Christianity. In the year 313, he issued a decree called the "Edict of Milan," which granted freedom of worship to all religions in the Roman Empire. He made several reforms, such as returning all confiscated property to Christians and giving church bishops the same rank as senators. He also gave presents, endowments, and property to the Christian churches and built basilicas, including St. Peter's in Rome. Under Constantine, the church and the state became one. In the year 380,

---

13   By the time of Constantine, the Roman Empire was divided into a Western part and an Eastern part.

the Emperor Flavius Theodosius made Christianity the state religion of the Roman Empire.

During and after Constantine, church planting and mission followed the pattern of the Roman military orders. In the fourth century, the relatively simple structure of pre-Constantine churches became much more complex with elaborate liturgies. The church also constructed magnificent and ornate buildings. As the church modeled itself after Roman governmental forms, the local church began to take on the form of a diocese. The word "diocese" was not originally a Roman Catholic Church term—it was a Roman governmental term. Rigid structure began to replace congregational life and vitality, especially after Constantine. For example, deacons were able to perform the Eucharist and lead church functions before Constantine, but a ruling at the Council of Nicaea deprived them of the authority to preside over the Eucharist. The church developed a strict clerical hierarchy. Only bishops and priests could perform the sacraments. In fact, as clergy were given special privileges by Constantine, their power and status increased. Unfortunately, this predisposed clergy to corruption and abuse as the church became increasingly wealthy.

In reaction against the secularization of the church, several groups of Christian men and women established communities called monasteries, where they could pursue piety and community. The first monastic community was started by Pachomius in 320. They formed religious fellowships throughout the empire, especially in wastelands and deserts. By separating themselves, they could take vows and search for God by meditating, fasting, and remaining celibate. They met on Sundays for the Eucharist and often met daily for common prayer. These hermits became known as monks. In Italy, Benedict of Nursia established a monastic order that became known as the Benedictines. He lived in a cave for three years because he was drawn to prayer and meditation. He began to attract followers and eventually set up twelve monasteries before he founded the famous monastery at Monte Cassino. He wrote the "Rule of Benedict"—a simple spiritual guide for his monks to follow. It included their day of prayer, manual work, study, and rest. The Benedictine order became very significant in the Catholic Church.

By the medieval period (between 450 and 1500 A.D.), the congregational model continued to diminish. By this time, local churches had adapted too much of the form of the Roman government. When the Roman government fell, the church was faced with serious problems. The only thing that saved the Christian movement was the monastery. The mission structure had taken the form of the monasteries. They maintained not only Scripture but also the life and vitality of the church. As the church moved into the medieval period, the expansion of the church was maintained not at the local level but through the monastery.

At the end of the sixth century, the church was still centered in the Mediterranean world and the Near East. Because of barbarian invasions, much of Rome was destroyed. In the year 590 A.D., Gregory the Great became pope. Pope Gregory realized that he needed to make allies with the barbarians. Having been a monk, he knew the importance of the monasteries. He saw monks as missionaries and as spiritual soldiers of the church. He ordered monks to go into barbarian lands to establish monasteries. Through the monasteries, monks converted barbarian tribes to the church and taught them Christianity. In particular, Pope Gregory dispatched a monk by the name of Augustine to lead a mission to the pagan Anglo-Saxons. As barbarian tribes gradually converted to Christianity, the Roman Catholic Church absorbed them into the church along with Arian and Celtic Christians.

As Philip Jenkins points out, Christianity has never truly been synonymous with the West alone.[14] In fact, Christianity was the official religion in Ethiopia and Armenia before the time of Constantine.[15] However, Armenian Christianity became increasingly detached from the Western Church. In the East, missionaries were sent out during this period to preach the gospel to the Slavic peoples. In 864, the Bulgarian czar was baptized into the church, along with his people. In addition, people from Romania and Serbia entered the Eastern Church. In Russia, the emperor Vladimir converted to Eastern Christianity in 988 and ordered all his subjects to be baptized with him. Meanwhile, Moravia, Bohemia (now the Czech Republic), and Poland converted to the Western Church. Overall, the church in the East was stronger than in the West until Muslim armies overran the Byzantine Empire in the East and

---

14   Jenkins, *The Next Christendom,*18. In addition to *The Next Christendom*, I recommend reading *The Lost History of Christianity: The Thousand-Year Golden Age of the Church in the Middle East, Africa and Asia—and How It Died*. In that book, Jenkins focuses on centuries of church history east of the Roman Empire.

15   Christianity became the official religion of Armenia around the year 300. Jenkins, *The Next Christendom*, 18.

the conversion of the Barbarians in the West. By the year 800, the church in the West had little contact with the Eastern Church. Christianity became bitterly divided during this period between Western and Eastern forms of the church.[16] According to the *Eerdmans Handbook to the History of Christianity*, the differences were not as much about basic Christian doctrine as about "a long list of incidental matters, such as customary expressions of faith, the way to worship, and details of practical, everyday administrations."[17] The final break between the West and the East occurred in the year 1054. The church in the East would become known as the Orthodox Church, and the church in the West as the Catholic Church.

The rise of Islam obviously affected the growth of the Eastern Church. Despite Muslim control, ancient Christian cities like Alexandria, Constantinople, and Antioch continued to be vital centers of Eastern Christianity for several years. As Jenkins clarifies, there were limits on religious liberty and on any kind of Christian growth in the Middle East.[18] Because the church insisted on maintaining Latin as an ecclesial language in most of North Africa, they never effectively evangelized beyond the cities. As a result, the North African churches did not survive Islamic conquests. However, Egypt was different— the Coptic Church survived. They were native Egyptians who held to their liturgy and indigenous Coptic language. According to Jenkins, the Coptic Church in Egypt today claims over 10 million members.[19] Large Christian communities continued to survive and even thrive in other places in the Middle East such as Syria, Lebanon, Palestine, Iraq, and Turkey.[20]

The church grew in the West, but often by forced conversion. During this period, the Western Church retained the forms of diocese. Each diocese received tithes from every citizen and distributed the funds to the bishop, clergy, maintenance of the diocese, and the poor.[21] The church provided education, and each diocese maintained at least one hospital. Throughout the medieval period, there were times of schisms, abuses, and plagues, but the church was also responsible for the revival of faith and art. The church developed a mon-

16   Ibid, 18.
17   Dowley, *Eerdmans Handbook,* 237.
18   Jenkins, *The Next Christendom,* 20.
19   Ibid, 21.
20   For example, Jenkins reports that Christians and Jews may have consisted of 30 percent of the population of the Ottoman Empire (modern Turkey) in 1900. *The Next Christendom,* 22.
21   Collins and Price, *The Story of Christianity,* 82.

archy and ruled through a strict hierarchy, which led to great corruption and abuses. The Crusades and the Inquisitions were horrendous.[22] By the late 14th century, there were significant attempts to reform the church. For example, there was a lay movement called "the Brethren of the Common Life" that evangelized, did pastoral work, and ran schools. The movement was supported by several German and Dutch bishops. Others started churches and movements outside of the church structure, such as the Lollards (followers of John Wycliffe), the Hussites (followers of Jan Hus), and the Waldensians. These and other groups started new churches outside the structure of the Roman Catholic Church and attempted to return to congregational life. However, they were targeted by Inquisitions and thus heavily persecuted.

----

22 Historically, there were four Inquisitions: (1) the Medieval Inquisition (also referred to as the Papal or Episcopal Inquisition), (2) the Spanish Inquisition, (3) the Portuguese Inquisition, and (4) the Roman Inquisition. During the Middle Ages, inquisition was ordered by the Roman Catholic Church to inquire into the spread of heresy. There was a growing number of groups in Europe that were crying for reform in the Roman Catholic Church. The church deemed it to be for the public good to remove heretics from the public, or at least to correct them. Clergy in the Roman Church believed that the eternal good of one's soul depended on its adherence to the teachings of the Holy Catholic Church. Tribunals of Catholics were held to secure repentance. The early inquisitions were influenced and initiated by church leaders, but secular rulers administered the trials, torture, and killings of unrepentant persons. Although it was originally the state that began the reprimanding of heretics, it eventually fell into the hands of the church by the late medieval period. In reality, "Inquisition" refers to a judicial technique, not an impersonal organization. "Inquisitors of heretical depravity" were individuals throughout western Europe assigned by the pope to inquire into heresy in specific areas. They were called such because they applied a judicial technique known as *inquisitio*, which could be translated as "inquiry" or "inquest." There were different forms of punishment, but the most severe punishment was burning at the stake. Though created to deal with Christian heretics, the Inquisitions eventually targeted Jews and Muslims. The Crusades were a series of nine religiously sanctioned military campaigns waged by much of Latin Christian Europe, particularly the Franks of France and the Holy Roman Empire. They were fought over a period of nearly 200 years (between 1095 and 1291). The Crusades originally had the goal of recapturing Jerusalem and the Holy Land from Muslim rule and were launched in response to a call by the Christian Byzantine Empire for help against the expansion of Islam. Crusaders took vows and were granted penance for past sins, often called an indulgence. The Crusades were fought mainly against Muslims, although campaigns were also waged against pagan Slavs, Jews, Russian and Greek Orthodox Christians, Mongols, Cathars, Hussites, Waldensians, and political enemies of the popes. Because of internal conflicts among Christian kingdoms and political powers, many of the crusade expeditions were diverted from their original aim. The Fourth Crusade, for example, resulted in the sacking of Christian Constantinople and the partition of the Byzantine Empire between Venice and the Crusaders. The Crusades were a failure and had far-reaching political, economic, and social impacts for Europe and the Middle East, some of which have lasted to the present day.

During the 13th century, two monastery orders were established that would spread and defend the faith and the Roman Church for the following few centuries. In 1217, a Spanish priest by the name of Dominic de Guzman established the Order of Preachers in Toulouse, France (eventually approved by Pope Honorius III) to preach the gospel, save souls, and combat heresy. After the 15th century, the order would become popularly known as the Dominicans (Dominican Order). These Dominican "friars" were trained to preach in the native languages of the people. They spread quickly in Western Europe. Eventually, the Dominicans would spread to England, Northern Europe, Africa, and Asia.

Another priest by the name of Francis of Assisi in Italy heard a sermon from the Gospel of Matthew (Matt. 10:9ff) and decided to devote himself wholly to a life of apostolic poverty. He began to preach repentance on the streets. Like Dominic de Guzman, Francis of Assisi saw the need for a new type of organization within the Catholic Church. The brotherhood of Assisi succeeded in gaining the approval of Pope Innocent III in 1209. In fact, Francis of Assisi would establish three orders that followed his teaching, but the most prominent group was the Order of Friars Minor, which became commonly referred to as the "Franciscans."

Both the Dominicans and Franciscans grew rapidly during their first century of existence and made an impact on the spread of the gospel in and beyond Europe. Unlike the Benedictines and other "contemplative" orders, the Franciscans and Dominicans were "active" orders, meaning they had more direct interaction with the world. In addition to prayer, these and other active orders devoted their "work" time to teaching, preaching, missions, and other activities. They were less bound by the walls of a monastery. Such activity included the sending of members (friars) to different locations to establish missions. As Western powers expanded globally, the Dominicans and Franciscans established missions in Africa, Asia, and eventually the New World (including the famous California missions). These missions were religious outposts (and sometimes also served as military outposts) to spread the gospel to indigenous peoples around the world, such as Africans, Indians, Chinese, and Native Americans.

Spain and Portugal completed their conquest of the Americas by 1580. According to Philip Jenkins, "the greatest long-term Catholic successes" were in Central and South America.[23] Unfortunately, it is argued that much of this success was associated with brutal colonization. As Christianity took local roots in the New World, the indigenous peoples mixed Catholicism with local beliefs. Despite the controversial aspects of colonization, Jenkins claims that "the conversion of Central and South America was steady and impressive."[24] By the 1520s, there was an "extensive network of bishoprics looking to metropolitan sees at Mexico City and Lima, and Lima was ruling congregations spread over what would later be the nations of Peru, Ecuador, Bolivia, and Chile. Natives were baptized in vast numbers, on occasion running to thousands in a single day." Jenkins adds that as the numbers grew, the Dominicans and Jesuits "struggled heroically to prevent natives from being exploited by greedy European colonists."[25] Nevertheless, the church made little effort to educate or evangelize. As a result, the growth of Christianity was limited beyond the main cities. In addition, native converts "were granted admission to communion only on the rarest occasions, a policy that acknowledged the shallowness of conversions."[26]

Colonization by Spain, Portugal, and other European powers also occurred in Africa and Asia. For example, Spain established a trade sea route from Mexico to Manila in the Philippines as part of their global strategy, which was supported by the popes in Rome. The Roman Catholic Church established archdioceses in Manila in 1595. As Jenkins points out, Mexico, the Philippines, and the Congo received Christianity only a century after the conversion of Europe.[27]

Catholic missionaries worked beyond the reach of European colonization. For example, they penetrated into independent kingdoms in Africa, such as Angola and the Congo. In fact, a Congolese king was baptized as early as 1491, and for the next couple centuries Christianity spread throughout the kingdom.[28] One Christian king in Congo by the name of Mvemba Nzinga was described in the 16th century as "one of the greatest lay Christians in

---

23 Jenkins, *The Next Christendom,* 27.

24 Ibid, 28.

25 Ibid, 28. Jenkins cites several sources, including David Chidester, *Christianity: A Global History*, 434-51; and Stephen Neill, *A History of Christian Missions*, 183-87.

26 Jenkins, *The Next Christendom*, 38.

27 The conversion of Europe was completed by the submission of Lithuania. Ibid, 27.

28 Ibid, 29.

African church history."[29] The success of Christianity in Africa during this period was due largely to the fact that it penetrated the local society without supplanting traditional lifestyles.[30] Catholic missionaries also labored in Asian nations. As they established missions, they strove to adapt Christianity to local cultures, but with varying degrees of success. In 17th century India, for example, Jesuit Robert De Nobili posed as a Hindu guru as he taught Christianity. Adapting the gospel to local cultures was often the path of growth.

Matteo Ricci, a Jesuit priest, followed this path in China. He respected Chinese traditions. For example, he learned to read, write, and speak Chinese and dressed in classical Chinese robes. As he established missions, Ricci used Chinese concepts, such as the Chinese term "Lord of Heaven" for God, to explain Christianity. Rather than introducing Christianity as a foreign religion, he presented Christianity as the completion of Chinese faith. Catholic missionaries during this period, especially the Jesuits, had much success in China, India, and Japan. Unfortunately, the popes politically turned against the Jesuits near the end of the 17th century, and by 1704 the Vatican ruled against the Jesuits, "prohibiting the Chinese Rites and ordering the suppression of recent Bible translations."[31] For at least a century, the new cultural rigid policy by the Vatican tremendously hindered the spread of Catholic missions around the world.

Orthodox Christianity in the East remained significant during the Middle Ages. Because the East was more densely populated than the West, there were more Christians in Eastern nations. More important, the Eastern Christians held to a cultural and spiritual life that was "at least" as active and vibrant as the West. However, although Russia, Bulgaria, Romania, and Serbia accepted Christianity in the 10th century, several other nations in Eastern Europe, like Lithuania, did not convert until the 14th century. Incidentally, Jenkins reports that in the 13th century, "there may have been more Christian believers on the continent of Asia than in Europe, while Africa still had populous Christian communities."[32]

29   Bengt Sundkler and Christopher Steed, *A History of the Church in Africa*, 51. Also quoted in Jenkins, *The Next Christendom*, 29.
30   Jenkins, *The Next Christendom*, 30.
31   Ibid, 33.
32   Ibid, 23.

In the early 15th century, the Renaissance took root in Italy and spread throughout western and northern Europe. During the Renaissance, there was progress in science and the arts. In addition, several intellectuals encouraged the development and growth of humanism. The term came from the Latin word "humanitas," which described the civilizing force of art, science, and literature. The emphasis of humanism was on searching, studying, and writing. A major factor for the spread of humanism and reform was the printing press, which was invented by Johannes Gutenberg in 1450. Because the printing press was faster and more accurate, it allowed for a mass-production of ideas. As a result, people were inspired to write and read books. The Roman Catholic Church began to lose its central role in Western society and continued its excesses, abuses, and corruption. The events of this period led to the decline of the church, giving pressure for greater reform. Reform came in the year 1517 when a German theologian by the name of Martin Luther publicly challenged the practices of the Roman Catholic Church.

III. Church Planting During and After the Reformation

In the year 1500, the diocese model of church, with its strict clerical and liturgical structure, remained well institutionalized in the Western and Eastern churches. There was unity within the Roman Catholic Church, with the pope as the supreme authority on faith and morals. However, because of rigid power and continual corruption and abuse, sectarian groups emerged throughout Europe. These sectarian groups included the Lollards, Hussites, and Waldensians. Despite the control of the institutional church, often maintained through persecution (i.e., the Inquisitions), sectarians increasingly started churches with congregational models outside the institutional church. Eventually religious unity was shattered by the Protestant Reformation. The Roman Church would forever lose its influence in northern Germany, Great Britain, Scandinavia, and parts of Switzerland and the Netherlands. Groups in other parts of Europe, such as France, accepted the new teaching and understanding of salvation by faith from the Reformers, such as Martin Luther, John Calvin, and Ulrich Zwingli.

The churches that broke off from Rome reformed their church liturgy, tradition, and theology (*Sola Scriptura, Sola Fide, Sola Gratia*), but in practice the churches still basically had a diocesan model. In essence, the Reformation was a renewal movement of Christendom (institutional and cultural Christianity). Church historians today debate whether the Reformers did or did not encourage the practice and study of mission. The claim is that the Reformers did not send missionaries or plant churches. On one hand, it is true that for several years the Protestants did not have the structures to send out missionaries like the Catholics had. According to the argument, the causes for the lack of mission and church planting zeal included (1) ecclesiology (belief that the Great Commission was already fulfilled), (2) lack of sending structures, and (3) lack of colonies (Protestants lacked overseas colonies in the early years of the Reformation).

Other historians, such as Erroll Hulse, Sidney Rooy, and others, argue that mission was important to the Reformers. In fact, though Protestants did not usually send missionaries to Asia or Africa to plant churches, they did plant churches throughout Europe. Dr. K. Deddens writes that he "who reasons that there was a complete lack, a vacuum in respect of the idea of mission in the mind of the Reformers, is absolutely wrong."[33] Deddens points out that Luther stressed that all Christians should be involved in the spreading of the gospel. Despite accusations regarding Luther's treatment of Turks and Jews, Deddens claims that Luther was the first to understand the need to bring the gospel to the Jews. In the book *Lutero y La Misión*, Sidney Rooy also affirms that the Reformers did in fact have a theology and practice of mission.[34]

Hulse also disputes the claim that Reformers were not involved in missionary activity during the 16th century. In particular, he underscores how Calvin and his followers sent church planters into France: "From 1555 to 1562, we know for sure that 88 preachers were sent from Geneva into France. Of these, nine laid down their lives as martyrs."[35] Because of the secrecy of church planting and mission at the time (due to security reasons), historical data is difficult to find. Nevertheless, the evidence does show that early Reformers planted churches throughout Europe. Calvin was the leading church planter. His followers planted five churches in France by 1555. By 1562, there were 2,150 constituted churches ("dressed churches") established in France.[36] Hulse is correct that this represents "growth of extraordinary proportions." There were eventually over two million Protestant church members in France, a nation of

---

33   K. Deddens, "Reformation and Mission."
34   Sidney H. Rooy, *Lutero y La Misión: Teología y Práctica de la Misión en Martín Lutero*, 9. In this book, Rooy explains Luther's missional passion, practice, and theology.
35   Erroll Hulse, "John Calvin and his Missionary Enterprise."
36   Ibid, 3.

about twenty million at the time. The Reformers also sent missionary church planters into Italy, the Netherlands, Hungary, Poland, and the city-states of the Rhineland (modern Germany). It is also recorded that Calvin sent two missionaries to Brazil in 1557.

The church planters in France were "exceptionally gifted men." Hulse describes the church planters in his article. Some were from aristocratic families, and most were from a well-educated upper middle class background. Very few were from artisan or peasant backgrounds. Church planters were obligated to conform to rigorous standards set up by Calvin.[37] Only when the church planter was judged by Calvin to be a person of "necessary fibre and stamina" was he sent into France to preach and plant churches. According to Hulse, each church began by a group gathering in a home, out of which a fully disciplined church would eventually be constituted. At that point, they were considered a "dressed church." The same pattern was likely followed by church planters who were sent into other countries in Europe.

Church multiplication among the Protestant movement occurred despite persecution. The Protestant Reformation resulted in religious wars. In France certain kings persecuted the Protestants (Reformed followers of Calvin), called Huguenots. According to Hulse, 70,000 Protestants lost their lives in 1572.[38] Because of zealous persecution in France, the Protestant believers had to worship in houses, caves, and in the mountains. They would host congregations in homes and then quickly transform a person's house from a sanctuary to a home to avoid detection. For example, water and wine barrels became pulpits. In the south of France, Protestants would worship in the mountains. As in the early church, simple congregational churches started very organically—wherever they could. The Huguenots planted churches as they were dispersed to other parts of Europe and to the New World.

There were other Reformers who wanted even more radical change, and they became known as the Radical Reformation. The radical Reformers were called Anabaptists because they believed in the baptism of believing adults

---

37   Ibid, 3. Hulse describes that the moral life, theological integrity, and preaching ability were subject to careful examination. Pastors were responsible to other pastors. The church planters had to be proficient in Latin, Hebrew, and Greek to know and understand Scripture. They were trained in church history and systematic theology. Character training was critical, for as Hulse points out, many church planters in France had to face the reality of martyrdom.
38   Ibid, 3.

rather than child baptism. The majority of Anabaptists came from lower classes and were persecuted by Catholics, Lutherans, and Reformed. The movement grew. As they were persecuted, they were scattered and started new churches and Christian communities that separated themselves from the main society. These Anabaptists would eventually become the Mennonites and Amish. Many fled Europe altogether to settle in North America, where they started their own churches and communities.

In response to the Reformation, the Catholic Church also experienced a "Counter-Reformation." This was also known as the Catholic Reformation, in which many internal grassroots reforms emerged throughout the Catholic Church. Many of the reform-minded church leaders established new religious orders, such as the Society of Jesus (founded in 1534 by a Spanish priest known as Ignatius of Loyola), better known as the Jesuits. The Jesuits vowed obedience to the pope but also emphasized deep spirituality, education, and missionary work. They were not only able to bring about internal reform, but many Jesuits also led missions to India, China, Japan, and the New World. Jesuits and other Catholic orders, like the Dominicans and Franciscans, had a lot of success in winning indigenous peoples of North and South America, mainly by establishing missions in new villages. The missions provided schools and held mass baptisms. The Jesuits, Dominicans, and Franciscans would set up missions as they followed European colonial expansion, especially Spanish and Portuguese expansion into the New World.

Throughout the years, Protestant churches continued to develop and divide into many splinter groups. For example, the Puritans, Separatists (from which "Baptists" emerged), Episcopal churches, Plymouth Brethren, Friends (Quaker) churches, and Methodists all came out of the Anglican Church. From out of the Lutheran Church came the Moravians. As the movements rose up and split off from one group or another, they started new churches and congregations.

IV. Church Planting in the 18th and 19th Centuries

As new churches were started by the growing number of Protestant groups, and as missions were established by the Jesuits and other Catholic orders, the church grew in Europe and beyond. Churches were started around the world because of several important evangelistic movements, including the Great Awakenings in the 18th and 19th centuries.

Within a century of the Reformation, the movement began to wane. The Protestant state churches were influenced by a cultural and institutional form of Christianity, which many missiologists today call "Christendom" (a form of Christianity still influenced by Constantine). However, though God still worked within the institutional churches, there were several renewal movements that began to emerge in the late 17th century. During the 18th and 19th centuries, the followers of these growing movements established new and vibrant churches throughout Western Europe and North America.

The renewal movements rose up with a call to return to Scripture and "pure" Christianity. The Puritans and Pietists were examples of such movements. In England, Puritanism was a reform movement that centered on simplified worship patterns, biblical preaching, and conversion. They believed they had to separate from the formalism of the Anglican Church to complete the Reformation. As a result, such groups were called Separatists. They planted churches that were more simplified (congregational) and missional (seeking to convert the lost to Christ). One of the Separatist groups that emerged during this period was the Baptists, who emphasized the baptism of adult believers. Other Puritan groups, such as the Quakers (also known as the Friends), separated from the formal mainline churches and started their own movements. The Quakers were followers of the Puritan George Fox. The nickname "Quakers" was given by a judge in 1650 after he had exhorted the magistrate to "tremble at the word of the Lord."[39] As the Puritans planted churches throughout England, they pursued a righteous society.

Pietism in Germany was a movement that developed in reaction to the more secular and institutionalized state churches. Like the Puritans, the Pietists centered their teaching on Bible-centered morality. They emphasized conviction of sin and conversion in their teaching. Both English Puritanism and German Pietism were holiness movements. Faith was very personal and their worship services were emotional. Though they were not a denomination, they were a transforming agent within Christian traditions, including the Catholic Church.[40] Though Pietism was a reform movement within the estab-

---

39 Clouse, Pierard, and Yamaugh, *The Story of the Church*, 207-08.
40 Collins and Price, *The Story of Christianity*, 161.

lished denominations, especially the Lutheran Church, there were separatist groups that started new churches. The Brethren and Moravians were such separatist groups within Pietism. Alexander Mack started the Brethren Church in 1708 when he baptized eight adults. He believed that the New Testament required that believers return to the apostolic practices of the early church.

The Moravians were a group of radical Pietists led by Count Nikolaus Ludwig von Zinzendorf. In fact, the origins of the Moravians are from the Brethren movement (the name of which comes from the official name *Unitas Fratrum*). They were heavily persecuted. By the 18th century, the Brethren and other Protestants were finding refuge on the estate of Count Zinzendorf at Herrnhut, Germany. Zinzendorf stressed a "heart religion."[41] The Moravians, also known as the Zinzendorfs, pursued worldwide evangelism and intimate Christian community. Although the Moravians had been persecuted and were a separatist movement, Zinzendorf worked toward reconciliation of Protestant, Roman Catholic, and Eastern Orthodox churches. The Moravians were especially known for prayer and their missionary work. Zinzendorf taught three principles to his missionaries. J. D. Payne quotes Zinzendorf:

> You are not to aim at the conversion of whole nations: you must simply look for seekers after the truth, who, like the Ethiopian eunuch, seem ready to welcome the Gospel. Second, you must go straight to the point and tell them about the life and death of Christ. Third, you must not stand aloof from the heathen, but humble yourself, mix with them, treat them as Brethren, and pray with them and for them...... And how is it that missionaries have failed in the past? They failed because, instead of preaching Christ, they have given lectures on theology.[42]

The Moravians focused on evangelism and discipleship. However, Zinzendorf preferred to connect disciples into established churches rather than starting new churches. Nevertheless, as the Moravians experienced conversion growth, they needed to develop methods of church planting. Payne tells about twelve such methods from which we can learn today:[43]

---

41 "Heart religion" meaning a deep, mystical experiential faith. Clouse, Pierard, and Yamaugh, *The Story of the Church*, 214.

42 J.D. Payne, *Discovering Church Planting: An Introduction to the Whats, Whys, and Hows of Global Church Planting*, 255.

43 Ibid, 256-61.

1. *Mission stations:* They established living residences where they went to practice communal living.
2. *Team approach:* They went as teams throughout the world. No one went alone.
3. *Acts of need:* They went to pioneer areas where they could find neglected peoples.
4. *Keeping it simple:* They were encouraged to preach a very simple message of Jesus Christ.
5. *Long-term perspective:* Many spent their entire lives working among a particular people and place. They made great sacrifices.
6. *Cultural acquisition and language learning:* They immersed themselves in the cultures of the people and learned the people's language.
7. *Bible translation:* Because of their emphasis on the Bible, they translated Scripture for the people.
8. *Missionary zeal:* Their zeal for the Lord drove them to leave Herrnhut to do missionary work.
9. *Priority of prayer:* They emphasized prayer. For example, Moravians at Herrnhut set aside an hour a day, around the clock, for one hundred years to pray for missions.
10. *Sheep stealing was not allowed:* They were not permitted to pull people from other churches. Their goal was to "win souls for the lamb."
11. *Tent-making expected:* The early Moravian missionaries worked where they did missionary work. Eventually, the churches at home helped support missionaries.
12. *Missionaries were the norm, not the exception:* They saw missions as the normative life of a follower of Christ.

The Moravians were a model for future generations of missionaries and church planters. Their influence was quite significant. In fact, they had a major influence on John Wesley and William Carey.

During the 18th century, the brothers John and Charles Wesley were ministers who studied at Oxford and made missionary journeys to North America. Attempting to minister to colonists and Native Americans, the brothers struggled with depression. Returning to England, they experienced what they called a "true conversion" at a Moravian church and found inner peace. After this experience, John Wesley spent time with Count Zinzendorf and the Moravians in Germany. Upon his return to England, he and Charles preached boldly in local churches, on the streets, and in other public places. They launched the Methodist revival that would make an impact on England and North America. John Wesley was criticized by the Anglican Church, and he eventually established the Methodist movement outside the established church. Wesley organized a more simple form of congregational life by putting his converts into groups called "societies," and societies were further divided into smaller groups called "classes" with "class leaders." Methodism grew rapidly through revivals that saw conversions, social ministry, and new churches. Another preacher by the name of George Whitefield helped ignite revival in Scotland and Wales. Although a friend of the Wesley brothers, Whitefield remained in the Anglican Church. Revival spread throughout Great Britain. From these revivals, many churches were planted, especially Methodist churches.

While there were revivals in Scotland and Wales, and as Methodism was bringing revival in England and Pietism was flourishing in Germany, the First Great Awakening was a major revival to hit North America in the 1730s. The Anabaptist and Moravian groups that settled in North America, especially in Pennsylvania, initiated the revival. However, the revival actually took off through the preaching and ministry of a German Pietist by the name of Theodore Frelinghuysen. Whitefield and the Methodists helped spread the revival. Another significant person in the First Great Awakening was a Congregational minister named Jonathan Edwards. During the Great Awakening, there were many conversions and churches planted. Revival spread throughout North America.

There were two more waves of revivals in the United States—the Second Great Awakening (1790-1840) and the Third Great Awakening (1858-1904). The Methodist movement saw enormous growth during these revivals. The Methodist Church became the largest denomination in the United States. Because of their missional success in planting churches in North America, J.D. Payne wrote about Methodists' convictions and missionary methods. According to Payne, their convictions included (1) a strong belief in preaching a simple gospel message and (2) maintaining highly reproducible and simple structures.[44] Their methods included circuit riders who went out to visit settlers, wherever they were, and preached the gospel and started churches.[45] In addition, they held camp meeting gatherings that lasted for days and consisted

---

44   Ibid, 268.
45   Ibid, 269-72.

of worship and preaching. Third, Payne points out that the Methodists also provided "class meetings" to provide pastoral care to the people. From their success, church planters and missionaries today can learn from their fervent preaching style, evangelistic zeal, contextualization, and sacrifice.[46]

Although many Methodist churches were planted throughout North America, Methodism would eventually split into several denominations. During the second half of the 19th century, despite the fact that Methodists established schools, founded the YMCA (and YWCA), and planted churches, many believed that the Methodist Church was becoming too liberal in theology and practice. As a result, there was a movement of American Methodists that pursued Christian perfection and a more vibrant "holy" Christianity. Two early leaders of the Holiness Movement were Phoebe and Walter Palmer. In 1835, Palmer's sister, Sarah A. Lankford, had started holding Tuesday Meetings for the Promotion of Holiness in New York. In 1837, Palmer experienced what she called entire sanctification. Eventually, Methodist bishops and hundreds of clergy and laymen began to attend the Tuesday Meetings and had the same experience. The Holiness Revival spread throughout North America and eventually to England by the end of the 19th century. As the revival spread, many churches were planted following the methods that the Methodists had already been using.

The Baptists also planted churches in North America in the 18th and 19th centuries and experienced unprecedented growth, especially on the American frontier. Though there is little detailed information on the methods that the Baptists used to plant churches, Payne highlights a few overarching factors for their success. First, he makes it clear that growth did not come from intentional evangelistic efforts.[47] According to Payne, much of the initial Baptist evangelistic and church planting activity on American frontiers occurred as the Lord worked primarily through the economy of the day—that is, the migration of people from the east toward the west. In addition, the Great Awakenings, especially the First Great Awakening, fueled the growth of the Baptists. Many of the early Baptist church planters in North America were "farmer-preachers."[48] Farmers during the week but preachers on Sunday, these preachers/church planters usually did not have much education. Rather, they

---

46   Ibid, 272-75.
47   Ibid, 280-81.
48   Ibid, 281.

were simple men who primarily "lived off the land and worked among the people they served."[49] These farmer-preachers contextualized ministry at the time as they lived incarnationally among the people.

In 1835, the Baptist Home Mission Society was established to help organize Baptist mission work in North America. Their church planting methods included the following:[50]

1. *Mother churches:* Congregations that planted other congregations.
2. *Hiving off:* A group of believers from a mother church would intentionally separate to begin a new congregation in a different location.
3. *Arms and branches:* A few new churches were independent, but they remained an arm of the mother church. They remained under the care of the mother churches until they developed a separate identity.
4. *Traveling churches:* During the westward migration of peoples, churches migrated together, replanting themselves on the frontier.
5. *Colonization:* Similar to the traveling churches, these pioneers would move, resettle, and then gather together a church in the new location.
6. *Nonprofessional church planters:* As we saw with the farmer-preacher, many Baptist church planters did not have theological education. They were men who felt a call to plant a church and were recognized by their congregations.
7. *Missional pastors:* Some pastors were sent out on itinerant evangelistic trips into other communities to preach and plant churches.
8. *Plant and pastor:* Pastors of the new churches were the individuals who planted the church and began to pastor immediately.
9. *Gather the scattered:* As people migrated westward, they found themselves isolated from other Baptists. Church planters would find those Baptist groups and begin to gather them into a new church.
10. *Associations:* As the Baptist churches increased, they would gather together to form associations for fellowship, accountability, encouragement, cooperation, and evangelism.

Also influenced by the Moravians, a Baptist minister in England named William Carey became the founder of the modern missionary movement. He realized that missions to reach the lost in other parts of the world was what

49   Ibid, 282.
50   Ibid, 286-92.

the Protestants needed near the end of the 18th century. As a result, he wrote and preached about and argued for a mission society. He wrote about the "means" to do this in his famous essay, "An Inquiry into the Use of Means for Propagation of the Gospel Among the Heathen." In 1793, the Baptist Missionary Society was formed. Carey sailed that year for India as the first modern missionary. These events began the Great Century of Missions of the 19th century, which saw a great expansion of the spread of the gospel by Protestants "into all the world."

During the Great Century of Missions, missionaries were sent into Africa, Asia, and Latin America. Groups like the Puritans, the Pietists, the Moravians, and the Methodists were very active in mission work. The majority of missionaries during this period went to India, China, and Africa. One of the most well-known missionaries was a British missionary by the name of James Hudson Taylor. He went to China and became the founder of the China Inland Mission (CIM, now OMF International). He was a missionary in China for 51 years. The CIM society was responsible for sending more than 800 missionaries to China. The missionaries established 125 schools and realized 18,000 Christian conversions, as well as establishing more than 300 stations of work with at least 500 local helpers in all eighteen provinces of China.

The 19th and early 20th centuries were the period of colonial missionary expansion under the empires of Germany, Great Britain, and France. Just as Catholic missionaries had followed Spanish and Portuguese colonial expansion a couple centuries earlier, the advance of the Protestant missionary movement in this period took place under the protection of European colonial powers and later under the spreading influence of the United States. This was a period of massive recruitment of pioneer missionaries and financial support. Western missionaries started orphanages, schools, and of course, churches. When the missionaries planted churches, those churches often looked like their home churches in the West. During this period, the missionary was very much in charge. As a result, the period has been criticized for spreading as much of Western culture as the gospel. Nevertheless, the gospel did spread throughout the world. Despite the mistakes of many early pioneer missionaries, we can now see the fruit of their work as we realize the growing strength of the church in Africa, Asia, and Latin America. However, as Philip Jenkins identified, Christianity in the global South is actually returning to its earlier roots.[51] By the 21st century, the church in the Majority World would become the missions force.

V. Church Planting in the 20th Century

The Pentecostal Movement emerged in the early 20th century from the Holiness Movement and revivalist movements. There were several revivals in places like India, Korea, Wales, and North Carolina in which people began to experience a new phenomenon of "being baptized in the Holy Spirit." There was one particular revival in a mission church in Los Angeles that caught the attention of the world. It was the Azusa Street Revival in 1906 that brought public awareness to the Pentecostal Movement and propelled it forward. It also birthed a fresh push for missions and evangelism. For the early Pentecostals, there was a strong association between the baptism in the Holy Spirit and an endowment of power for Christian witness. William Seymour, leader of the Azusa Street Revival, charged those in attendance: "Now do not go from this meeting and talk about tongues, but try to get people saved."[52] The statement indicates that mission was a core missional value in Seymour's spirituality.

The emphasis on mission was due to a strong belief in the soon return of Christ. However, Pentecostal mission from North America was chaotic in its first twenty years. People at Azusa Street would sense a call from God and go out by faith without any organizational or financial covering. As the Pentecostal Movement matured, more attention was given to preparation for the foreign fields and to sound financial support, especially in the Assemblies of God foreign missions program. The early Pentecostal missionaries usually chose traditional sites of Protestant missionary endeavors, such as Africa, India, and China.

The early Pentecostals focused more on individual salvation through evangelism than on planting churches. After a few years, Pentecostals became more deliberate in planting churches. Since many church planters came out of Baptist and Methodist churches, they followed patterns similar to those of the Baptists and Methodists in the previous century. Fervent church planting continued in North America until about the 1980s. Pentecostalism is still

---

51 Jenkins, *The Next Christendom*, 15.
52 Quoted by Pentecostal missiologist Grant McClung in *Azusa Street and Beyond: 100 Years of Commentary on the Global Pentecostal, Charismatic Movement*, 3.

growing in Africa, Latin America, and parts of Asia. However, church planting within classical Pentecostal denominations in the West has followed similar patterns as other Protestant and Evangelical denominations and have begun to wane in the past twenty years.

In addition to the Pentecostal movement, there were other "waves" of the Spirit in the 20th century. In the book *Third Wave of the Holy Spirit*, Peter Wagner describes three historical periods of the activity of the Holy Spirit. The first "wave of the Holy Spirit" was the rise of the Pentecostal Movement at Azusa Street and other revivals around the globe. The second wave of the Spirit was the Charismatic Movement during the 1960s. The Charismatic Movement of the second wave spread throughout many Protestant denominations and the Roman Catholic Church. The "Third Wave" of the Spirit was the neo-Charismatic movement during the mid-1980s. The movement included independent indigenous Charismatic movements around the world (like in Africa and South America) and the Vineyard movement (John Wimber).[53] According to Vinson Synan in *The Century of the Holy Spirit*, each "wave of the Spirit" dwarfed the previous with "explosive" growth.[54] Since many Charismatic Christians of the Second Wave were already members in existing churches, they did not seek to plant new churches. On the other hand, the majority of the Charismatic churches and groups associated with the Third Wave were independent and indigenous. As a result, these neo-Charismatics fervently pursued church planting around the world. Incidentally, the models and strategies for Charismatic church planting were not much different from those of other Evangelicals.

Pentecostalism has deep roots in Latin America. Many of the independent churches were planted before the First World War, but growth became more prevalent after the 1950s. According to Philip Jenkins, Pentecostals account for eighty to ninety percent of Protestant growth in Latin America.[55] He gives

---

53   C. Peter Wagner, *The Third Wave of the Holy Spirit: Encountering the Power of Signs and Wonders Today.*
54   Vinson Synan, *The Century of the Holy Spirit: 100 Years of Pentecostal and Charismatic Renewal, 1901-2001,* 382. Synan listed the approximate number of adherents for each wave in 2001:
- First Wave (classical Pentecostals) = 63 million
- Second Wave (Charismatic movement) = 175 million
- Third Wave (neo-Charismatics) = 295 million.
55   Jenkins, *The Next Christendom,* 63.

several examples of successful church growth throughout Latin America. In Brazil, Assemblies of God missionaries brought the Pentecostal movement in the early 20th century, but the surge of growth began during the 1950s and 1960s. The "third wave" of Pentecostal evangelism and church planting came in the last twenty years of the century. The majority of those churches have been indigenous.[56] However, other Protestant and indigenous groups are also planting churches and experiencing growth. In addition, the Catholic Church has responded to Pentecostal and Protestant growth by becoming more missional and charismatic. In fact, Jenkins claims that "the Catholic response to these changes may be as far-reaching as Protestant expansion itself."[57]

Church planting continued to decline among most Protestant denominations in the Western world in the latter half of the 20th century. In contemporary "missional church" literature, the Protestant and Evangelical denominations in the West, and now classical Pentecostal denominations, are declining because they no longer emphasize church planting and missions. There are a few exceptions, but the overall trend among church denominations has been the development of a mindset to maintain their institutions. In general, denominations have lost the missional mindset that was prevalent in the 18th, 19th, and early 20th centuries. Since the 1950s, institutionalism has choked out much of the zeal to reach the lost and to plant churches in the West. When they have attempted to plant churches, denominations have often sent church planters or couples out alone without much support, training, or mentoring. The denominational church planters would then often clone models that had worked in other contexts, but such attempts failed because they were not contextualized. One size does not fit all, even in the same nation.

In addition to the impact of institutionalism, the Western Church has struggled to respond effectively to cultural changes in the West. The West has become post-Christian, meaning the church has been marginalized. As a post-Christian society, the church no longer has a privileged position because it is only one claim of truth among many. Alan Hirsch claims that middle class values of Western culture now seem contrary to authentic gospel values.[58] The West is experiencing a de-Christianization of culture, or what missiolo-

---

56   Ibid, 64-65.
57   Ibid, 66.
58   Hirsch, *The Forgotten Ways*, 219.

gist David Bjork calls the "*ex*culturation of Christianity" of the West.[59] The reality is that Western society is in a historical and cultural shift. The most common label is that we live in a historical period called postmodernity. A few sociologists in the West call the historical/cultural transition a shift from solid modernity to a liquid modernity due to the instant flow of information from the internet, rampant consumerism, and constant cultural changes. Globalization, accelerated by the internet and technology, has the West in the midst of a "digital" or "information age." Finally, secularization and individualism has also created major challenges for denominational church planting and growth in the late 20th century, especially when the Church has not adjusted its methods and strategies and way of being church in the world.

Although Christianity has been declining in the West, the church in the Majority World (Asia, Africa, and Latin America) grew tremendously in the second half of the 20th century.[60] During the years of decolonization (1950s-1960s), Western denominations were concerned about how the new African and Asian churches would survive the transition to independence.[61] Although Western missionaries were the church planters in the 19th and early 20th centuries, the vast majority of new churches planted in the latter half of the century were indigenous.

One example of successful indigenous church planting is in China. In 1922, a pastor named Watchman Nee started a church in Fuzhou. Watchman Nee was a church leader and Christian teacher and writer during the first half of the 20th century. During his thirty years of ministry, Nee planted churches throughout China and trained many Bible students and church workers

---

59   There is an interesting article by David Bjork called "The Future of Christianity in Western Europe" in a 2006 issue of *Missiology: An International Review,* 309-324. He speaks of the de-Christianization of Europe, which he calls the "*ex*culturation of Christianity." In the article, he agrees with a French sociologist, Danièle Hervieu-Léger, that Christianity has lost its influence in Western society in the process of secularization. Bjork claims that the de-Christianization of Western Europe has gone even further: "the very tissue underlying secular European culture is coming undone." He explains that Europeans are not concerned about the afterlife. For Bjork, the future of Christianity in Western Europe will be largely determined by the ability of churches there to recruit and incorporate new members in a manner that creates and maintains their identity as Christian communities. This will require fervent church planting in Europe and throughout the West that will be able to incorporate the Christians influenced by postmodernism and secularization.

60   According to Jenkins, Christianity in the Majority World, inside and outside the Catholic Church, is "becoming steadily more Pentecostal." *The Next Christendom,* 67.

61   Ibid, 56.

through his writing and teaching at conferences. He wrote and published several books on ministry and the Bible. After the Communists came to power in 1949, Nee was persecuted and imprisoned for his faith. By the time he was imprisoned in 1952, approximately 400 churches were planted in China through his ministry and the "Little Flock" movement. After twenty years of prison, he passed away in 1972. Despite the impact of his writing and ministry before 1952, "Watchman Nee touched more lives for Christ from the obscurity of his prison cell than he ever had as a free man."[62] Watchman Nee is considered a hero of the faith for China.

Since Western denominations were expelled from China after the Cultural Revolution in 1966, church planting in China has exploded. The indigenous Chinese churches became underground house churches due to persecution by the government. The Cultural Revolution sought to eliminate religion, calling it, in Karl Marx's terms, the "opium of the people." Since the underground Chinese churches were not part of a structured institution, they became a network of house churches that continue to grow and multiply. Consequently, church planting has been very simple and organic. Institutions do not clone churches artificially from the top down, but rather house churches grow to the point where they need to divide into two groups, or they send someone out to begin a new church. Many church planters have simply felt a call to go out and start a new group. Pastors of existing churches often start a second church while still pastoring the first. It is typical for Chinese pastors to shepherd two or three churches. The house churches multiply very naturally. It is estimated that there are now anywhere from 80-150 million Christians in China. In fact, the church in China now envisions sending church planters to all the nations between China and Jerusalem to win the lost, including Muslims.

The Chinese are not only planting non-registered house churches, but they are also planting registered churches recognized by the government. There are registered Protestant churches in the People's Republic of China that are affiliated with the China Christian Council and belong to the Three-Self Patriotic Movement. The three principles of the Three-Self movement is self-governance, self-support (i.e., financial independence from foreigners), and self-propagation (i.e., indigenous missionary work). The principles originated in 1892 during a conference of Christian missions in Shanghai. In 1951, a Chinese Christian leader initiated the Three-Self Patriotic Movement

---

62   Bob Laurent, *Watchman Nee: Sufferer for China*, 10.

to remove foreign influences from Chinese churches and to assure the government that the churches would be patriotic to the newly established People's Republic of China. In 1954, 138 Chinese Christian leaders presented a "Christian Manifesto," pledging support of Christians for "anti-imperialism, anti-feudalism, and anti-bureaucratic capitalism." According to the non-registered churches, the movement has allowed the government to infiltrate, subvert, and control much of the registered church. In 2004, the Chinese government announced that "for the first time under Communist rule, two new churches would be built" in Beijing.[63] There are now over 13,000 churches throughout the People's Republic of China that are permitted to operate legally because they are recognized by the Three-Self Movement (China Christian Council). These churches serve more than twenty million Protestant believers. Church services in the official registered churches are often packed to capacity. The services in most of the churches include robed choirs and headsets for translation into English. The teaching is normally orthodox Christianity. In addition, a few of the registered churches have bookstores that sell Chinese Bibles and devotional materials. According to David Aikman, one of the major differences between the services in the registered churches and those in the underground house churches is that in the Three-Self churches, "there is unlikely to be any Charismatic expression—e.g., praying in tongues, joyful hand-waving, or even dancing."[64]

Within the Catholic Church in China, there are both registered and non-registered churches. In 1991, there were 1,000 priests and seventy bishops. According to John Tong, over 3,000 Catholic churches and prayer centers, sixteen seminaries, and approximately twenty convents were reopened by the 1990s.[65] Overall, there were between five and six million Catholics in China.[66] That number has grown in both the official and unofficial Catholic churches. Though they are not multiplying and growing like the house churches, the registered churches, both Catholic and Protestant, do grow. However, due to historical factors, there has been tension between the registered and unregistered churches. From the perspective of the unofficial house churches, the registered churches are controlled by the government. Therefore, they claim they are not allowed to practice true Christianity. For example, they are not al-

---

63   David Aikman, *Jesus in Beijing: How Christianity Is Transforming China and Changing the Global Balance of Power*, 136.
64   Ibid, 137.
65   John Tong, "The Church from 1949 to 1990," 24.
66   Ibid, 25.

lowed to proselytize. In addition, many of the pastors and leaders of the house churches have experienced persecution, so they do not trust the registered churches. On the other hand, the growth of the unofficial house churches has positively influenced the registered churches. As Aikman claimed, Chinese evangelicals in the registered churches are becoming increasingly eager to spread the Christian message.[67]

Church planting exploded in Africa in the 20th century. African Protestants, Catholics, and Pentecostals have planted churches throughout Sub-Saharan Africa. Though the many methods of church planting have followed the methods learned from Western missionaries, the churches have increasingly become indigenous. In fact, there has been a growing movement of new churches in Africa called the African independent churches (i.e., the AICs).[68] Many of these independent churches adapt Christianity to local cultures and traditions. They "are African churches with African leaders for African people."[69] The current movement of independent denominations and churches began to emerge around the 1880s. Because of racial segregation in many European-founded churches, scores of Africans defected and started their own churches. As Jenkins reveals, the "so-called Scramble for Africa marked a scramble out of inhospitable White churches, with the resulting formation of new independent denominations."[70] The Africans continue to have an incredible passion and urgency to plant churches to win the lost. After a century of church planting and multiplication, most of the churches in Africa are still vibrant and missional.

New churches in the Majority World are succeeding for various reasons. In the book *The Next Christendom*, Philip Jenkins highlights a few of those factors.[71] For example, the new churches (Protestant, Pentecostal, and Catholic) provide a sense of family and community. Jenkins calls this factor "radical community." The new churches also fulfill social needs and provide a refuge

---

67   Aikman, *Jesus in Beijing*, 137.
68   According to Jenkins, the acronym of AIC can also be understood as "African initiated churches" or "African indigenous churches." He explains that the term covers a wide range of groupings, including groups ranging from highly Africanized variants of recognizably European or American churches to tribal groups that loosely borrow Christian thought. *The Next Christendom*, 51.
69   Ibid, 52.
70   Ibid, 52.
71   Ibid, 74-78.

during the social change occurring in the global South. Because the churches planted in the late 20th century were among the poor, they are very appealing to the masses. Churches also provide a "very practical setting in which people can improve their daily lives."[72] As the Majority World also experienced modernization, older Protestant denominations have appealed more to the middle class. David Martin believes that these Protestant churches have provided "channels of mobility" out of poverty.[73]

Another appeal of the churches that have emerged in the Majority World in the 20th century was the supernatural realm. Simply, people in the global South are particularly open to the supernatural. As a result, they seek miracles, such as healing of mind and body. "The seemingly diverse Southern churches have in common many aspects of belief and practice, and these characteristics differentiate them from older Northern Christianity."[74] People in the global South have responded to the promises of supernatural blessings "in this life as well as the next." Many Christians in the Majority World have also responded to the "Faith Gospel." People are seeking health and prosperity, "or at least, economic survival." Unfortunately, the Faith Gospel has also promoted abuses and materialism.

Many churches in the Majority World have grown and become megachurches with thousands of members. Megachurches in nations like Honduras, Guatemala, Colombia, Argentina, Brazil, Chile, Nigeria, Zambia, Kenya, Tanzania, the Philippines, South Korea, Singapore, and Indonesia, just to name a few, have sent out numerous church planters and missionaries to start daughter churches in their countries and around the world. Churches are flourishing in the global South. It was clear by the end of the 20th century that the Majority World (also known as the global South or Two-Thirds World) had become a mission force, planting churches around the world, including among secular post-Christian Westerners (North Americans, Europeans, Australians, and New Zealanders) and unreached people groups in the 10/40 Window (North Africa, the Middle East, Central Asia, and East Asia). The face of missions and church planting has been transformed.

---

72 Ibid, 76.
73 David Martin, *Tongues of Fire: The Explosion of Protestantism in Latin America*, 230.
74 Jenkins, *The Next Christendom*, 77.

VI. Church Planting in the 21st Century

In the 21st century, church planters are going around the world to plant healthy missional churches in most contexts. In Africa, Latin America, and parts of Asia, church planting is occurring at an impressive rate. The church will continue to stress reaching the lost and establishing churches among unreached people groups in the 10/40 Window. In the West, denominations and new missional movements are discovering new ways—and old ways—to plant healthy churches. In many cases, rather than putting new wine in old wine skins, they are going beyond institutional church to reconstruct church planting for a postmodern culture.

Missional church leaders are calling for the Western Church in the 21st century to return to "the forgotten ways" of being church. They look back to the strategies, models, and passions of the early church as a role model. Alan Hirsch encourages Western Christians to discover their "truest nature as an apostolic people."[75] By adding missional leadership, radical discipleship, and relevant forms of organization and structure, he believes that the situation in the West, as it is in the global South, can still be ripe for remarkable growth. However, the situation will require the kind of church planting as seen in the early church, China, and other historical church planting movements outlined in this chapter. Missional church leaders and writers call for church planting in the West to be more organic (natural and simple), incarnational (living among the people and contextualizing the kingdom), and missional (having a missional mindset and passion).

Church planting will continue to move forward in the Majority World. However, the churches will need to learn from the mistakes of the Western Church and not lose their missional passion due to institutionalism. Many church leaders and missiologists believe that the historical and missional situation in the 21st century is much like that of the first three centuries. As a result, the global church must plant churches in the 21st century with the same fervor as the early church before Constantine. In the book *Extending God's Kingdom*, Craig Ott agrees that we have seen some of the most dramatic changes in world history, "encompassing technology, geopolitics, globalization, world religions, and the growth of Majority World Christianity."[76] He

---

75 Hirsch, *The Forgotten Ways*, 20.
76 Craig Ott, "Church Planting in the 21st Century: Seven Developments," 243.

believes that these changes are having a major impact on missions in general and church planting in particular. He highlights seven developments facing church planting in the 21st century—each development requiring wisdom to maximize the opportunity for "kingdom impact in the global church among the unreached and underreached:"[77]

1. *Church-planting support systems.* These support systems that assist church planters include church planter assessment, boot camps, training centers, internships, coaching systems, resources, books, conferences, and support networks. The systems help increase the effectiveness of church planters.

2. *Short-term missions and church planting.* Short-term mission trips have become incredibly popular in the Western Church, but are now becoming more common in the Majority World as Koreans, Latin Americans, and others are volunteering to do short-term missional ministry around the world. Ott believes that this is having a major impact on global mission.

3. *Internationalization of missionary sending and church-planting teams.* The Majority World is becoming a major missionary-sending force. Mission and church-planting teams today are being formed from every continent.

4. *Migration and diaspora church planting.* Human migration and globalization have increased the needs and opportunities to plant ethnic and multicultural churches, especially in the cities. Ott points out that there are enormous opportunities for the church as cities and communities are increasingly composed of peoples from unreached or restricted-access people groups.

5. *Holistic mission and church planting.* New and existing churches are increasingly doing ministry to the whole person spiritually, physically, and socially.

6. *The uncertain role of Western missionaries in church planting.* The role of Western missionaries is in flux. They are increasingly serving under or alongside national churches. On the other hand, the nations of the Majority World are sending out more missionaries. Partnerships, humility, and teachability are foundational for the role of missionary church planters in the 21st century.

7. *Continued need for contextualization and new forms of church.* Church

---

77   Ibid, 243-48.

planters need to avoid one-size-fits-all strategies and models. Rather, though church planters can learn from strategies and models in other places, they need to study and assess the local context of their church plant and evaluate what methods and strategies are best for that particular situation. Ott makes it clear that this must be done in a spirit of openness.

CONCLUSION

In his concluding remarks, Ott states that there is "nothing new under the sun, just new arrangements."[78] Church planters throughout history have responded to their divine call and passion to reach the lost and make disciples. On one hand, it is clear that God is doing a new thing, but on the other hand, it would seem that the missional zeal to plant churches in the 21st century has brought us back full circle. It will require the same passion, prayer, dedication, flexibility, incarnational living, missional mindset, and possibly even the same organic approaches to plant churches in this century as in the first three centuries of the church. We can realistically see the kingdom of God go forward in every context and among every people group in the 21st century. In light of that possibility, we pray, "Your kingdom come, your will be done on earth as it is in heaven!"

---

78   Ibid, 247.

Questions

1. What was church planting like in the early church? Describe what the churches may have been like. Where did they meet? What may have the services looked like?

2. How and why did Constantine change the church, and how did that affect church planting?

3. What were the monasteries? Why did they come into existence? Who were the Benedictines? Who were the Dominicans and Franciscans? What were the differences between the earlier and latter religious orders? How did they effect the preservation and spread of the church?

4. How did the Renaissance affect the church? What factors led to the Reformation? What were the local churches inside and outside the Catholic Church possibly like?

5. Did the Reformation impact church planting? Did the local church look different? How did persecution affect church life? How did the Radical Reformation impact starting new churches? What was the Catholic response?

6. Who were the Puritans and Pietists? What groups emerged from these movements? How and why did they plant churches, especially the Moravians?

7. How did the Great Awakenings affect church planting? How did the Wesley brothers influence church planting? What did their new churches possibly look like? How did the First Great Awakening impact church planting?

8. How did the Methodists and Baptists plant churches in North America during the 19th century? What methods did they use?

9. How did the Great Century of Missions have an impact on church planting around the world? How did it start? Who planted churches? Who sent missionaries? Where did they go?

10. Who were the Pentecostals? How and why did they plant churches? Why did the movement grow in North America and around the world? What were their motivations? What were the three "waves of the Spirit," and what were their differences? How did they affect church planting?

11. Why did church planting decline in the West in the latter half of the 20th century? What challenges have developed in the Western churches and in Western society?

12. Why did the church grow in the Majority World (Africa, Asia, and Latin America) in the latter half of the 20th century? What does church planting look like and why has the church been so successful in multiplying churches in that part of the world? What is church planting like in China?

13. What does church planting look like in the 21st century? What are the trends, developments, challenges, and opportunities? How can the church adjust, especially in the West? What can we learn from the early church and the various movements throughout church history?

5 PLANTING THE CHURCH: HISTORICAL MODELS

Sidney Rooy

From its beginning, the Christian church has been a missionary church. Most world religions have not. As the Swiss theologian Emil Brunner put it, "The Church exists by mission, just as fire exists by burning."[1] Our purpose in this essay is to identify the different ways in which the church has carried out its mission. More specifically, we want to concentrate on the methods by which the church shared the gospel committed to it. How did the church become relevant to human need and gather those who believed the message and became disciples of the Lord? Gospel communities proliferated because the church was faithful to its mission.

The complexities of culture, the ambiguities of history, and the constantly changing political reality required the sensitivity and adaptability of God's people in its response to new opportunities. One has only to think of racial diversity, of the dire effects of storm and disease, of dictatorships and persecution, of crusades and colonialism, to be aware of the cost of discipleship. All these, and more, shaped the evangelization and establishment of the Christian church across the centuries.

---

1   H. Emil Brunner, *The Word and the World*, 108.

Some elements that we need to consider for the definition of the methods of evangelization and the planting of churches across history include knowledge of diverse languages and cultures, an intuition of the religious feeling and mindset of specific people groups, the capacity of adaptation to new personal and community contexts, and a timely sense of the gut needs to be confronted. The diversity of times, needs, and places certainly require different methodologies. However, once used, they reappear now and again in the expansion of the church.

One more aspect of church planting needs to be defined. What is the gospel message that is proclaimed? That question can best be answered by a consideration of historical models themselves. As we proceed, it will become clear that the method of evangelism used reflects the interpretation given to the gospel message in that historical moment. Our premise is that no single human interpretation exhausts the significance of the message. Parallel to that premise belongs this one: the new understandings of the reaches of the gospel call across time enriches our faith in the wholeness and integrality of God's message for every church and every believer. So we are still learning while we give consideration to the ways in which the Spirit has led the church in past times.

I. Historical Models of Evangelization and Church Planting

A. Testimonial Model

No single method for evangelism and church beginnings was used in any period of church history, certainly not by the earliest Christians. We will call their way of sharing the faith the *testimonial model*. That needs to be understood in broad ways. Ordinary disciples shared the new meaning and purpose they found in their lives and relationships. Not only the Twelve apostles but also their helpers, as well as others, felt called to spread the good news. Some were merchants, and as they traveled, they shared their new faith in Jesus. The commission he gave to those assembled the night of his resurrection became the practice of the Christian community as a whole.

In the post-apostolic age, sometimes the community found it necessary to identify and authenticate those commissioned to speak on its behalf. Instructions are found not only in the Epistles of the New Testament but in very early preserved writings. The *Didache*, Clement of Rome, and Ignatius the Martyr (c. 90-120 A.D.) all give rather specific instructions about such messengers and leaders. The concern was first of all the desire to maintain high moral standards and holy living, both in order to follow scriptural guidelines and to free new groups of Christians from official and civilian criticism. Such a lifestyle gave powerful testimony that attracted others to the Christian faith.

This testimonial method was exercised on various levels. First of all, there were frequent public testimonies given by preachers and "prophets" in the streets and synagogues. Though some were well received by the general public, others were disdained by the authorities and religious leaders.

Some, though a small minority, were arrested and tried for opposition to the Roman government. When martyrdom occurred, often leaders were chosen to dissuade the populace from choosing and adhering to the Christian faith. This happened occasionally and in varied regions, except for three brief periods of wider imperial action against the growing Christian movement, especially after 250 A.D. However, opposition to the faith encouraged growth and the beginning of new communities. From this came Tertullian's famous adage: "The blood of the martyrs, the seed of the church."

The testimony of leaders in addition to preaching included the instruction given to seekers and new believers. This was foundational and essential for the founding of the budding church movement. Early documents show that the essentials of the doctrine and life of Christ formed the heart of the instruction; however, foremost was the testimony to the radical change the Christian experience brought about in daily life. In this way the home and occupation of the new believers stood out in the community where they lived. Already in 112 A.D., Pliny writes to the Emperor Trajan that Christians are "many in every period of life, on every level of society, of both sexes . . . in towns and villages and scattered throughout the countryside." With both the Jewish and the Roman centrality of the home as a general broad group of persons including parents, elders, children, slaves, relatives, freed persons, and often close friends (compare Cornelius, Acts 10), the opportunity for "family" conversions provided rich ground for evangelism. Their refusal to worship the Roman gods (such as Aesculapius, the god of healing), patronize image art, and render obeisance to emperors, marked them off from the general population. But more attractive were the Christians' strengthened family loyalties, acceptance of the very poor, refusal to abandon girl babies, sacrificial care for the sick (including unbelievers), and new moral and ethical standards for all of life. The Roman philosopher Celsus lamented that Christians cared not only for their own but also for the forgotten needy of the general population. Such family loyalty to the Jesus way became a powerful testimony that won many to the faith.

How can it be explained that the church was extended so rapidly? True, there were missionaries like Paul, but not many. Rather, there were many traders, soldiers, slaves, and even governmental workers who gave enthusiastic testimony to their newfound faith as they traveled. Often they carried letters from fellow believers to distant friends and relatives when they visited different regions of the Roman Empire. We do not have a great amount of literature from this early period, but we have enough to know part of the story. Some indeed sold their lands and became itinerant witnesses to the gospel. Personal accounts of the martyrs' experiences, the persecutions, the internal conflicts among the believers, the exhortations to the good life, the call to receive the suffering ones in the spirit of Christ—all these remain to remind us that the faith received strives to reach out to others. Not long afterward, Christian writings became the means by which the faith was presented to the literate part of Roman society.

The late first and early second centuries witnessed a wide variety of ways in which the gospel was presented to the Roman world. We have classed them together as the *testimonial model*. It is indeed a broad category: commissioned missionaries, self-appointed itinerants, heads or members of home groups, traveling emissaries, written experiences and communications with distant relatives and friends, and more—all had their part. They were convinced of the authenticity of the message, they had experienced the presence of Christ in their lives, and they were enthusiastically committed disciples of the Lord who wanted nothing more than to have others share this joyous certainty of faith with them.

B. Apologetical Model

There are few sharp transitions from one period of history to another. We can speak of tendencies and movements that come into prominence while preceding ones continue. As the Christian church grew and reached the limits of the Roman Empire, so also did its self-identity and sense of rightful place and belonging. Its membership mirrored the diversity of the general populace of which the overwhelming majority were the poor and disadvantaged members of society. However, during the second century, the church's representatives from the upper and educated classes presented a changed public face. They mounted an offensive on behalf of the Christian faith and a vigorous defense of its adherents. Here, then, we introduce the rise of the *apologetical method*, which refers to the rational defense of those who professed faith in the gospel.

In the Roman and Greek world, great uncertainty reigned, despair about entrenched immorality prevailed, general anxiety about immortality produced insecurity, and a multiplicity of mystery religions proliferated. To this profound sense of lostness, no convincing answer was supplied from the philosophers and writers in the Empire. Indeed, in this period of history, literary voices were few.

Within the ranks of the faithful, voices arose that proclaimed loyalty to the Roman Empire, gave witness to the truths and practice of the Christian communities, and decried the injustices being committed against its innocent and morally upright members. Noteworthy is that these defenses were made to the highest authorities of the provincial governments and to the emperor himself. Some of their prestigious number included Justin Martyr, Tatian, Irenaeus, Tertullian, Clement of Alexandria, Origen, Cyprian, and Athenagoras.

The defense was basically a three-pronged offensive. First, there was a full-fledged denunciation of the polytheism of the Greek and Roman traditions while affirming the truth of monotheism. Though Christians were being judged responsible for disasters and catastrophes that plagued society, the Apologists argued that the fault lay with the irrationalities and the immoralities of the gods. Belief in the gods had indeed been shaken, but popular belief in the state religions died hard. Even the highly respected philosophers of the past, including Plato and Aristotle, were subjected to the harshest of criticisms for misleading the people on fundamental issues. Some of the Apologists were recent converts to the faith, and as such, some of their recriminations may be subject to debate. Yet their affirmations of God the eternal Creator and Sustainer of all appealed to many who inclined to some sort of monotheism.

Second, Christians ought to be judged not from their rejection of certain religious rites expected of the general populace, but by their lives and conduct. There were horrific accusations with the gravest of moral and civil denunciations that needed to be answered. Among these were claims about drinking the blood of child victims, promiscuity, atheism (refusal to recognize the Roman gods), secret associations, being destructive to the state, and being enemies of civilization. Apologists responded by pointing out the high moral character of Christians' lives, their unstinting care for the downtrodden and poor, and their loyalty to and prayers for the state. Rather, they declared, it was the Christians who were the saviors of society, while the pagans were the real danger for their failure to honor God.

Finally, their defense centered on the person and ministry of Jesus Christ. Though some Apologists believed that Christianity had come to fulfill what the ancients sought and what humanity in its essence had always believed to be the goal of history, others had less patience with religious beliefs and practices of the past. Still others, like Tertullian, rhetorically cried out: "What does Jerusalem have to do with Athens?"—expecting the answer to be, "Nothing at all!" Yet all were in the mainstream of the faith, witnessing to the uniqueness of Jesus, that he had brought the truth, suffered voluntarily, and sacrificed himself for the salvation of the world. They represented what became the orthodox way. No religious synthesis with other faiths was proclaimed. Other religions might have elements of the truth, but only Christianity was the final and full faith.

This last position gave the Apologists another task: the defense of the Christian faith from those who sought a synthesis with other religious forms, such as the then current mystery religions. Especially viral was the offensive against the Gnostic emphasis on the authenticity of only the spiritual while condemning the material world either as illusory or the embodiment of evil. Some still sought to defuse Jewish opposition and to win over the declining number of Jews who were open to their message. Others, such as the Marcionists, questioned the acceptance of much of the Scriptures followed by the orthodox current that predominated in the Christian community.

To sum up, as more of the educated class were converted and became vocal defenders of the faith, the *apologetical model* became a new mode by which the Christian church claimed its place in the Roman world. The Apologists established schools at which new defenders of the faith and evangelists were trained. Some became outstanding evangelists like Gregory Taumaturgos, student of Origen for five years, who was ordained as bishop of his native city, where under his leadership a mass conversion of the populace occurred. However, Christians remained a minority in the empire until the edict of toleration issued by Constantine in 313 A.D. They were scattered unevenly in the Roman Empire and may have been about ten percent of the total population. Significant growth continued also by the testimonial model throughout the second and third centuries.

C. Monastic Model

Due to the breakdown of the Roman Empire, the invasions of Eastern clans, and the destruction of much of Western civilization, monasteries thrived both in the Western and the Eastern churches. First, individual ascetics, often referred to as the "desert fathers," began their particular forms of ministry, especially in Egypt, where the Coptic Church was founded. Soon, however, the communal type gained ascendency and proliferated in both the Eastern and the Western churches. For the next centuries, the dominant mission was through the *monastic model.*

Some have called the extension of the gospel by non-orthodox Nestorian groups the "golden age" of missions for the East Syrian churches. They evangelized in multiple cultural forms and liturgies, such as the Coptic, Syriac, Ethiopian, Abyssinian, Nubian, Armenian, Indian, and even Chinese. Their multireligious context included traditional groups (Turks, Mongols, Huns), long established religions (Manichaeism, Buddhism, Zoroastrianism), Asian faiths (Hinduism, Confucianism, Taoism), and the burgeoning Muslim movement.

Missionary monks, steeped in the ascetic tradition, invested their spirituality in sacrificial ministry to their neighbors and in itinerancy to the far-Eastern reaches of Asia. Their preparation included science, medicine, education, and philosophy. In their travels, they shared their learning, while at the same time they received the Eastern treasures of astronomy, mathematics, and classics, which they in turn eventually made available to the later Western Renaissance. By the end of the first millennium, their witness and establishment of Christian communities had reached all the way to Mongolia, Korea, and Japan. However, these Christians in Asia were but a small minority and were often plagued by persecution and eventual extinction in areas where missionaries had achieved significant advances. Also the strident advances of Islam in the seventh and early eighth centuries made Christians second-class citizens and proscribed its missionary impetus. In Africa and Asia Minor, the Christian churches suffered their greatest losses, with the isolation of the Christian kingdoms of Nubia and Ethiopia and their consequently turning more conservative with the loss of missionary spirit.

The *monastic model* functioned differently in the West, due to the conversion of Constantine (313) and the destruction of Rome (486). The model took different forms in distinct contexts. In the following centuries, Irish monks made multiple pilgrimages in Britain and to the Continent, preaching conversion to Christ and founding monasteries where the faith was taught. Ascetic practices were instituted, and ministry to the social context, especially for the peasants and poor, was carried out. Besides such notables as Columban, Wilfrid, Leoba, and Willibrord, Boniface shared the gospel and established beachheads in the lowland countries and Germany for forty years before his martyrdom for the faith with thirty of his coworkers in Frisia.

Much of the early mission was achieved through the alliance of state and church, usually through monks. Sometimes they, both men and women, also founded convents for women. Especially Charlemagne in his conquest of the Saxons in central Europe required the acceptance of the Christian faith, sometimes by offers of benefits but often as a condition for survival. After conquest, monks were sent to the reaches of the empire to establish monasteries and churches, where baptism was effected, then the Christian faith taught, and ethical norms established—in that order! The monk Alcuin of York was Charlemagne's principal minister to implement this lengthy process. To his credit, he objected to the forced conversions and baptisms required by the king. Though there was nominal acceptance by many at first, progressively through preaching, adoption of Christian rites, and education, the general populace accepted the Christian faith as their religion.

The bishop of Rome who claimed universal jurisdiction in the West sent and consecrated missionaries for the task of converting England and northern Europe. Notable was Augustine, sent around 600 A.D. to England on a mission. He was instrumental in the conversion of King Ethelbert of Kent. Augustine by correspondence asked the Pope what should be done about the pagan sacrifices, their temples, and the idols in them. Illustrative of the principle of accommodation was the advice to use the temples for worship if they were well constructed, destroy the idols, and convert the sacrifices of animals into feasts to which all the people should be invited to share in the joy and thanksgiving of the Christian life. Itinerant monks traveled to villages and distant hamlets, everywhere calling the poor folk to heavenly themes, both through preaching of the Word and by their virtuous example of love. Many sought their consecration by the Pope in Rome, and some were named as bishops to the regions they evangelized. In this way the *monastic model* was carried out by dedicated monks, sometimes by martyrdom but usually by royal favor and by church authority vested in the Pope. Despite repeated invasions and destruction of the monasteries with their surrounding villages, the patience, dedication, and perseverance of the monastic movement gained Western Europe for the Christian faith.

D. Communal Model

Contemporary to the monastic movement, the *communal model* of evangelization gained whole tribes and people movements for the Christian faith. The pattern for this type of conversion occurred primarily through the decisions of kings and princes, or leaders and elders, to accept baptism and to become Christian, who then called upon their people to follow their example. During this period of perhaps more than six centuries, mass conversions occurred, and then it took generations to digest the meaning of this process in which people were baptized and then taught catechisms. The usual catechisms included the teaching of the meaning of the Apostles' Creed, the Lord's Prayer, and the Ten Commandments. Nominal Christians would wait for the arrival of monks and teachers to lead them into an understanding of their newly accepted faith. Though that may seem strange to us, in cultures where the communal values take precedence over the individual, religious decisions were part of an integral mindset that controlled the tribal destiny.

This happened in some cases by peaceful means, such as the conversion of the Bergundians, who sought baptism and the power of its God to overcome the invading Huns. Of far more importance was the baptism in 496 of Clovis, king of the Franks, which marked the alliance of state and church and ushered in the period of acceptance of the faith by the non-Roman invaders of Western Europe. Progressively they were conquered by successive kings, baptized, and slowly assimilated into the faith, often with much of their culture and spirit incorporated. But Germanic leaders were required in defeat to accept the faith. Charlemagne reigned for more than thirty years, extended the empire, and required baptism as a sign of defeat. It happened on occasion that when the conquered refused, they were put to death.

Though methods varied in the mass conversions to Christianity during the first half of the medieval period, from the fourth to the tenth centuries A.D., church growth was significant and the future course of its history altered. State domination of churches, more in the Eastern Church than in the West, the verticalization of clerical leadership, and the emphasis of orthodoxy in doctrine—all of these grew steadily.

There was a significant difference between the West and the East in the methodology of evangelization, with more adaptation to local languages, the adoption of more culturally sensitive rites, and a more localized form of church government in the Eastern churches. Illustrative are the early adoption of the gospel in the kingdoms of Nubia and Ethiopia, mentioned above, and in the Coptic church—as well as in the later mission of the brothers Cyril and Methodius to Russia in the 10th century. Their adaptation of the faith to national languages and to the culture of local people in an understandable way was considered revolutionary and was countered fiercely by Western Latin religious leaders. Cyril and Methodius created the Slavonic alphabet, translated the Scriptures into the language of the common people, and adapted the liturgy.

Examples of the communal model can also be given for the late evangelization of some Scandinavian countries as well as Russia, Poland, Moravia, and Bohemia. For many people groups of this period, leaders either decided for or greatly influenced their conversion, so the communal model predominated. In these areas, a conscious commitment to the Christian faith became progressively realized, with sectors remaining nominal but with the community as a whole eventually adhering to the Christian understanding of discipleship.

At the turn of the millennium, new movements began to appear in the known Christian world. The Muslim faith had by then made initial conquests, changing the face of world history. The increasing number of maritime and land caravans, the interchange of knowledge between East and West, a sharpened virulent opposition against other faith groups, the breakup of the empires of East and West into more national loyalties, and the tragic division symbolized by Rome and Constantinople—all contributed to the confusion of spiritual and political ends. In this latter half of the medieval period from the tenth to the fifteenth centuries, a diversity of methods sought to further the extension of the Christian faith.

In a general way, the thought forms and rites in the church during the first millennium tended to affirm a Greek understanding of the faith. In other words, the spiritual aspect of existence more closely defined the approach to God and the understanding of the gospel. The material aspect of existence had little, or, in some interpretations, no permanent value or reality, as affirmed by early ascetics. The monastic model, in its life of service to the peasant poor and to persecuted minorities, had always affirmed the importance of earthly existence. Yet church theology grew more and more defined with far greater emphasis given to the spiritual realm. Especially the Order of Cluny, founded in 910, sought to maintain the spirituality of the church by seeking internal reforms and claiming its dominant role in society and also over the state.

Due to interchange with the East from trade, travelers, and commerce, new Aristotelian thought forms challenged the Platonic spiritual worldview, especially in the tenth to the twelfth centuries. Now the reality and inherent value of the material world was affirmed. Some religious leaders, such as Abelard, lectured in universities on the goodness of the physical creation and the Aristotelian worldview, and gained the following of many students and thinkers. They were strongly opposed by such conservative leaders as St. Bernard, who was able to secure the condemnation of Abelard in two synods of the church.

E. Teaching Model

Two new movements arose at the beginning of the 13th century that gave weight to these claims and formed new models of evangelization. These were the mendicant orders: Dominicans and Franciscans. They were not called monks because they did not separate themselves from the world. Rather they were friars or brothers who spent most of their time among the people and in society, and were known for their reforming zeal as inspired agents of mission.

The Dominicans represented the *teaching model* and are often known as the "Order of the Preachers." Founded by Dominic de Guzman, its members were among the great Schoolmen (or Scholastics) who taught in the universities of southern Europe from the twelfth to the fifteenth centuries. Among them were Albert the Great and Thomas Aquinas. The Systematic Theology (*Summa Theologica*) of Aquinas became the official doctrine of the Roman Catholic Church, pretty much to this day.[2] Dominicans began preaching in the north of Spain and in the southern region of France, especially trying to win back to the faith those who were considered heretics. Later they traversed the world as missionaries, converting, baptizing, and establishing schools, often commissioned by colonial governments.

Aquinas' acceptance of the material world as good revolutionized church thinking. Aquinas held that if anyone errs in his teaching concerning creation, he is bound to be wrong in all his theology. However, material existence of nature is secondary and subservient to the spiritual. To understand nature, one uses reason; to understand divine truths, one is dependent on revelation. Non-Christians can be addressed through natural concepts, through reason. Therefore the proper method in mission is to prove the existence of God and transcendent truths through reason. His three-volume mission theology, *Summa Contra Gentiles*, sets forth rational arguments for the Christian faith intended to train missionaries working among Jews and Muslims. To this he adds at the end a description of Christian truths received through revelation. Coercion should never be used for conversion.

Though the great missionary Raymond Lull never became a member of the Dominican Order, he followed this method. His was a mystical love for the Savior that sought concreteness of expression. First, he believed that one must learn excellently the language of the other. For this he tried to convince the universities, with limited success, to teach the languages of the Jewish and the Muslim peoples. Then, one must demonstrate rationally the truth of the Christian position. His many writings presented such a defense and were widely circulated. Finally, one must be a faithful preacher to non-believers though one's life be at risk. His third attempt to convert the Muslims of North Africa ended his fifty years of sacrificial mission with his death in 1316. Nota-

---

2 See Thomas Aquinas, *Summa Theologica, First Part, Question 47*, where he affirms the goodness of creation.

ble was his desire to evangelize the invading Mongols from the Far East and to secure their conversion before they succumbed to the Muslim religion.

Though Dominicans emphasized learning, by the beginning of the 14th century they had organized "the company of brethren dwelling in foreign parts among the heathen for the sake of Christ." Later, Dominican missionaries followed the teaching and preaching model in Latin America, Asia, and Africa. Their method required many years of intellectual preparation. Noteworthy was the long defense of the Indians of the Americas by Bartolomé de Las Casas in the 16th century. He strenuously opposed the Spanish imposition of Christian baptism by force and of slavery conditions on conquered peoples. Rather, he believed that the Indians should and could be converted by reasonable and persuasive arguments, as he affirmed in the title of his principal work: "the only way to bring all peoples to the true religion." Bartolomé explained that all are created with the *natural* capacity to choose the Christian way. Preachers, he said, not soldiers, are the proper agents of conversion. Unfortunately, the majority of his fellow Mendicants did not support his protests, and later generations tended to accept the *status quo* of oppression.

F.   Servant Model

Though the Franciscans share with the Dominicans the apostolic model of "being sent out," their incarnation into the world, especially with ministry to the needs of the poor, makes theirs the *servant model*. Francis of Assisi received approval to form a new Order from Pope Innocent III in 1215. Some of their number also achieved fame as university professors—for example, the famed mystic Bonaventura, Occam, and Duns Scotus. Yet the gentle and humble simplicity of Francis won for him the most cherished memory of generations. The popular art that shows him preaching to birds and caressing animals symbolizes his love for the good in all creation, including his poetry praising "brother sun" and "sister moon."

For new recruits to the Order, a year of probation was required, washing the wounds of lepers and caring for the sick and dying. His was an austere poverty, and those nearest him were called "spirituals," while others of his movement became "conventuals." But for all his followers, group holiness and poverty, service to the most neglected of society, and zeal for missions characterized the Order. The last chapter of the constitution or Rule for the Order, written by Francis himself, mandated the mission of preaching the gospel to all lands and peoples.

The Franciscans, perhaps due in part to the extreme austerity prescribed by Francis, suffered many divisions. Though subscribing to the authority of the church, frequently severe criticisms raised by the Order against the corruption and riches of those in power resulted in proscriptions and restrictions in its ministry. Dominicans were admired for their erudition and sometimes criticized for their harshness, while Franciscans were loved by the poorer and despised segments of society. The more "evangelical" or "spiritual" Franciscans were requested by the Catholic King Fernando for the mission in Latin America. In the spirit of the humility of Christ, Martin of Valencia and his companions, called the Apostles to Mexico, walked barefoot from their boats to their place of residence in the Capital. For their humility, adoption of poverty as a way of life, and rigorous observance of the religious life, they were greatly admired by the Indians. Wherever the Order has gone, Francis' prayer has served as a guide: "Lord, make me an instrument of your peace!"

G. Artistic Model

Following the rise of the mendicant orders and the destructive character of the Crusades, the growing interchange between the East and the West brought signs of a renaissance in the 14th and 15th centuries. True, the gospel continued to spread by the word of teaching, Dominican style, and by the act of serving, Franciscan style; however, in the Middle Ages other media and forms communicated the gospel as well. Let us describe them as the *artistic model*. By "artistic" we refer to the general world of the arts, those areas of life that were used for communication in the world of the illiterate and very poor, as were the vast majority of the population in this period. To adapt the words of a contemporary writer: "the medium was the message."

First, in the late Middle Ages there was the cathedral with its powerful arches and majestic steeples pointing heavenward and dedicated to the glory of God. In the drab world of the suffering and poor, everything beautiful to enrich human existence was there: carvings in wood and stone made by great artisans, stained-glass windows through which light streamed in many colors, richly embroidered tapestry for altars, gold and silver candlesticks and sacred vessels, sculptures of the greatest saints of the church—all for the glory of God and the happiness of those who came to share these treasures. Then there was the mystery drama of the mass offered by the priest in another tongue that in some way expiated sin and guaranteed heaven to those who came. Just to be there and to be counted worthy of participation gave new meaning to the lives of everyday people and gave them a feeling of the transcendent.

When the church was faced with the challenge to present a new religion to large illiterate populations brought as groups into the Christian realm, priests began to stage dramatized events on special feast days during the year. Symbolic actions and objects were used to recall meaningful moments of biblical history celebrated in Christian liturgy: censers, vestments, pantomime, all used to communicate with illiterate audiences. The so-called "Mystery Cycles," which dramatized central biblical events, were performed on stationary wagons placed around the town, and the audience would move from one to the other. Miracle plays presented events, often focusing on miracles, from the life of Christ or from the life of a martyr or saint.

In *The Hours,* Bible stories were dramatized, often with music incorporated, and sometimes were sung antiphonally. Favorites included Mary at the Tomb, the Conversion of Paul, Daniel in the Lion's Den, and the like. First they were presented in the church in Latin and initially not in verse, but later they were played in the streets and in public places, changing gradually to use verse and the vernacular. In "The Wise Virgins," a French drama of the early 12th century, the choir speaks Latin, while the virgins and Christ speak both Latin and French. Gradually, while the church liturgy remained in Latin, public drama became vernacular so that the common people could understand.

In the century before the Reformation, morality plays became popular and widely used to teach the basics of the faith to the largely illiterate masses. By allegory, difficult themes could be communicated more clearly. The central message taught that man was created in innocence, falls before temptation, repents, and is saved from judgment. Its intent was to teach the greater concepts of sin and virtue. Typical was the popular *Everyman,* including the characters God, Death, Everyman, Good-Deeds, Angel, Knowledge, Beauty, Discretion, and Strength. The story communicates that God is displeased with Everyman for seeking wealth and material possessions, which bring Death, rather than the virtues of true Knowledge and Beauty. The morale highlights the opposition between good and evil and the strong presence of God in the life of Everyman.

A wide variety of medieval art forms presented the call of the gospel and the need for the divine presence in people's lives: mosaics, paintings, fresco wall artistry, illuminated manuscripts, stained-glass scenes, and symbolic metalwork. Byzantine and other Eastern Orthodox churches, which rejected the use of images (iconoclasm), retain monumental church mosaics that appealed to the masses and commanded their religious loyalty. When Cyril and Methodius missionized Russia, emissaries of the prince were enthralled by the glory and beauty of St. Sophia Cathedral in Constantinople and chose the Eastern rather than the Roman version of the Christian faith, a decision which affected the spread and organization of the Christian faith in the East.

Perhaps the greatest effect of the arts was in the realm of painting, where the Christian message was presented visually to the world. Those that presented biblical figures inspired others to follow in their footsteps. Those that presented the birth, ministry, death, and resurrection of Christ enlisted disciples. Those that depicted vivid scenes of the saints in Paradise, often on the same canvas as scenes of those burning in the agony of hell, terrified the guilty and innocent alike. Those that accented the beauty of nature and the passion of love furthered the acceptance of this world as a good to be preserved. One has only to remember the names of Rafael, Michelangelo, and Rembrandt to confirm the power of art for good or evil. The *artistic model* effectively kept alive the flame of the gospel during exceedingly difficult and troubled times.

H. Mystical Model

Quite different from the preceding model based on the arts was a contemporary contrasting current that accented the internalization of the Christian relationship to God. The *mystical model* bridged the medieval and renaissance periods with a great impetus for the spread and the message of the gospel. Though the related word "mystery" does not occur in the Old Testament but does occur many times in the New Testament, it is used in the sense of revealing more clearly something that had previously been hidden. This is in contrast to the mystery religions that preceded and were contemporary to the birth of the Christian faith and in which mysteries referred to esoteric truths and ecstatic relations to their deity revealed through an elite priesthood. The purpose was to achieve mystic union with the divine and thus to attain immortality.

In the Christian tradition, this model had similarities, at least in phraseology, to ancient religions, and sometimes it was tempted to follow ways similar to those of such ancient beliefs. There were great Christian mystics who held that a divine spark resides in every person, and that in giving oneself wholly to this holy presence one enters into union with God. In this giving of oneself, love and justice reign in life. Ecclesiastical rites may be of some use, but an interior birth of union with God is superior in every way. This was the position of Maestro Eckhart and his disciple Juan Tauler, whose practical counsels of comfort and guidance were an inspiration to Martin Luther. Some dedicated their theology and life to a practical mysticism: contemplation and mission.

Francis of Assisi (*Rule*) and Raymond Lull (*The Book of the Lover and the Beloved*) accentuated the mystical aspects of their faith both in their writings and in their action. Like others who followed them, their inward visions and transformation resulted in an extraordinary mission to the world. Theirs was a lived experience of the love of God. Mysticism professes that there is a subjective experience, for some perhaps an intuition or insight beyond ordinary understanding, of the transcendent reality, of God and his call to specific discipleship. Someone has said that all the great Christian mystics were prophets with a vision for God's mission in the world.

Most of the early Spanish mystics, such as Cisneros of Spain, Teresa de Avila, and John of the Cross, felt that their spiritual exercises were a place where discursive thought is left behind to seek a loving encounter with God. Their visions and contemplations were carried out within monastic orders, but they were actively planting new communities for the reform of the church. Such efforts sometimes brought ecclesiastical judgment upon them.

However, others, such as Ignatius of Loyola and Antonio Ruíz de Montoya, challenged this mystical way by showing how the calling could and perhaps ought to be an engagement with an active life of ministry to the world. Loyola wrote the well-known and still used *Spiritual Exercises* and Montoya the *Firestone of Divine Love*, profound books of a mystic call to the contemplative life. Action without contemplation, they believed, will fail to accomplish the mission. But the Jesuit mission, as we will note below, and the Indian villages of Paraguay established by Montoya, evidence some of the most far reaching, dynamic, and successful missions in Christian history.

The connection between mystic contemplation and mission certainly was not limited to these leaders. The mystic disciple of Montoya, Juan Miguel Marin, felt the call to become the apostle to black slaves in the Americas. How many have not felt the compelling desire to seek closer union with God and had a burning desire to minister to their fellows in their suffering and life! John Wesley's "strange warming" at Aldersgate signaled the beginning of a most devout pilgrimage of contemplation and an itinerant ministry of world-wide scope.

Sadhu Sundar Singh, born into a Sikh Indian family, experienced as a boy twice weekly the presence of an ascetic *sadhu* (mystic). When he was four-teen, his mother died, and he despaired and became angry. He hated the local Christian missionaries and publicly burned a Bible page by page. In his de-spair he planned suicide but prayed for God to appear or give some sign: a vision, a trance, a voice? One night a light of growing intensity engulfed him, and he saw not one of his traditional gods but the Lord Jesus Christ. Later he had more visions of the presence of Christ. He took on the saffron robes of the *sadhu* and spent his life spreading the gospel of love, peace, and rebirth through Jesus. On his journeys he carried no money or other possessions, only his New Testament. He traveled in India, China, Ceylon, Malaya, Burma, and Tibet—and twice to the West, including the United States and Europe, in 1920 and 1922. In the West he was appalled by the materialism and lack of religious zeal in comparison with Asia's awareness of the divine.

Singh became a sadhu because he felt that Christianity would not enter into Indian life and culture unless he evangelized in an Indian way. So he chose the humble way of Jesus. He said, "I am not worthy to follow in the steps of my Lord, but, like him, I want no home, no possessions. Like him, I will belong to the road, sharing the suffering of my people, eating with those who will give me shelter, and telling all men of the love of God."[3] While train-ing at an Anglican college, he felt ostracized for being different, and his studies seemed irrelevant to the gospel in India's great need. He left. His spiritual life was built around his mystical visions, which continued throughout his life,

---

3   Sadhu Singh, *Wisdom of the Sadhu: Teachings of Sundar Singh*. See also Janet and Geoff Benge, *Sundar Singh: Footprints over the Mountains*.

and some believed that his life paralleled that of Jesus. Many were converted to the faith through his testimony and his widely circulated spiritual writings. Numerous followers and others consider Singh to be a formative spirit of the church in India.

More difficult to evaluate was the movement initiated by Simon Kimbangu in the Congo around the same time that Singh had his first vision of Christ. Converted through the Baptist Mission in 1915, he became a catechist and religious leader before having a vision of an encounter with Jesus Christ and receiving a divine command to preach and to heal the sick in 1921. His ministry of only six months was astounding. He healed many sick, reportedly resurrected someone, appointed 12 disciples, and claimed that he was the comforter promised by Christ in John 14. Literally multitudes came from their villages, plantations, and sick beds to hear the prophetic message and to be healed. Many believed that the missionaries hid secrets of the faith that gave power and wealth to the European colonists. Kimbangu, as one of their own who had spoken with God, could reveal the secret knowledge. He identified God with the Congolese Supreme Being, which he presented as close to the local people.

The Belgian authorities and some Christians were fearful of a rebellion, so Kimbangu was arrested on sedition charges and condemned to death. But after an appeal from the Baptist missionaries, King Albert of Belgium commuted his sentence to 150 lashes and life imprisonment. He was sent 1,000 miles away to the other side of the country, and he never saw his wife and three sons again. There he died thirty years later in 1951. All admired his mystical sense of piety, his personal deep holiness, and his quiet submission to his fate as Christ had accepted his condemnation.

Kimbangu's movement was proscribed by the governing colonial power, and his followers went underground. Under the leadership of his wife and sons, the movement took on monumental national and extra-national proportions and transcended tribal limits. With the independence movement in 1960, it emerged with several million members. Named "the Church of Jesus Christ on Earth," it is often referred to as an African Independent Church (AIC).

Its African leadership teaches the main Christian doctrines but also includes elements of spiritual African beliefs and rites. As a member of the World Council of Churches, it enters into and is influenced by dialogue with the broader Christian church. Though not strictly Pentecostal in origin and character, it reflects some Pentecostal characteristics: healing, speaking in tongues, and prophesying. Current estimates of membership range as high as 5 million members.

Mystical experiences have a powerful effect, both on the subject and on those to whom mission comes. The one who receives the vision, dream, or trance becomes possessed by a spirit of divine certainty of calling that is felt by all to whom they subsequently minister. The authenticity of the messenger convicts those who experience his presence and message. The confluence of factors that make such a mass movement possible certainly include the contextual felt need, whether economic, political, or religious. The mystical visionary provides the spark that ignites pent-up passions, deep religious hunger, and also nationalist expectations. *Mystical models* have spawned some of the greatest movements of the expansion of the gospel in history.

I. Kerygmatic Model

In the 16th century, the Renaissance in the West, expanding horizons through maritime discoveries, a sense of the value of the individual, new scientific views, and religious humanism, gave birth to a critical reevaluation of the spiritual life. The ensuing Reformation, led largely by Martin Luther and John Calvin and the Anabaptists, called for a personal confrontation with sin and with the Lord for forgiveness.

In all of mission history, there are what some historians call "constants." By that we understand the abiding reality of God's actions in the world, the nature of the human respondents, and the relationships that hold them together. However, changing mindsets, the spirit of new epochs, and new historical perspectives define the ways in which these constants centered on the gospel are mediated to persons and groups. So in the transition from the Medieval to the Modern period of church history, many factors contributed to the birth of the new age in the West. They included the following:

- the arrival of long-forgotten (or unfamiliar) knowledge of classics from the East
- the increase of commerce between the West and the East
- the religious crusades to regain holy lands from the Turks
- the birth of a new worldview involving science and the planets
- the exploration and conquest of Africa and the Americas
- the invention of movable typesetting and printing of books
- the breakdown of papal supremacy in the West
- the rise of nationalism in England, France, and Spain

Consequent was the increased recognition of the value of the human person, of the created world as good, and of the use of the arts and sciences to discover and express truth. These constitute the movement called Humanism, which in northern Europe had religious depth while in southern Europe there grew a more secular non-religious version. In this context new opportunities for and methods of evangelization were born.

In the 16th century the Reformers basically believed that most necessary for the church was to announce the gospel of the kingdom (reign) of God, what we call the *kerygmatic model*. *Kerygma* is the Greek word that refers to the good news of the kingdom of God (i.e., the gospel), the proclamation and announcement of God's action in Christ for our salvation.

Given the widespread illiteracy of the pre-Reformational priesthood, the liturgical announcement of the gospel in a language not understood by the majority of the people, and the shortage of priests in rural areas, the Reformers did not believe that the gospel had really arrived among the common people. Luther repeatedly charged that not one person in ten knew the gospel of Jesus Christ. Though Calvin and Zwingli were more optimistic, and while the Anabaptists were less so, all affirmed the urgent need to spread the Word far and near.

For this reason the Reformers accented the centrality of the Holy Scriptures. Less emphasis was given to what they believed to be secondary means of worship and religious rites, such as sacraments, religious symbols and saints, priestly intermediation and apostolic succession, monks and nuns, images and icons, gothic architecture and stained-glass windows. Access to God, they believed, was more direct, personal, and simplified. The hearing of the Word of God and personal response to it became central to faith and worship. Also, with the printing press, reading was a way of communicating, so the Reformers insisted on education for boys and girls, for priests, for men and women. The message spread as well through congregational singing with experiential words and simplified music. But whether in reading or singing or preaching or home Bible study, central was the *kerygma*, the announcement of the gospel, the preaching of the good news, the spread of the Word of the Lord.

As true religious humanists, the Reformers affirmed the urgency of a personal response to the *kerygma*, the communication of the gospel. Many British and U.S. mission historians insist that the Reformers had no mission interest, no theology or practice of mission. German and Dutch historians disagree. They point out that while the Reformers' mission began in their home territory (or in Great Commission language, "in Jerusalem, and . . . Judea"), their view and their concern was that the spread of the gospel reach "to the ends of the earth" (Acts 1:8). As Luther in a classic passage put it: "As when a pebble is thrown into a pond, the ripples continue expanding until they reach the farthest edge, so when the gospel is preached, the ripples begin in the center and continue expanding until they reach the farthest ends of the earth."[4]

Calvin sent a coded message to the struggling mission churches in France: "Send me the wood, and I will send you the arrows," which meant, "Send me the men, and I will send you the trained evangelists and pastors."[5] He emphasized the work of the Holy Spirit both in the conversion of persons and in renewing "the face of the earth." As the theological foundation for mission, he proclaimed an active Christ whose reign in human history set the church as the appointed instrument for conversion and cosmic renewal. This theme was later taken up by Gisbertus Voetius (b. 1589), the first Protestant theologian of mission, in his *Plantatio Ecclesiae*. He affirmed the threefold goal of missions: the conversion of the Gentiles, the planting of the church, and the glory of the manifestation of divine grace in history. This definition proved to be more inclusive than that of succeeding centuries and predated what we now

---

4   Sermon on Mark 16:14, Ascension Day, 1522, *Weimar Ausgabe*, Vol. 10, III, 140. Cited in Sidney Rooy, *Lutero y la Misión: Teología y Práctica de la Misión en Martin Lutero.*
5   *"Donnez-moi du bois, et je vous envoie les fleches."* Cited in Robert Kingdon, *Geneva and the Coming Wars of Religion in France, 1555- 1563.* See also Rooy, "La Pastoral de los Refugiados Franceses en Ginebra: 1546 – 1565," 127.

call *missio dei* (God's mission). According to this understanding of missions, great advances were made for the progress of the church during Reformation times. The gospel reached out and claimed loyalties not only to the peoples of Europe but also to those of other known lands.

Following the originality and creativity of the Reformers, several generations tried to preserve their teaching. We call this period "Protestant Scholasticism" because the theologians systematized what they had received rather than to creatively bring the Word of the Lord to new challenges and generations. The Roman Catholic Church did the same at the definitive Council of Trent (1545-1564). There the theology of Thomas Aquinas was declared to be the permanent interpretation of the faith, and the work of the Reformers was condemned. This hardening of the teachings of both the Reformers and the Roman Catholics tended to stifle new attempts and understandings of the faith.

J.   Pietist Model

In the 17th century new spiritual movements blossomed first through a group of poets in the Netherlands called the "Further Reformation" (*Nadere Reformatie*). Later, Phillip Spener in Germany organized small Bible study and prayer groups to deepen spirituality and extend concern for the poor. They were cells that acted as a renovation movement within the state Lutheran church. Related to this movement was the University of Halle, led by August Hermann Franke, an institution in which missionaries were trained to announce the gospel. Many were sent to the farthest reaches of the world.

This *pietist model* was furthered by Conde Ludwig von Zinzendorf, who provided room on his estate for a Moravian Community called Herrnhut ("the Lord's House"). The Herrnhutters sent out more than three hundred missionaries between 1730 and 1764, the year of Zinzendorf's death. Missionaries were sent out two by two, following Jesus' way, but were chosen by prayer and the casting of lots. They were outfitted with necessary goods and sent by boat to many newly discovered lands throughout the world. This was a community project that in turn cared for family members left behind, not knowing if their loved ones would return. The missionaries, upon arrival at their destinations, would build homes appropriate to the locale, find work to support themselves, begin Bible studies and prayer groups in their homes, and so establish church groups. Some of their church plants continue to the present, notably the significant churches in Surinam.

K. Imperial Model

When Portugal and Spain controlled shipping on the seas in the 15th and 16th centuries, their kings were given authority by the Pope in Rome to conquer and to extend the church in Africa and Latin America. We could call this the "royal patronage" model, or, perhaps better, the *imperial model*. When Portugal explored African coasts in the mid-15th century, the Pope authorized the king's right to subdue and Christianize the native peoples. Later the same right was given to the Spanish king in 1493 for Latin America. A divisory line known as the Line of Demarcation was established at one hundred miles west of the Azore Islands in the mid-Atlantic. Later it was discovered that this line intersected Brazil, of which Portugal became the official "Patron." In this model the king controlled the church and the missions. He appointed the bishops, divided bishoprics, collected tithes, paid for churches and seminaries, authorized who could travel to the new lands, and gave the rights of missionizing native peoples to four different monastic orders at first: Dominicans, Franciscans, Jesuits, and Augustines—and then later granted similar rights to Cistercians and other orders. The "secular" priests served the colonists, the "regular" (monastic) priests evangelized the natives.

The methods varied under this model according to each monastic order, but, even more, each missionary had his own view with respect to evaluating the local native culture and beliefs, the best method with which to approach the natives, and how to Christianize those who had never heard the gospel. Of course, the missionaries were also locked into a system of conquest and practical slavery. Usually an attempt was made to reorganize the local peoples into communities, either near cities or towns where they could be servants for the colonists, or in the interior of the country (most of it at that time!), where they operated as isolated communities, often under the jurisdiction of two or more priests.

First, it was deemed necessary for soldiers to subject the natives to Spanish or Portuguese rule. In these wars, many of the people were killed by the superior weaponry of the invaders. Missionaries accompanied the troops and participated in the "pacification" process. They assumed charge of the internal organization of the villages, the teaching, and the administration of baptism and other religious rites. Insurrections and rebellions were frequent and were put down by the military.

In the first stages of conquest, mass baptisms were common. Natives were assigned by the hundreds or thousands to the conquering soldiers to till and care for the land areas conceded to the soldiers for their faithful service to the king. The land owners were required to offer instruction in the Christian faith by the priests. Certain rights for the natives were stipulated by the king but were poorly observed. The native peoples were treated as slaves, punished severely for perceived faults, and restricted to assigned limits. More died from imported diseases and were decimated within short periods of time. For the most part the *tabula rasa* (erase and start over) method of religious teaching was followed, in which native beliefs were negated as evil and a transplanted Christian set of views and values were imposed. An attempt was made to stamp out native ways, culture, writings, ethical standards, and religious rites, and to replace them with Roman Catholic doctrines about the church, the sacraments, the saints, Mariology, the priesthood, and moral values.

However, some priests and bishops worked tirelessly to defend native rights and to denounce the established domination and treatment of the semi-slaves. This minority group of priests saw the futility and sinfulness of evangelization by force and of holding of the natives in slave-like conditions to Christian masters. Bartolomé de Las Casas was called the "Apostle to the Indians" for his lifelong struggle for native rights. The only way to gain converts to Christ, he insisted, was by persuasion of the will, not by force. He achieved *New Laws for the Indies* from the king in 1542, but found it impossible to gain its acceptance by the colonists. By and large the *imperial model* over the centuries brought many Indians into the Christian faith, but its methodology has been rightly condemned.

L. Cultural Adaptation Model

Noteworthy was the contribution to the theology and practice of mission initiated by the Jesuit Order. The Portuguese Ignatius of Loyola won its adoption as a mission order by the Pope in 1540, certainly in part because of its vows of absolute obedience, not to imperial powers but to the Pope. This was the first step in the long struggle between "the Crown" and "the Cross" to regain ecclesiastical control of the mission, control that had been given to kings under the patronal system. The Jesuit mission to Asia adopted what may be called the *cultural adaptation model*. Its missionaries viewed the Japanese and Chinese civilizations as similar to that of the Greco-Roman world of apostolic times and therefore to be considered as worthy recipients of the gospel in their own cultural forms. Decisions had to be made about the name to be chosen for God, ancestral veneration, and sacramental rituals. This accommodational approach rejected the *tabula rasa* model and incorporated the favorable acceptance of the cultural rites and values of the receiving society.

The second step in the recuperation of papal control of mission was the organization of the Sacred Congregation for the Propagation of the Faith in 1622 by the Pope. At first this Roman Catholic agency approved the accommodation of the faith to the new cultural rites and values adopted by the Jesuit missionaries in Asia. The Congregation's remarkable instructions to the Jesuit Order in 1659 counsels the missionaries,

> Do not regard it as your task, and do not bring any pressure to bear on the peoples, to change their manners, customs, and uses, unless they are evidently contrary to religion and sound morals. What could be more absurd than to transport France, Spain, Italy, or some other European country to China? Do not introduce all of that to them, but only the faith, which does not despise or destroy the manners and customs of any people, always supposing that they are not evil, but rather wishes to see them preserved unharmed.[6]

The great missionaries of this period include Francis Xavier (India and Japan), Alesandro Valignano (papal visitor to Asia), Matteo Ricci (China), Robert de Nobili (India), and Alexandre de Rhodes (Vietnam). Valignano called their method the "gentle model" (*il modo soave*). They learned local languages, studied and translated religious and philosophical works of local culture, empowered local leaders, brought scientific advances of the West (clocks, mapmaking, astronomy, mathematics), and worked with the upper classes as well as the lowest. De Nobili organized two groups of missions in India, one for the upper and another for the lower castes. The missionaries entered into dialogue with local religious leaders, often adapted their priestly garb or

---

6   Stephen Neill, *Christian Missions*, 179.

hairstyles, accepted the caste system, and adapted local social customs. Some adopted the austere lifestyle of holy persons of that culture. Jesuits were expected to be open and responsive to the context to which they were assigned.

One area of difficulty, especially in China, was the rites associated with obedience to and veneration of ancestors: Was it an embedded cultural practice or a form of worship of elders? The Jesuits by and large judged that the rites were largely social and cultural, and, with some alterations, local Christians could participate. However, when Dominican and Franciscan missionaries arrived, they considered this syncretistic and idolatrous. Their complaints reached the Pope, who altered his judgments more than once on the subject, depending on which group was reporting. In response to the problem with the Jesuit model of missions, the Chinese Kangxi emperor declared in 1700 that the ancestral rites were civil, not religious, practices.

Part of the problem stemmed from the national loyalties of the missionaries, the Jesuits from Portugal and the other orders from France. A papal legate from France was sent to investigate, and he condemned the Jesuit practices. In 1715 a final decision was made to forbid the Jesuit practices of accommodation. The Chinese emperor was incensed and responded two years later by forbidding Christian worship, by ordering the closure of all churches, and by expelling all other missionaries, including the Dominicans and Franciscans. By this time there were 200,000 Christians in China and an estimated 300,000 in Vietnam. Thousands had been baptized in Japan, but severe persecution reduced the number. By and large, it must be said that the *cultural adaptation model* brought in large numbers of baptized Christians, but these were mostly subsequently eliminated by persecution.

We can only speculate about what might have resulted if the Jesuits had been given a free hand to continue with their evangelization project. Several principles are evident here: severing the link with foreign powers, dialogue between equals in the study of local religions, seeking a contextual foundation for an indigenous church, and recognizing the person to be evangelized as a subject worthy of respect and dignity. These principles served as guiding norms also for persons such as Bartolomé de Las Casas and the establishment of the reductions among the Guaranis in Paraguay and elsewhere in Latin America. However, some of the missionaries took a more moderate position and conceded that a critique of social and cultural phenomena was necessary to purge doctrinal and ethical inaccuracies, but that this could better be attained as a second step after commitment to the Christian faith.

M. Colonial Model

Near the end of the 16th century, the British defeated the Spanish Armada. This feat signaled the end of the Spanish and Portuguese domination of the seas. The Protestant lands of Great Britain and the Netherlands gained control and began their own explorations and conquests. The significant difference between the Spanish and the Protestant expansions was religious. The Spanish Conquest was considered by their king and the church as an expansion of the kingdom of God. There was an identification of the Roman Catholic Church with the political kingdoms within its spiritual jurisdiction. In the Protestant world, a separation between the sacred and the secular had been drawn. The church was under the state in secular matters but claimed its own jurisdiction in spiritual matters. This was often contested by kings and secular authorities, though in principle it was true.

The *colonial model* became the chief method of missions for the extension of Christianity both for Roman Catholicism and for Protestantism in the 16th, 17th, and the 18th centuries. In both cases the missionaries traveled with the military and with the commercial interests of the dominant land. Within this general class we do distinguish several of the methods that surpass this mold, but it is safe to say that in this period the Christian gospel arrived in more countries and among more different peoples groups than in any former period. More often than not, the mission agents needed approval from the civil and/or military authorities to travel; they often traveled with their nations' boats; they were more often than not subsidized and supported financially by the state; and their permission to stay or the obligation to leave depended on conformity to the trading company's regulations and the approval of the resident colonists.

However, there was a significant difference between the Roman Catholic *and* the Protestant methodologies. In the Americas the dual interest of the former was commercial and religious—that is, to secure gold *and* the conversion of the inhabitants. Since the Spanish invasion of Latin America was under the queen, who was deeply religious, she established norms to assure the humane treatment of those conquered, their education in the faith, and sufficient means to live. Her husband, the king, continued this policy after her death. But these norms were rarely respected in Latin America. After subjecting the native peoples to a severely conscripted existence, members of the religious orders tried to give some religious training, and baptisms *en masse* occurred. Although all of Latin America became predominantly Roman Catholic in form and name, a two-layer theology and religious practice resulted for many.

Yet there were conscientious priests and bishops who worked for the good of the native peoples and defended them with a modicum of success. Such were the thirty Jesuit villages in Paraguay with 150,000 inhabitants, referred to earlier, which existed over a span of 150 years, with each village under the tutelage of two or more priests (1610-1754). Solid advances were made in the indoctrination of the faith, in culture, in agriculture, and in the arts. However, the failure to train native clergy and community leaders caused the whole amazing project to fail when the Jesuit priests were forcibly removed by the royal authorities of their respective countries after the mid-18th century. In this particular village model there were excellent aspects: respect for the community ethos of the people, work through the natural leadership and kinship lines, and the use of drama and the arts in education. However, the leadership was paternalistic, and native leaders were not given adequate training and authority. Without the Jesuit presence, the missions largely disappeared. Though much formalism and superficiality resulted, large sectors of the newly encountered areas became and now remain mostly Roman Catholic.

For Protestants, the *colonial model* suffered some of the same defects. Here the trading was done by commercial companies (both in the East and West Indies Companies), which also were sometimes accompanied by soldiers or armed personnel. The companies were closely tied to the ruling authorities of their respective homelands. Pastors accompanied the traders to care for early colonists who had settled in the various new lands. Soon many of them began to contact indigenous peoples, learn their languages, and act as missionaries in spreading the gospel. The Netherlands East Indies Company established a seminary in 1721 to train missionaries for Indonesia, Ceylon, and Formosa (now Taiwan). A number of significant books on missions were published in the Netherlands during the 17th century, one by Gisbertus Voetius called *Plantatio Ecclesiae* (Church Planting)! There were also mass baptisms, more than 10,000 in Formosa in the early 1700s. But after training some twenty missionaries, the seminary closed down around 1734, probably because the

East Indies Company realized that too much instruction was not good for their commercial interests. For the most part these were forays on the coast and into some nearby interior areas without a conscientious effort to reach the population as a whole. Though once again this model needs to be viewed critically, some missionaries at this time pressured for native rights and for the right to share the gospel. Notable were the efforts of some missionaries in the Caribbean region on behalf of blacks in militating for their freedom from slavery in the early 18th century.

In the 19th century, when the center of Africa was opened by the intrepid itinerant missionary David Livingstone, numerous European countries established colonies there. Once again soldiers and imposition were the order of the day, however, and in this setting missionary societies soon played an important role. We discuss those groups in the following section. Lands were carved into nations, often separating sectors of the same people groups, subject to the commercial and political interests of the "Christian" colonial power. Though Livingstone hoped that the winning aspects of civilization would be a stepping stone to Christianization, the approach left much to be desired.

Similar problems occurred with the British colonies in North America. Though the establishment of colonies was often to escape religious persecution in their homelands, the colonists used the invasion of Native American lands for economic purposes. In general, no meaningful relationship between the colonists and their native subjects was established, and no cultural affinity was found. In New England only a few, such as John Eliot and the Mayhew brothers, initially sought to evangelize the local native peoples. Eliot translated the Bible into the Narragansett language and established fourteen self-governed Indian Christian villages. The native nations lived apart from the settlers, managed their own affairs, and were visited weekly for religious instruction by Eliot. His was a teaching model, but the context militated against its success. Wars and forcible occupation of lands by the expanding colonies destroyed the work rapidly there as well as in nearby coastal islands. The theocratic justification for the new colonies as the crowning of divine providence and evidence of his favor hardly reflected what God's kingdom ought to be in scriptural terms. For the most part, the Native Americans simply did not count as worthy recipients of divine grace. Fewer indigenous people survived in North America than in lands to the south.

N. Mission Society Model

To support John Eliot in his admirable work, the first of the *mission societies* was established. The Roman Catholic Church had at its beck and call an in-house natural supply of missionaries: the monastic orders and the convents. They were and continue to be effective missionaries across the earth. But the Reformers in the 16th century, one and all, rejected the belief that the contemplative life of separation from the world was spiritually superior to living and working in the world. For them the spiritual life was not separated from the natural world; rather the two were integrated into the one kingdom of God. This meant that monastic orders and convents for nuns were abolished in Protestant lands. For the next two centuries, missionaries were sent by rulers, accompanied traders to new lands, and/or went out to foreign lands on their own. There are numerous examples in which the Reformers were heartfelt participants.

In 1649, Christians in England formed the Society for the Propagation of the Gospel in New England in order to further the work of John Eliot and associates in evangelizing the native peoples. The *mission society model* was the dominant Protestant way to do missions in the next two centuries as dozens more societies began in England, France, Germany, Russia, China, Africa, and North America. Some were Bible societies. Some were formed to evangelize specific people groups: Jews, Native Americans, and blacks. The societies were voluntary agencies, made up of Christians concerned about the spread of the gospel, sometimes from one denomination, sometimes from various churches. Their purposes included prayer for the specific mission for which they were organized, selection and sending of missionaries as their representatives, and financial support to maintain the work and to carry on the mission. By the time of the World Missions Conference of Edinburgh of 1910, there were 44 mission societies in the United States sending persons just to Latin America, and many more mission societies were founded in England and Europe. It is significant that at least in the North American experience, women were more active than men in organizing mission societies, particularly when, and perhaps because, other leadership positions were closed to them.

The methodology of the many societies varied widely in some respects. Missionaries worked hard to translate the Scriptures for the many language groups. To this goal, the British and Foreign Bible Society (1804) and the

American Bible Societies (1816) stretched their resources, as did their counterparts in Europe. At this time only 7 percent of the U.S. population were members of the churches. Both of these Bible societies were broadly interdenominational, representing Christians from a majority of the denominations in existence at the time. Their method accented literacy, using the Bible as text. Concurrently with the liberation movement from Spanish domination in its colonies came the colporteurs (Bible distributors), especially from England and the United States, some using the Lancaster method of education. In this methodology, a more advanced group read and studied texts in the morning. Then each participant taught a group in another part of the city in the afternoon.

Significantly, in Latin America the British Bible Society used a Catholic version of the Bible (Padre Scio Version) for its first twenty years, one with the deutero-canonical books included. The military liberators from 1810 favored the spread and teaching of the Bible, and they accepted its use in the literacy programs. However, when both Bible societies were forced by some local branches to remove the deutero-canonical books from the Padre Scio Version, resistance from Catholic clergy grew to the reading and discussion of the Bible either publicly or as a tool in learning to read in the education of the masses. Then in 1837, when the Pope condemned the work of the Protestant Bible societies, Roman Catholic participation lessened but did not end. The political conflict between the liberal and the conservative wings of the church made some continuance possible.

During the 19th and 20th centuries, the *mission society model* was dominant for Protestants in Asia, Africa, and Latin America. However, given the wide variety of sending churches, the methodology varied across the spectrum from imposition and *tabula rasa* on the one hand to alleged inculturation and syncretism on the other. Many of those methods have already been considered above. With the mission society model we need to recognize especially the voluntary character of each, the grassroots movement to share the gospel which had not been recognized by the leadership of the organized churches, and the sacrificial ministries of many missionaries who plunged into unknown territory and peoples to fulfill their sense of the Lord's calling. We cannot but give thankful praise to those who sponsored and carried out this means of church planting in the far reaches of the world. Their varied approaches in mission make clear that it is futile to establish a single method for this task—or to select some few that will give success. What is required is sensitivity to the contextual situation, the cultural and religious character of the recipients, and the already present work of the divine Spirit in each *ethne*, or people group.

O. Church Model

Here we should interject that in the first half of the 20th century, many of the established churches recognized a failure on their part to be primarily oriented to the missionary call. In these communities the method transformed into a *church model*, what could be described as "the church planting churches." We return to a point made at the beginning of this chapter by Emil Brunner: "the church exists by mission as fire exists by burning"—what many church groups recognize as *missio dei*, "the mission of God." God is the agent and source of mission. The church has been formed and is called permanently to participate in that mission. Our guidance in this task comes from the Scriptures and the direction of the Holy Spirit. Divine providence goes before the church and prepares the way for the messenger.

The mission societies were incorporated into the church organization as the mission branch or the mission division of the church's ministry. Admittedly, sometimes the mission could be relegated to secondary importance, but that was not the intention or the vision that brought about the change. Symbolic of the larger movement was the organization of the World Missionary Conference (1910) in Edinburgh, Scotland, by more than 150 mission societies, the subsequent birth of the World Missionary Council (and the publication of the prestigious *World Review of Missions*), its world conferences on mission, and finally in 1964 its incorporation into the World Council of Churches. So the mission societies of numerous churches evolved into a core part of the world communion of churches. Many conservative churches likewise adopted the mission societies into their structure in their recognition of the mission as the heart and soul of the church of Christ. However, many of the mission societies were interdenominational and thus have continued their worldwide ministry to the present.

The *church model* differs in many ways from the *mission society model*. Frequently this has meant that more academically prepared candidates have gone to the mission field. This raises the question of efficacy: Did these do more effective work than the lesser trained, or did the vocabulary of the lesser trained give better communication and yield a better response from recipients of the gospel? Normally the sending church has assumed the financial responsibility for the missionary, spouse, and children, though that may be in process of change. Also the church department of mission has often assumed a more direct role in determining foreign mission policy. This has frequently caused resentment on the part of the growing national church as well as with a denomination's own missionaries on the field. Both the national church and often the missionaries questioned whether the sending church board could understand and impose policies and properly determine budgets for distant fields of mission of which their knowledge and perception was scant.

Neither the *mission society model* nor the *church model* perceived the vast changes that were occurring in the postmodern world. They tended to assume that theology, ethics, and church formation were already defined. Their calling as mission agents was to bring the defined truth and the gospel to lands and peoples who had not heard. So the missionaries, the churches they represented, the systematic theologies they had created, and the resources they brought held center stage in the whole evangelization effort. Whether, as the more progressive churches held, the approach should be a comprehensive one with education, health clinics, social betterment seminars and participation in government, or, as the more conservative missions and churches held, preaching the gospel and evangelism crusades should be the approach, the direction was one-way. The West brought what the rest of the world needed. The underdeveloped peoples needed what had been attained elsewhere. Not recognized was the realization that what was brought was itself culturally conditioned: the theology and the Western understanding of the gospel. Unquestioned were the effects of colonial domination, the feelings of cultural superiority, and "manifest destiny" beliefs, upon the gospel and the whole missionary enterprise.

One of the universal problems for the Christian mission has been the preparation of effective leaders for emergent churches. This is especially true where there has been excessive dependence on imported leadership and insufficient incorporation of new Christians into positions of leadership. The foreign missionary model has nearly always brought with it the feeling and judgment that he who evangelizes knows best. This may be because he or she comes from a culture that has more educational and cultural possibilities. Often the missionary has more economic resources to finance and lead new projects, whether for schools, hospitals, church facilities, or agricultural projects.

P. Institutional Model

The 19th century spawned a wave of optimism and new hopes for human improvement. A new spirit and mindset grew in the West that the era of progress would usher in a new age of peace and prosperity for all peoples. Some of the contributing factors included the wave of industrialization in the West, the scientific advances, the hopes for social and economic improvement, a Deistic mindset that humans have been given the mission to achieve the good, an optimistic anthropology that sees mankind as inherently good, the theory of the evolution of the cosmos, and the conviction that the kingdom of God was beginning to be realized on earth. Jesus was considered to be the prophet of these better times, and following his teaching would bring us heaven on earth. This mindset and belief with its myth of progress we call "nineteenth century liberalism."

For those of a more conservative mindset, the optimism and belief for human betterment translated into the development of revival movements and messianic cults. It was firmly believed and publicly preached that the harvest of souls would contribute to ushering in the millennium. In the United States there were also many specific predictions about Christ's imminent return as Seventh Day Adventists, Mormons, Jehovah's Witnesses, and other movements formed. In Africa, Latin America, and Asia, other messianic movements appeared, their leaders claiming to bring in the promised restoration of all things. Progressives and conservatives alike tended to accept a sort of post-millennialism—that is, that the progress of the gospel contributes directly to the hastening of the return of Christ and the establishment of his millennial kingdom, however that might be defined.

What is important for our theme of models of mission was the incorporation of these liberal values into the concept of evangelism. In the later 19th century, emphasis gradually came to be placed on an *institutional model* of missions. Across the globe, it was felt that education, medical assistance, social help for the poor, democratic government, and personal responsibility for decisions would bring people to accept the message of the Scriptures. As Diego Thomson, the first missionary to come to Latin America after the liberation from the Spanish yoke, put it: "Ignorance must be made to feel ashamed to exist. This enemy of humanity must be exterminated. Without education, there is no human society."[7] So Thomson proposed the learning of English for "the progress of the nation from every point of view!" Education was the principal mode of evangelism for many mission societies of the period.

The result of this mindset was the establishment of schools, hospitals, and other centers created for the improvement of the culture and the perceived ignorance of native populations. These institutions were headed up by doctors, teachers, and specialists of many sorts in order to bring others to accept the gospel. It was thought that when people were educated, healed of their diseases, instructed in new vocations and possibilities for a better life, they would be attracted to the Christian way. Many were. But in their culture, this often meant ostracism from their own families and faith groups. To be baptized as a Christian often meant excommunication from the former life and family.

In many countries the missionaries tended to live on communal property, and progressively so-called missionary enclaves or compounds came into being, especially in Asia and Africa. Many of the newly converted came to work for the mission, according to their potential. Some were trained to be teachers, medical assistants or even doctors, mechanical or agricultural workers, and helpers in families. This created encapsulated church communities cut off from the broader life of the society and culture. The phrase "rice Christians" came to be used in China to signify those who came to the missionaries in order to find a better life for themselves and their families.

Near the end of the 19th century and the beginning of the 20th, this whole "liberal" mindset came under severe criticism, challenged both by conservative and more liberal Christians. Likewise this *institutional model* was rejected by many missionaries, though its effects carried over in various ways. Even among the most conservative churches, missionary enclaves and compounds continued right up to the great emancipation decades of the 1950s and 1960s, when colonial powers granted independence to many nations in Africa and Asia, or were forced by revolutionary forces to do so. As a reaction, these new indigenous forces often required missions and missionaries to leave their lands and to turn over their hospitals and schools to national control.

---

7   Exact bibliographic source unknown.

Q. Catechist (Evangelist) Model

In the new nations, often the rapid spread of the gospel outpaced the possibilities of a pastoral presence among new groups of seekers and believers. This has been equally true for Africa, Asia, and Latin America. How then should the church answer this challenge?

In Africa, the proportion of pastoral staff to congregants and seekers has been disproportionate to the task. For the Roman Catholic Church in many rural areas, it was more than 5,000 people per priest. The Roman Catholic Church adopted what could be called a *catechist (or evangelist) model* in which non-ordained men functioned as representatives of the local churches. Celibacy was not a requirement. They pastored the great influx of new members in the latter part of the last century. Their task included forming and baptizing their fellow Christians. During bitter and cruel dictatorships they strengthened the faith of many who were suffering—and many of these lay leaders suffered imprisonment, torture, and death for doing so. Lay catechists have become the life blood for millions of their fellow believers in the global South, where most Catholics now live. Sixty-nine percent of Roman Catholic pastoral workers are catechists today.

Among evangelical Christians, the need for more workers gave rise to the commissioning of lay evangelists or pastors, many of whom planted new churches. They may have continued as the pastor once the church was organized or they turned these churches over to trained, ordained leaders.

R. Contextual Models: Adaptation and Inculturation

Churches and mission agencies alike have often been slow to recognize that the old models were breaking down. With the development of the new human sciences of anthropology, ethnology, psychology, and sociology during the 20th century, as well as linguistics and semiotics, better methods of understanding and interaction among human groups have emerged. The spirit of nationalism has grown rapidly, as has the maturation of mission churches where frequently new independent churches are being organized. New concepts and words have entered our vocabulary to express some of these nuances. One of them we call the *contextual model*. At first questioned by some groups as suggesting a sort of relativism, it has since been universally accepted as essential in a meaningful approach to others in evangelism. At our point in history we cannot credit one group for the new understandings that the above-mentioned sciences have given us. Nor is this model to be understood universally in the same way.

We humans have a way of importing our own meanings and judgments in such a way that we come to widely varied conclusions. But there is agreement that the *contextual model* requires first and foremost an analysis of those to whom we go with the gospel, with a number of significant questions (to which others could be added):

- What does the other understand by the name *God* or by the phrase *transcendent being?*
- How does the other consider the relation of the transcendent to present reality?
- How does the other express his or her religious actions, whether in ritual, prayer, or action?
- How does the other relate to family and community in terms of ethical norms and duties?
- Is the other more conceptual, intuitive, or emotional in the reception of transcendent guidance for life decisions?
- Are there sacred texts accepted by the other or the community, and, if so, with what literalism or symbolism are they accepted?
- Who makes religious decisions with and for the other, and to what extent are they communal and/or personal?

The *contextual model* thus begins where the other person is located, and with the willingness first to listen and learn who the other is and what the questions are for which he or she seeks an answer. Once a relationship is established and contact points are confirmed, not primarily intellectually but through a personal relation of mutual trust, questions and testimonies from both parts in mutual dialogue may be in order. The way in which the process of communication follows will be as different as the unique varieties of human beings to whom the Lord has given life. Evangelism and church planting become a surprising and ever evolving journey; only sensibility to the guidance of the Spirit of Christ and faith in his leading will suffice.

Adaptation.

There are two chief ways in which the *contextual model* has been developed and is being used in missions today. The first is the *adaptation model*. Here we could use the analogy of the coconut with its sizeable husk and its hard shell center (the heart of the fruit). In this model, one's culture, societal structure, racial and psychological character, and so on, are like the husk of a coconut. These external features change and are adaptable to the transmission of the gospel into new cultures and peoples. They might include, for example, rituals for worship, use of the Bible in one's own language, modes of prayer and spirituality, ethical applications for daily living, and types of music and instruments used for adoration. Liberty should be given for members of new *ethne* to make such adaptations as seems fit in their situation and for the personal and social needs of the community. All these are part of the "husk" of the gospel.

The *adaptation model* affirms, however, that the basic truths of the gospel, like the hard center of a coconut, are constant and permanent. What the Bible teaches, what the church has always defined as the truth, and what the missionary brings and proclaims in the spread of the gospel has the kernel, the solid core, of the truth. The nonnegotiable, which must always be maintained, are the doctrinal truths of the gospel about God, the church, and the Christian life.

A question that naturally arises is why different missionaries bring a variety of interpretations of the core text of the Christian faith to the mission field—for example, different views of church government, of baptism and the Lord's Supper, of the kingdom of God (here in the present or only in the future?), of the millennium, and hundreds of other issues that have caused church divisions across the centuries. Earlier theologies of mission spoke of the three-self character of the church: self-support, self-governance, and self-propagation. The prevailing controlling thought was basically pedagogical. The truth of the gospel and its implications needed to be taught, sometimes admittedly through a long and arduous process, to peoples that were far from gospel concepts and even the possibility of understanding. Often in the history of missions it was believed to be necessary to civilize peoples in order to Christianize.

The churches of the West believed that they possessed the truth and that others needed to learn what it was. The "younger" churches had to learn from the "mature" ones what the Christian faith and its demands really were. In time they would become able to fulfill the three-self character of the churches. Often it was questioned as to why mission churches did not grow from dependence on their mother churches. While there were political colonies in the world, ecclesiastical colonies continued.

Inculturation.

After the Second World War, the situation changed rapidly. One author called it "the coming of the third church." Equally in Roman Catholic and in Protestant churches came the realization that the three-self movement had to be expanded to include a new self: "self-theologizing." Though this was for the most part a new understanding, it had occurred throughout church history. The theology of the Euro-American West was precisely that—their interpretation of the original Eastern gospel. The differences among the various Christian church families—that is, the Eastern Orthodox churches, the Roman Catholic churches, and the Protestant churches—must be understood in this light. As the translation of the good news had occurred across the centuries, often in different forms, so now with the spread of the gospel in new cultures, new translations (that is, new theologies) were being formed. This interpretation of the contextual model moves beyond that of adaptation to an *inculturation model.* Attempts toward this model occurred earlier in history, notably in the accommodation model of the Jesuits in the 16th and 17th centuries.

David Bosch, in his book *Transforming Mission,* points out several ways in which this new model functions.[8] The agents of mission are not exclusively the Western mission; rather, the Holy Spirit and the local faith community also are involved in the dialogue. However, these are also in conversation with the broader regional and intercultural situation. Christ says, "As the Father has sent me, I am sending you" (John 20:21). He came by way of the incarnation, born into a specific people, culture, and time, to identify himself with the Jewish and Roman cultures. So the missionary enters the new cultural situation and allows not only self but also the gospel to do its sifting, purifying, and redeeming action in that culture and time.

The announcement by life and word of the gospel becomes a principle that transforms and remakes that culture into a new creation. This activity

---

8   David Bosch, *Transforming Mission: Paradigm Shifts in Theology of Mission,* 453ff.

occurs on the local level but is at the same time universal—that is, it interacts with other transformations and is corrected by them. So a new theological form is born yet is not alone but comes with its significant contribution to other theologies. In this sense, no one culture, church, or race becomes the sole interpreter of the gospel and the reign of Jesus Christ but is led by the Spirit of truth; each contributes what is needed to make the universal church significant and meaningful for its time. In this sense, the Church worldwide has been enriched by the discourse and dialogue of black theologies, Asian theologies, and liberation theologies as well as for Eastern Orthodox and Western ones.

Missionaries need to realize that they are "temporary, secondary, and advisory" in the "one holy catholic church" professed in the Apostles' Creed.[9] Local theologies contribute to the wholeness of the Christian church, and the universal church shares its diversity and unity with local communities of faith. This sharing of the truth comes only with the humility that recognizes that our personal and local formulation of the faith has arrived through the filter of our limited capacities and sometimes perverted individualism. As such, our "knowing in part" with the final dream of being known by our Lord stimulates and encourages us to always be true disciples—that is, learners of the divine will.

Constant is the living gospel, transmitted to us by the Holy Scriptures, inspired by the ever-present Spirit, and interpreted by the community of local believers in the light of Christian history and tradition. No one person or group stands or worships alone; we are all tempered by listening to other believers and sharing with them the insights the good Lord has given to us. Each new group sees and experiences the truth of the gospel through the providential lens of its own culture and time, knowing that it too sees only in part. That is why God gives us the grace of each other—to understand more, to love more, to worship more.

S.   Spontaneous Evangelism Model

Here we need to mention a phenomenon that completely eclipses our human efforts to plan and calculate methods and models of evangelization. It ought also to remind us of the secondary character of our efforts at mission.

9   Ibid, 456.

This is God's mission (*missio dei*), and as such the Holy Spirit precedes us in all cases, preparing the way, opening cultural and human doors, and softening hearts so that the seed that sometimes arrives mysteriously bears its fruit in the fullness of time. Perhaps the only appropriate phrase to describe this is the *spontaneous evangelism model*, by which we mean that the church growth and planting of churches is not intentionally orchestrated by those who sometimes make elaborate programs and optimistic calculations. This may happen when there is a constellation of favorable circumstances, accompanied by a movement of the divine Spirit, that result in a great influx into the community of the faith. Though others could be mentioned, there were three of special significance in the past century.

First, let us note the amazing growth of the African Independent Churches (AICs) from 1950 to the end of the century. Several factors coalesced to bring this about: the uneasy truce of charismatic individuals with missionaries, the political tension with a sense of social struggle, discontent with the imposition of missionary control and the presence of gifted leaders like Kimbangu and others. Beneath and behind all this there seemed to be a tension in existing structures and a sense that important societal changes were coming in the near future. By the end of the century, the AICs constituted 31 percent of Christians in Africa. Some estimates affirm that the various AICs of Africa have about 20 million members.

Second, the great Pentecostal movement in Latin America surpassed the highest imagination by the rapidity of its growth. Beginning in Chile in 1910, it spread slowly until the Great Depression occurred. Thereafter it began to reach into the slums of major Latin American cities and into rural areas. However, it was during the epoch of cruel military dictatorships in most Latin American nations—from 1954 in Brazil to 1990 in Guatemala—that the growth of this movement exploded. It should be noted that this movement was not dependent on the arrival and service of Pentecostal missionaries from the North. Though the movement reached across all social classes, the overwhelming source of growth came from the lower economic and racially dominated sectors. Leadership came not from the theologically trained but from ordinary workers, beginning with meetings in homes and storefronts, and with concentration on immediate human need, and with mutual help for spiritual ways of coping with human suffering. Services emphasized healing for body and spirit, acceptance in community, and direct participation in worship to people who in daily life were restricted or denied acceptance. Current statistics vary widely in the various countries, but most church statistics indicate that Pentecostals now make up 70-80 percent of Protestant Christians in Latin America.

Third, after the expulsion of all Christian missionaries and their staff by the conquering Communist take-over in China, grave fears were current about the continuing state of the Christian churches there. That was in 1949. More than thirty years later, when visitors began to visit China, there were at first questioned reports about the growing number of churches and Christians there. In order to control the many trends in society, the Communist government ruled that churches should officially register. But it was evident that there were many, many, house churches that did not do so. Progressively the news that the church had grown by great numbers during the period of closed doors was confirmed. Persons who had worked as missionaries and who were permitted to return as visitors after thirty years of absence were astounded at the new situation of the church. It became evident that the church had grown much more without the presence of Western missionaries than it had for a century with their missions and work. Conservative estimates now affirm that there are more than 80 million Christians in China, and some estimates are considerably higher.

The *spontaneous growth model* calls us to the humble recognition that the mission is not ours and that we are not the directors and inspiration of God's mission in his world. Pope Gregory I (590-604) proclaimed: "We are the servants of the servants of God" (*servus servorum dei*).[10] True, no more and no less. Man proposes, God disposes. We study the soil and plant accordingly; God in his own way and time gives the harvest. But study the soil we must. Plant and care for the seed of God's love we will. And for the strength to do so faithfully we pray. And then we wait.

II. Principles for Use of the Models

This survey has shown numerous ways in which the Spirit of God in wisdom has led the church to fulfill its double mandate: "to go and to do" in order

---

10   Gabriel Adeleye with Kofi Acquah-Dadzie, *World Dictionary of Foreign Expressions: A Resource for Readers and Writers,* 361.

to make God's love known and lived. Several principles come to light that we need to affirm in order to use them aright.

The wonderful diversity of the models of evangelization used throughout history makes clear that no single method can exhaust the possibilities for the spread of the gospel. Each new historical and cultural opportunity creates the openness for unique responses to the implicit call to witness.

The unrepeatable historical circumstance in which any of the models occurred means that the model as such can only be called upon formally to respond to the challenge of a new moment and event. The models are descriptions of living events in the lives of real people and therefore must be adapted to the needs and times of each people in their context.

The varied models of Christ's encounter with the people and events of his day confirm that there is no single approach mechanism that assures success in the evangelism encounter. Likewise, his instructions to the sent out ones during his ministry varied widely, with no key to explain such a diversity of methods. Sometimes it was healing; other times it was ministry to fulfill needs; other times it focused on forgiveness; still other times it centered on preaching of the Word.

The quality and authenticity of the models vary a great deal, and we must learn from them to choose those that most nearly express the quality and depth of God's love for all his creatures. The success strategy is never used by Christ when it does not adequately express the priority of his love for the sinner and for his kingdom.

The variety of models, which sometimes represents divergent theologies and ecclesiologies, should not diminish the oneness of the church or deform mission. Our common calling to mission follows from the Pentecostal experience of the one Spirit who qualifies all to be authentic witnesses to the truth of the gospel "that the world may believe" (John 17:21).

The distinction between sending and receiving mission agencies used in many of the historical models of evangelism is overcome to the extent that the incarnation of the gospel in every culture is recognized. When the church is present in different cultures, there needs to be a listening and sharing dialogue between equally inspired and committed disciples.

CONCLUSION

The birth of new models and their use will never come to an end as long as history endures. The mysteries of divine providence will continue to perplex, to cause tensions, sometimes to confuse, and often to inspire believers about which model can best accomplish effective communication of the gospel. When difficulties occur, the cause usually rests in human limitations and excessive claims of insight.

The purpose of mission exemplified by the numerous models extends to the role of sacrificial and unconditional service to human need wherever present. The models speak to the fullness of life and often by silent and loving care achieve what the multiplicity of words and deeds cannot do: the communication of the generous and gracious love of God.

Questions

1. What determines whether a model of mission is acceptable or not? List some of the criteria that you would use in its evaluation.

2. Of the many models of mission, mention three that you consider appropriate for today, and state your reasons for your choice.

3. Do you consider some of the models used in the history of the church contrary to the meaning and spirit of the gospel? Name three and explain why they should be rejected.

4. What underlying worldviews of the first millennium made the models of mission significantly different from those of the second millennium?

5. Do you feel that the models used in the history of the church improved as time went on, or not? Give reasons and use examples for your answer.

6. Make a typology of the models of mission discussed in this chapter by grouping together from the different chronological periods those that are similar and basically the same type.

7. Sometimes a distinction is made between the quality and the quantity of conversions achieved by different models of mission. In your opinion, what do the different models teach us with respect to this distinction? Give examples to illustrate your answer.

8. What are the virtues and the limitations of the nonverbal methods of church growth evidenced by the models explained in this chapter? Do they have a place in missions in your context today?

9. List some of the principles and lessons that you have learned from this survey of models used by Christians and churches in history.

10. Project your thought and vision into the future and state in a paragraph or two what steps you should take to achieve an effective planting of the church in your cultural context.

6 WHO SHOULD PLANT CHURCHES? LEADERSHIP IN CHURCH PLANTING

Gary Teja

Introduction

When Farmer José wants to plant seeds to produce, for example, sunflowers, he must prepare the land. He must add to the soil a mixture of phosphorus, nitrogen, and potassium, which together make a good fertilizer. The combination of these chemicals will vary, depending on the time of year and the results the farmer wants to achieve. The desired result is a plant with deep roots, a strong stem, and a beautiful flower. Without the correct mixture, the plants will be weak, lack deep roots, or will not produce the desired flower or fruit.

The planting of new churches also requires a good mix of elements. In order to be effective, church planting begins with prayer and requires a planter with skills, abilities, knowledge, and passion. Church planting is not for everyone. Only those who have the correct combination of characteristics, confidence in the Holy Spirit, and the effective prayers of believers can be successful as new church planters. In this chapter we will study these characteristics. It is worth noting that those who possess these skills can be graduates of seminaries or Bible institutes. They can also be recruited and trained members of the community who have shown potential within the ministry of the local church. There are people who have the gifts for being a church planter without having studied in a formal program, and there are those who need a lot of academic preparation. What is good is that God can use many types of people who have open hearts to plant his church. Having said this, it is good to identify the people with the correct combination of characteristics, seeking God's guidance through a filtering process. In addition, we will confirm in these people the qualities that will help them become successful church planters.

In this chapter we will study how to pick out a new church planter. We will begin with the essential characteristics of a successful planter and will consider two useful tools for evaluating a candidate. Then we will speak to the roles that formal institutions and nonformal organizations play in equipping future church planters.

Dr. Charles Ridley, a professor in the counseling psychology program at Texas A & M University, is recognized as a specialist in assessment and selection of ministerial personnel. (Formerly he served as a professor and training director in the doctoral program in counseling psychology at Indiana University.) Ridley designed an evaluative method that helps determine the characteristics of an effective church planter. A questionnaire given to church planters from many denominations yielded statistical results in terms of church planter characteristics. It was determined that thirteen of those characteristics are indispensable. In a formal assessment of those who wish to be church planters, the candidate is allowed to continue with their plans if the following thirteen characteristics are present:[1]

1. Has the capacity of vision
2. Shows personal motivation
3. Is inclusive in ministry
4. Reaches out to nonbelievers
5. Has the support of their spouse
6. Has the capacity to establish relationships with others
7. Is dedicated to the growth of the church
8. Responds to the community
9. Uses the gifts of others
10. Is flexible
11. Maintains unity within the church

---

1   Charles Ridley and Robert Logan, *Training for Selection Interviewing.*

12. Shows adaptability
13. Lives out their faith

It is not possible to reduce the number of characteristics to a magical list of ten (as in "Ten Characteristics of a Successful Church Planter"). According to the statistical study, these thirteen were shown to be indispensable in the majority of cases studied, so these are the characteristics that evaluators of candidates look for in formal assessments—the "non-negotiables" as it were. Following is a brief description of each one.

—Graph according to Charles Ridley in *Training for Selection Interviewing*

1. *Has the capacity of vision*

This capability requires that the church planter have a vision for the church that is to be established. It is a vision that the planter receives from God. It is a vision that he or she must present to those who wish to support the founding of the new church. The planter should have a clear vision, something that can be shared with those recruited to be part of the launch team. If the planter does not have a defined vision, the church will develop erratically without a singular focus and purpose. A Hispanic church planter in Chicago walked into an abandoned youth center and told his colleagues that he felt God wanted them to buy this place and establish a church there. The price of the building was more than $350,000, and they did not have the money. One of his ministry companions said to him, "Brother Peter, if this is your vision and it comes from God, he will provide the funds." The next time he visited the building, accompanied by a wealthy believer, God provided the money. The wealthy brother-in-Christ was so impressed by Peter's vision that he wrote a check for the total amount. In less than one year, the building was renovated; many activities during the day and night were developed for the youth of the community. Now weekly services are offered, and Bible studies bring in approximately 150 people.

2. *Shows personal motivation*

All church planters should testify to the importance of being highly motivated. Planting a church requires self-discipline and a great deal of energy in order to accomplish each day's tasks, even when it can be difficult at first to see the desired results. There are times when there is no one to accompany the planter, motivating him to do the necessary work. On other occasions, the planter works alone, without a lot of direction or push. Of course, the Holy Spirit is there, but, humanly speaking, at times no one is there to offer encouragement. There is a direct relationship between one's motivation and accomplished work. Church planter and author Ed Stetzer emphasizes the planter's responsibilities, especially when the church is more than a dream and is already a reality.[2] He says that the planter's planner is an expression of the priorities in the ministry. If the planter works full-time in ministry, Stetzer suggest that the church planter should dedicate no less than 15 hours a week to evangelism. If the planter works part-time in ministry, it should be

2   Ed Stetzer, *Planting New Churches in a Postmodern Age.*

three hours a week. The planter should dedicate ten hours full time (FT) or two hours part-time (PT), or 10FT/2PT hours, each week to studying and sermon preparation; 10FT/2PT hours each week doing administration; and 15FT/3PT hours a week to pastoral care. It is clear, therefore, why a planter or new pastor has to be self-motivated!

I know a planter who got very frustrated when he did not see the results he wanted. He went home and sat in front of his computer to put together bulletins and newsletters, as if this would attract people. He became discouraged and lost the motivation to hit the street, knocking on doors and visiting shopping centers in order to establish relationship with others. The church plant, of course, went from bad to worse and ultimately had to shut its doors. The work was not successful. One has to be motivated to do what is necessary in order to achieve the desired results in the short term and the long term.

3. Is inclusive in ministry (creates a sense of responsibility)

Delegating is key in forming a committed group to work together to found a new church. One cannot do it all alone. Nevertheless, many pastors try to. By being "bossmen" or "chiefs," many tend to plant a new congregation by their own efforts, without taking into account the resources and talents of those surrounding them. A successful planter motivates and involves others. As the Bible says, "Two are better than one, because they have a good return for their labor: If either of them falls down, one can help the other up. But pity anyone who falls and has no one to help them up. . . . Though one may be overpowered, two can defend themselves. A cord of three strands is not quickly broken" (Eccles. 4:9-12). In other words, when working together, one must stand firmly in the church plant and also have people with whom to share the good and the bad. Additionally, a committed group will take hold of the process of establishing the church, thus creating a nexus of belonging. If one intends to do it all by himself, the group will never be committed. They will see the ministry as a work of only the church planter. If the pastor does not delegate, he will have to do everything, and the success or failure of the ministry lies in his own hands. How many pastors have expressed their frustration with members who do not want to do anything and only wait for the pastor to do it all! In many cases, there is a lack of delegation, of involving others in the decisions and in the planting process.

One committed person with responsibility in the new church is more effective and hard-working than ten who are not committed. Steve Ogne points out that many church plants fail precisely because the planter does not have a committed and equipped team. He affirms, "A church planter who is incapable of motivating a launch team or volunteers, will never be able form a stable congregation."[3] I know a planter who did everything by himself. He visited the sick, bringing them food and clothes; he attended to the necessities of the members and even gave people rides in his own vehicle when it was needed. He always complained about his lack of time and that he was always running around. When I asked him why he didn't ask the leaders to help him, he responded, "They all have their own work to do. Only I have a flexible schedule that allows me to help." What was the result of all his solitary effort? By not involving the other leaders, the church shut down. There was no commitment to the ministry. No one felt obligated to help. No one else felt responsible for the ministry. Stetzer talks about involving other brothers and sisters in the ministry from the very beginning.[4] When the church is ready for launch, the leaders should already be in place: the pastor (or planter), the worship leader, the children's leader, the coordinator of the program that incorporates those who come to know the Lord; one or various others who lead evangelism and one or more who help members identify their gifts and put them into practice in the local body. You can count on committed people if these leaders are in place.

Pastor Peter, in Chicago, sold the vision of his ministry to the persons he discipled. He trained them to minister in the community. He sent them into the streets to use their gifts. He also gave them responsibilities in the local church. Not only did the church grow, but three of those leaders became ordained as pastors, opening more churches. The church has such an abundance of leaders that it continues to function well while Peter continues his theological studies and directs the vision of the established church toward their future.

4. Reaches out to nonbelievers

When I was a child, someone told me a story about a drunk person in the street who was looking for money under a lightpost. A passerby asked him, "Where did you lose your money, sir?"

---

3   Steven Ogne and Thomas Nebel, *Capacitando a Líderes*, 95.
4   Stetzer, *Planting New Churches*.

The drunken man responded, "Over there, about five meters from here."

"Well, then, why are you looking here?" asked the other man.

The drunken man answered, "Because there's better light here."

If the purpose of planting congregations is to look for the lost, we must look for them where they can be found. If we want to fish for trout, we must fish in a river, not in a well or a puddle. The planter needs fortitude and perseverance in order to go to nonbelievers and not stay with believers, where life is more comfortable and less complicated.

Reaching out to nonbelievers should be the planter's main focus, especially at the beginning of the church plant (although this work should never stop). If this essential characteristic is not present, one cannot call himself or herself a church planter. Jesus said to his disciples, "I will send you out to fish for people" (Mark 1:17). He knew what the disciples had to do. This was of utmost importance in the ministry with which they were entrusted. The ministry did not consist of nicely published bulletins or electronically prepared presentations; it consisted of reaching out to the unbelieving with the good news of Jesus Christ. Gary McIntosh, in *Biblical Church Growth*, defines church growth as essentially evangelism.[5] Roger Greenway writes, "Christ wanted missions to be the responsibility of the whole church and to continue this way until he returns."[6] There has to be a commitment to evangelize and transform converts into the local body of Christ.

A planter, especially in the first two years of planting, must dedicate 60 to 80 percent of the time forming new relationships, chatting with neighbors, and going into the streets to look for nonbelievers. When a planter tells me that he has not been successful in attracting people and nobody has responded, I ask him to show me his schedule of visitation. Usually, this complainer does not show many hours of visitation. They want the "fish" to come to them without much effort on their part. Juan Pablo is a planter in the great city of Miami. He is on the streets every day. He has formed small group Bible studies

---

5   Gary McIntosh, *Biblical Church Growth: How You Can Work with God to Build a Faithful Church.*
6   Roger Greenway, *¡Vayan! Y Hagan Discípulos*, 7. Libolt translation.

in the neighborhood. He teaches them the Word of God. Many people have been converted. He already has 125 believers attending church services.

5. Has the support of their spouse

The planter needs the cooperation of his spouse. The experience of the author confirms that without this cooperation, the planter fights two battles, one with the devil and the other with his spouse. I know various planters whose spouses did not want to be married to a church planter. They wanted more stability and did not want to leave their relatives. For various reasons, they opposed their spouses at the expense of the ministry. I remember one case in particular. The wife of a missionary planter confessed to my wife that she did not want to be a missionary or a pastor's wife. She said that when she married her husband, he was not a pastor and that perhaps, had she known he would become one, she would not have married him. She was ashamed of her attitude, but it was the reality of her life. She felt like a failure. When she did not become pregnant, she felt that God was punishing her for her lack of commitment to the ministry. Each time I would visit this couple in their home, the first thing she did was give me a list of complaints, even before greeting me. She also did not open her home to the members of their new work. It was very rare for her to accompany her husband on visits. She was bad tempered. One time she threatened two employees of the power company with a hose when, by mistake, they tried to shut off their electrical service. Imagine the newspaper headline: "Wife of Church Planter Electrocutes Power Company Employees When They Try to Cut Power to Her House." Her testimony was horrible. It was not until she returned to the United States, living through more bitter years in ministry, that she began to participate in an in-depth Bible study. Through this she became a completely different person, willing to help her husband in ministry. One cannot underestimate the importance of a spouse's cooperation. Without it, the planter soon becomes weak in the battles involved in planting a new church.

6. Has the capacity to establish relationships with others

The planter needs to be sociable. He should be able to relate well with different people. He needs to relate with those who collaborate in the church planting, with those who he wants to reach out to, with the authorities in the community, and so on. There is a saying that states, "People won't care how much you know until they know how much you care." The planter should know the community and should relate well with people, showing an interest in them as people and not just potential converts.

The planter who does not know how to relate well with others is not capable of forming a launch team. Therefore he must be very relational with everyone. In this regard, it is very helpful to be an extrovert. If one is an introvert, he must force himself to be more sociable. He must dedicate more time to being with people, chatting even about insignificant things. What one says to people is not necessarily important. The act of taking time to relate to them is what is important. I know a church planter who does not like to visit people. He prefers to isolate himself in his office, preparing attractive pamphlets. His wife is even less cordial. She does not greet people at church. Rarely does she welcome visitors. And those who visit generally do not return a second time because of the lack of friendliness on the part of the pastor and his wife. Michael, on the other hand, was a pastor par excellence. He always had a smile on his face, a word of welcome, a firm handshake. His wife was his "twin" in her ability to socialize. The door of their house was always open to visitors. They had a very fruitful ministry in Costa Rica.

7. Is dedicated to the growth of the church

An integral part of planting a church is making it grow. This book, of course, has to do with church growth, the planting and development of the church. The Great Commission says, "Go and make disciples . . . teaching them to obey everything I have commanded you" (Matt. 28:19-20). Believers should grow *spiritually* through discipleship, just as a seed in fertile ground. The church also must grow *organically* with structures and leaders in its ministries. And, without a doubt, it should grow *exponentially* through evangelism. This should be the principal focus of believers while their own faith and the church itself grow. A congregation should never be satisfied with its size or level of spirituality. On the contrary, it should look at how it can grow as a congregation, while at the same time exploring how to found more churches. The church planter must take church multiplication very seriously. It is only through this that we will see the good news deeply rooted throughout the world.

Planting churches is not an end in itself, but, through the will of God, it honors the *missio dei* [God's mission], something more than simply evangelism. Gene Mims and Ramón Martinez, in their book *Principios del Reino para el Crecimiento de la Iglesia*, list five components of church growth: (1) evangelism, (2) discipleship, (3) ministry, (4) friendship, (5) worship. According to them, the Great Commission is the driving force for church growth, and these five functions are essential to make it grow. "If we practice these five functions, we experience . . . four results," they report.[7] These are (1) numerical growth, (2) spiritual growth, (3) ministry expansion, and (4) missionary advancement.

Consider this example. In an intensive seminar that we sponsored for planters of new churches, the participants engaged in a reflection exercise regarding recent converts. They had to note all of the ministries they might establish that would help a recent convert grow in maturity in Christ and become one who disciples other recent converts. The planter does not want people just to sit and warm the benches in their church; instead, the planter wants discipled believers who later disciple others. The spiritual growth of believers is the counterweight of evangelism, or in other words the continual numerical growth of the local church. I remember one brother-in-Christ who said, "My work is to preach the good news to unbelievers. It's up to someone else to disciple them." This works only if one is an itinerant evangelist, who goes from place to place, leaving the work of discipleship to the local pastors. But if one has the title of church planter, his work is to plant churches in every sense of the word, not just in planting the seed.

8. *Responds to the community*

Jesus, seeing the hungry, gave them food. When he was with the multitude by the lake and night was coming, he gave them fish and bread. He responded to the needs of the multitude. The planter, in the same way, should respond to the needs of the community. He cannot ignore what happens in it. He must worry about the problems of the community and see how the church can respond. Some candidates only worry about the spiritual when, at times, the daily needs of the people are evidently much more physical and mundane. At times, attending to these needs opens the door to hearing the good news.

---

7   Gene Mims and Ramón Martínez, *Principios para el Crecimiento de la Iglesia*, chap. 4, 72-94.

In the intensive seminars that we give, each planter writes his own "Mission Statement." The planter has to determine the group they are going to reach, their needs, and how they think they are going to attend to them. If they do not know the community, they do not know the people's needs, and, therefore, they cannot scratch the people where they itch. Greenway comments, "Missions—in word and deed—give a powerful testimony of Jesus Christ. Having homes, villages, and nations open to the good news, in imitation of Jesus, who 'went through all the towns and villages, teaching in their synagogues, proclaiming the good news of the kingdom and healing every disease and sickness' (Matt. 9:35)."[8] The Christian Reformed Church of San José in Tipitapa, Nicaragua, is an example of a congregation that responds to the community. Pastor Freddy Ordoñez convinced an international aid NGO to help them respond to the needs of those affected by Hurricane Mitch in the areas surrounding Tipitapa. In addition to responding with food and medicine, they built new houses. Establishing a revolving loan fund for microbusinesses, they helped form a cooperative for businesswomen and other similar initiatives. At the same time, they were able to establish a new church in this community because of their good testimony through helping the community.

9. *Uses the gifts of others*

The planter should know how to encourage others to use their gifts in the work of establishing a new church. The planter cannot found a new congregation alone. The planter cannot and should not be a "do-it-all." He must use the gifts of others in the various aspects of ministry. Pastor Peter is a good example of a planter with this characteristic. As I mentioned before, he trained three brothers in Christ, and they are now pastors. While they were being trained, they helped him in his church. Peter also trained various men and women to be small group leaders. Many of them are already elders and deacons in the local church. Peter recognized their gifts and potential and put them to work for the Lord. The church is not dependent on Peter. It has a leadership body that is well equipped. Each leader goes through a period of training. Peter assigns them responsibilities, according to their level of maturity. Little by little each one earns more responsibilities. Eventually they become the pastor's "right hand" in the Humboldt Park ministry in Chicago. Peter followed the example of Jesus, who sent his disciples into the mission field. They learned from their mistakes and successes until, by the power of the Holy Spirit, they

8   Greenway, *¡Vayan!*, 132.

were able to bring the good news to the known world of that time after Jesus' ascension and the Spirit's outpouring.

10. *Is flexible*

One cannot be a planter and at the same time be inflexible. Things never go the way one might prefer them to go, and it is much less so when planting a church. In ministry, one has to ebb and flow like the waves on a beach. That is to say, a church planter must be ready to change plans. There is a saying that rings true: "Man proposes, God disposes." The secret to happiness in planting a church is to follow the plan of God. He is building the church, and we want to be in line with his plan. This implies that at times we have to change our plans when we notice they go against what God wants.

Working with human beings also requires flexibility, since everyone has his or her own will, ideas, and desires. We cannot impose our thoughts at the cost of hearing out and at times implementing others' ideas. I remember one very inflexible man. He wanted everything to conform to his vision and wishes. He was not receptive to the suggestions of others. For a time he had a ministry that appeared successful. But after a while, people started to leave, frustrated with his inflexibility and his authoritarian ways. A church that grew to 125 parishioners with this inflexible, authoritarian leader decreased to 20 in less than two years.

11. *Maintains unity within the church*

A shepherd knows that in order to protect the sheep, he has to circle them. Only when they are together are they a flock of sheep. Outside of this, they are weak, subject to adversity and danger.

Jesus said, "I will build my church" (Matt. 16:18). The word *church* connotes a group of believers, making up a body, like a flock. Paul refers to this body, the church, in Romans 12:4 and also in 1 Corinthians 12. In Romans 12:5, he affirms that "in Christ we, though many, form one body, and each member belongs to all the others."

We all have distinct gifts and functions within the body of Christ, the church. As Paul expresses in 1 Corinthians 12:12, there is diversity in ministries and functions, and although we are made up of "many parts [we] form one body." Christ is what makes us one. The planter has to be able to form one body, a cohesive whole, of the many believers, with the same vision, mission, purpose, and reason for existence. The planter then needs administrative organizational skills or the wisdom to know to look for someone who has those skills. The body, in order to function well, has to work in unity, with the same sense of cohesiveness. This is a coming together of parts, like bones and ligaments. They do not operate apart from each other but together. The church is a cohesive body of individual believers who need structure, purpose, and a reason to come together and serve. If they continue as individuals, they will not get to experience brotherly love and will not be able to stand against adversities. The planter should not only be concerned about bringing in new "sheep" to the flock but also about how to make them come together as one body.

12. *Shows adaptability*

There are animals that adapt quickly to their environment. There is a type of fish that can survive during the dry season in mud, when water almost disappears for months. There is also another fish that can "walk" from river to river. The salamander changes color in order to protect itself from predators. A type of butterfly has markings that imitate those of a poisonous butterfly, so birds maintain their distance from both. Another type of butterfly has the design of an eye on its wings, and this also drives birds away. These animals, by God's design, adapt to their environment and survive.

Planters should also be adaptable to their environment. They should be "Roman among Romans and Greek among Greeks." This means that the planter should be able to identify with the community that he wants to reach. He must adapt positively to changing situations and be able to "read" the culture in which he walks and serves. He should adapt to his environment, as the butterfly or salamander do. Pastor Gianni is a good example of a planter who knows how to adapt to his environment. He knows how to communicate with the local youth in their language. He understands their culture and their needs, and he can respond adequately. With a Cuban he can speak like a Cuban. With Nicaraguans he can be like a Nicaraguan. With the elderly, he can identify with their sicknesses and weaknesses. He adapts to his circumstances in an effective way without setting aside his convictions and principles.

Paul required that Timothy be circumcised (Acts 16:3) even though he was Greek, so that he would not offend the Jews they would encounter in their travels. Timothy had to adapt to his circumstances. Paul had to adjust to the Gentiles, eating their food, leaving behind orthodox practices of the Jews, in order to reach out to the Gentiles. In a sense, a good planter also must leave behind his citizenship, culture, and preferences in order to adapt to the group he is going to minister to, speaking their language, understanding their surroundings, and accepting the changes needed in order to reach the lost.

13. *Lives out their faith*

The final characteristic, not necessarily in order of importance, is that planters must live out their faith. No legitimate planter lives by his or her own strength but only through the power of God. Trust in God. Like Paul, declare that "he who began a good work in you will carry it on to completion until the day of Christ Jesus" (Phil. 1:6). He lives by faith and plants a church by faith. At times, church planting can seem very slow. The end results can seem very distant. The planter has to trust that his vision is from God and must live each day with this confidence, this faith, until God produces the fruit of his labor. The planter cannot doubt that God will provide the fruit. He must continue to trust that it is God who will establish the church. The planter is simply a participant in this beautiful, divine plan.

Are These Thirteen Characteristics Essential?

Given this list of thirteen characteristics that identify a successful church planter, can we allow a candidate with only twelve or less of these characteristics to plant churches? That may be very tempting, but whenever we have allowed it, the results have been disastrous. For example, after participating in an assessment center, several times we recommended couples for church planting, knowing that the planter really did not have the full support of his spouse. When we ignore those observations, later we have to admit the error and pay the price of a bad decision. The couple suffers in their ministry, which often ends in failure, and they may even suffer the breakup of their marriage.

In another case, a candidate did not demonstrate a good presentation of the good news in an activity in an assessment center. Nevertheless, we certified him as a planter. Later we admitted that he did not know how to evangelize.

He had not evangelized in the past. He was not evangelizing in the present and most likely would not evangelize in the future. His work failed.

What can we learn from these sad lessons? The thirteen characteristics are *essential*. The list is a result of significant social and psychological evaluation and of many concrete experiences. The list was formed from a broad statistical study and is reliable, proven in practice. These thirteen characteristics are non-negotiables. Lack of any of these thirteen key characteristics should disqualify a person for church planting, at least until that characteristic becomes a part of the person.

Other Lists

Do you have these thirteen essential characteristics of a church planter? Each one is indispensable. Has God called you to be the next planter? While you think about your answer, I want to share some other lists of characteristics that come from those who evaluate candidates for planting new churches. Here I would like to present six more compilations of lists to show how they agree or differ from the characteristics listed above.

1. The first list comes from the mouth and pen of the man who first used the term *church growth*, Dr. Peter Wagner. For him, the success or failure of a church plant lies mainly on the shoulders of the planter. The planter is "key."[9] The planter, according to Wagner, is characterized as being (a) a committed, Christian worker, (b) a self-initiator, (c) one who is willing to begin alone, (d) adaptable, (e) one with a high level of faith, (f) supported by his spouse and family, (g) a natural leader, (h) a friendly personality, and (i) called by God to plant a church.[10] This list compares well with Ridley's list, and Wagner's was done without investing in a statistical study!

2. Stetzer comments on the diverse forms of evaluation, including Ridley's.[11] He suggests that the candidate should be evaluated regarding his spiritual gifts, his passion, his abilities, his personality type, and his ex-

---

9   Peter Wagner, *Church Planting for a Greater Harvest: A Comprehensive Guide*, 51-55.
10 Ibid, 51-55.
11 Stetzer, *Planting New Churches*.

periences. A combination of the evaluations creates a profile that is more complete than an evaluation without these elements.

3. Daniel Sánchez and his colleagues, in *Cómo Sembrar Iglesias en el Siglo XXI*, suggest a profile similar to those outlined above.[12] They catalogue these general characteristics under three main categories: spiritual, personal, and administrative. They are presented as such:

Spiritual
- Has a call from God to plant a church
- Shows a high level of faith
- Exhibits spiritual maturity
- Is gifted spiritually

Personal
- Is intrinsically motivated
- Has a friendly personality
- Shows psychological maturity
- Has the support of his spouse and family
- Shows flexibility and adaptability
- Is healthy
- Relates well with nonbelievers
- Is committed to church growth
- Is responsive to the community
- Values others

Administrative
- Is desirous of and is capable of leading
- Is a servant leader
- Is an effective action planner
- Maintains and extends financial support
- Is a visionary
- Encourages ownership of the ministry
- Uses the gifts of others
- Promotes unity
- Has evangelism experience
- Is experienced in discipling others

12 Daniel Sánchez, Ebbie C. Smith, and Curtis E. Watke, *Cómo Sembrar Iglesias en el Siglo XXI*, chapter 7.

A good evaluator (or assessor) should be able to discern if the candidate has these qualities and if his experience in the past shows that these characteristics exist. Sánchez adds other qualifications for a planter that he considers specialized: capable of experiencing loneliness, shows initiative, is empathetic in his context, capable of adapting socially, able to minister interculturally when necessary and can adjust to these changes. The book and workbook that Sánchez prepared will help those who are considering being a church planter to determine if God has really called and equipped them for this task.

4. The *Church Planter Manual* from Redeemer Presbyterian Church in New York includes a section on the characteristics of a planter.[13] It presents a list of personal, ministerial, and interpersonal characteristics. In addition, it adds a component that is often ignored, *the characteristics of the planter's spouse.* The manual divides the profile of the spouse into three sections: personal, supportive, and interpersonal. According to Thompson, a spouse should show five qualities in their personal life: in their family life, in their integrity, in God's calling, spiritual vitality, and prayer. In other words, the couple has to come to an agreement as to the role each one will have in the ministry, and they must agree on the spouse's level of involvement. At times, this can be more or less what others hope for. The spouse should be a model of integrity, fulfilling his/her promises and commitments, above reproach in their personal and private dealings. Spouses should sense the calling to serve God and support their spouse in planting the new church. They should also demonstrate a vital walk with God. Prayer must be integral in their life. They should share the same vision with their spouse in regard to the church and should also help with the work. Many ministries fail when there is not spousal support.

Thompson expects much from the planter's spouse. When we did not pay enough attention, during assessment, to the spouse or to the personal problems between the planter and the spouse, we had to intervene later, sometimes shutting down their work. The spouse is as important in the evaluation of a future planter as is the candidate himself.

5. Recently a study from seven denominations in the United States was conducted by Stanley Wood, director of the Center for the Development of

13   J. Allen Thompson and Timothy Keller, *Redeemer Church Planting Manual*, 65.

New Churches at Columbia Theological Seminary. This broad study was funded through a subsidy from the Lilly Foundation. The results will be published in a book soon to be released. The focus of the study was to "identify and analyze key factors found in pastoral leaders in the effective development of new churches."[14] The survey group was composed of Anglo-Saxons, African Americans, Latinos, Asians, Koreans, and Native Americans from the United States. The period studied was almost twenty years. The study participants had to answer one main question: *"Thinking about the role of a church planter, can you identify some necessary leadership competencies and functions and behaviors required in the first stages of developing a new church?"*

With this information, the study established qualities of conduct organized on two scales. The first consisted of the following qualities:
- innovative and catalyzing work habits
- a personal life of faith with devotional habits
- visionary skills with the ability to share this vision

The second scale presented the following qualities:
- recruitment skills
- ability to form teams
- ability to delegate
- passion for evangelism
- passion for people
- inspired preaching and worship
- healthy spouse and family

The study also asked another question: *"The leadership that is needed later on in the development of a new church, does it differ from the leadership needed at the beginning of a church plant? If it differs, how does it differ?"* According to the answers given by those questioned, in the later stages the planter should show an ability to change his leadership style. He should be able to delegate more and more, to empower people, to understand the dynamics of change yet continue declaring the unchanging vision. In other words, one who can launch a new church as a "catalytic planter" should be flexible in his ability to develop other gifts and abilities and then operate in

14 H. Stanley Wood, "New Church Development for the 21st Century: Sharing Initial Research Finds and Survey Data Insights."

a different way when the church plant is more mature. It is interesting to distinguish between the necessary qualities to found a church and those that are necessary to bring it to maturity.

6. In his book *Planting Growing Churches in the 21st Century,* Aubrey Malphurs enumerates some primary and secondary areas for evaluation. The primary are spiritual gifts, passion, temperament, leadership, and administrative capabilities. The secondary areas are natural gifts, talents and abilities; unique ways of thinking, learning, and making decisions; and evangelism.[15]

"Of the listing of qualifications, there is no end." Each person has his preferred list of qualifications. There are similarities between all the lists, and there are some points of departure. One list emphasizes the qualities of a spouse, while others do not even touch on that topic. No list will be enough if it is not used in a more complete program of assessment for church planters. There needs to be a method of identifying those who possess these characteristics or mixture of gifts. In the following section, we will discuss specific tools that Ridley's list uses to identify candidates who are suitable for planting new churches.[16]

Tools to Evaluate a Candidate's Potential

Two principle tools for determining whether one has the skills for planting new churches are the "Behavioral Interview" and the "Assessment Center." Various denominations use both tools. They serve to determine whether or not the candidates for church planting really have the necessary abilities, passion, and knowledge.

One could ask, "Why conduct an assessment?" Stetzer, in his book *Planting New Churches in a Postmodern Age,* gives us an excellent answer: "Church planters who have gone through a Ridley assessment interview lead churches that are larger in attendance than those who do not. . . . A new church is more

---

15 Aubrey Malphurs, *Planting Growing Churches in the 21ˢᵗ Century: A Comprehensive Guide for New Churches and Those Desiring Renewal.*

16 If you do not have access to these tools, you can design them with what has been learned in this chapter. Also, what follows may or may not work in your context. These behavior assessments may be more or less complex and empirical than your culture may require for determining who should plant churches.

likely to fail when it is started by a planter who has not been assessed. All other factors being equal, an assessment assures the selection of better church planters with a higher likelihood of success."[17]

I can attest that identifying a planter's potential can help to avoid lots of problems. For many years in my denomination, we tried to plant churches without a systematic program of evaluation. The success rate in starting new churches was very low. When we incorporated a program of identifying planters into the process, the percentage of plants that continued to last after five years went up. In addition, when one includes a program with a mentor for the first two years of planting, it has been noted statistically that there are more churches that survive and flourish. Today we have a success rate of 85 percent.

I will present and briefly describe the two tools we use to identify planters for new churches: the "Behavioral Interview" and the "Assessment Center."

Behavioral Interview

Dr. Charles Ridley designed what has become a well-known interview process.[18] Based on research conducted in 13 denominations, the Behavioral Interview is premised on the following principle: "Past performance is a good indicator of future performance." The interview lasts from three to five hours and consists of questions that lead the candidate to share past experiences, commenting on specific past behavior. The interviewer says, for example, "Tell me about a time in which you were involved in a conflict in your church or job. What did you do, and what were the results of your involvement in the process?" With the help of questions, the interviewer wants to see the potential the candidate has in successfully resolving conflicts as a planter. The interviewer wants to establish a profile of the candidate and the answers to the questions help formulate this profile. The interviewer is trying to establish the candidate's behavior because behavior does not just happen. It is a reflection of who we are. If someone conducts himself in the same way in various situations or experiences, we can deduce that there is "behavioral congruence," meaning that a behavioral pattern is present that predicts how the planter will respond in a given situation. Every time this person confronts a similar situation, it is most probable that he will respond in the same way. According to Ridley, one

---

17 Stetzer, *Planting New Churches*, 79.
18 Ridley and Logan, *Training for Selection Interviewing*.

must focus on the behavior and not on the experiences themselves because, apart from the behavior, they do not tell us anything about the candidate.[19] They are events that give us the opportunity to get to know the candidate according to his behaviors.

It is worthwhile noting that all the questions do not necessarily have to do with the candidate's actual ministry. Their behavior is applicable in various situations. Therefore, what one wants to determine is their behavior in various contexts and not necessarily just in the ministry context. According to Ridley, behavior is transferable. Because of this, the interviewer asks a series of questions to get at their behavior in various contexts. The conduct we are looking for in the interview is based on the thirteen characteristics or norms that we mentioned previously in this chapter. For example, we want to establish how a candidate will react to complaints and to critics. Their answer shows their level of flexibility to give others authority in making decisions, and so on. "Tell me about a time when someone criticized you. What did you do? What did you say?"

On the other hand, we want to understand how the candidate adapts and if they have the strength to stand firm when problems arise. "Has there been a situation with which you were frustrated and discouraged? How did you overcome your frustration? How long did it take you to feel better?"

Oftentimes the Behavioral Interview is used as the first filter in the process for identifying candidates for planting new churches. This filter can also be combined with the Assessment Center. In my denomination, we begin with the Assessment Center, opting to use the Behavioral Interview when a candidate for various reasons cannot attend the assessment or in order to reevaluate a candidate two years after the assessment if the first one was provisional and the candidate had to experience more ministerial life before being evaluated again.

Assessment Center

The Assessment Center for church planters consists of various exercises and simulations for two to three days. These activities are used to discern the candidate's ability to plant churches. The candidate and his spouse under-

19 Ibid.

go in-depth activities in a retreat context. The Center is different from the Behavioral Interview in that it is not based on past actions but on real-time observations. This only serves to predict the potential for success in planting a church based on their real-time behavior in the moment of participating in the Assessment Center.

The event is deliberately intensive and fast-paced so that we can see how the candidates respond under pressure. In real life, the planter has to accomplish many tasks without reprieve, practically without stopping for breath. Through these simulations, we can discern if the planter has what it takes to endure.

About a month before the Assessment Center, the candidate fills out a series of written questionnaires. These consist of "Personal Profile System, DiSC" which determines behavior styles, a gift inventory,[20] and "Skills, Abilities, and Gifts of New Church Planters," a self-perception tool made up of twenty statements that help determine if one has the passion and abilities for planting a church. The DiSC can be found on the internet or in your local library. If you live close to a university, you can consult with a psychology professor regarding this inventory. The webpage may change but the date of publication for this book exists on a site with others for the DiSC: https://www. discprofile.com/what-is-disc/overview/. In addition, this site has instruments that measure one's susceptibility to stress, behavior in the workplace, and type of leadership. The tools *Discover Your Gifts* and "Skills, Abilities, and Gifts of New Church Planters" can be found at www.multiplicationnetwork.org.

The results of these questionnaires are received and studied by assessors in order to establish a preliminary objective profile of the candidate. The assessors are people experienced in church planting who also have been trained in evaluative methods. We try to have a minimum of three assessors at each retreat. Upon arrival at the Assessment Center, each assessor is put in charge of getting to know one or two of the candidates and their spouses. They review material that was filled out before the candidates came to the Assessment. The assessor will be key when the time comes to determine the candidate's eligibility for the ministry of planting new churches.

---

20   *Descubriendo Mis Dones* (*Discover Your Gifts*).

During the three days of the Assessment, the assessors observe the actions and reactions of the candidates participating in seven activities. These are described in more detail later in this chapter. In each activity the assessors grade the candidates in accordance with their behavior, their participation in the exercises, and the way in which they relate to others in their group, including their behavior toward their spouse.

Ideally, there are three or four couples per table and two or more tables, which allows for quality observation of their behavior in each activity. The couples change tables with each activity so that the assessors have the opportunity to see how well they relate with the various couples.

At the end of the assessment, each assessor privately determines the score for each couple, using a point system. All of the assessors then come together to put their scores for each category on the board and then come up with an average. In addition to their score, the assessors write up a profile for each couple, noting not only their strengths but also any areas for growth. The assessors assign each couple a biblical passage as a key text. The assessor who was assigned to a particular couple meets with them to give them the results of the Assessment Center.

At the center, we want to establish a positive situation for the candidate. If the assessors determine that the couple does not have the gifts or abilities to plant churches, we offer them other ministerial alternatives and options. Perhaps the couple has shown abilities or a passion for youth ministry or chaplaincy. At times, the assessors encourage them to consider support ministry, serving as helpers to a pastor in an established church, or as the right hand to a church planter but not as the main person establishing the new church. The couple leaves the center affirmed as people and ministers so that they can find their place of service in God's kingdom. The denomination invests in this process so that they can better use the support money they receive for a higher probability of success in church planting.

The activities in the Assessment Center are divided into seven exercises and are as follows:

1. *Survival Situation.* This is a group simulation in which the participants have, for example, survived a shipwreck. The participants receive a list of

tools they have, such as a mirror, compass, gun, rope, and canvas. On their own, each person notes the order of priorities in regard to each tool. After this, each participant shares his or her list with the group, and together they make up a new list of priorities. Following this, they are told what an expert in survival would have done. The object of this activity is to observe the behavior of each person and to teach all of them the importance of collective decision making. Normally the group arrives at a better set of priorities than they did as individuals. This speaks to the synergy of working in a group. As the planters negotiate to solve the situation, one can see many characteristics of each person.

2. *Zonal (or geographical) Investigation.* Each couple receives a demographic study (a zone description) and other statistical documents (real or fictitious) describing a community. With this information, the couple needs to determine the profile of the community they want to reach. What are its characteristics? Its needs? How are we going to satisfy these necessities? Each couple presents their community profile to the others at the table. Then they all need to determine which profile will be presented in the plenary session. One couple per table, chosen by the moderator in the moment, presents the group's results. The goal of this activity is to determine if the candidate can "read" or interpret the community where he wants to plant a new church. Those who will present are named "on the spot" in order to observe their reaction to being assigned the presentation without any prior notice.

3. *Vision.* Each couple must write their vision for a new church. They must share it with their colleagues. One per table is selected to share their vision with the group at large. These people need to "sell" their vision to the others. This helps with measuring their vision and with seeing how they communicate with a group.

4. *Strategy Design.* In this exercise, the candidates have to note, one by one, the steps in planting a new church. Although they do this in groups, the assessors observe each couple in order to see their ability to collaborate in the exercise and their behavior in the group. One spokesperson per table, representing the rest of the group, presents their work plan.

5. *Conflict Resolution.* In small groups, the candidates read a case about a specific conflict. As a group they must figure out a solution. For example, the participants receive a case about an elder in the church who loudly argued with another member just outside the church immediately following a church service. The participants are asked to outline a process to resolve this conflict. The assessors observe each person's participation in the conflict resolution process and the options each one presents. They also observe the interaction between the participants, the concessions that some have to make for the good of the group, whether one tends to dominate or impose their point of view, and so on.

6. *Gospel Presentation.* Each candidate has to present the gospel to another person. There is role-play involved in this activity. For example, a man has a motorcycle accident, and his mother asks you to visit him in the hospital. The candidate makes the visit and has to use the situation to present the gospel. As this happens, the candidate's main assessor observes and afterward comments on the presentation. Afterward, the "nonbeliever" switches roles with the evangelist, using another case. Often the participants are hesitant to present the gospel at the prescribed time. They almost always say, "It's only the first visit, and I don't want to offend the person. I want to establish a relationship with him before I present the gospel to him." As an assessor, he must insist that time is of the utmost importance. Perhaps the man will die soon of his wounds. It's now or never!

This exercise allows one to observe how the candidate will play the role of an evangelist as well as that of a nonbeliever, in order to assess if he understands the culture of nonbelievers, if he knows how to relate, speak their language, and present the gospel in a way they can understand.

7. *Message for the Grand Opening.* The candidates come prepared to give a message as if it were the sermon prepared for their first public church service, or the grand opening of their new ministry. The assessors rate the message and the delivery, and they evaluate how the candidates share their vision for the new ministry, their spouse's involvement, and so on.

After three days of in-depth assessment, the candidates are usually tired and worn out. We try to make the final interview as pleasant as possible so that the candidates can be affirmed in their gifts for a specific type of ministry.

Through the use of this questionnaire, the mentioned tools, and the Assessment Center, one can get to know the candidates for church planting quite well. Perhaps you can use some of these ideas for your own situation.

The Role of Formal Institutions

When recruiting candidates for planting new churches, some denominations first look at established academic institutions, such as seminaries and Bible institutes. They assume that with academic preparation one is equipped to plant churches. The truth is that many institutions can give someone academic preparation, but that does not mean the person is ready to plant churches. Institutional preparation should be combined with a *practicum* or experience within a local church or with participation in the planting of a new congregation. Academic preparation should be paired with something practical. Many seminarians, upon graduation and taking on the work of ministry in their first church, confess to being ignorant about a lot of things, those that the seminary did not train them to do. George Hunter, in *Radical Outreach*, points out that many formal academic institutions are not capable of holistically preparing candidates for planting new churches.[21] Many institutions will have to change their focus and ministerial philosophy or pedagogical paradigm if they are going to participate in the preparation of new church initiators. We must ask ourselves—those of us who are in the teaching profession—if we are preparing church planters or fish tank guardians. Our answer to this question determines the training focus that we offer and reveals the paradigm of "pastor" under which we operate.

Academic preparation needs to be supplemented with other forms of training. In my church, for example, we offer internships to potential planters. (Understand that an internship is a work experience for a time with an experienced person in this line of work. Generally it includes study, practice, and reflection.) We offer three options: (1) a nonformal internship of six months to a year which trains future evangelists (for those in nonformal programs);

---

21   George Hunter, *Radical Outreach: Recovery of Apostolic Ministry and Evangelism.*

(2) an academic-practical internship of six months to a year for those involved in a formal seminary or Bible institute program; and (3) a practicum of one year for seminary graduates. The internships and residency allow a candidate to put into practice what they are learning or have learned in the formal or nonformal program. The combination of formal studies with a supervised practicum allows for a better integration of what a candidate needs in order to be able to plant new churches. The practicum is based on the needs of the candidate. It focuses on areas of weakness, giving the candidate necessary experience in order to develop their skills, reflecting on theory in practice. This also serves as additional training for the candidate. At times the internships function as additional filters in determining whether one has the "makings" of a church planter. Not all who begin the internship process leave with the qualifications for planting churches.

An adult learns better when he can immediately apply what he has studied, and our interns are given the opportunity to integrate everything. According to Malcolm Knowles, "Adults are motivated to learn as they experience needs and interests that learning will satisfy."[22] Robert Havighurst defines this disposition as "teachable moments" when the candidate is more disposed to learning something.[23] Times when the planter is in the thick of planting or preparing himself for planting could be those teachable moments. In order for that to happen, the denomination needs to assign a mentor to the new planter. The mentor will help the planter consider alternatives, think about options, point them in the right direction, and so on. Once a church planter has been identified, assigning him a good mentor helps in predicting the future success of a church plant.

The Role of Nonformal Institutions

If we only depended on seminarians for planting churches, we would never fulfill the work of evangelizing the whole world. Candidates, therefore, are not limited to those in formal programs such as seminary programs or internships for church planting. There are unaccredited programs in which a future planter or new planter can receive basic training. For more than 30 years, Theological Education by Extension (TEE) has been offering courses and workshops in Latin America and in the United States. Since the begin-

---

22   Malcolm Knowles, *The Adult Learner: A Neglected Species*, 30.
23   Robert Havighurst, *Development Tasks and Education*.

ning of this movement in Latin America—with pioneers such as Ross Kinsler and Kenneth Mulholland—we have prepared and offered training, bringing courses to the homes and churches of the candidates themselves. This is an effective way to train pastors and church planters without their having to leave their work settings. It is a form of "vocational training," or training in actual ministry, and not training for a future ministry. This allows for training to occur within the context of ministry and as an apprentice. This strategy makes more sense than taking the student out of their daily context and sending them to a distant institution to learn how to minister in their community, far away from their community. Other programs, such as SEAN and FLET, also offer preparatory studies for ministry. Many people in Latin America have taken advantage of these programs and today serve as pastors, evangelists, and new church planters and occupy leadership positions in their local churches.

We have already talked about formal institutions. We recognize, however, that today many denominations and large churches opt to identify and send out their own candidates for planting new churches. At times, these groups send their candidates directly into the missionary field, like paratroopers. Perhaps some institutions and ecclesiastical associations have tended to be too theoretical and academic in preparing candidates. However, the idea of dropping a planter on the field without some preparation is not the answer. Without basic preparation, a new planter can fall into many errors and frustrations. Both a paratrooper-style planter as well as a planter with three or four seminary degrees can benefit from some sort of basic training for church planters, such as a *Bootcamp*, an in-depth and practical seminar sponsored by the Church Multiplication Training Center (CMTC) or other similar organizations. The planter, either a seminary graduate or someone sent directly to the field by his church, continues learning in the "school of life." With a good mentor and participation in events such as *Bootcamp*, a church initiator has a better possibility of harvesting better fruit after planting seeds. Other organizations, such as Dynamic Church Planting International, are also becoming known for their system of training modules. Many denominations have also started their own training programs. Multiplication Network Ministries (MNM) has also been partnering with major denominations in training church planters in a 12-module approach, supplemented by mentor/coaches who meet with the church planter-in-training between modules. See www. multiplicationnetwork.org.

Some Caveats

The Romans had a word in Latin, *caveat*, which is equivalent to *"Look out!"* in our vocabulary. It means that we have to qualify what we have said. We have studied a lot regarding the characteristics of a new church planter. We have talked about qualities and abilities. It is obvious that whatever assessment is used, there must be an evaluation of the planter's spiritual character. Perhaps we assume that those who go to an Assessment Center or who go through a behavioral interview arrive with an acknowledged level of spiritual preparation for ministry. We believe that generally, the local church, pastor, denomination, or someone else has qualified the candidate in regard to their spiritual character. Although the assessment for planters has to do with some spiritual areas—such as living out their faith—we know the spiritual formation of believers is a process and not something that can be measured by one event. Because of this we recognize that we must rely on others most of the time to measure a candidate's spiritual preparation. Once measured, the candidate is ready for the Assessment Center—and not before. We have seen cases of spiritual brokenness, immorality, and spiritual immaturity in planters who were sent to be evaluated as church planters but were not sufficiently discipled. In the battle of planting churches, one's faults and spiritual weaknesses come to the surface, contributing to their failure in ministry. One's faith life is of utmost importance. It must be seen and confirmed by others. This is not for the Assessment Center or the Behavioral Interview to determine. The candidate, upon enrollment in one of these events, must come with the testimony of witnesses (Acts 9:27) regarding their spiritual depth and the confirmation of their calling.

A second caveat is the need for a call. No one should consider planting a church unless he truly senses God calling him to this vocation. God will equip those whom he has called to be church planters—whether using formal programs or nonformal means of preparation. Oftentimes when everything seems to be going wrong in the church plant, the only thing that keeps the planter plodding along is his sense of call. One couple who went to live among a tribe in a distant land felt they had a call from God to live among these people and to eventually translate the Bible into that language. At least four times their home was burned, or ransacked, or dismantled by those who did not want them to stay. What kept them faithful to the task was this extreme sense of call. Some 20 years later, they were able to see the Bible read in this language. Early on they could have left when faced with such opposition, but, as the husband said, "I sensed that God had called us here, and we were not about to disobey."

Do you have that sense of call? No amount of training and preparation will help you to plant a new church if you do not have God's call on your life. Please be certain that God has called you to this task, and then never look back! Like Paul, you want to be able to say that you have been called to be an "apostle to . . ." (Rom. 11:13). Paul knew to whom he had been called and what his calling was. This is what kept Paul going, despite the oppositions he faced on many fronts. In the end he could write to his disciple Timothy from prison, "I have fought the good fight, I have finished the race, I have kept the faith. Now there is in store for me the crown of righteousness, which the Lord, the righteous Judge, will award to me on that day—and not only to me, but also to all who have longed for his appearing" (2 Tim. 4:7-8).

A third caveat deals with biblical qualifications. There are no qualifications listed in the Bible that are church planter-specific. Nevertheless, we can look at the biblical qualifications for office found in 1 Timothy 3:1-7, among other passages. Consider also 2 Timothy 2:15-16 and Titus 4:1-2. Look carefully at these passages and do a personal inventory. Do you meet these spiritual qualifications for leadership?

CONCLUSION

We began this chapter asking, who should plant churches? We saw that not everyone is capable of doing this. Although all of us have the responsibility to share the good news of Jesus Christ, not all of us have received the call to be church planters. Not everyone is equipped by the Holy Spirit with the necessary characteristics to be effective in this missionary work. Only those who have the mentioned characteristics should make the decision to plant churches. *A warning, however:* It is easy to conclude that all who have the thirteen characteristics outlined by Ridley or the nine mentioned by Wagner will be successful in church planting. If it were only for the characteristics, that might be true. But the truth is that only God can plant the church. He equips the planter, but he also brings forth the fruit. Remember the words of Paul: "Neither the one who plants nor the one who waters is anything, but only God, who makes things grow" (1 Cor. 3:7). We are God's partners. The church will only be planted if we work with him, trusting in his power and good will. The Lord will build his church. No matter how much training and assessment a planter has, he will not be successful in his planting endeavors if God does not lead the planting. To him be the glory and honor.

Questions

1. Why is it important to consider the question, "Who should plant churches?" Can just anyone plant a church? Explain your answer.

2. According to Ridley, what are the 13 essential characteristics of a person gifted to plant a church?

3. Choose three of these to describe in more detail, with your thoughts on why each one is important.

4. Should we move ahead with the calling of a church planter if he or she does not meet all of the characteristics? Why or why not?

5. Name two or three other characteristics that you feel are important.

6. What are the two ways by which we can evaluate if a person is gifted for church planting?

7. Describe each way and how they are different.

8. Explain why doing an assessment of potential church planters does not minimize the role of the Holy Spirit in equipping each person who has been called.

9. Where do you see yourself regarding these 13 characteristics? Are there areas in which you might need more time before offering yourself as a church planter? Explain.

7 FIVE COMMITMENTS OF A HEALTHY CHURCH

Tim Koster & John Wagenveld

Editor's note: Chapter 7 and 8 are available in a more complete book version which can be downloaded for free at www.multiplicationnetwork.org.

> God's intent was that now, *through the church*, the manifold wisdom of God should be made known to the rulers and authorities in the heavenly realms, according to his eternal purpose which he accomplished in Christ Jesus our Lord.
>
> Ephesians 3:10-11

"Through the church…" What a key phrase. Through the church God is unveiling his redemptive purposes in the world. Through the church he is revealing his manifold wisdom. Through the church he is declaring the good news of salvation in Christ Jesus. Through the church God is demonstrating the reality of his transforming power. Through the church God lays claim to the kingdom that was inaugurated in the life and ministry of Jesus Christ. Through the church God models a vision for what life can be under the Lordship of Christ. Through the church God communicates redemption, brings restoration, and provides a foretaste of the community that works with hope as it anticipates a new heaven and a new earth. The main actor is God. The Church is his agent.

God's intentions for the church are huge, particularly when we stop to recognize that the church is a gathering of very ordinary people, complete with warts and blemishes. To even begin to live out God's dreams for us, we require an infusion of the life-giving Spirit, an awareness of how he has gifted us and where we need more of his healing grace.

To understand a healthy church, one must first recognize that the church does not exist for itself. It is a creation of the Spirit and at its core reflects the nature and character of God.[1] Only when we recognize the truth that God is the primary agent in mission and that both the church and the gospel it carries are for the sake of the world does our human effort, led by the Spirit, make sense. From that understanding flows the purpose, function, and organization of local communities of faith. These participate with God in his mission as the body of Christ, his feet and his hands.

The Redemptive Reign of God Through the Church in Mission

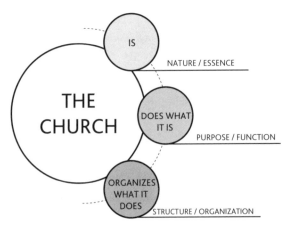

Viewing the church as the Body of Christ gives us a helpful way to develop an awareness of how the Holy Spirit is at work in a congregation. When someone visits the doctor, the appointment always begins with the collection of certain basic data: pulse, temperature, blood pressure, oxygen levels, weight, blood sugar, and cholesterol levels, etc. Those simple tests offer

---

1   Adapted from Craig Van Gelder, *The Essence of the Church: A Community Created by the Spirit.*

insight as to what is happening inside the body. If something is wrong, the tests also offer direction as to treatment—or at least the next round of tests.

In the same way, there are 10 simple vital signs that offer insight into the health of a congregation. The list is neither definitive nor exhaustive, but it is sufficient to recognize a movement of the Spirit or a problem that needs to be addressed. Every church lives out these vital signs at some level. A healthy church will have them operating in an effective and balanced way. The context will determine the form in which they are expressed. The ten vital signs are:

In this and the next chapter,[2] we discuss each vital sign and explain how it contributes to greater ministry effectiveness. These vital areas of a healthy church can be divided into two parts. In the first part, we present the five essential commitments, defined by the Spirit, that every congregation should have. This will be chapter 7. The second part, or chapter 8, explains the five vital functions, led by the Spirit, that should be considered as areas in which the church must work. All of these arise from God's command to proclaim, announce, and embody the good news of the already present reality of God's kingdom in Jesus Christ, empowered by the Holy Spirit, which will bring transformation to all areas of life for God's glory.

---

2   Chapters 7 and 8 are a condensation of the book *Take Your Church's Pulse: Ten Characteristics of a Healthy Church,* by the same authors, offered as an ebook by Multiplication Network Ministries. A free download can be obtained by going to www.multiplicationnetwork.com.

10 Characteristics of a Healthy Church

FIVE COMMITMENTS	FIVE FUNCTIONS
CLEAR AND INSPIRING VISION • Mtt. 9:36-38; Luke 4:14-21 • Acts 1:8 • 2 Cor. 5:14-21; 2 Tim. 2:15, 22-24; 2 Tim. 4:1-7	COMPELLING WITNESS • Matt. 28:18-20; Luke 24:45-48 • Acts 5:42; Acts 10:34-43 • Rom. 10:13-15; 2 Cor. 4:5; 2 Cor. 5:20-21
MOBILIZING LEADERSHIP • Mark 10:42-45; John 13:1-17 • Acts 6:1-7; Acts 13:1-3; Acts 20:28-31a • 2 Cor. 2:17; 2 Cor. 4:1-2; Eph. 4:11-13	COMPREHENSIVE DISCIPLESHIP • Matt. 28:18-20 • Acts 17:11; Acts 19:9b-10 • 2 Tim. 2:2; Titus 2:7-8; 2 Pet. 3:18
MOTIVATED MINISTERING BODY • Luke 10:1-2 • Acts 6:1-7 • Rom. 12:4, 6-8; Eph. 4:11-13; 1 Pet. 4:10-11	COMPASSIONATE SERVICE • Matt. 6:1-4; Matt. 20:25-28; Matt. 25:31-46 • Acts 6:1-7; Acts 20:35 • Gal. 6:10; Heb. 13:16; James 1:22, 27; James 2:14-17
PROPER STEWARDSHIP OF RESOURCES • Luke 19:11-26 • Acts 2:44-46; Acts 4:32-35 • 1 Cor. 4:2; 2 Cor. 8:1-7	CARING AND WELCOMING COMMUNITY • John 17:20-23 • Acts 2:42, 44 • 1 Cor. 12:25b-26; Gal. 6:1-2; Eph. 4:32; Heb. 10:24-25; 1 John 1:7
INTEGRATION OF TEXT AND CONTEXT • John 1:14 • Acts 17:18-28 • 1 Cor. 9:19-23	DYNAMIC WORSHIP AND PRAYER • Matt. 28:8-9; Luke 24:50-52; John 4:19-26 • Acts 13:2 • Heb. 12:28-29; Rev. 5:9-14

The first five indispensable *commitments* (also called elements) upon which a healthy church is built are:

1. a clear and inspiring *vision,*
2. a mobilizing *leadership,*
3. a motivated *ministering body,*
4. the proper stewardship of *resources,* and
5. the integration of the *text* to the *context.*

I. FIRST KEY COMMITMENT: A CLEAR AND INSPIRING VISION

What is a vision?

A vision is a clear mental picture of a preferred future. It is not a pithy slogan or motto on a T-shirt or mug. It is not a generic paragraph fitting every other church in the community. It is not a strategic goal to accomplish in the next 1-2 years.

A vision will ultimately work itself out into specific goals. Yet instead of getting bogged down in the details, it holds out for a dream of what could be as we join God in bearing witness of the full reality of God's kingdom in our midst.

A vision is a congregation's answer to the question, "What is that preferred future God is leading us into? God has us here in this place, at this time, with these particular people, gifts, and challenges. What is that clear mental picture of the place where God is taking us as a congregation?"

3 Key Ingredients In Clarifying Your Vision

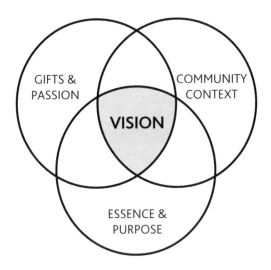

Or to put it slightly differently: What has God created the church to be and what is God's general purpose for the church as a whole? How has he uniquely equipped us as a local body? Where has he placed us in this broken world?

When we can state a clear answer to those questions, the resulting vision will propel us to pursue Christ and his kingdom. The element of vision has to do with perspective, with how we "see" our role within the greater purposes of God for our community.

A clear and inspiring vision empowers the church by providing urgency and unity. The church without vision is not only blind but also prone to being shaped primarily by tradition and surrounding culture. It ends up drifting without direction, comfortable and complacent. It has no sense of urgency to carry out the task to which God has called it. New churches generally begin with great enthusiasm and with a contagious vision. Church planters should take advantage of this moment to further develop that vision and to communicate it with conviction to prospective leaders and the broader community.

A danger of not having a clear vision is that in the absence of visionary leadership, people will fill the vacuum with their own visions. More than one focused vision causes division (divided vision). A clear vision puts every member of the congregation on the same page. It draws people together and aligns the congregation so that each member can serve in ways that build the Body of Christ (cf. Ephesians 4:1-16).

Normally the vision is the first factor to consider when evaluating a ministry's progress. In the sport of soccer, midfielders are the strategic motor of the team. Midfielders link all the players together to both defend and attack. Often, the play in the midfield wins or loses games. The importance of the vision of a congregation is similar to the strategic importance of the midfield. Just as inadequate midfield execution causes problems for a soccer team, many of the problems that arise in new congregations arise from an inadequate vision. Winning teams and healthy congregations will have a clear and inspiring vision.

In our More Churches, Stronger Churches trainings, we teach eight key elements for a vision:

Eight Key Elements of Vision
- It projects a clear framework of an ideal future.
- It focuses on the future through God's eyes and provides direction.
- It is based on the redemptive purposes of God.
- It does not conform to the status quo.
- It requires faith. It is ambitious, yet realistic.
- It communicates clearly to others.
- It motivates people to act. It provides a sense of urgency.
- It is a shared vision.

Define the vision

The first step is defining the vision that God gives. To do this, faithfully pray for the Lord to show you what he wants to develop in the congregation or ministry to which he has called you. Then take an inventory of your gifts, abilities, and interests and think about how you could put them into service for God. Remember that Scripture shows us God's purposes for the whole Church. The vision you will be defining is the particular expression of the way that God's purposes can be worked out in your local context and according to the gifts, passions, and personality that he has provided for you. The vision can be adjusted and changed according to the context—that is, the needs, challenges, and opportunities of the area of ministry—but it must always be rooted in God's purposes for his Church.

A firm and clear vision will correctly guide the leadership team and the new congregation and will foster the wise use of resources. It will also give direction to the church's other work areas. The persons responsible to steward the development of a vision for the community of faith are the leaders. They are the vision's crucial vehicle, the first ones to dream, the first to implement it, and the first in challenging others to see new horizons and to join the team to reach the stated goal of establishing a healthy church that gives witness to the gospel of Christ. Visionary leadership, rooted in Biblical values, will often end up in a Christ-centered church.

Share the vision

You should share the vision that has been developed with others to seek confirmation by the wider community of faith. It is important to have people who are mature and wise within your community who confirm the vision God is giving you. Without their affirmation, it is too easy to put your words in God's mouth and pretend he was the one speaking all along. You can motivate others by sharing the vision in a contagious way. To effectively communicate the vision and get other people excited about it, take the following steps:

A. Share the vision with clarity and conviction

You should communicate the vision clearly and with a sense of urgency. People will be more ready to work with you on common goals if they understand what the final objective is. The kind of vision that compels people is a clear, biblical, and achievable but challenging vision.

Some examples of a clearly defined vision:

To cross two or more cultural barriers: geo-political, ethnic, linguistic, world-view, socio-economic to plant indigenous churches and promote social justice.
(**Xenos Christian Fellowship**)

We see an active congregation reaching the unchurched with the good news of Jesus; equipping them with a faith that works in real life; sending them out to serve the world in the name of Christ. **(Faith Lutheran Church)**

New Life Christian Church will reach the lost people of Ciudad Juárez, disciple the chosen, serve the community, show Christian fellowship, and worship God in all aspects of life for the honor and glory of his name. **(New Life Christian Church)**

Exercise: Each of the vision statements above was designed for a unique congregation. Rate each one on its ability to unite and create urgency. How would you rework them to make them clearer and more compelling?

B. Create an environment in which others can identify and participate in the vision

A true vision is a shared vision. People can take ownership only if they invest something of themselves in the fine print of how the vision works out in real life. To foster the vision, there should be an atmosphere of clear communication, transparency, honesty, respect, participation, and unity.

C. Foster a team held together by the vision

Every day we become more aware of the importance of working as a team. Our Lord Jesus Christ brought together the twelve disciples and with this group revolutionized the world around his vision for the Kingdom of God. He sent out his disciples to preach the gospel in teams of two. In the church today, we should also work as teams and not as lone rangers. The common vision, centered on the person of Jesus Christ, will be the unifying factor for the team.

D. Allow for experimentation and failure

For the vision to become a reality, it may be necessary to try several strategies. There should be a place for new ideas, and there should be openness to the possibility that some initiatives will fail. Other people will be more willing to join with the vision if they know they have the freedom to fail when working for the desired goal.

E. Keep the vision in everyone's sight

Churches should use all means possible to communicate the vision: preaching, teaching, literature, signs, banners, pamphlets, etc. Remind the congregation and the leaders regularly about the vision. Always look for new and fresh ways to keep the vision in front of the people who are involved.

F. Develop a concrete plan ("Put feet on the vision")

The vision must eventually have an operational plan that becomes the blueprint for making it a reality. Too many visions stay as dreams and are never put into practical action. Healthy churches will discover their clear and compelling vision, understand their mission, clarify their values, and convert all this into a practical operational plan supported by the available local resources.

Now that we have discussed the importance of a clear and inspiring vision, we can turn to those who are supposed to formulate and communicate it—mobilizing leaders.

II. SECOND KEY COMMITMENT: MOBILIZING LEADERSHIP

Leadership is the essential link between the vision and the mobilized church body. A chain is as strong as its weakest link, but the leadership link should be one of the most trustworthy components in the entire ministry. The church needs leaders to communicate a clear vision and to formulate pertinent strategies.

Church planters have the advantage of being able to begin a new entity that reflects their personal vision (i.e what God wants to accomplish in a church planting effort). As they develop a team of leaders around them, it is essential to make sure new leaders share the vision with those already on the team.

A. Biblical Characteristics

Throughout Scripture, God reveals the characteristics of godly leaders. One key passage on leadership is found in Ephesians 4:11-16:

> It was he who gave some to be apostles, some to be prophets, some to be evangelists, and some to be pastors and teachers, to

prepare God's people for works of service, so that the Body of Christ may be built up until we all reach unity in the faith and in the knowledge of the Son of God and become mature, attaining to the whole measure of the fullness of Christ. Then we will no longer be infants, tossed back and forth by the waves, and blown here and there by every wind of teaching and by the cunning and craftiness of men in their deceitful scheming. Instead, speaking the truth in love, we will in all things grow up into him who is the Head, that is, Christ. From him the whole body, joined and held together by every supporting ligament, grows and builds itself up in love, as each part does its work.

The ENTIRE congregation and all God's people, not just the leaders, do God's ministry. The leadership's function is to help the congregation find its place, with each member carrying out work corresponding to his or her gifts and talents. The most explicit epistles about leadership in the church are 1 and 2 Timothy and the letter to Titus.

Jesus as the Leader Exemplar

Jesus was the Son of God who became flesh. He possessed all the gifts of the Spirit. What Jesus did individually, the church lives out corporately through the complementary gifts of the leaders and the congregation. Jesus models leadership for us. The Holy Spirit anointed and prepared Jesus for ministry. He also washed the feet of the disciples and said that he came to serve and not to be served (John 13:1-17). He taught with authority that being a leader is to serve. He led with humility. Whoever wanted to be first among the disciples was to be the last. Whoever wanted to be greater was first to be the least. While our leadership styles may vary depending on the situation, our character should be shaped by the character and the person of our Lord Jesus Christ.

Christian leadership requires personal time with God, offering him the opportunity to do his work. Our study of Scripture and time in prayer ought to include some time to be agenda free – not focused on preparing the next sermon or solving the next problem. We need time with God designed simply to be with him, letting him teach and shape us. We can end our personal prayer time with 5 minutes of silence, holding back our incessant need to speak to give God the opportunity to speak to us.

In addition, we need to have the humility to let others speak into our lives. First, we should listen to people of wise counsel who we trust. As the writer of Proverbs puts it, "Wounds from a friend can be trusted (27:6)." Yet even our critics may have a truth we need to hear if we are willing to listen.

Lastly, leaders should remember that character development is not just an exercise in self-discipline. The qualities we desire are fruit of the Spirit, which we can cultivate, but he must grow. The fruit is developed together in community. We should not rely on our own strength but rather on the grace of God. We hold on to God's promise to the Apostle Paul: "My grace is sufficient for you" (2 Corinthians 12:9).

B. Missional characteristics

Mobilizing leaders must be missional— they must be leaders who see the world through the eyes of the triune God; leaders who seek to participate in God's mission in the world; leaders who call sinners with the Word of God and the power of the Holy Spirit. It is helpful to note three key aspects of missional leadership.

1. **Engaging the world.** Our communities are mission fields and the locus of God's redemptive and transformative activity! The most effective ministries are those in which the leaders do not only feed the sheep in the sheep pen but are also concerned, just as Jesus is, for the lost or missing sheep. This characteristic is essential in planting new churches and should not be lost in established ones. Jesus went to have dinner with many tax collectors and sinners. When the scribes and Pharisees saw it, they asked the disciples why Jesus was doing this. "On hearing this, Jesus said to them, 'It is not the healthy who need a doctor, but the sick. I have not come to call the righteous, but sinners'" (Mark2:17).

2. **Motivating and involving the members**. A study of churches in Latin America by John Hall demonstrated that one of the most important characteristics of a leader is being able to motivate and involve the

congregation.[3] The traditional role of the "do-everything pastor" will rarely work in the postmodern context in which we live. Good leaders want to broaden, improve, channel, train, and delegate. Effective leaders are those who multiply themselves in others and who help all the members find their places in the ministries to which God has called them.

3. **Seeding mission into every area of ministry.** God's mission has a church, therefore every dimension of church life needs to incorporate a focus on mission. We intentionally need to cross-pollinate across areas of ministry. A missional focus should saturate all of a church's activities: worship, fellowship, counseling, finances, and all the church's systems. Every element of our communal life is about something bigger than we are.

A missional focus is the key!

C. Differentiating characteristics

Recently there has been greater understanding of the variety of leaders needed for the diverse and complex ministry in God's work.

The Lord uses different types of leaders in diverse places. What follows is a discussion of some of the wide variety of skills and abilities that are useful to greater or lesser degrees, depending on the context.

Authors David Shenk and Ervin Stutzman, in their book *Creating Communities of the Kingdom: New Testament Models of Church Planting,* describe four types of leaders.[4] One person may have several of these characteristics, but generally, one characteristic is most prominent.

1. **Catalyzer.** This leader works optimally when he or she must begin from nothing. These leaders almost never need others to motivate them to work; they motivate themselves to start projects and can be very effective in planting new churches for a denomination. These

---

3   John Hall, *Urban Ministry Factors in Latin America,* 161-62.
4   David Shenk and Ervin Stutzman, *Creating Communities of the Kingdom: New Testament Models of Church Planting,* 176-78.

people are often extroverted and confident and have the necessary charisma to attract others and begin a group or a new ministry.

2. **Organizer.** This type of leader can take something that is in disorder and organize it to maximize its effectiveness. These leaders like the challenge that coordinating and promoting a complex system brings. Many church planters identify with this type; they are able to structure things with the gifts and spirit of a businessperson.

3. **Operator.** Operators maintain the course of the church as long as there are not drastic changes in the environment. The majority of leaders fall into this category, although they may share characteristics of other styles. Operators make limited use of the more entrepreneurial aspects of the other styles and the more visible leadership behaviors associated with those styles. Nevertheless, every established church needs the talents and gifts of people who know how to lead through administrative skills.

4. **Revitalizer.** This person has certain characteristics of the previous three categories that allow him or her to mobilize and "resuscitate" a church even when it is declining. These leaders have many qualities similar to the catalyzer, but they begin with something that has already been established. Revitalizers frequently have gone through a variety of experiences and can use the many lessons they've learned in the new context in which they find themselves.

III. THIRD KEY COMMITMENT: MOTIVATED MINISTRY BODY

The key commitment of a mobilizing leadership links vision to the element of a motivated ministering body. The effective leader knows how to motivate and involve the congregation and how to multiply the number of leaders in that congregation. This is the discipleship model in 2 Timothy 2:2, in which Paul instructs young Timothy: "And the things you have heard me say in the presence of many witnesses entrust to reliable men who will also be qualified to teach others." Paul's instructions to his disciple indicate that Timothy was likely quiet and shy. The Bible demonstrates that God frequently uses the person we least expect to do his greatest work. Nevertheless, charismatic or shy, the truth is none of us accomplishes God's purposes alone. God established the church as a community of believers so we could participate in God's mission together and learn to love each other in the process. Therefore it is essential to challenge the congregation to unite in reaching its established goals and objectives.

An effective leader delegates to others not just to get out from under the work, but above all because it allows others to use their gifts to minister to others as they grow in responsibility. We are only stewards in growing God's people. Moses, in Exodus 18, had to accept the advice of his father-in-law and stop doing everything by himself.

For new churches, some experts suggest that church planters should spend eighty percent of their time with twenty percent of their congregation—their key leaders—once a core group has been formed. These new leaders will shepherd and mobilize the rest of the emerging church. One of the reasons there are so many churches of between thirty and fifty people is that most of the work is left for the pastor to do alone. Thirty to fifty people is, in the majority of cases, the number of people that one person can pastor without much help.

There are too many inactive Christians in established congregations. There are many consumers and few contributors.

The attitude of a church body that is not active in ministry is reflected especially by communities of faith that think of the church as the physical building where they meet. Church for them is a place one visits or an event one attends.

Other churches, once established, are simply too comfortable and satisfied with things the way they are. They are self-centered congregations. Their programs and budgets serve those who are "inside." When there is no mission with what the Spirit is already doing in the community, there are far fewer places to serve, and therefore there is less need to mobilize the entire congregation in ministry— with just a few people, things can move along.

The Priesthood of All Believers

It is time for the whole church to be set free to minister. It is time to mobilize all of God's people in each local church to serve him with the gifts he has given them. The body of a missionary God is a missionary church. The principle of the priesthood of all believers, proclaimed in the letter to the Hebrews and restated during the Protestant Reformation of the sixteenth century, should be rescued and put into practice. The church is most effective at fulfilling its calling when everyone is working for the same purpose.

Gift-Based Ministry

The Apostle Peter tells us in his first letter, "Each one should use whatever gift he has received to serve others, faithfully administering God's grace in its various forms" (1 Peter 4:10). Christians who do not use their gifts are, in general, bored believers because they are not doing the things the Lord created, equipped, and called them to do. Doing ministry motivates people. People become enthusiastic about their faith when they are doing things and learning things in the crucible of ministry and mission in and toward the world.

A good leader, a good church planter:

- Helps people identify their spiritual gifts.
- Helps people identify their passions. God has wired everyone differently.
- Listens to people's stories and helps them trace their history.
- Mobilizes people according to their gifts.
- Works as a team.

Bottom line, it is important for Christian leaders to realize that one of their principal functions is "to prepare God's people for works of service, so that the Body of Christ may be built up" (Ephesians 4:12). Healthy teams with healthy leaders can go a long way toward forming healthy churches.

IV. FOURTH KEY COMMITMENT: PROPER STEWARDSHIP OF RESOURCES

We are not the owners of anything in God's Kingdom. We are simply stewards. God is the creator of heaven and earth and is the rightful owner of the entire cosmos. God has created human beings who carry the image of God to be stewards over all creation for the glory of God.

When we talk about resources, we almost always think about the three "T's": the time, talents, and treasure of the church, all of which belong to God.

A. Time

Time may be one of the least used resources for the Lord's work in most congregations. The time that members can use to serve in ministry to others is extremely valuable. It is the leaders' responsibility to challenge the members to get more involved and to mobilize them to use their time responsibly.

B. Talents

Some leaders do not have the slightest idea of the amount of "hidden" talents in their own congregations. If we could maximize the use of each member's talents, we would revolutionize the way we do things. It is a good idea to conduct a survey of the members periodically to create an inventory of the talents and abilities in the local church.

You can ask the following questions of each member:

- What gifts do you feel the Lord has given you to serve others?
- What things do you like to do that others have confirmed you do well?
- If the church were to help place you in a ministry, what would you prefer to do?
- Would you be willing to take an inventory to discover your gifts?
- When could we meet to talk about the results?

C. Treasure (Facilities, and Finances)

Location for new meeting places

The decision about where to locate a meeting place is almost always made after studying the area and the people you hope to reach with the gospel. In rural areas, people may want to attend the church that is closest in proximity, but in urban areas they may be more willing to travel to find a congregation that they like and where they may already know people. Some church planters have used valuable information regarding a large multifamily housing project that was going to be built in the area to help plan for the future.

However, David Hesselgrave gives us something else to think about besides geographic location—the spiritual state of the area. He says that we need to seek a place where the Holy Spirit has been preparing people; otherwise, we may face years of frustration and little fruit.[5] In *Experiencing God*, Henry Blackaby describes the same factor another way when he says, "Find out where God is at work and join Him there."[6]

When the decision is to be made regarding where to locate the meeting place once the congregation has been established, it is important to look for a place with excellent visibility. Choosing a main street versus a small side street or a dead-end road can make all the difference in how many people will be able to find the meeting place.

Some communities of faith prefer a structure that stands out. Other contexts may require a building that looks like all the neighboring buildings, unlike the traditional idea of a church. This is why it is so important to first determine the needs and the customs of the people you are hoping to reach. It is essential to ask people who live in the community what they think about the location being considered.

Another important resource is the building or facilities that the congregation uses for its worship services and its church programs. Some congregations create a list of primary elements they need for their facilities. These include good lighting for evening activities, sufficient parking if people come in cars, a place that is adequate for teaching, good childcare, and clean bathrooms. A church in a rural area may not face the same expectations as one in the city, but it will have its own details to take care of to maximize the impression it makes on visitors.

Most consultants recommend expanding the meeting place once it is eighty percent full during worship services. A visionary church planter will invest the resources, even when it may cost a bit more, to find a place with enough

5   David Hesselgrave, *Planting Churches Cross-Culturally: North America and Beyond*, 227.
6   Henry Blackaby, Richard Blackaby, and Claude King, *Experiencing God*, 73.

capacity to carry out the programs that the church plans to develop and to allow for future growth.

Having said all this, we believe many Christians put too much of an emphasis on buildings, almost as if they truly believe God inhabited the building. Scripture is clear that the church is the people of God and that the Lord does not need a special edifice (See 2 Samuel 7:4-7). We see the desire for a building distracting many church planters from focusing on the task of building up the "living stones" where God truly inhabits— with His people.

Finances

The church, in practical terms, needs financial resources to achieve its goals of evangelization and bearing witness to God's kingdom. Without money, the church will have serious difficulties in doing the work to which it is called. The advantage we have is that when God sends us to do something, he also provides the tools we need to do the work. Good finances require certain efforts on the part of the church planter:

- *Communicate the vision.* Money almost always flows where there is a clear, motivating, and well-communicated vision.

- *Provide transparent accounting.* It is the leaders' and the treasurer's responsibility to give a clear accounting for the income and expenses and to tell how this has contributed to a fuller participation in the mission of God.

- *Teach on tithing and stewardship.* It is important for the church's leadership to lead by example in the matter of giving. It is part of responsible leadership to teach about the blessing of tithing and stewardship.

V. FIFTH KEY COMMITMENT: INTEGRATION OF TEXT AND CONTEXT

The Centrality of the Text

The fifth commitment of a healthy church is that Scripture is taught and lived out in appropriate ways in the local and global community. Psalm

119:105 celebrates the wisdom of life based on God's instructions and has the oft-quoted verse, "Your word is a lamp unto my feet and a light for my path." A healthy congregation nourishes itself by reading and studying Scripture together. Apostle Paul wrote to Timothy, the young pastor of the church at Ephesus, "All Scripture is God-breathed and is useful for teaching, rebuking, correcting, and training in righteousness, so that the man of God may be thoroughly equipped for every good work" (II Timothy 3:16-17). In Colossians 3:16, he wrote, "Let the word of God dwell in you richly as you teach and admonish one another with all wisdom..."

This task requires that we spend focused time with God in God's Word and prayer, both as a community and also individually. So often the pressures of ministry compel leaders to use Scripture simply as a tool rather than as God's voice speaking into our lives. We will study the Bible to help us write the next sermon, prepare the next Bible study or minister to someone in crisis. We run from responsibility to responsibility until we are out of time, with the result that we are prepared just enough to explain the words to others but not enough to really listen and apply them to our own lives. In the midst of it all, we may assume that we have learned what Scripture has to teach us, when in fact we have not taken the time to let God use it to shape us.

When we set aside responsibilities just to be with him, our relationship with him has the opportunity to grow stronger and deeper. That depth of relationship will later feed ministry, but only if it is flowing from our affection for God.

Leaders of healthy congregations know Scripture well, they are shaped by it, and they apply biblical principles in their decision-making, handling of conflicts, strategic planning, evaluation of worship, and other aspects of church life. They read Scripture together and use it to nurture their life with God and to disciple church members. They study it, meditate on it, and memorize it. Scripture shapes the values of the congregation, and members use it to hold each other accountable.

Good leaders, good church planters:

- *Know the context.* Knowing Scripture isn't enough to enable a church to successfully reach its community. The church must also understand its cultural context in a variety of different dimensions: religious, socioeconomic, cultural, geographical, political, etc. This comes from listening to people, building relationships with them, living among them, and learning everything possible from and about them. For biblical examples, see Acts 17:22-23, Acts. 22:3-4, Acts 23:6. In each case, Paul took into consideration who he was speaking to and the cultural context they were from.

- *Enter a culture.* Entering a culture is all about immersing yourself in a culture to understand its worldview: the questions it asks, the things it values the most, the way it reasons and thinks and argues, along with its sources of hope and belief. Are they influenced by logical debate, a well-told story, or communal debate? Do they make major decisions as individuals or as a group? Understanding the process a culture uses to make a decision is critical if you hope to help people in that culture make a commitment to follow Christ.

- *Challenge the culture.* One of God's primary goals is to bring his redemptive power to bear transforming the surrounding culture through the church. The church actively cultivates a worldview where God is king, Christ is at the center and everything else finds its place in him (cf. Colossians 1). That requires the prophetic task of challenging the culture in which we live.

- *Appeal to the listeners.* The third step of contextualization is making an appeal to those who will listen in a manner they will find compelling. That is why it is so important to determine how particular cultures come to decisions during the "entering" step.

As congregations "sink deep" both into God's Word and also into the community they are a part of, they become increasingly able to share biblical truth in actions and words that make sense to the community. Just as Jesus spent time in prayer but also went out into communities with the announcement of God's Kingdom (Matthew 4:23), we are called to spend time with God in order to be sent into the world (Matthew 28:18-20). In the book of Acts, the Holy Spirit–empowered people of God were to carry the gospel to Jerusalem (their immediate community), all Judea (their immediate region), Samaria (the neighboring, culturally different region), and the ends of the earth (Acts 1:8). Healthy churches will connect the text to the context being both faithful to Scripture and relevant to the culture in which they minister.

LIVING WORD

CONTEXT

CONTEXT

HOLY SPIRIT

CHURCH IN MISSION

CONTEXT

Integration of TEXT & CONTEXT mediated through Scripture, the Holy Spirit and the Church in mission

CONCLUSION

In this chapter, we've presented the five vital commitments for effective ministry: (1) clear and inspiring vision, (2) mobilizing leadership, (3) motivated ministering body, (4) proper stewardship of resources, and (5) the integration of text and context.

Each pastor should evaluate with his leadership if the church is living up to these commitments. If not, it should serve as a wake up call to make improvements in order to nurture a healthy church.

Now, with this foundation, we can transition to the next chapter, where we will discuss the five vital functions that have to be developed in a healthy church.

Questions

1. Explain your understanding of Ephesians 3:10-11 and its importance for issues of church development.

2. What are the three key ingredients in clarifying your vision according to the authors?

3. Choose your favorite element of the Eight Key Elements of Vision and explain why you think it is critical.

4. List the three Missional Characteristics of mobilizing leadership and provide your own definition.

5. How is the revitalizer leader different than the operator leader? How are they similar?

6. Do you think most Christians know what their spiritual gift is? Support your answer with some examples.

7. What do you think is the biggest challenge in your setting in terms of management and administration of resources?

8. What does being faithful to Scripture mean to you? How would this be evidenced in congregational life?

9. What does being relevant to culture mean to you? How would this be evidenced in congregational life?

10. Which of the five key commitments do you think needs more attention in your particular context? Why?

8 FIVE FUNCTIONS OF A HEALTHY CHURCH

Tim Koster & John Wagenveld

Editor's note: Chapter 7 and 8 are available in a more complete book version which can be downloaded for free at www.multiplicationnetwork.org.

The five indispensable functions upon which a healthy church is built are:

1. a compelling *witness* (the evangelistic function),
2. a comprehensive *discipleship*,
3. a compassionate *service*,
4. a caring and welcoming *community*,
5. a dynamic *worship and prayer*.[1]

Introduction

"Those who accepted his message were baptized, and about three thousand were added to their number that day. They devoted themselves to the apostles' teaching and to the fellowship, to the breaking of bread and to prayer. Everyone was filled with awe, and many wonders and miraculous

---

1   Chapters 7 and 8 are a condensation of the book *Take Your Church's Pulse: Ten Characteristics of a Healthy Church*, by the same authors, offered as an ebook by Multiplication Network Ministries. A free download can be obtained by going to www.multiplicationnetwork.com.

signs were done by the apostles. All the believers were together and had everything in common. Selling their possessions and goods, they gave to anyone as he had need. Every day they continued to meet together in the temple courts. They broke bread in their homes and ate together with glad and sincere hearts, praising God and enjoying the favor of all the people. And the Lord added to their number daily those who were being saved" Acts 2:41-47.

The Bible, from Genesis to Revelation, contains abundant evidence that God has a plan for his creation. But when we reflect on the function of the Church— God's central instrument for bearing witness to his kingdom and reign—we think of the Church that is described in this very familiar passage. On Pentecost, the Church receives power from on high to achieve God's purposes. God's Spirit is poured out on the Church so that it can carry out Christ's orders. This Church is dynamic, joyful, and enthusiastic; it is also obedient, suffering, and faithful to its Lord. But we only have to read the rest of the book to see that it also faces conflicts, false teachers, deceivers, jealousy, and pride. However, in Acts 2:41-47, the Church is seen in its first love, fulfilling the functions and purposes for which Christ established it. We remember that Christ himself said, "I will build my Church" (Matthew16:18). Jesus glorifies the Father by building his Church and extending his mission. In the following pages, we will identify the purposes of the Church in this passage from Acts 2 and suggest some ideas for healthy conversations in the local congregation.

I. FIRST FUNCTION: COMPELLING WITNESS (The Evangelistic Function)

The Church announces the good news of Jesus Christ in word and in deed and invites people to be a part of the Kingdom of God.

"And the Lord added to their number daily those who were being saved" (Acts 2:47).

We are compelled to obey the biblical imperative to go and make disciples of all nations. The last command Christ gave us before he ascended into heaven should be our first priority. We cannot settle for merely a testimony of presence; rather, when and wherever possible, we have to verbally proclaim the good news of Jesus Christ. Jesus' initial invitation to his disciples affirms that he calls us for this purpose: "Come, follow me, and I will make you fishers of men" (Mark 1:17).

The New Testament uses derivations of the Greek word for witness (*martys*) more than two hundred times. One who testifies (*martyreo*) and gives his testimony (*martyrion*) fulfills the biblical command for all Christians (Luke 24:48 and Acts 1:8). It is interesting to note that the word "martyr," one who dies for a cause, is derived from *martyreo*. Giving testimony to the Lord Jesus Christ in many cases has meant suffering, discomfort, and even death. Some have said that the blood of the martyrs is the seed for new converts.

Each local church should find a method that is appropriate to its context and put it into practice. There are too many conferences on this topic and too little implementation. A lady once criticized the evangelism methods used by Dwight L. Moody, the famed 19th century American pastor, to win people to saving faith in the Lord Jesus Christ. In response Moody replied, "I agree with you. I don't like the way I do it either. Tell me, how do you do it?" Moody's critic answered, "I don't do it." Moody quipped, "In that case, I like my way of doing it better than your way of not doing it."[2] *What is important is for the church to choose some way to evangelize and to practice this evangelism in a consistent fashion that is relevant to its community and faithful to the gospel!*

A. Know the People You Hope to Reach

Getting to know the people you are hoping to reach happens on two levels. The first is in a more clinical, demographic way. Define the characteristics of your culture. Where is it spiritually? Is it Christianized so that even if the members of your community aren't believers, they still have an awareness of God, respect Scripture, and treasure basic Judeo-Christian values? Is it a post-Christian secular community where notions of God are dismissed, truth is defined by science, and values are relativistic based on "what's working for me right now"? Does your community have Islamic, Hindu, Buddhist, or other religious roots? Is it an honor/shame culture or an individualistic one? What are its idols: family, success, fame, wealth, scientific truth, military strength, sexual prowess? Where do its mores diverge from Christian values? Who in society is valued and who is devalued? How are the vulnerable–women, children, poor, disabled, minority groups–treated?

---

2 James Hewett, *Illustrations Unlimited*, 178.

B. Identify a Niche Group

In the end, these observations, bathed in prayer, should lead to two discoveries. The first is whether there is a particular niche group in your community whom God is calling you to reach.

Prince of Peace Church, a church plant initiated by John in Puerto Rico, decided to concentrate on young couples with small children because there was a great need to help this group of people. Emmanuel, the church Tim pastors, was led in a different direction. He chose drug addicts and alcoholics as the niche group. As you get to know your community, God will make it clear whom you are to reach.

C. Identify Stumbling Blocks

The second discovery is the identification of the stumbling blocks the people in your community are likely to face, either on the path to believing or immediately after believing as that fledgling faith is tested. Odds are that there will be 10-20 predictable mini- questions that will need to be addressed on the way to the Big Question of "What will I do with Jesus?" Some will be universal to human nature: Am I ready to admit I am broken and sinful and need God's help? Others will be more culturally specific. For example, in a Christianized society, God's existence may not be a question at all. In a secular community, it may be a big hurdle. In an Islamic community, the shift in the concept of God from a God of hard, unyielding demands to a God of grace may become the stumbling block. Do I dare break with the traditions and expectations of my family? Is the Bible literature, ancient wisdom, or God's Word? Am I ready to shift from business practices that made me wealthy? What do I do with this new set of sexual boundaries?

The point of laying out the map of potential objections is to be prepared to help those you hope to reach count the cost and have a clear picture of the decision they are making. In addition, the map will help you design your ministry in such a way that not just what you say but what you do and how you do it will break down all barriers except the barrier of the gospel itself.

D. Decide How the Whole Church Can Participate

When Jesus sent the disciples out to visit the villages, he sent them out in pairs. No one went alone. In the same way, it is wise to work together as a congregation. We are always more effective as a team than as a group of individuals. The key is to have a plan for getting as many members as possible involved and training them to play their part.

There are many models for accomplishing this teamwork. Many churches now use small groups as a point of entry. Ideally, anyone can invite someone new, but each member in the group adds something to the mix: hospitality, prayer support, explaining Scripture, refreshments, or readiness to serve in other practical ways. Still others try to get as many members involved in targeted ministries to the community with training for identifying opportunities that point back to Christ. One church used a strategy they called Servant Evangelism, in which they went out in groups doing small acts of kindness for strangers: handing out cans of refreshment on a hot day, putting change in parking meters so others could park for free, etc. Every once in a while, this act of kindness would spark a conversation that would start a friendship, and eventually, get someone on a path towards Christ.

Another approach that has long been popular is an invitation model, where the congregation hosts either a unique event or a designated worship service at a regular interval where the primary responsibility of the members is to invite others so they can hear the gospel explained by someone gifted to do it well.

A third approach involves equipping every member with a simple gospel presentation, often in booklet form, that they are trained to explain themselves, with an invitation to worship as a follow-up step. Evangelism Explosion, Four Spiritual Laws, and Steps to Peace with God are classics. Though they work best in a culture with some Christian understanding, they can be modified to fit a number of different situations.

E. Tell Our Story and God's Story

One of the most helpful gifts we can offer members of the congregations we serve is the ability to see their own personal stories as they fit in God's story with its themes of Creation, Fall, Redemption, and Restoration. Part of understanding this happens as they come to faith, repenting and believing in Christ. Discipleship fleshes out the larger picture. While salvation is very personal for people, their salvation is only one small piece of God's comprehensive plan.

When members grasp the connection between the two stories— their own story and God's larger plan—they have a natural way to witness in a compelling manner. They simply tell their own story, making connections to the larger story and turning it into an invitation to others to come and join the larger story as well. This transforms a "canned or prepackaged" gospel presentation into a personal, practical account of God's love.

Because the themes in most gospel presentations are rooted in Scripture, any of them could profitably be used to help members draw the connections. But to illustrate, we will use "The Big Story" presentation, adapted from James Choung.[3]

F. "The Big Story"

The Big Story starts with the world the way it is: messed up. Parts are missing, parts are bent, and parts are broken. Relationships are strained and even disrupted between us as human beings (divorce, crime, competition, jealousy, war), between us and God (feelings of guilt, shame, and lack of purpose or meaning), and us and creation (pollution, global warming, natural disasters). It is fairly easy for us all to agree that this is not life the way it ought to be.

LIFE:
THE WAY IT IS

---

3   James Choung, "Big Story."

That very sense that "this is not the way it ought to be" suggests that we innately know that there is a way that it should be. Either it once was something much better or we anticipate that it one day will be much better. Christians believe both to be true. We call the ideal world, the way God made it to be, Creation. We call life the way it is now, the Fall, because by our own selfish desires and greed; we tried to grab control and use it for our benefit, and in the process, we have warped and distorted the world into something less than it could have been.

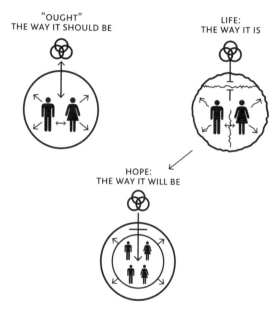

However, we also live in hope that one day this world will be restored. Life will be better. We will experience joy and all the parts of creation will live in harmony again. In fact, you see a great number of organizations out there striving for just that. They are trying to save endangered species, prevent global warming, stop human trafficking, offer marital counseling and job training, etc. There are thousands of ways to improve our world. Yet with all that effort, nothing seems to improve. It's like throwing rocks in the ocean in order to build a bridge between Europe and the Americas—it is simply beyond our capabilities. To see true restoration, we need to turn to the one who created the world in the first place. He is the only one with the resources to do the job, mostly because we have not mastered our own souls or conquered our own selfishness.

The good news is God sent Jesus into our world. Jesus became one of us yet never yielded to selfishness or sin. Instead of grasping for fame, power, or comfort, he sacrificed himself for the rest of us. He invites us to a renewed relationship with God and with each other. He offers forgiveness for the places we have messed up and the power of the Holy Spirit to transform our lives. All we need to do is admit to ourselves and to him how badly we have messed up, invite him to do his work for us and in us, and trust him enough to live life his way instead of our way. That's Redemption.

CREATION
THE WAY IT WAS

FALL
THE WAY IT IS

RESTORATION
THE WAY IT WILL BE

REDEMPTION
THE WAY IT CAN BE

The reality is that God isn't just redeeming and restoring us as individuals. He is drawing us together as his family, Christ's body, the Church. And he doesn't just leave us sitting on the sidelines as an audience watching while he works. We don't sit on our hands waiting for Christ to return and sort it all out. We have mission, purpose, and meaning. God invites us to join him in what he is doing. We are his agents as he remakes this world.

G. Helping Others Tell Their Stories

Here are some questions that will help people connect their personal story with the Big Story.

1. How is your life messed up and "fallen?" In what ways is it less than it ought to be?
2. How does that differ from the potential God had for you when he made you? What could have been? What are the circumstances of your life that set you on the path to your personal fall? What are the choices you made that helped bring you down?
3. How did God step into your life? How did you first learn the story of Jesus Christ? How did it move from being a story to a personal conviction that Jesus lived, died, and rose again for you?
4. How has God restored your life? What broken parts have been healed? Which parts are still awaiting healing?
5. What has it meant to you to be a member of God's gathered community? How has he invited you individually and as part of the body to make a difference in this world? How are you an agent of restoration for him?

Finally, once members can tell their stories in the context of God's story, ask them to share it with you and with each other before they share it with the world. This accomplishes three things. First, it gets them used to saying the words aloud. Second, it builds confidence as they encourage each other and recognize they are not alone in this. Third, it helps them discern how God works differently in different people's lives within the same framework.

The best part of this approach to training is that members never have to struggle to remember what part comes next or worry about missing an important element. All they need to do is tell their story and what they know already.

H. Pursue a Total Encounter with Jesus

There are at least three kind of encounters between a person and Christ. R. Daniel Shaw and Charles Van Engen summarize Kraft's typology of encounters in *Communicating God's Word in a Complex World*.[4]

Kraft Types Of Encounter

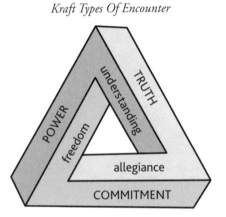

I. A Power Encounter

This encounter recognizes that God is reconciling the world to himself and that—in Christ—Satan, the enemy, has already been defeated. Through the Spirit of God, the gospel confronts every culture, the power of sin, and the evil one. This reality becomes even more obvious as the second coming of Jesus approaches, when all things will be brought to completion in the new heavens and the new earth. In the meantime, we are in a spiritual battle. The result of a power encounter with Jesus is freedom in Christ. Biblical texts like Ephesians 3:10 and 6:12 make it clear the Church is involved in the struggle against the principalities and powers and not just "against flesh and blood." The battle occurs at cosmic, community, and individual levels. Christ's victory over death, Satan, and evil equips us against the pride still evident in human rebellion and the idolatries of our time (misuse of good things like power, wealth and sex, for example).

---

4   R. Daniel Shaw and Charles Van Engen, *Communicating God's Word in a Complex World*, 179-80.

Many people in different parts of the world are guided by power. Many respond favorably to the gospel when they understand the changes Christ can make in their lives, their marriages, their families, and their communities. Only Christ fills the emptiness they have and gives them eternal life.

Declaring victory in Christ over the enemy and over sin is a very effective weapon in the church's evangelistic work, but it is incomplete if a balance is not maintained with the other two types of encounters that follow.

J.   A Truth Encounter

Here the concept is to know Christ in a true and correct way. This may include academic and theological/philosophical understanding, although it also includes the personal truth of subjective experience. The vehicle for this type of encounter is good teaching. The knowledge of the truth in Jesus Christ allows Christians to interpret and understand the other types of encounters. When the Lord gave a demonstration of his power, he almost always used it to teach his followers. Teaching is what leads a disciple into the truth. It is interesting to note that the favorite title of Jesus for the Holy Spirit is "the Spirit of Truth" (see, for example, John 15-16). What a difference it would make if this biblical truth were recognized!

K.   A Commitment Encounter

This is the most important of the three encounters. It demands total faithfulness to Jesus Christ and focuses on the person's submission to the lordship of Jesus. This involves a lifelong journey of obedience and service to God. Believers submit their will to the Lord through his Word, and after recognizing the power of God and being taught in his ways, they submit their lives to God through a serious and faithful commitment. This is the command of discipleship.

II. SECOND FUNCTION: COMPREHENSIVE DISCIPLESHIP

The Church helps people to see Jesus clearly and to know his will for their lives. It equips them to follow him in all aspects of life.

"They devoted themselves to the apostles' teaching..." (Acts 2:42)

The early church understood clearly that its foundation was the teaching of Jesus. The word "doctrine" means teaching. The disciples studied the teachings of the apostles, repeatedly reviewed them, and practiced them. They used the framework of those teachings to evaluate every new idea. Even the Jews of the synagogue in Berea analyzed what Paul had told them according to the Scriptures (Acts 17:11). The passage continues: "Many of them believed!"

"Disciple" (mathetes in Greek) means one who learns, but more akin to apprentice than student. The disciple follows Jesus and learns from him, but not just head knowledge. Discipleship requires absorbing behavior, character, attitudes, perspectives—a total worldview. When Jesus gave the Great Commission in Matthew 28, he commanded the apostles not only to baptize but also to teach to fully follow Christ's teachings. They were not to simply dispense doctrine but also instruction in how to live out truths from God's Word. Being a disciple, therefore, requires one to persevere in both the study of God's Word and the incorporation of those truths into one's life. This was the foundation of the early church. And it should be the foundation today for every congregation that is serious and committed to the Lord.

In Ephesians 4, Paul calls us to Christian maturity. The Gospels say that we should be like children in terms of our faith, but this does not mean that we are to be childish or immature. Paul says we should no longer be "infants, tossed back and forth by the waves," but rather we should grow up into Christ, who is the Head (Ephesians 4:14-15).

At the same time, it is important to note the vital connection between evangelism and discipleship. They flow from one directly to the other. The process is largely the same in both. Both work incarnationally as both unbelievers and growing believers see and experience the teachings of Christ animated in the lives of believers. Both are communal, becoming richer and more fully balanced as the body of believers each invest their strengths and insights into the mix. Both happen in stages, often messy stages, as we relinquish parts of our lives to Christ while continuing to retain, often subconsciously, other portions. While our salvation may be secure in Christ, even mature believers continue to require a fresh application of the gospel as the Spirit continues his saving work.

A. "Persons who learn"

As we saw previously, mathetes means one who learns. The word "mathematics" is derived from this word. We may not like to learn mathematics, but those who say they are Christians must learn to follow the Lord. We are apprentices and followers of the Lord. Luke 6:25-35, perhaps one of the most demanding passages about discipleship, orders us to renounce everything in order to be Christ's disciples. Jesus says, "Anyone who does not carry his cross and follow me cannot be my disciple" (Luke 14:27). Discipleship, therefore, has to do with a total surrender to the Lord Jesus Christ, a surrender that includes all aspects of the relationship between the believer and God.

Dimensions Of Discipleship

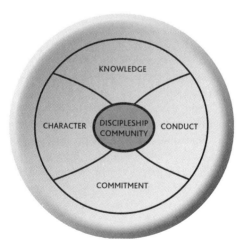

To remember the central aspects of the process of spiritual maturity, it can be helpful to recognize that discipleship consists of knowing, doing, being, and willing; also, it promotes growth using head, hands, and heart. These are simple ways of expressing that there cannot be spiritual growth if one is not growing in knowledge, conduct, character, and commitment.

B. Knowledge: Knowing

Biblical knowledge always develops on two different levels. One is focused on the content. There are a variety of biblical concepts we need to comprehend and tuck away in our brains: that there is a God, that he made us and the world we are in, that the human race corrupted his creation including ourselves by our sin, and that he sent his Son into this world to set things right. The list goes on: the Trinity, the Holy Spirit, providence, grace, resurrection, and so on. Long term it is difficult to grow in faith without growing in an understanding of the content of that faith.

Part of the task of discipleship is coming to the realization that all of those wonderful biblical doctrines are true for me personally. That is the type of knowledge that becomes transformative in every area of life, hands and heart as well as head.

C. Conduct: Doing

Conduct is one of the most evident ways to show the fruit of what God is doing in our lives. We should create good habits that shape our lives, such as dedicating time to prayer, to Bible study, and to family recreation. Sometimes we replace obedience with merely the knowledge of biblical teachings. James instructs us: "Do not merely listen to the word, and so deceive yourselves. Do what it says" (1:22). Our conduct should complement our biblical knowledge. The way we conduct ourselves in the Christian life will be one of the methods that God will use to make his gospel known. We are, in a way, the open Bible before the nonbelieving community.

D. Character: Being

This aspect of our personhood is being forged blow by blow on the anvil of life and in the context of community. Character is often described as who we are when no one else is looking. The Christian's character grows in maturity in the measure that the person submits all of his or her life to the lordship of Jesus Christ. The person sees things with the eyes of Christ and develops a perspective on life and the world—a worldview—more in tune with that of God and his Word. Character goes much deeper than an isolated action that we perform. It is something that we work on long-term. This old proverb sums it up well: "It takes a second to make a hero, but it takes an entire life to make a good man."

E. Commitment: Willing

When we submit our will to Christ, we turn everything over to him. In this endeavor, commitment is necessary because we often balk at following Christ. What he asks of us may not make sense to us, may require sacrifice, or may be contrary to our own desires and plans. In such moments, it requires a Spirit-aided act of the will to steel ourselves to do what we know is right. Jesus evidenced that kind of determination as he came down from the glorious experience of the Transfiguration in Luke 19. In that moment, Luke tells us, Jesus "set his face" to go to Jerusalem and face the cross. The early Christians also inspire us: with their blood they planted the seed of the gospel. In a time like the one in which we live, it is even more important to take note of the commitment that arises from a real transformation in Jesus Christ. It is God himself who is perfecting us and strengthening us through committed discipleship. Let's listen to what the Word of God tells us:

> Be self-controlled and alert. Your enemy the devil prowls
> around like a roaring lion looking for someone to devour.
> Resist him, standing firm in the faith, because you know that
> your brothers throughout the world are undergoing the same
> kind of sufferings. And the God of all grace, who called you
> to his eternal glory in Christ, after you have suffered a little
> while, will himself restore you and make you strong, firm,
> and steadfast (1 Peter 5:8-10).

F. A Profound Transformation

Discipleship also depends on a change of worldview—a new way to see and interpret the world and reality. A biblical worldview covers all areas of life and does not allow the segmentation of faith. The following diagrams show the difference between a segmented and an integrated view of faith and life.

A Segmented View vs. An Integrated View of Faith and Life

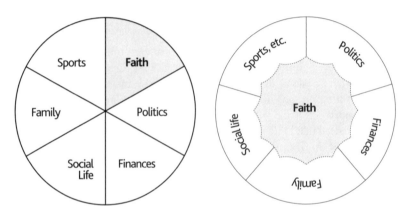

Faith should affect and influence every sphere of life. A biblical world-view should affect the values that drive our actions, our behaviors, and our attitudes. These in turn will have consequences that should glorify God. The consequences of a biblical worldview are generally good and positive. For example, an alcoholic changes his way of thinking and seeing life and now treats his wife better, teaches his children, and takes care of his finances. But sometimes the consequences of having a biblical worldview can bring suffering or persecution, as in the case of a person who converts to Christianity in a Muslim context and is then rejected by the rest of the community. In any case, the goal of discipleship is to bring about a radical change in a person's worldview, leading to the transformation of the rest of his or her life.

BIBLICAL WORLDVIEW AS FOUNDATION FOR DISCIPLESHIP

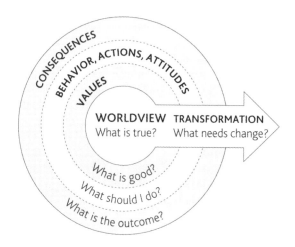

Adapted from John Wagenveld, *Sembremos Iglesias Saludables*, 275.

G. Putting It All Together

Developing a comprehensive, congregational approach to discipleship that effectively mixes all of the ingredients listed above is as complex and varied as the people it hopes to cultivate. However, the task becomes more manageable when visualized in terms of tools and outcomes.

H. Tools

Discipleship tools fall into two basic categories: Information and Practice. Think of it in terms of learning a musical instrument. There is an element of knowledge. There are notes and chords, scales and rhythms that need to be firmly planted in one's head. Still they are not mastered until they are practiced frequently enough that one's fingers can play them smoothly without deliberate thought.

So too discipleship starts with content. Followers of Christ need to have a grasp of Scripture, particularly the story of Christ himself. His birth, his character, his teaching, his miracles, his love, and his anger, his death and his resurrection--all are lessons to be absorbed. The basics of Christian doctrine are also essential lessons used to understand the Christian faith.

This leads to the second tool of discipleship: practice. The disciple can engage in activities that develop the "muscle memory" of Christian habits. Disciples can pray together in worship, in small groups, in family settings, as well as one-on-one. This way they can learn the feel and rhythm of prayer. They can tackle a portion of Scripture together devotionally so they have a sense of what personal time in God's Word can feel like. Christian service, working side- by-side with someone, is also a key ingredient in the formation of a disciple. Reflecting afterwards, noting not only results but attitudes, can also be helpful. Engaging in Christian fellowship in small groups and with the congregation as a whole also nurtures the habits of the heart.

I. Outcomes

While information and practice are both vital to discipleship, the goal is never to pass a Bible test or to be an expert in spiritual disciplines. A comprehensive discipleship process will seek two outcomes.

The first is Christ-shaped lives. As Paul puts it in Ephesians 4:23-24, "[You were taught] to be made new in the attitude of your minds; and to put on the new self, created to be like God in true righteousness and holiness." Our measure is not whether we know the right things or do the right things but whether we reflect the character of Christ. After one year or five, will the people we disciple exhibit more of the fruit of the Spirit: love, joy, peace, forbearance, kindness, goodness, faithfulness, gentleness, and self-control (Galatians 5:22-23)? Will their spouses, children, friends, and co-workers endorse a positive change? Over and over the New Testament indicates that true discipleship will be reflected in how we treat others, from our brothers and sisters in Christ (1 John) to those with a different ethnic and religious background (parable of the Good Samaritan). Jesus' ultimate litmus test is how we treat the most vulnerable and powerless when no one else is looking (Matthew 25:31-46). Discipleship is rooted in the teaching of scripture and the formation of Christian habits, but it finds its home in our hearts and relationships.

Yet there is a second outcome that discipleship aims for as well: passing it on. Gospel-centered formation will lead to multiplication. When we integrate Christ into our lives or ours into Christ, the natural result is a desire to let others in on our discovery, to share our story, to share HIS story. There is no room for spiritual gluttony where we keep absorbing more and more of Christ's blessings without spilling that life over into others. For some, this expression is direct and verbal as they share their faith evangelistically. Others show their gratitude forward by discipling others. Paul teaches his disciple, Timothy: "And the things you have heard me say in the presence of many witnesses entrust to reliable men who will also be qualified to teach others" (2 Timothy 2:2. See also Ephesians 3:16-17).

III. THIRD FUNCTION: COMPASSIONATE SERVICE

The Church meets people's needs in the name of Christ and invites them to be disciples.

"Selling their possessions and goods, they gave to anyone as he had need" (Acts 2:45).

The early church shared its goods among the faithful and also gave to people in need. This impressed the people living around the church and testified to the strength of Christian love. The internal change Christ had made in their lives showed in external works that changed society. Spiritual transformation carried with it a social and community commitment. Although we know from other texts that not everyone sold their property, many did so to help the common good. This is very much in agreement with what we read in the book of James, when he says that "faith without works is dead" (2:17). Works demonstrate one's transformation by grace in Jesus Christ. And although works do not contribute to salvation which is by grace alone (Ephesians 2:8-9), they help us to live the Christian life in a dynamic and edifying way. In theological terms, works do not fall under justification, but under the sanctification of the believer. Sanctification—holiness—involves being *set apart*. Unfortunately, a large part of the church has only focused on being *set apart FROM* and has neglected the other dimension of being *set apart FOR*. In other words, a true vocation of holiness is not just a separateness "from the patterns of this world" (Romans 12:2) but a call into mission and service in the world, joining the Spirit in his transformative activity in the world.

Models of Church in Relationship to the World

ESCAPE
Emphasizes separateness from the world.
Holiness means "stay clean."

ENGAGE
Emphasizes cultural engagement.
Holiness means participating in
God's redemptive reign and
restoration of all things in Christ as
salt and light.

ACCOMMODATE
Emphasizes identification with the world to
the extent that the gospel is compromised.
Holiness is exchanged for cultural conformity

The graphic above helps explain there are churches whose self-understanding is to be separate from the world. These churches usually emphasize the "other-world" aspects of the gospel. On the other extreme are churches who want to identify with the surrounding culture so much that they compromise the integrity of the gospel. A healthy church will have a balanced and contextual approach to incarnating the values of the gospel and engage culture with the claims of Christ. There is a wide range of callings for the church that span from evangelism to working for justice and creation care.

Serving others in a fallen world, led by the Spirit, is a way of participating with God in bringing about redemption and recreation within the world. The biblical narrative bookends the role of God's people as participation in God's mission to bring back all things into right relationship with God (fixing the mess of the Garden) but, more than that, looking forward in hope to the beautiful, ordered society in the new city where all things will be as they should be.

Bringing all things to right relationship with God involves unmasking the principalities and powers which were disarmed in Christ's death and resurrection. The Holy Spirit empowers the Church to do this work in all kinds of ways. Ephesians 4 tells us that each member of the body is gifted for a particular kind of activity of service and testimony. The entire body, working together, is involved in helping to build one another up and in sharing with those who are in need. Ephesians 2:10 tells us, "We are God's workmanship, created in Christ Jesus to do good works, which God prepared in advance for us to do." The command to serve is clear. Jesus himself said that he did not come to be served, but to serve (Matthew 20:28).

A. Without Service, It's Worthless

The church that worships and maintains good communion among the flock but does not serve others is incomplete. All Christians should find their place of service to God by finding ministries that use their God-given gifts. Whether it's something simple, like sweeping a meeting place, or very complex, like fighting against oppression and injustice, each Christian must participate in an area of service individually and corporately. This function of the church cannot be missing in a congregation that wishes to grow in a holistic and healthy way.

We need a holistic strategy that understands evangelism and social activism as the two parts of a pair of scissors or the two wings of a bird. With just one side, scissors do not cut; with one wing, a bird doesn't fly. What happens if we row on just one side of a boat? The boat will just go in circles. It won't move forward. Likewise, we cannot present a compelling testimony to the world if we do not integrate social action with evangelism.

The evangelical world, with representatives from many countries, came together to discuss the issue of social action and evangelism in the International Consultation on the Relationship between Evangelism and Social Responsibility, held in Grand Rapids, Michigan (USA), in 1982. This meeting was sponsored by the Lausanne Committee for World Evangelization and the World Evangelical Fellowship.[5] During this event, the representatives agreed that the divorce between evangelism and social responsibility reflected a dualistic thinking, dividing the spiritual and the physical. While the Bible distinguishes between the two, it teaches that they are related and should be kept together.

At the conference, the relationship between evangelism and social responsibility was discussed in depth, and the participants recognized that social action can have three types of healthy relationships with evangelism:

1. Social action as a CONSEQUENCE of evangelism. God changes people when they are born again, and their new life is made evident in the way that they serve others. In 1 John 3:16-18, the Scripture teaches us to show the love that God gave us by loving our brothers

---

5   James Scherer and Stephen Bevans, *New Directions in Mission and Evangelization*, 278-80.

and sisters, serving their needs, and being ready to give our own lives for them.

2. Social action as a BRIDGE to evangelism. Many times Jesus healed or acted with mercy toward people before proclaiming to them the good news. Social action for our neighbors causes them to pay more attention when we speak to them about the gospel but is good in and of itself. Helping nonbelievers when they are going through material problems allows us to get to the more profound needs of eternal salvation. As an African proverb says, "Empty stomachs do not have ears." Social action opens doors and ears, and it builds bridges to those who haven't heard the gospel.

3. Social action as a COMPANION to evangelism. In the letter of James, we see that faith and works go together. We know that we do good works in gratitude for the faith that God gives us, and that they facilitate a living and productive faith that benefits others. In the same way, *diakonía* (ministry of service and mercy) and *kerygma* (proclamation of the gospel) are united.

Transforming salvation not only includes people who are forgiven of their particular sins, but it also seeks to change unjust structures that promote systemic and institutional sin (like racism, economic oppression, unethical legal systems, etc.). Look for the way that your church can participate in service to your community according to its needs, and you will see the Lord transforming lives and communities with a holistic gospel.

B. New Heaven and New Earth

Isaiah 65 and Revelation 21 teach us that God is bringing about a new heaven and a new earth. This is the end game: the renewal and restoration of all things in Christ. While only God can make this happen, he invites the Church to participate with him in this recreation activity and to be a foretaste of the kingdom that Jesus inaugurated with his coming to Earth. The Church acts as a demonstration plot for the wider world.

IV. FOURTH FUNCTION: CARING AND WELCOMING COMMU-NITY

Members help each other with their burdens, thus showing the love and compassion of Christ.

"They devoted themselves...to the fellowship... All the believers were together and had everything in common... Every day they continued to meet together... They broke bread in their home and ate together with glad and sincere hearts" (Acts 2:42, 44, 46).

Christian life is sharing with others in fraternal love. The important thing is to never forget the missionary purpose of koinonia, as Jesus prayed: "...so that the world may believe that you have sent me" (John 17:21).

Without a doubt, one of the biggest reasons for new converts to join and remain in a congregation is that they feel the fellowship of their brothers and sisters in Christ. If there is no authentic fellowship, people leave and look for alternatives that can satisfy these basic needs that God created in us.

Theologically, we believe God is Triune: Father, Son, and Holy Spirit. They form the first and perfect community—diversity in unity. Man is made in God's image. Therefore, it stands to reason, we are made for community as well! We are designed this way by the Creator.

A. "One Another"

It is interesting to note the number of commandments in the New Testament that deal with how people are to treat each other in community. Let's look at some examples.

"Dear friends, let us love ONE ANOTHER..." (1 John 4:7).

"So then, my brothers, when you come together to eat, wait for EACH OTHER..." (1 Corinthians 11:33).

"...So that there should be no division in the body, but that its parts should have equal concern for EACH OTHER" (1 Corinthians 12:25).

"Be kind and compassionate to ONE ANOTHER, forgiving EACH OTHER..." (Ephesians 4:32).

"Submit to ONE ANOTHER out of reverence for Christ" (Ephesians 5:21).

"But encourage ONE ANOTHER daily..." (Hebrews 3:13).

"Therefore confess your sins to EACH OTHER and pray for EACH OTHER..." (James 5:16).

It is evident that the Christian faith should not be lived in solitude or isolated from the brothers and sisters of our community (Hebrews 10:25). Sadly, the entire world is now influenced by individualistic Western culture, a culture that seeks to make us self-sufficient and, with new technologies, isolates us, both through entertainment and faceless communication. The individual spends more time producing and consuming and less time relating to others.

People are made to relate and the worship gatherings should be no exception. It is impressive to note the enormous difference there is between two Christian meetings, one in which people depart as soon as the service has ended, and another where people look for each other, talk, and share. Churches that grow know how valuable it is for the members to have good relationships where they can practice the love and friendship they share in concrete ways. Unfortunately, there are some churches that do many things well, but have this serious problem: they are cold when it comes to expressing love and fellowship among the leaders and the congregants. Church leaders should cultivate the presence of God in our midst, through community, from the launch of the congregation. While we cultivate this characteristic, it is good to be aware that it is God actually doing it!

B.   A Community Ministering Together

Healthy church leadership knows how to incorporate new arrivals adequately into the life of the church. When one is planting a new congregation, the pastor should have thought out what the enfolding process will be for accepting people as members and engaging them in ministry. In trainings for church planters, we have participants write out on a large piece of paper the steps that new people arriving at the church can pass through to mature in the faith and grow until they become leaders. What ministries are there in your church to help Frank and Maria become a part of the work? How will they be received in the congregation? Who will make sure they feel at home? Who will train them? How will they become involved?

Then we ask the leaders to make a diagram, as shown here, with the logical sequence of existing ministries. Later we ask them to identify the gaps where they see they need more ministries. The idea is to have a specific plan to welcome people in with fraternal love and to provide ministries in which they can develop and have a sense of belonging and purpose.

POINTS OF CONTACT	POINTS OF RECEPTION	POINTS OF TRAINING	POINTS OF SERVICE
"Bring a Friend" Event	Intro to Bible Seminar	Women's Bible Study	Deacon
Community Service project	Weekly Worship	Discover Your Gifts Workshop	Children's Ministry
Small Group Friendship	Small Study Group	Ministry Apprenticeship	Community Development

Take a moment to design a diagram to show the steps that would be available in the church that you are planting or leading. Identify the ministries that you need, and ask yourself the following questions:

Do we have sufficient doors of entry for Frank and Maria?

Do we have enough ministries in a logical sequence, so that Frank and Maria can become trained leaders in our church?

What aspects should we improve, based on what we can see in the diagram?

To understand the role that different ministries in the church play in moving a person toward spiritual growth, it is helpful to think in four basic categories:

1. *Points of contact*

These are all of the church's ministries, formal or informal, through which the church can enter into contact with people who may be introduced to God and his people. These doors of entry may be special services, concerts, service to the community, or just contact with friends. In the graphic, one can see the different ways people can find entry into the church.

2. *Points of Reception*

These are all of the church's ministries, formal or informal, that enfold and incorporate new people into the congregation. If doors of entry are about reaching new people, points of reception are about helping them stick. One might ask, besides the Sunday worship service, what alternatives does the flock have to involve a person in the life of the congregation? Some examples may be a discipleship group, a class on basic doctrine with the pastor, or a shared meal at a member's home. Most of the time, it is about relationships.

3. *Points of Training*

These are all the ministries that help people grow in their knowledge of the faith and in their ability to live the Christian life according to biblical principles. They also help people to understand their spiritual gifts and use them for the extension of God's kingdom. Some examples include discipleship classes, small group workshops, guitar classes, conferences on family finances, Bible courses, or preaching classes.

4. *Points of Service and Ministry*
   These are all of the ministries that provide positions of service for new believers. It is very important for the church to find places of service and ministry for new members according to their gifts as soon as possible. It could be that a woman prepares food for poor people in the church's kitchen, or a young person could pursue training in how to use the Word to lead Bible studies. It is good to also provide service opportunities for people who might have a physical handicap or are mentally impaired. It is vital to have multiple entry-level points of service so that even those new to the faith have an opportunity to contribute.

C. Membership

We have talked about being a caring and welcoming community. People belong to a family as a covenantal community. This manifests itself in people wanting to become members of the local body of Christ. This membership implies certain privileges and responsibilities. Some traditions avoid formal church membership, embracing all who attend worship regularly as members. More frequently, congregations will have formal membership to avoid spiritual drift and clarify commitments to both Christ and his body. Either way, it is important for the church to clearly define expectations for new members and the steps they are expected to follow. In many congregations, people who accept the Lord go through classes of basic doctrine and sign a covenant of commitment when they join the church. Church planter Ralph Moore recommends asking five questions of all who desire to become members of a church:

1. Do you love Jesus Christ and recognize him as Lord of your life and of all creation?
2. Do you respect the leaders of this church and the church's vision?
3. Are you willing to spend time with your new faith family?
4. Do you promise to support the church financially?
5. Are you ready to serve God according to how the Spirit leads you?[6]

---

6 Ralph Moore, *Starting a New Church: The Church Planter's Guide to Success*, 225.

D. Small Group Ministry

One of the greatest tools for creating community is small group ministry. Many churches are recognizing the need to enfold and continue discipling new members through small groups so that they become more mature in the faith and continue to be nourished. Small groups of Christians provide opportunities to grow spiritually, to experience friendship and fellowship, to get advice, to serve others in times of need, to pray together, and to find support to face the situations of life. Small groups allow for intimacy that leads to mutual trust and deep life sharing, something that does not happen in large groups due to their different nature.

Some Advantages of Small Groups

• Flexibility for scheduling
• Flexibility in meeting location
• Less need for infrastructure (building, furniture, etc.)
• Greater companionship and sense of belonging
• More communication and participation
• More possibilities for intercession
• A better teaching process
• Ability to respond to specific needs
• More personal attention
• Easier development and multiplication of leaders
• Better geographic coverage

What do I do in a small group?

There is a significant amount of material and training to promote a very simple but effective agenda for healthy small groups. The agenda presented here is being used successfully in thousands of small groups in Latin America, Africa, Europe, and China. This agenda has some basic steps:

1. *Ice Breaker*

   This is a brief, non-threatening activity that is used so that those attending are integrated into the group, participate immediately, and put aside the possible distractions of their daily life. The ice breaker may be an activity in which they learn others' names or everyone shares something--for example, people's favorite foods, interesting anecdotes, or places they have visited. At this time it is not necessary to refer to biblical topics. The principal reason for the ice breaker is for everyone to have a chance to speak during the first few minutes of the meeting. Studies show that this will prompt people to share more openly during the Bible study time.

2. *Brief Prayer*

   Taking into account that those attending may not be familiar with prayer, the prayer should meet three requirements. It should be Audible, Brief, and Christocentric. This is the ABC of prayer. Remember that new people may imitate you in prayer, so the idea is to pray as briefly and simply as possible so that they feel that it is easy and they can do it.

   This could be a recommended prayer to begin the Bible study: "Thank you Lord for this day. We are here to study your Word and we ask that you help us to understand it. Open our minds and our hearts. In the name of Jesus. Amen."

3. *Song*

   Prepare this part ahead of time, choosing a simple song that is easy to learn, or have a way for people to read the words. Be mindful of the new person who does not know these songs.

4. *Testimony*

Have someone in the group give a brief testimony of God's work in their lives during the week. This will encourage people and provide an environment where they can share a story of what they are learning in their walk with the Lord.

5. *Bible Study*

This is generally the most important part of the meeting, and it should last half an hour to an hour. We recommend that meetings not go more than an hour and a half, so that new people can adjust to this new habit. Meetings that are too long can cause people to leave and not come back. For the study, you might choose a passage of the Bible and do an inductive study of it, or you might choose some appropriate Bible study material such as a denominational series.

6. *Intercessory Prayer*

Dedicate some time before ending the meeting to pray for each person in the group. This will strengthen the meeting and will build the sense of belonging for those who attend. Remember the prayer requests during the week and ask the participants in later meetings if the Lord has answered their prayers. The simple act of remembering their requests communicates that you are concerned for the members of your small group.

E. Counseling or Pastoral Care

When a church has small groups, much of the work that a pastor normally has to do is shared among the leaders. Many problems are solved at the level of the small group. The close relationship the members have with their leaders allows for intensive and adequate care among the members of the cell group.

F. Conflict in the Community

Every congregation will experience problems at some point in its ministry. A community can appear to be uncaring and unwelcoming due to internal conflicts. When mishandled, conflict can drive people from the church. When handled wisely, conflict can make a congregation stronger. It is likely that all of us have felt some conflict in our lives or witnessed it in our church. The first thing we need to recognize is that conflict is something that is real and normal. Even the apostles experienced conflict (Acts 6 and 15)!

The first step in resolving conflict is to identify the problem that is causing the conflict. If it can be identified and clearly defined, you've taken a big step towards resolving it. It is not constructive to say the other person is the problem. Both sides should analyze the situation as objectively as possible, trying to reach a solution through clear and effective communication in order to reach an outcome in which everyone wins and God is glorified.

After the problem is identified, follow the pattern of Matthew 18:15-17. We should first talk with our brother or sister in Christ. If the person does not listen, we should return with one or two other brothers or sisters in Christ. If the person still will not listen, we should take the situation before the community of faith.

There are extreme cases in which we find people who refuse to change and who only want to destroy the work of the church. You should treat them with respect and love, but firmly. If, after you've worked to resolve conflicts many times, they continue their destructive and divisive path, you must let them go so that they do not disturb the work and vision of the congregation.

V. FIFTH FUNCTION: DYNAMIC WORSHIP AND PRAYER

The church meets as the family of God with the Father in worship, confession, and gratitude, as well as dedicating itself to service and prayer.

"They persevered…in the breaking of bread and in prayer… praising God" (Acts 2:42, 47a).

The first Christians persevered also in the breaking of bread, in prayer, and in praise. A dynamic community like that of the first Christians gets its focus and vitality through worshiping and praising God. The preaching of the Word, as Peter had just finished doing in his first speech after Pentecost, was central. The breaking of bread is the equivalent of what we know today as the Lord's Supper or Communion, within the context of a larger meal. Remembering with the meal what the Lord Jesus Christ had experienced in his death and resurrection, the disciples were spiritually strengthened with the sacrament. They participated in Communion accompanied by a love feast that built community with each other as well as with Christ. Thirdly, through their prayers they were able to center their lives on the most important things without being distracted. Prayer was the lubricant that reduced friction between the brothers and sisters, so that they were able to face opposition, the sword, and even the lions in unity. Prayer included praise, gratitude, confession, and supplication. Prayer also prepared the group for the work of evangelization.

In its worship, the church needs to reach a balance between celebration and reverence to keep the worship service centered on the Word. "Celebration," because we Christians have the best reason in the world to celebrate and rejoice in thanks for what Christ has done for us. "Reverence," because we have a God who is not only our friend, but also our King and ruler. When there is a biblical balance, we can celebrate the love of God at the same time that we revere his power and majesty!

A. Worship in Established and Church Planting Contexts

For most of those who study church growth, church health and the missional church, worship is of primary importance in measuring progress in a congregation once it has been established; it is the time when the people of God meet to worship him and listen to his Word. Although worship is not limited to the time or the location of the public worship service, it is at that time that we can measure how certain things are going in the congregation. We observe the level of attendance in the service and we can gauge the level of commitment of the people to being the church gathered. We see the offerings and we can measure how the finances are doing.

We see the number of new visitors and see the results of evangelism. We see those who confess to the Lord, we observe the spirit of worship, and we see many parts of the system functioning at the same time. In *The Church Growth Handbook*, William Easum says that few factors influence church growth as much as the quality of worship. When worship meets people's needs and proves to be a true encounter between God and his people, the church tends to grow.[7]

---

7   William M Easum, *The Church Growth Handbook*, 49.

Worship is also key in church planting. Church planters first begin by making contacts through evangelism, and then they bring together the new converts in Bible study groups, seek commitments from the new believers, and identify and train leaders. Eventually the group begins to hold worship services. In most cases, it is recommended that church planters delay the beginning of worship services until they have consolidated good disciple-making in small groups. However, many people's first contact with a church happens at a corporate worship service. That is why we need to make a good connection. There will never be a second chance to make a first impression! We should consider, therefore, all the details to create an environment that leads to dynamic worship—reverent and celebratory.

B. Planning Worship

When a pastor wants to start having worship services, one of the best things to do is to establish a planning team. This team designs the services to fulfill the purposes of worship and the proposed worship style. It is great to see how some churches have Bible readings, songs, prayers, and the message synchronized around a particular theme. They then transmit it coherently through all these vehicles of communication. This requires careful planning, but it unleashes amazing creativity. Worship planned by a well-orchestrated team is more likely to be fresh and inviting.

C. The Desired Result of Worship

The worship service should be something that elevates and inspires. The deepest fiber of our being gets excited when we come before a God who has done marvelous, powerful things in the past, who assures our present, and who guards our certain future. We should appropriately take advantage of music, poetry, drama, and other artistic means to enrich our liturgy and order of service. Every church should create a dialogue in worship that includes all of the following points in some responsible way:

- God calls us to worship. The congregation of believers responds with jubilation.
- God calls us to repentance. All respond by confessing in prayer.
- God speaks through his Word. The community of faith responds with songs and offerings.
- God gives his blessing. The body responds by going out to serve.

D. The Worship Service and the Culture

When traveling to different continents, one quickly notices that worship can look very different from place to place. Some may ask how this can be, when we have the same God and the same Bible. The answer has to do with the fact that all worship occurs within a local culture. All belief and theology travels through a particular language and culture. The Lutheran World Federation Nairobi Statement on Worship and Culture proposes a framework that is helpful in understanding some of these meaningful aspects of worship.[8]

Worship should be...

Contextual: In the same way Christ humbled himself (Philippians 2) and identified himself with humanity in the form of a Jewish baby, people express their worship of God within their particular cultural context identifying with the local environment. All cultures of the world can worship God. A classic example is the use in Andean countries of musical instruments called the *charango* and the *bombo* to praise God.

Countercultural: In the same way that Christ turned over the tables of the vendors who were profaning the temple with their avarice and called the Pharisees a "brood of vipers," worship of God is expressed by confronting the aspects of the culture that go against the values of the gospel. Jesus Christ came to transform all cultures. The Word calls us not to conform to this world, but to be transformed by the renewing of our minds (Romans 12). Therefore, the worship service should reflect the culture but also confront it.

Cross-cultural & Multi-cultural: The book of Revelation (5:9;7:9) shows us that there will be people from every language, tribe, and nation in the kingdom of God. Jesus came to be the savior of every nation and not of just one while excluding others. Our worship service can also reflect the universality of the gospel and can make use of art, music, architecture, customs, and values of other cultures to enrich the liturgical act. How do we express the universality and intercultural nature of the gospel in our church?

Transcultural: In the same way the resurrection of Christ demonstrates a power and truth that goes beyond our understanding and culture, the worship

8   "Nairobi Statement on Worship and Culture."

service also reflects something beyond one or even the sum of all cultures. The gospel has supracultural aspects. The triune God and all his works (creation, redemption, sanctification, etc.) exceed human comprehension and take us beyond the possibility that any one culture or even all cultures together could express faith completely or perfectly. The Word says that even the peace of God "transcends all understanding" (Philippians 4:7), and 2 Peter 1:4 says, "...He has given us his very great and precious promises, so that through them you may participate in the divine nature and escape the corruption in the world caused by evil desires." What aspects of our worship help us to connect with a God that transcends every human culture?

Worship and Culture

TRANSCULTURAL

Reflects the mystery of faith
that goes beyond the
sum of all cultures

COUNTERCULTURAL

Confronts culture in a
biblical and prophetic way

CROSSCULTURAL

Learns from and is enriched by
the crossing of borders

CONTEXTUAL
Identifies with the culture,
seeking its transformation

Church leaders who take these four elements of the relationship between worship and culture into account will enrich the worship experience of the people with whom they work. The most important thing is for the worship service to reflect that God is alive, present, and in communion with his people. This will help in reaching the desired end: that through the experience of worship, the worshipers will leave to transform their culture for Christ.

E. Basic Considerations

The welcome visitors and congregants receive to the worship service is essential. This is the important part of *the ushers' ministry*, as they welcome people with a smile and with a desire to serve. It is key is to have some way to get to know the people and offer hospitality. Remember that many first time visitors decide that day if they will return to the worship service or not; therefore, receive them well. We should make every effort so the visitor feels the warmth of the Christian community and hears clearly the good news of salvation Christ offers.

The follow-up team is responsible for recognizing and taking advantage of each opportunity to find a date to visit the new attendees. If possible, it is good to send a note or make a telephone call to the new people, showing sincere interest in them and inviting visitors back to worship together.

Another consideration is *the size of the sanctuary and the number of seats that are available.* Sadly, many meeting places are built with very little vision for the future. Some churches limit their growth indefinitely because their buildings are too small or their property has no room for expansion. They choke off their growth before they even begin. When people arrive at a place that is nearly full, they feel squeezed and begin to be uncomfortable. When a congregation reaches 80 percent of its seating capacity, it should consider the options to enlarge its capacity: adding services, expanding the meeting place, or moving to a bigger location.

Biblical, solid preaching is essential for a healthy church. The messages should reach both the head and the heart. Challenges from the pulpit should be applicable to daily life and should strengthen today's family with healthy doctrine. Always craft your message, and the entire service, on the assumption that you are addressing at least one long term Christian and one person exploring the faith for the first time.

Adapt the program to your liturgical style, and encourage and urge people to take steps of faith in response to the spiritual transformation that God is carrying out in them. People appreciate challenges to action and opportunities to respond to the call of God. The answer to the call may be private or public. It is also good to provide opportunities so that during the course of the service (before, during, or after), people who desire prayer for special needs can come to the front or go to a special room where someone can accompany them in prayer.

Promote participation by the leaders and the members of the flock. Use their talents and gifts for the edification of the body during the worship service. The worship leaders are key people. They should be mature people, respected, having a good testimony, and they should be worshipers who want to lead others in the worship of God. Music is one of the areas in which a good number of people can be involved.

Make use of the testimonies of people who have known the grace, mercy, and transforming love of God. It is important to let people share their spiritual pilgrimages in public for the edification of everyone. When others see what God is doing in the community, it is contagious and they begin showing interest in participating and contributing to the work.

F. Baptism and the Lord's Supper

The sacraments are an integral part of the worship service. Church planters should read books and literature that their denomination recommends to learn the theology and practice of baptism and the Lord's Supper. Teaching should accompany the sacraments. Leaders should also know the varied forms of ritual (in the good sense of the word) permitted in the local context. But beyond protocol, church planters should know how to create meaningful experiences that deepen believers' faith and open opportunities to give testimony with these sacraments.

Baptism provides an excellent opportunity to celebrate the entry of a new believer into the family of faith, to explain its importance, and to call those who have not yet taken that step. It is even better when this ceremony can be accompanied by a testimony. With the Lord's Supper, there is also an opportunity to explain the profound meaning of the work of Jesus and the communion of the saints that this work makes possible.

G. Prayer

Practical Steps
1. Begin a discipline of personal prayer in private.
2. Find prayer intercessors to support you.
3. Pray regularly with the leaders of the church in small groups.
4. Develop a prayer ministry in the entire church.

Let's highlight some relevant points. First, prayer reminds us daily that the work belongs to God and not to us. Our prayer, confession, requests, and petitions assure that the solid base on which the church is built is the triune and true God. By putting the brakes on our activity and stopping ourselves to pray, we recognize that we depend on divine grace and we do not rely on our own understanding nor our own strength. One pastor said, "If we are to prevail over men in public, we must prevail with God in private."

Second, prayer is the lubricating oil that allows all the "machinery" to work well. The machine not maintained with oil soon becomes rusty and useless. The same thing happens with the church that does not pray. We should center ourselves on God's will, bathing all the ministries in prayer, seeking the presence of God, so that he blesses our efforts. Poetically we may say, "Prayer moves the hand of God." However, in reality, prayer does not change God as much as it changes us!

Third, prayer unites the leaders and the congregation. It is difficult for conflicts, anger, jealousy, disagreements, and annoyances to take root in the soil of people's hearts watered constantly with prayer. We do not know a better activity to unite a team than praying together. Prayer maintains the harmony between brothers and sisters. Prayer unifies and maintains us in the will of the Lord. As a colleague says, "Prayer keeps you far from sin and sin keeps you far from prayer."

Fourth, prayer strengthens the church to reach out to the community. Saturate all evangelistic projects with prayer. We need to be under the protective hand of God, centered in the love of Christ, and wrapped with the impulsive energy of the Holy Spirit when going out as ambassadors of the Lord. Nevertheless, it is not enough to talk. We should work at it, put it into practice.

A church's practice of prayer is usually a reliable indicator of the spiritual level of a church. The absence of prayer characterizes a stagnant or sick church. This Christian discipline can be the contagious spark that starts the biblical fire in the hearts of lifeless people and that shines the way for those who are wandering on mistaken paths.

In some ways, prayer is the beginning of all ministry and worship is its chief end. Together, as bookends, they invigorate all the other aspects of holistic ministry mentioned in these two chapters. Evangelism, discipleship, service, and fellowship can all come together in the acts of prayer and worship, which nurtures us to keep on with the task. At the same time, we simply accept prayer and worship as gifts from the Lord. His gift to us becomes our task.

H. Reproducing the church

The good thing about church planting is that the five functions reproduce themselves again and again with new congregations. Each church has the responsibility to multiply these functions in new disciples and, when possible, in new churches. Once a brother in Christ in Nicaragua told us that we were missing a function. He said that function was reproduction, and he was right. We need to be reproducing these functions constantly, and one of the best ways to do this is to plant new churches. If we have a fruit tree, taking very good care of it will help it produce more fruit, but it can only grow so big. If we want to produce more fruit, it is better to use the seeds of some of the fruit to plant new trees that will produce their own fruit. The key question is therefore: When you lead a church, will you instill in it the vision for reproducing the vital functions of the church by planting other daughter churches?

CONCLUSION

This chapter gave us insights into five functions of a healthy church: (1) compelling witness, (2) comprehensive discipleship, (3) compassionate service, (4) caring and welcoming community, (5) dynamic worship and prayer. How does your church fare when compared to these five vital functions? Is there an area in which your church needs to improve? Together with the five vital commitments of the previous chapter, all 10 of these elements are vital for a growing, healthy, reproducing congregation.

Questions

1. What do you like or not like about the definition provided for the function of compelling witness?

2. How did the graphics in "The Big Story" help you better understand or explain the Christian story?

3. Describe the three kinds of "Encounters" needed according to Kraft's typology of evangelism.

4. Describe the four Dimensions of Discipleship as presented by the authors.

5. What examples of a segmented view of faith do you notice in your own context?

6. What could your church do to teach a fuller, more integrated approach to faith and life?

7. Which of the five key functions do you think needs more attention in your particular context? Why?

8. Which of the five key functions do you think is best practiced in your particular context? Why?

9. Which of the ten vital signs of a healthy church do you think your own ministry needs to celebrate and why?

10. Which of the ten vital signs of a healthy church do you think your own ministry needs to address as a challenge and why?

9 CONTEXTUALIZATION ISSUES

Todd Benkert, Gary Teja, and Blayne Waltrip

Introduction

As we consider the planting of a new church, we are reminded of the principles established by early missionaries like Roland Allen, John Livingston Nevius, and Nelvin Hodges:[1] we want to see a church established that is self-sustaining, self-propagating, and self-governing.[2] This implies a church that has "taken root" within the community in which it has been planted. It cannot be a transplant. Oftentimes transplants do not take root. The soil is not conducive to the plant's healthy growth. It may take root, but it may be stunted in its growth or mutate and be unproductive. Likewise, we need to be careful about our preconceived ideas of what the church should look like in any given community. This is because the church needs to be planted within a particular *context*, a context that may be different from that of the community from which the church planter comes.

---

[1] Roland Allen, *Spontaneous Expansion of the Church;* John Livingston Nevius, *The Planting and Development of Missionary Churches*; and Nelvin Hodges, *The Indigenous Church*.

[2] A newer concept is *self-theologizing*, in which the church's theology is developed in the context of a particular culture. Scripture is read through the eyes of the culture. This means, for example, that its understanding of church governance may look different from how churches in another church govern themselves. Some churches have governing elders while others call them deacons, for example.

As a church planter begins to make plans for planting a new church, he/she needs to take into account this context. If we were to draw a continuum, we would have those on the far left who say, "Just preach the gospel!" and on the other end we would have those who say, "Whatever wins some."

"Just preach the gospel!"   "Whatever wins some."

←———————————————————/———————————————————→

Both of these attitudes toward church planting are extremes. The former does not take context into account, while the latter goes beyond contextualization to syncretism. In this chapter, we want to take a balanced approach and place the church plant within a particular context where it has the possibility of not just surviving but thriving, responding to the contextual needs of those being reached with the gospel and expressing itself within that context.

Objective

The student will describe the contextualization issues that face the church planter who contemplates planting the church in a new community, and will reflect on how the context will impact the way the new church worships, presents the gospel, and demonstrates love to its neighbors.

Outline
    I.   Critical contextualization—a review of Hiebert (Todd Benkert)
    II.   Cross-cultural issues (Gary Teja)
    III. Church/context—Niebuhr, Kraft (Blayne Waltrip)

I. Critical contextualization (Todd Benkert)

Church planting is not merely an idea, but a practice. This means that church planting does not happen in the abstract, theoretical realm but in real places among real peoples. The task of taking the gospel to the world involves communicating the gospel to people of different cultures. The task of proclaiming and living out the gospel in a particular setting requires a process called *contextualization*. Through contextualization, we are able to communicate the message of Christ in language and forms that meet people where they are, in their own cultural context. In this chapter, we will introduce the concept of contextualization, outline parameters for contextualization, and offer some practical considerations for church planting.

What is contextualization?

The primary function of contextualization is to proclaim Christ and plant the Christian faith among people in a particular cultural setting. Contextualization helps us to share the gospel in ways that most effectively communicate the good news in a particular culture and to help new believers practice their Christian faith in ways that both transform and make sense within that culture. Contextualization may refer to the proclamation of the gospel message itself, the adaptation of behaviors of the church planter, or the entire way that a Christian community practices their faith in their particular cultural setting.

Contextualizing the Gospel Message

Church planting begins with evangelism, and thus the church planter must first learn to contextualize the gospel message so that he can communicate the message of Christ clearly. David Hesselgrave and Edward Rommen describe contextualization of the gospel as "any action that puts the gospel into a more understandable, culturally relevant form by including elements from a target culture's customs, language, and traditions."[3] The church planter, and later the believers who form the new church, will need to be able to communicate the gospel in such a way that the hearer can both understand and respond to the gospel message.

What is involved?

Contextualization is not a change in the substance of the message. The gospel is unchanging and universal. While the content of the gospel message remains the same, the expression of that message will be different in each context. Contextualization requires an understanding of the cultural context so that we communicate the unchanging gospel in a way that meets the hearer where they are and leads them to Christ.

---

3   David Hesselgrave and Edward Rommen, *Contextualization: Meanings, Methods, and Models,* 1-2.

Identify the worldview. In order to communicate the gospel effectively, you must first decide where to begin. As one reads the New Testament, it becomes clear that no two witnessing encounters begin or develop in the same way. Each hearer comes to the cross from a different vantage point. Thus, the gospel messengers in the New Testament approach each person and culture differently. Each hearer of the gospel had certain worldview barriers that needed to be overcome so that they could understand and consider the gospel message.

Paul's speech to the Jews in Acts 13, for example, is radically different than his witness at the Areopagus in Acts 17. Why? Because the worldview of the hearers was drastically different in each context. In Acts 13, the hearers were already familiar with and believed the Hebrew Scriptures, the one true God, and its promise of a coming Messiah. Paul's sermon began with that common belief and revealed Jesus as the promised Messiah crucified for their sins. In Acts 17, a completely different worldview was present. Here, the audience was polytheistic and had no familiarity with the Bible or its message. Paul found a starting point in the monument to an "unknown God" and from there built a bridge to introduce the one true God of Scripture.

Contextualization of the gospel begins by identifying where the people are and building a bridge to where they need to be. An important step in evangelization, then, is selecting what aspects and emphases of the gospel to deliver first. The gospel messenger should identify worldview barriers that must be overcome for a person to understand and consider the gospel message. Further, understanding the worldview helps to know how the gospel answers the big questions particular to that culture and provides clues for questions and objections that might arise.[4]

When planting a church within one's own cultural context, this task may be simpler and involve assessing each individual and their personal barriers to belief. When church planting cross-culturally, the task is more challenging. The greater the cultural distance, the more important it will be for the church planting missionary to understand the worldview of the people and to work hard to craft his message to meet people where they are. Whatever the cultural

---

4 Hesselgrave, *Communicating Christ Cross-Culturally: An Introduction to Missionary Communication*, 152-54.

distance, the worldview of the hearer should guide the starting point and focus of the gospel presentation.

How can I best communicate the message?

Once I know where to begin, I must think through how I will present the unchangeable message. In the New Testament, Jesus and his followers used stories and metaphors to explain the theological content of the gospel message more clearly. As Jesus preached to the agrarian villages of Palestine, he commonly used word pictures and stories from farming and fishing and everyday village life to explain his message. Similarly, Paul used pictures relevant to Gentiles living in Roman cities. A church planter will need to ask what pictures, symbols, and metaphors might be meaningful in communicating the message to the people he is trying to reach.

The church planter must also keep in mind that what works in one culture may not work in another. For example, a common metaphor used in the West is a cliff and chasm so large that no bridge can cross. This "bridge" illustration provides an effective metaphor for sin and the separation between man and God that only the cross of Jesus Christ can span. Yet how would this illustration need to be modified in a context that knew nothing of cliffs or chasms or bridges? The illustration would be meaningless to a culture in which these symbols were unfamiliar. The task of the evangelist is to find those pictures and metaphors that can serve as "points of contact" and "redemptive analogies"[5] to illustrate the gospel message in ways that are relevant to the people being reached.

Similarly, one must also consider what concepts might be difficult to explain in a particular context. How do you explain the rural elements of Scripture to a people who know nothing of rural life? How do you explain that Jesus is the "Lamb" of God to a people who have never seen a sheep? Contextualization involves identifying these potential barriers to understanding and finding ways to make them understood.

---

5   Ibid, 154.

What should we avoid?

Whenever we take the gospel to the world around us, we face inherent dangers. In the process of communicating the message in ways that are relevant to the culture, we must be certain that we do not alter the message itself. The gospel, though communicated in different ways, is unchanging. Thus, contextualization of the gospel must be done in such a way that the message is both culturally communicated and biblically sound.

The danger of watering down the gospel or falling into heresy is real and should be taken seriously by those who wish to communicate the gospel in any cultural setting. It is not enough to be contextual if the gospel message is compromised or is so unclear and imprecise that it no longer communicates saving faith. We must clearly communicate and never compromise the message that Jesus died for our sins and rose again and that one must repent and believe the good news. At the same time, the danger of being culturally irrelevant should not be taken lightly. It is not enough to be faithful to the content of the message if we fail to communicate the content clearly to the lost around us. A gospel that does not communicate is no gospel to the one who hears it. Biblically sound contextualization takes effort. But the effort is worthwhile in being able to faithfully share the message of Christ to the people God calls us to reach.

Contextualizing the Messenger

A second and important aspect of contextualization is the contextualization of the messenger himself. This kind of contextualization involves helping the messenger fit in to the new culture and create opportunities for gospel ministry. Here the church planter must evaluate the practices chosen. What actions or behaviors might create obstacles that keep the message from getting a hearing? How can the church planter remove these unnecessary barriers to the gospel message?

Again, we see the example of Paul and his evangelization in both Jewish and Greek contexts. In 1 Corinthians 9:19-22 (ESV), Paul states:

> Though I am free from all, I have made myself a servant to
> all, that I might win more of them. To the Jews I became as

a Jew, in order to win Jews. To those under the law I became as one under the law (though not being myself under the law) that I might win those under the law. To those outside the law I became as one outside the law (not being outside the law of God but under the law of Christ) that I might win those outside the law. To the weak I became weak, that I might win the weak. I have become all things to all people, that by all means I might save some.

We have already seen examples of Paul contextualizing his message, but Paul also contextualized his behavior in order to remove cultural barriers to the message being heard.

When Paul spoke of being "all things to all people," one of the things he was talking about was removing cultural barriers. He was referring not only to the message but also to being sensitive to cultural barriers to the gospel. Paul was willing to adjust his language and behavior to cultural norms so that he might gain an audience for his message.

For example, Paul states that "to those outside the law I became as one outside the law." Though Paul was culturally Jewish, his aim was to reach non-Jews. To do so, Paul was willing to adopt new eating practices and to abandon Jewish purity laws that forbid eating with Gentiles and entering their homes. Conversely, Paul states that "to the Jews I became as a Jew, in order to win Jews." Thus, when Paul sought to reach Jewish people, though he was not scripturally bound to keep the Jewish law, he was nevertheless willing to keep the law to gain a hearing among Jews. In doing so, Paul was engaging in contextualization—changing his actions to remove cultural barriers to the gospel and gain a hearing for it.

The role of the church planting missionary includes evaluating one's own practice. What changes will a church planter need to make to participate in the target culture? What things might a planter need to give up or begin practicing in order to remove social barriers to the gospel? Once again, this means that the church planter will need to understand the culture of the people being reached and contextualize the behavior so that a hearing for the gospel can be gained.

Contextualizing the Church

A third area of contextualization concerns the local church. When people come to faith in Christ and new churches are planted, those churches must function in ways that make sense within the culture. The church planter will initially be concerned with contextualization of the gospel message. As new believers are won and a church is planted, contextualization will include the practices of the church and all aspects of the Christian life in that culture. The question moves from "How do I communicate the gospel in this cultural setting?" to "How do I live out the gospel in this particular time and place?" Gailyn Van Rheenen explains that "a contextualized church is like planting 'God's seed' in new soil and allowing the seed to grow naturally, adapting to the language, thought processes, and rituals of the new culture *without losing its eternal meanings.*"[6] Contextualization helps the new church to be a healthy church within the culture.

What is involved?

New churches will want to live out the functions of church life in ways that make sense within the cultural context. Many questions will need to be asked and answered. The questions may vary from place to place, but will address matters such as music, preaching, order of worship, and the forms and activities of the worship service. Here, there will be both continuity and discontinuity with other expressions of the Christian faith. In every church, for example, we might expect to find in common certain biblical expressions of worship, including prayer, singing, and the preaching of the Word. At the same time, the forms that accompany those expressions will vary according to the culture in which they are expressed. Such things as the posture of prayers, the length of the worship service, the style of music and instrumentation, and the form and structure of the sermon will vary from one setting to the next.

Similarly, new churches need to understand how they will live out their faith in the particular culture. Every Christian church will teach its people biblical principles like the importance of modesty and loving one's neighbor, yet the particular applications of those principles may vary widely. Churches will need to evaluate the elements of their present culture in light of their new-found faith. Further, cultural customs may or may not be consistent with the

---

6   Gailyn Van Rheenen, "MR #17: Transplanted and Contextualized Churches."

Christian faith. Churches will need to determine, for example, what elements of their culture may be retained, what elements will be given new Christian meaning, and what elements will be replaced with "functional substitutes." These are all part of the contextualization process which the new church will need to work through biblically. Paul Hiebert calls this process "critical contextualization."[7]

Critical contextualization begins as new believers recognize that the Bible applies to every aspect of life. Forms of expression, entertainment, everyday behaviors, traditions, celebrations, and rites of passage must all be measured by and conformed to the Bible. With that conviction, the first step is to examine old practices and customs for each area of life. In order to apply the Bible, the new church must neither uncritically accept nor reject old cultural forms. Rather, they must examine each custom and identify its meaning and function so that they fully understand their old practice. Then, with this understanding, the pastor or planter can lead the church to study what the Bible has to say about the particular area of life. Finally, the new church evaluates each custom from a biblical perspective and either accepts the cultural form, adapts and gives new meaning to it, or replaces the old form with a functional substitute. In this way, the Bible evaluates and transforms the culture of the new believers. This process of critical contextualization allows the new church both to practice their new faith in a way that makes sense within the culture and to "deal biblically with all areas of life."[8]

What should we avoid?

The Christian faith can be planted in any cultural soil and be practiced within that cultural framework. Yet one of the dangers of contextualization is that either the message or the practice of the church becomes distorted so that it is no longer a biblical expression of Christian faith. The guiding principle must always be the Scripture and not the culture. Contextualization is a tool that will help us to plant more churches. Critical contextualization will help us to plant *healthy* churches by helping to avoid the danger of syncretism.

---

7   Paul G. Hiebert, "Critical Contextualization," in *Anthropological Insights for Missionaries,* 187-89.

8   Ibid, 183-90; quote, 186.

Contextualization is the communication and practice of the gospel in ways that are understood and appropriate to each culture. Syncretism, on the other hand, takes place when elements of culture blend with the Christian faith in such a way that there is a "replacement or dilution of the essential truths of the gospel through the incorporation of non-Christian elements."[9] Thus, rather than the gospel being communicated in and through the culture, the gospel is *changed* by the culture and you end up with something other than authentic Christianity. Syncretism is a constant danger in church planting because each of us is influenced by the culture in which we live. We must continually evaluate our contextualized methods of church planting and make every effort to conform our thought and practice to Scripture. Ultimately, we must be concerned not only that our ministry is contextual but also that it is biblical. With Scripture as our guide, we must approach contextualization carefully and with discernment.

Conclusion

Faithfulness to the Great Commission demands that church planters faithfully proclaim the gospel in a way that both communicates to the world around us and remains faithful to the biblical gospel. Faithfulness means that we aim to plant more churches and to plant healthy churches. Contextualization helps us to do just that. In the rest of this chapter, we will examine some practical helps for contextualization.

II. Cross-cultural issues (Gary Teja)

How do people view their world?

As we go into a community, we need to first ask ourselves, "How do people view their world?" The way in which a people view their world may not coincide with the way we view the world. In fact, our views of the world may be diametrically opposed. Let's say that you come from Culture X, which puts a high value on education. A pastor in this culture is respected because of the education he has. He prides himself on placing Rev. Dr. John Doe on his business card. Those in his culture respect him for his education and will listen to him because he is an educated person. In Culture Y, most people only have an eighth-grade education. The pastors in Culture Y come from the

---

9   A. Scott Moreau, "Syncretism," 924.

same educational level as the average member of the congregation. A person with a higher education may appear to be haughty, seeing himself better than everyone else. His sermons would be too erudite with vocabulary over the heads of the average attendee. He would probably win few converts and would not plant a healthy, growing congregation in Culture Y. What we are dealing with is a conflict of cultures. Culture deals with what we value, including our worldview (how we see the world around us). When a church planter from Culture X is working cross-culturally, he needs to take the context of the other culture into account. Richard Brislin writes,

> The product of a culture's influence, then, is a residue of behaviours, ideas, and beliefs with which people are comfortable and which they consider 'proper' or 'the right way.' In intercultural contact, however, people interact with others who also consider certain behaviours desirable. Often, the same behavior is considered desirable to people from one culture and distasteful to people of the other.[10]

This is our conundrum.

Why are we asking this question?

You may be thinking, "I'm not going to plant a church in another country." Often when we think of ministering cross-culturally, we think of going from one country to another. Nevertheless, a church planter can remain in the country of origin and still find oneself working cross-culturally. There are differences, for example, in the United States between geographic regions: the north, the south, the west coast, New England, the southeast.[11] There are differences between those who live in rural areas and those who live in the suburbs and those who live in urban areas (or even what we once termed "the inner city"). There are also differences between those who have lived in a city for many years and immigrants, recent arrivals from another country. Europe is a prime example of ongoing immigration and the need to work cross-culturally. In Africa, there are different worldviews and languages within large countries. Also, an African church planter going from southern Africa

---

10   Richard Brislin, *Cross-Cultural Encounters: Face-to-Face Interactions,* 6.
11   Even as early as 1785 these geographic differences were noted. In a letter addressed to the Marquis of Chastellux, Thomas Jefferson remarked on the differences between "the North" and "the South," referring to the United States. Cited on page 14 of Sarah Lanier, *Foreign to Familiar: A Guide to Understanding Hot- and Cold-Climate Cultures.*

to northern Africa would find significant cultural differences. There have also been cases of African Americans from the U.S. going as missionaries to Africa and being judged according to African standards because of their race, though they have been raised in a culture completely different from their host country. There are also generational differences.[12]

In one particular culture, a young missionary, Don Richardson, attempted to share the gospel story with the Sawi people of New Guinea.[13] One of the Bible stories he told was about Judas' betrayal of Jesus, handing him over to the Roman authorities. All of a sudden, Richardson's audience began to smile and clap and cheer for Judas. In their culture, treachery was a valued skill. Imagine Richardson's chagrin when he realized this story was not going to have the effect on the people that he hoped it would.

All of this to say that *context* matters. The context, the cultural milieu in which the planter will work, needs to be understood if one is to be successful in transmitting the good news in ways that are understood and accepted. The goal is to see a healthy church that is indigenous to the culture. J.D. Payne writes, "These churches spring from the soil, manifesting the cultural expressions and traits of the people, couched within the biblical parameters."[14]

What are some of these differences?

Many good books and articles have been written on the subject of cross-cultural issues. A person could take a semester just reading through the literature. We will try to summarize some of the best readings in this section of this chapter on contextualization issues.

Sarah Lanier has written a succinct book on ministering cross-culturally.[15] She discusses the differences in her title, *Foreign to Familiar*. What is familiar to us may be foreign to the culture we want to reach with the good news. She looks at differences between what she calls *cold-climate cultures* and *hot-climate*

---

12 See Part 3, "Understanding Cultures and Models," of Ed Stetzer's book, *Planting New Churches in a Postmodern Age*.

13 Don Richardson, *Peace Child*.

14 J.D. Payne, *Discovering Church Planting: An Introduction to the Whats, Whys, and Hows of Global Church Planting*, 188-89.

15 Lanier, *Foreign to Familiar*. The contrasts between hot-climate and cold-climate cultures are extrapolated from this book with personal applications from the author's own experiences.

cultures. These terms refer to the different ways in which those from a one climate view life and act upon in comparison to the other climate. It's a world-view, as it were. It looks at, for example, how a culture views time. Lanier looks at the following differences: relationship vs. task orientation, direct communi-cation vs. indirect communication, individualism vs. group orientation, inclu-sion vs. privacy, views on hospitality, high context vs. low context, and views on time and planning. For each item, we will first look at how a hot-climate culture views it and then follow up with how a cold-climate culture looks at it. In both cases we will talk about *tendencies,* since not everyone within the one culture or the other necessarily exhibits all of the traits. For example, although hot-climate culture people tend to be more relational than task-oriented, some individuals may very well be more task-oriented than relational. The opposite holds true for some cold-climate culture individuals.

As you go through the two sets of bullet points for each of these items, ask yourself, "Where do I seem to fit? Am I more a hot-climate culture person or a cold-climate culture person?" If you are already beginning to work in a church plant, ask yourself, "Do the people I am reaching out to tend to be more a hot-climate culture or a cold-climate culture?" Knowing your own tendency and the tendency of the culture you want to reach will help you in planting a healthy, growing church.

Relationship versus task-orientation

Hot-climate cultures tend to be more relational than task-oriented. Cold-climate cultures tend to be more task-oriented. See bullet points below.

Hot-climate cultures (relationship-based)
- Communication must create a "feel-good" atmosphere.
- Though the individuals may be otherwise, the society is feeling-ori-ented.
- Efficiency and time do not take priority over the person.
- It is inappropriate to "talk business" upon first arriving at a business meeting or when making a business phone call.

Cold-climate cultures (task-oriented)
- Communication must provide accurate information.
- Though individuals may be otherwise, the society is logic-oriented.
- Efficiency and time are high priorities and taking them seriously is a statement of respect for the other person.

How does this play out in real life? As a missionary in Nicaragua, I had to quickly learn the importance of relationship-building over accomplishing tasks. Pastors would stop by the house uninvited at any time day or night. I initially was frustrated and felt resentful. I had work to accomplish, and I saw their visits as an interruption. Eventually, I learned to put those tasks aside and see those visits as opportunities to get to know the pastors better.

Several became very close friends over time. Had I put them off, we never would have become friends.

Direct versus indirect communication

Hot-climate cultures tend to be more indirect than direct in their communication. Cold-climate cultures tend to be more direct in their communication with each other. See bullet points below.

Hot-climate cultures (indirect communication)
- It's all about being friendly.
- Every question must be phrased in such a way as to not offend by its directness.
- Use a third party for accurate information if you sense that a direct answer will be too harsh, or will not get the results you are seeking.
- A "yes" may not be an answer to your question. It may be the first step in beginning a friendly interchange. Or verbal compliance may be required by the culture. Therefore, avoid yes-or-no questions.
- Avoid embarrassing people.

Cold-climate cultures (direct communication)
- Short, direct questions show respect for the person's time, as well as professionalism.
- A "yes" is a "yes," and a "no" is a "no." There are no hidden meanings.

- An honest, direct answer is information only. It does not reflect on how the person feels about you.
- You can say what you think (nicely), and it will usually not be taken personally.

I quickly learned that if a pastor had something to say to me, he would normally do so through another pastor. It would have been impolite for him to speak to me directly if it involved a chastisement or complaint. I soon got over asking, "Why doesn't Pastor Enrique tell me himself?" I also learned that responding positively to my suggestion did not necessarily mean that the person agreed with me or would actually carry out the suggestion. He was being polite and saving face. I had to pick up on other nonverbal cues to determine if this was a "Yes" or something else.

Individualism versus group orientation

Hot-climate cultures tend to emphasize the group more than the individual. Cold-climate cultures tend to emphasize the individual more. Others call this the difference between individualistic cultures and collectivistic cultures.[16] Paul Tokunaga calls these individual-centered and situation-centered cultures.[17] See bullet points below.

Hot-climate cultures (group-oriented)
- I belong, therefore I am.
- My identity is tied to the group (family, tribe, etc.)
- The group protects and provides for me.
- Taking initiative within a group can be greatly determined by my role.
- I do not expect to have to stand alone.
- My behavior reflects on the whole group.
- Team members expect direction from the leader.

---

16 Patty Lane, *A Beginner's Guide to Crossing Cultures,* chap. 6. Also, Gary Fujino, "Toward a Cross-Cultural Identity of Forgiveness," 22-28.
17 Paul Tokunaga, "Introduction: Learning Our Names," 9-15.

Cold-climate cultures (individual-oriented)
- I am a self-standing person, with my own identity.
- Every individual should have an opinion and can speak for himself or herself.
- Taking initiative within a group is good and is expected.
- One must know how to make one's own decisions.
- My behavior reflects on me, not on the group.

I remember a story I heard about church meetings among Navajo Christians. When in meetings with Western missionaries, items would be quickly put to a vote. While the Navajo were allowing for each person to think before answering, the Western missionaries were already voting, thus unconsciously showing disrespect to something very important within the Navajo decision-making culture.

In another case, I sat in a church service among Cubans in Miami. The pastor only had to look at one of his leaders from the platform, and they immediately knew what they had to do. In meetings where the pastors and elders got together to make decisions, the elders would look to the pastor to see how he would vote before they voiced their opinion. Their opinion was always in line with the pastor's view. Individualism was not something that was encouraged.

Inclusion versus privacy

Hot-climate cultures tend to emphasize inclusion. Cold-climate cultures tend to emphasize the need for privacy. See bullet points below.

Hot-climate cultures (inclusion)
- People tend to be group-oriented.
- Individuals know they are automatically included in conversation, meals, and the other activities of the group.
- Possessions are to be used freely by all: food, tools, etc.
- It is not desirable to be left to oneself.
- It is rude to hold a private conversation or to make plans that exclude others present.

Cold-climate cultures (privacy)
- People enjoy having time and space to themselves.
- People are expected to ask permission to borrow something or to interrupt a conversation.
- Each person is considered to be a steward of his or her possessions and has the responsibility to maintain and protect them.
- In a community setting, it might be common to label one's food, tools, etc., to set them apart from the group's common possessions.
- It is acceptable to hold private conversations or to make exclusive plans with a few people, not including everyone.

The American daughter of a friend of ours went to Costa Rica to spend a semester abroad, living with other friends of ours. After a week there, she came to us, complaining, "I can't seem to get any privacy. They want to include me in everything. Even my bedroom is a public area." What she did not understand was that she was a cold-climate person who relished privacy while they were a hot-climate family who wanted to make sure she did not feel lonely. Likewise, when she would come home from the university, she would want to go straight to her room. If visitors were present, she wanted to ignore them and go to her room. This was, of course, very insulting for the visitors and shameful for the host family.

Views on hospitality

Hot-climate cultures tend to be very hospitable, even to their own detriment. Cold-climate cultures tend to be selective in their hospitality. See bullet points below.

Hot-climate cultures (broadly hospitable)
- Hospitality is spontaneous, often without an advance invitation.
- It is the context for relationship (even a business relationship).
- Hospitality usually takes place in the home.
- The host fully takes care of the needs of the guest. The guest pays for nothing.
- A gift is usually expected.
- Food and drink are involved.
- Travelers are taken in and provided for.

Cold-climate cultures (selectively hospitable)
- Hospitality is taken very seriously and is planned for.
- It is usually not as spontaneous. The host usually appreciates advance notice of a visit.
- Travelers are expected to make their own arrangements other than what is specifically communicated to the host ahead of time.
- Guests need to expect to pay for their transportation and restaurants if visiting. If the host plans to pay, he usually will say so.
- Hospitality is a special occasion, taking the full attention of the host.

As Westerners, we have a lot to learn about hospitality. Those of us who have been on the receiving end of hospitality often feel chagrined, not knowing how to respond. I have many Laotian, Cambodian, and Thai friends who have extended hospitality to the extreme, leaving my wife and me non-plussed.

While traveling in Finland, where we were guests of the mother of a former exchange student, we were not allowed to pay for anything. We learned that when she came to the U.S., such hospitality should be reciprocal. We were honored to have her and her daughter in our home, and we returned her hospitality to the extent we were able.

Views on time and planning

Hot-climate cultures tend to have a flexible concept of time. Planning in advance is not a top priority. Cold-climate cultures tend to put more emphasis on being punctual and making plans well in advance. See bullet points below.

Hot-climate cultures (informal, flexible)
- People are generally event-oriented more than time-oriented.
- People tend to be spontaneous and flexible in their approach to life.
- It's important to respond to what life brings.
- Saving time is not as important as experiencing the moment.
- Informal visiting is part of the event.
- People recognize that structure is required in some areas of life (the military, for example).

Cold-climate cultures (punctual, plan-focused)
- People tend to be time-oriented.
- Structure is important in their approach to life.
- People like using time efficiently.
- Planning one's day and saving time are important values.
- People expect an event (dinner, arrival of a guest, or a meeting) to begin at the time announced. Visiting or informal chatting happens before or after the event.

How many weddings have we attended at which the ceremony did not start "on time"? According to our friends in hot-climate cultures, though, "on time" was when the bride came. It was similar for church services. A service advertised for 6 p.m. did not begin until 7 p.m. If we really wanted an activity to begin at a certain time, we learned to call it for an hour earlier so that everyone was there at the time we wanted.

High-context versus low-context cultures

Hot-climate cultures tend to be high-context. Cold-climate cultures tend to be low-context. A definition of these terms is probably in order before we proceed. These terms go back to Edward T. Hall in his book *Beyond Cultures.*[18] Jaime Wurzel and Nancy Fischman write, "Low-context cultures place a small amount of importance on the context while high-context cultures place a large degree of meaning on the context."[19] Context is defined as environment, processes like *how* we meet other people, body language, tone of voice, gestures, facial expressions, and a person's appearance, such as how they are dressed. See the bullet points below.

High-context societies (everything matters)
- Who you are related to matters.
- It is better to overdress than to underdress.
- Watch to see how others respond in a situation in order to apply appropriate behavior.
- Remember to honor the people you are dealing with; being too casual is insulting.

18 Edward T. Hall, *Beyond Culture.*
19 Jaime S. Wurzel and Nancy K. Fischman, *A Different Place: The Intercultural Classroom,* 38-43. Cited in Lane, *A Beginner's Guide,* 48-49. Chapter 3 in Lane's book is worth reading for a fuller understanding of high- and low-context cultures.

- Ask a local person who has lived overseas for a while what is important to know.
- Use manners.
- Respect the rules.
- Give attention to appropriate greetings.

Low-context societies (nothing matters; anything goes, within reason)
- Who you know matters, but not so much. What you know is more important.
- Do not be offended by a casual atmosphere.
- Lack of protocol does not mean rejecting, nor is it dishonoring.
- They do not know what your rules are, so leave your rules at home.
- Address people by their given names unless others use titles.

When visiting in a home in a high-context culture, we learned to identify the most important person in the room and to greet that person first. It might be the oldest person, or the one who was the community leader. Also, when meeting with people of a high-context culture, we normally wore suits and ties and then removed the tie or jacket if others were less dressed up. We found this true among many Asians as well as Latinos.

Individualistic and collectivistic cultures

Another way of looking at these cross-cultural differences is through the use of the terms *individualistic* and *collectivistic*. In Lanier's terminology, these were the differences between cultures that are group-oriented and those that are oriented toward the individual.[20] You can probably think of some cultures that would be more collectivistic (hot-climate) and those that are more individual-oriented (cold-climate). Chinese tend to be more collectivistic in their outlook. Dutch tend to be more individualistic in their approach to life. Lane writes about these terms under the rubric of *relationship lens*. She writes, "This lens is very significant in cross-cultural interactions. It represents a fundamental difference in cultural perspectives that impacts all relationships at some level and defines a major portion of one's identity."[21] In other words, how one sees oneself—as part of a group or as an individual—determines in broad strokes how we act.

---

20   Lanier, *Foreign to Familiar.*
21   Lane, *A Beginner's Guide,* 87.

Guilt-based, shame-based, and fear-based cultures

We can also look at cross-cultural issues in contextualization by examining how people view guilt, shame, or fear. These present themselves as dichotomous worldviews: guilt/righteousness, honor/shame, and fear/power. Many of us are not fully conscious of these dichotomies and how they play out in our dealings with people who are different from ourselves. Nevertheless, these differences are very important and can help us to understand a culture and how to penetrate it with the saving news of Jesus Christ. To be unaware of these differences could result in a lack of communication that could be crucial in our attempt to share the good news with another person. The message must be communicated in the heart-language of the person and in a context that makes sense to the person.

Roland Muller wrote a book called *Honor and Shame,* which looks at these three dichotomies.[22] Only about one-third of the world tends to look at the world through what we call guilt/righteousness. The rest of the world tends to interpret the world through honor/shame or fear/power or through a combination of the three different dichotomies. Muller writes,

> Many Western nations (Northern Europe, North America, Australia, and New Zealand) have cultures that contain mostly guilt-based cultural characteristics. On the other hand, much of the 10/40 Window is made up shame-based cultures. *[sic]* Most of the primal religions and cultures of the world (such as tribes in . . . Africa, Asia, and South America) are structured around fear-based principles.[23]

Let's look at all three of these sets of principles.

Guilt/righteousness

In the Western worldview, justice is determined based on guilt. In a court of law, deliberations are made to determine whether the accused is guilty or innocent of the charge. John Doe was brought before a judge and jury to determine if he was guilty or innocent of robbery. Both the prosecuting attorney and the defense attorney presented their case. The prosecutor tried to prove from evidence that John Doe had indeed committed the crime of robbery.

---

22 Roland Muller, *Honor and Shame: Unlocking the Door.*
23 Ibid, 20.

John Doe's attorney tried to show that Joe Doe had not committed the crime. In the end, the judge instructed the jury to determine innocence or guilt. When the verdict was returned, John Doe was declared guilty. The judge then pronounced sentence. Joe Doe had to spend the next 15 years in jail. Why? Because he was declared guilty. A guilty verdict demanded a punishment of 15 years in jail.

If a church planter is working in a culture that is guilt/righteousness-oriented, he can use Bible passages that reflect this view. For example, "All have sinned and fall short of the glory of God" (Rom. 3:23). "There is no one righteous, not even one" (Rom. 3:10). "The wages of sin is death" (Rom. 6:23). But not all countries work on the principle of guilt/righteousness. Says Muller,

> The danger comes . . . when we take our Roman understanding of the gospel and apply it to those who do not have a Roman-based culture. We fruitlessly spend untold hours and incalculable amounts of energy explaining to our contact that he is guilty of sin, and needs to be justified before God. The poor listener, on the other hand, may not even have a word for sin, or perhaps even a concept of sin, in his language. He struggles to understand guilt, and sees no need for justification. . . . We must put our Roman, guilt-based understanding of the gospel aside, and strive to understand other worldviews and their thinking.[24]

In this light, the church planter needs to look at the other two worldviews.

Honor/shame

In some cultures, the sense of what is good or bad can be based on what brings honor to an individual and his family or clan or community and what brings shame. Ahmed was caught stealing 10 dinares of bread. Ahmed felt ashamed and embarrassed. He was not repentant but ashamed for being caught. It was not the act of stealing that brought him embarrassment but the shame that came with being found out. (Though stealing was illegal, it was not necessarily considered shameful/bad/wrong if he was not caught.) Now he had lost honor in the eyes of his friends and family, and they in turn lost honor because of his act. No matter how rich or poor a person is in that particular culture, the important thing is to maintain honor and avoid shame.[25]

---

24 Ibid, 32-33.
25 See Christopher Flanders, "Fixing the Problem of Face," 12-19. Also, dealing with those

Timothy had performed poorly at work. His poor performance had cost his company a large contract. Timothy's boss had reprimanded him in front of his coworkers in the weekly meeting. After the meeting, Timothy went up to his boss and resigned. Had Timothy felt guilty for his poor performance and the subsequent loss to the company? No. Timothy had lost face in front of his coworkers when his boss scolded him in public. This was an honor/shame incident.

Lane points out that "saving face" is very important to those in an honor/shame culture. "The fear of 'losing face,' feeling shame or losing honor, seems almost innate, as natural as breathing and as devastating as not breathing. It is a guiding force behind most interactions, or at the very least, the principle on which decisions are made as to what is appropriate behavior."[26] She offers suggestions on how not to lose face and how not to cause someone to lose face. Here are a couple of examples:

1. Never ask questions that will force a person to admit making a mistake.
2. Don't ask questions that imply the other person is in need.

These two examples remind me of the proper way in Central America to ask someone if they understood what you were saying. It would be very impolite to ask, "Did you understand me? Did you understand what I said?" Instead, it is more appropriate to ask, "Did I make myself clear? (¿Me explico?)." Also, in grammatically correct Spanish, a person never says, "I broke the vase," or, "I forgot." An intransitive form of the verb is used so that it comes across this way: "The vase broke to me (Se me quebró)," or, "It was forgotten to me (Se me olvidó)." It seems to soften the issue and saves the face of the speaker.

It is obvious, then, that the church planter needs to consider issues of honor and shame when presenting the gospel to someone of this culture. Scripture allows for the gospel to be presented in other-than-guilt/righteousness terms. Paul said, "I am *not ashamed* of the gospel" (Rom. 1:16). Sin can be cloaked in the way it brings shame to oneself and to the community, and shame to God. The church planter need not talk about guilt and righteousness in a shame

---

who come to faith from an honor/shame culture, consider Jeanette Yep, *Following Jesus Without Dishonoring Your Parents.*
26   Lane, *A Beginner's Guide,* 88-89.

culture. Even Jesus' death on the cross can be discussed as a shameful act (Heb. 12:2) and how our condition before God has brought Jesus to this shameful point in his life. We have brought dishonor to Jesus by forcing him to die on the cross. Only by accepting Jesus' death on our behalf can this shame be lifted. We are honored by being called sons and daughters of God. Jesus' resurrection brought honor again to him as he had completed what his Father had required. Even 1 Peter 2:4-8 shares the good news that if we put our trust in Jesus, the cornerstone, we need not be ashamed.

Fear/power

Lastly, some cultures are overly conscious and preoccupied with fear and power. They are afraid of the unknown. They are afraid of spirits that live in dark places, or that cause illness, or that possess a person who appears to be crazy. They seek power to ward off the evil spirits, to cure illness, to cast out the demons. Most of these are animistic cultures.[27] The Scriptures also speak the language of those who live in a fear/power culture. The Bible talks of many power encounters. The gospel gives many examples of power over the things that cause fear in the hearts of mere humans.

At Jesus' birth, the angel told the shepherds, "Do not be afraid. I bring you good news that will cause great joy for all the people" (Luke 2:10). At the beginning of his teaching ministry, Jesus had a power encounter with the devil in the desert, and he was victorious over the devil (Matt. 4:1-11). Jesus healed two men possessed by demons (Matt. 8:28-34). Jesus healed a man with the dreaded disease of leprosy (Matt. 8:1-4). Jesus demonstrated his power over nature by calming a stormy sea (Matt. 8:23-27). Jesus even demonstrated God's power over death by being raised from the dead (Matt. 28:1-10). What's more, the resurrected Jesus said, "All *authority [power]* in heaven and on earth has been given to me" (28:18). And the apostle Paul adds, "The gospel . . . is the *power* of God that brings salvation to everyone who believes" (Rom. 1:16).

Muller makes it abundantly clear, though, that the Bible speaks to all three worldviews. "The three themes of salvation are woven together in the Scriptures, to present a complete picture of what God wants to do with mankind."[28]

---

27 For an excellent treatment of evangelism among those of a fear-based culture, see Van Rheenen, *Communicating Christ in Animistic Contexts.*

28 Muller, *Honor and Shame,* 102.

Summary

In this section we have looked at different cross-cultural issues that can confront a church planter. There are more than what we have dealt with here. Suffice it to say that a church planter needs to recognize the *context* in which he is working. That context may be very different from the one he normally operates in. The church planter, therefore, needs to *incarnate* in the other culture. As Jesus became flesh and dwelt among us, so the church planter needs to become embodied within the new culture. He needs to learn as much as he can about that culture in order to speak the good news into that culture in understandable terms.

III. Church/context (Blayne Waltrip)

Introduction

Mission happens in a particular context, as we saw in the previous section. A church planter cannot separate oneself from the context. If we plant new life in a particular context, we have to understand the context, including the society and the culture. Although the gospel does not change, the culture around is constantly changing. As a result, we have to constantly be students of culture to live incarnationally among those whom we want to reach and make disciples. That means we will have to contextualize the gospel so that those in the culture understand it. We also must contextualize discipleship and the way we do church so that people of the culture will grow spiritually and become mature missional Christians in that context. I will briefly define society, culture, worldview, and contextualization in light of "church/context" as we live out the kingdom of God. I will conclude by explaining incarnational church planting.

Society

Society is the context in which we live and serve. Society is a social organization made up of a group of people who share a geographical area and culture. Although society and culture are interdependent concepts, they are not the same. Society refers to people and their social organizations, whereas culture refers to their learned and shared way of life. When there are two or more people interacting with each other, there is the basis for society.

Culture

There are many definitions and theories on culture. Basically, culture is the way of life for the society. As such, it includes codes of manners, dress, language, religion, rituals, norms of behavior such as law and morality, and systems of belief. Charles Kraft defines culture as the integrated system of learned behavior patterns that are characteristic of a society and are not the result of biological inheritance.[29] Culture is learned and passed down. In a particular family and culture, we are "enculturated." Enculturation is the process by which people learn the cultural knowledge needed as they grow for physical survival, getting along with others, and interpreting the world around them.

There are four basic components of culture: (1) values, (2) norms, (3) institutions, and (4) artifacts.

- Values are ideas people have about what seems important in life. They guide the rest of the culture. How we view our relationships, money, work, and the unborn, for example, will guide us as a society.

- Norms are the expectations of how people will behave in various situations. For example, many cultures value marriage and family. As a result, the corresponding norms are for a man and woman to marry and have children. Each culture also has methods, called sanctions, of enforcing its norms. Sanctions vary with the importance of the norm; norms that a society enforces formally have the status of laws. According to our analogy, there would be social sanctions for a man and woman to live together outside of marriage. In addition, laws may be passed that only a man and woman could marry.

- Institutions are the structures of a society within which values and norms are transmitted (e.g., legal systems and law enforcement).

- Lastly, artifacts are the material things in the culture that derive from a culture's values and norms, such as clothes, tools, vehicles, and so on.

---

29   Charles Kraft with Marguerite Kraft, *Christianity in Culture: A Study in Biblical Theologizing in Cross-Cultural Perspective*, 46.

Worldview

"Worldview" is the central systematization of conceptions of reality to which the members of the culture agree. It originates from their value system. A worldview is imposed upon the young of a society by means of familiar processes of teaching and learning. As each young person is raised in a given culture, they are conditioned to interpret reality in terms of the conceptual system of that culture. Some of it is "taught," while other parts are simply "caught" by living in that society. The worldview is the central control box of a culture.

Here is a practical yet very poignant example of how a worldview permeates all of society. A Muslim's worldview, in which Allah is at the center of everything a Muslim thinks, says, or does, informs a Muslim consciously and unconsciously how he should act and react as a member of the umma (community of faith). This explains why a Muslim reacts violently to caricatures of Mohammed, for example. A Westerner's worldview tends not to be all-comprehensive, but compartmentalized. Religion for a Westerner normally is not all-encompassing. It is one compartment in his or her worldview. Westerners, therefore, experience cultural conflict in understanding the Muslim mind and a Muslim's actions because of this difference in worldview makeup.

Contextualization

Contextualization has simply been understood as the way to communicate the gospel effectively to others in a particular context (i.e., culture and society). The church planter takes the gospel to a new context and finds appropriate ways to communicate it so that it is understandable to the people in that context. The truth and message of the Word is eternal, but we must understand the meaning and message of Scripture and interpret it to the people of a particular context so that they can understand. This means that we not only contextualize passages and stories of the Bible, but we also contextualize the way we evangelize (i.e., communicate the gospel in a way that helps a person come to faith in Christ) and make disciples (i.e., continue to communicate the message of the Bible and kingdom so that the new disciple can grow in Christ and become fruitbearing in the local church). For example, the church planter can contextualize through redemptive analogies to tell the story of Christ in that culture. Redemptive analogies are stories, understandings or practices in a given culture that demonstrate the gospel. If no known story can be used, then the church planter can create a culturally appropriate story to tell the gospel story in a way that the listener can understand. Jesus constantly used redemptive analogies. For example, Jesus would often say, "The kingdom of God is like . . ." The church planter must find stories in the culture that can be used to relay the truths of the gospel. It may well involve a retelling of gospel stories in stories of that culture.

In relationship to church planting, J.D. Payne explains that contextualization addresses two areas.[30] The first, he explains, is related to the way the church planter communicates the gospel. The church planter must make sure that people understand the gospel. I would expand it to understanding the kingdom of God. The other area is related to the way the church planter teaches obedience to new believers. Payne explains that this area of contextualization is primarily "concerned with the cultural flavor the church takes as the new kingdom ethic in their communities." As the new believer matures to bear fruit, he or she will bear fruit for the kingdom in that context. A mature Christian is a missional Christian who seeks to continue the mission of God wherever they live.

The new church must be both biblically faithful and culturally appropriate. Although church planters cannot completely separate themselves from their own culture, they must avoid imposing their cultural preferences onto the new church. I agree with Payne that this will take prayerful discernment.[31] The goal is to have a truly indigenous church that is biblically faithful. In addition to being faithful in prayer, the church planter must live out the kingdom of God incarnationally, meaning they "incarnate" the kingdom of God, that which is eternal, into a new culture as they live among the people of that context. This will take understanding one's culturally learned way of doing church, and then learning the way of doing church in a new culture. This means that the church planter must learn the new culture in a holistic way (i.e., "acculturate").

Incarnational Church Planting

In order to contextualize the "flavor" of the new church, the church planter must acculturate into the new culture. As *enculturation* is the learning process

---

30   Payne, *Discovering Church Planting*, 184.
31   Ibid, 187.

of a culture while one grows up in their own context, *acculturation* is the learning of the appropriate behavior within another culture, a host culture. It involves learning a new way of life. Missionaries and cross-cultural ministers have traditionally had to acculturate into their host culture to do ministry effectively. Likewise, if a church planter starts a church in a culture other than his own, acculturation will be essential for them to be effective in the new culture. This kind of learning is not just an objective rational learning of facts about a culture, which is necessary, but also includes the learning of a culture through experience and relationships—what some call a *yada* learning.[32] I can know *about* you, such as how tall you are, your age, where you grew up, where you live, and so on; but in order to really know you, I must spend time with you. I must not only hear about the stories of your life, I must grow to understand your hurts, disappointments, hopes, joys, fears, and so on. I can know about Jesus from the Bible, but I really know him only with a relational knowledge by having a relationship with him.

We gain acculturation and learn with *yada* knowledge by living among people. This is incarnational living. Jesus serves as a model for us. In John 1:1, Scripture tells us, "In the beginning was the Word, and the Word was with God, and the Word was God." Verse 14 of that chapter adds that "the Word became flesh and made his dwelling among us." The eternal Word became flesh. Why? John 3:16 explains the reason: "For God so loved the world that he gave his one and only Son, that whoever believes in him shall not perish but have eternal life." God so loved us that he sent his only Son to take on flesh and live among us so that no one among us would perish, if we believe. Love was his motivation, for God is love (1 John 4:8). The incarnation is a result of

---

32 Cheryl Bridges Johns explains that the Old Testament word for "to know" is *yada*, referring to "a knowing more by the heart than by the mind, a knowing that arises not by standing back from in order to look at, but by active and intentional engagement in lived experience." This is in contrast to the Greek approach (i.e., *ginoskein*) of standing back from something to objectively know it. This Greek type of knowing is a rationalistic approach to scientific knowledge as opposed to a knowledge that comes from a relational and holistic engaging knowledge. In English, we have only one word for "to know," but other languages have two words for "to know" that better express the two kinds of knowing: "saber" (rational/objective) vs. "conocer" (relational/subjective = yada) in Spanish; "savoir" (rational/objective) vs. "connaître" (relational/subjective) in French; or "wissen" (rational/objective) vs. "kennen" (relational/subjective) in German. The idea is that we need to know God and others beyond a rational or objective knowledge to a more relational knowledge that is holistic and subjective—a knowing "more by the heart." This type of knowledge is expressed well in the Hebrew word *yada*. Cheryl Bridge Johns, *Pentecostal Formation: A Pedagogy Among the Oppressed*, 35.

love. Jesus came into the world, grew up as a Jew, learned Jewish culture, and lived among Jews. He was 100 percent human. However, Jesus was also 100 percent divine. His presence meant that the kingdom of God was at hand. He came, died, and rose again. The story does not end with the incarnation. In John 20:21, Jesus greets his disciples after the resurrection by stating, "Peace be with you! As the Father has sent me, I am sending you." The story continues with us. Because he went on to the Father, he sends us to continue his mission. Incarnational church planting is about being sent into a particular context to be agents, signs, and foretastes of the kingdom of God. That is best expressed in a loving community of faith. As Jesus learned Jewish culture (enculturated or acculturated? or both?) and lived among Jewish people, we also live among others and learn the culture of the people whom we love, to show them Christ in a contextualized way.

In the growing missional church conversation, there is much discussion on incarnation that has implications for church planting. Inagrace Dietterich is convinced that the mission of the church is to be a source of radical hope and a witness of a new life.[33] The new church is a community of Christ-followers that has become a new social reality (i.e., described as alternative community by others) in Christ through the power of the Holy Spirit. She calls this community *koinonia*, "incarnating a whole new order."[34] For Dietterich, "The church makes Christ visible in the world as a sign, foretaste and instrument of God's reconciling love and forgiveness."[35] According to Leonard Sweet, we "incarnate the timeless into the timely."[36] We do that by "double listening," which he describes this way: "Christianity is double listening—to God through the Scripture[37] and to the voice of humans around us."[38] When we plant a missional incarnational church in a new context, we must practice double listening.

George Hunsberger and Craig Van Gelder encourage us "to be less accommodating to the world, yet every local expression must be incarnated as

---

33   Inagrace Dietterich, *Cultivating Missional Communities*, 5.
34   Ibid, 5.
35   Ibid, 5.
36   Leonard Sweet, *Post-Modern Pilgrims: First Century Passion for the 21st Century World*, xvi.
37   I would add "through the Holy Spirit" as well.
38   Sweet, *Post-Modern Pilgrims*, xvi.

a witness."[39] Simply, their call is to encounter the culture with the gospel.[40] The Holy Spirit empowers us to incarnate our witness in a plurality of cultural forms. It is the Holy Spirit that forms mission communities so that "the gospel may be incarnated in particular places, to be the witness to Jesus Christ."[41] As a result, "the gospel freely enters all cultures and places all cultures in question. It is translatable as the witness and message of Jesus, who may be known, confessed, and followed in every human setting."[42]

Neil Cole would claim that is what the "Organic Church" is all about. According to Cole, church planters of organic churches are willing to abide in their space and even have church there. They have church meetings in restaurants, offices, homes, university campuses, high school facilities, beaches, bars, coffeehouses, parks, and locker rooms.[43] They have church in their space to reveal Christ. Cole understands incarnational ministry as follows: "Instead of bringing people to church so that we can then bring them to Christ, let's bring Christ to people where they live."[44] He warns that a new kind of church may grow out of such an effort. As we are in their midst, in their space, we reveal Christ because "we are now His feet, His hands, His eyes, and His mouth."[45] Because we are the body of Christ, Jesus is still incarnate. Cole describes the incarnation this way: "He came to us. He lived life on our terms and on our turf."[46] He became incarnate. *Incarnate* means he was "in flesh" or "in a human body." He was truth "fleshed out" for all to see. Now "we are His temple, and His Spirit dwells within our flesh."[47] So, "'the Church is sent into the world to continue that which He came to do, in the power of the same Spirit, reconciling people to God.'"[48]

Darrell Guder also writes about the term *incarnation* in his other book, *The Incarnation and the Church's Witness*. First of all, he establishes that to speak "of

---

39   George Hunsberger and Craig Van Gelder, *Church Between Gospel & Culture: The Emerging Mission in North America*, xvi.

40   Ibid, xvii.

41   Darrell L. Guder, *The Continuing Conversion of the Church*, 145-46.

42   Ibid, 93.

43   Neil Cole, *Organic Church: Growing Faith Where Life Happens*, xxvi.

44   Ibid, xxvi.

45   Ibid, xxviii.

46   Ibid, xxvii.

47   Ibid, xxviii.

48   Cole quotes Leslie Newbigin in his book, *Organic Church*, xviii.

the incarnation is always to speak of Jesus Christ, the Lord, the once-and-for-all event of God's saving work in the world and for the world."[49] He continues:

> The term *incarnation* includes the whole of that story, as it is described in the Gospels and expounded in the letters of the New Testament. At the same time, it is a concept that, in a very profound way, defines the "how" of gospel witness. There is a fundamental pattern to God's self-disclosure throughout the Scriptures.[50]

The "what" and "how" of God's mission are shaped by the "why" of God's love. In other words, our vocation is shaped by the great commandment (see Matt. 22:37; John 14:34; 1 John 4:7-19). Later in the book, Guder writes, "What the mission of the church is called and empowered to incarnate is God's love in Christ. This is the heart of the matter. Jesus forms the community to carry out its witness as the continuing and expanding embodying of God's love for the world."[51]

Summary

Church planters are sent by God to plant an incarnational community of faith in a particular context. They are agents of the kingdom of God sent by Christ. The new church becomes incarnated and contextualized as prophet and priest wherever they are to transform values and worldviews that are contrary to the kingdom of God. As such, the new communities of faith are countercultural. Our hope and prayer is "Thy kingdom come, thy will be done" in each and every culture. However, that is accomplished by planting new churches that incarnate the kingdom of God. They demonstrate the justice, peace, hope, love, and life of Christ—the *shalom* of God. To communicate the new reality of the kingdom in practical ways, the church planter must learn to contextualize the gospel and the way of doing church for that context. In conclusion, such an acculturation process of contextualization-incarnation for church planters would practically include the following:

---

49   Guder, *The Incarnation and the Church's Witness*, 3.
50   Ibid, 3.
51   Ibid, 39.

1. Discern where God has called you to plant the new church.
2. Know the Word in order to know the truths and meanings that the Holy Spirit intended to communicate.
3. Know your own culture. What values and norms of your culture are you bringing into the way you want to do church? Make sure that you do not judge the new culture on the basis of your own, which is easy to do during culture shock. As a church planter, do not do church in the new culture the same way you have always done church just because it is the way you learned it. Discern. Do not clone models. Rather, plant life.
4. Learn as much as possible about the culture, including values, norms, institutions, artifacts, history, demographics, language, and so on. Learn their perspective and worldview.
5. Live among the people and develop relationships.
6. Gain a relational knowledge of the people in their context through relationships. Practice "double listening" (i.e., listening to God and listening to the people in the culture). Grow to understand their stories, fears, hopes, hurts, concerns, needs, and so on.
7. As you know the people and learn the culture, find redemptive analogies in the culture and in people's stories. Discover where the Holy Spirit is already at work.
8. With the relational knowledge gained, contextualize the gospel to communicate it effectively in the new culture.
9. As people come to Christ, contextualize the way of expressing and living the gospel for that culture. Again, do not clone models of church just because a church grew in another context. What works in the United States will not necessarily work in France, Nigeria, or Japan. Listen to God and to the people and do not presume.
10. Contextualize the worship. People connect with God and are most comfortable when they worship in ways that make sense for their culture. For example, music styles will vary.
11. Contextualize your discipleship so that the new believers can learn, mature in Christ, and bear fruit. People learn in different ways. People in the host culture may not learn in the same way as in your culture.
12. Once the church begins to grow and serve their community, become a prophetic voice to the culture as an alternative community of the kingdom, but speak to the values of the culture (e.g., consumerism, individualism, hatred, racism, etc.) that are contrary to the values of

the kingdom (e.g., love, community, kindness, patience, hospitality, etc.). You must first earn the right to be heard.

13. Multiply by equipping new church planters and sending them out into your and other contexts.

This is not a magic formula to guarantee success. Rather, it is a suggested process that a church planter can follow to help contextualize the gospel and live out the kingdom of God incarnationally. The details of contextualization-acculturation-incarnation are hard work, but the rewards will be eternal.

CONCLUSION

In this chapter, we looked at three key areas of contextualization: (1) critical contextualization, (2) cross-cultural issues, and (3) church and context. In the first, we learned the importance of seeing society as the context in which church planting is being carried out. It is the locus of where the church exists. In the second, we learned about the differences between people—their values and beliefs—and their approach to things like time and relationships. These differences need to be taken into consideration as we plant a church in a particular context. Lastly, we saw the importance of understanding worldviews and of the need for the church to become incarnate in a particular context. The age-old message needs to be transmitted in language, symbols, and images that communicate without distorting the truths of the ageless gospel.

Questions

1. List three aspects of missions to which "contextualization" may refer.

2. Why is it important to identify the worldview of the person/group you are evangelizing?

3. What dangers are present when contextualizing the message of the gospel?

4. What are some questions the messenger should ask himself/herself in order to fit in to the new culture and create opportunities for gospel ministry?

5. Explain the concept of "critical contextualization." What are the steps involved?

6. According to Lanier, what are some of the categories that must be considered when dealing with cold-climate and hot-climate cultures?

7. A visitor comes to your home. You are very busy with a project, but you stop what you are doing to make the visitor feel welcome. You treat him with honor, serving him food and a cup of tea. You act as if you had nothing else in the world pressing on you. What culture are you representing?

8. You need to discuss a problem with an elder, but you do not want to talk to him face to face so that he does not lose honor. What kind of communication are you using?

9. Navajos tend to be very non-competitive in sports. No one would think of receiving an award that does not go to the community as a whole. Are they collectivistic or individualistic?

10. The church planter kept looking at his watch, wondering why people were slow in getting to the meeting. When they did arrive, nothing was said about the time. Everyone was ready to begin the meeting. What contexts are at play here?

11. Define "society" and "culture" in two or three sentences.

12. What is the "worldview" of a culture?

13. As we plant churches in a context, what do we contextualize? How?

14. How do church planters acculturate in a new culture? How is it related to the Incarnation?

10 Is There Another Way to Plant a Church?
Alternative Models for Church Planting

Ken Davis

New churches are planted in many different ways. Each has its own unique birth, and the circumstances surrounding its beginning are unique. Consequently, there is no single "right" way to establish a new church. God is limitless in his creativity, and his servants can also be creative in their ministries. In his sovereignty, the Lord of the harvest is blessing a variety of church planting approaches in our day. This should not surprise us. In an increasingly complex culture, many kinds of churches will be required to reach all kinds of people; therefore, no one church planting model will be appropriate in all settings.

In this chapter, we will start by surveying fifteen different options for launching and growing new churches. We will consider the benefits and drawbacks of each model, and then we will conclude with some suggestions on how to select the model that will best fit one's particular ministry focus group. The selection of the right birth model is crucial because it invariably affects the baby church's future growth and health.

For the purposes of our discussion, we will group the fifteen models under three general headings: Individual Models, Mother-Daughter Models, and Models Involving Several Churches. First, we will discuss three church planting models that are best described as the work of an individual, because just one person plants the new church. Second, we will consider seven models classified as the work of a mother, because they all involve, in some way, one local church giving birth to another. Third, we will discuss five models that are the work of several churches. Each of these first fifteen church planting models has its own strengths and weaknesses. After examining these fifteen models, we will present some additional models that are used less frequently, including models for multicultural or multilingual settings. Wise church planters will seek to understand and evaluate each of these models before beginning their faith adventure of starting a new community of faith.

I. The Independent Pioneer

In this model, a church is started from scratch, often in a remote, unreached area, through the initiative of a single individual who usually has no organizational backing or even local church approval. Pioneer church planters are simply convinced of God's call on their lives to begin a church. Perhaps a group of believers has requested their assistance. Or the pioneer simply sees the potential for a new church in a place where nobody else has ventured to go. So by faith they step out—all on their own. Humanly speaking, the success or failure of the planting project is determined largely by the dynamic personality, character qualities, vision, and leadership ability of the individual pioneer and their family.

Some individuals are natural entrepreneurs. They simply have to be starting things! They seem to naturally attract people and be risk-takers. If they were marooned all alone in a desert, somehow they would locate water and begin cultivating an oasis to draw people to them. Pioneers tend to see the potential where others see only problems. They see opportunities when others see obstacles.

Most independent church planters are aggressive and active. They find it difficult to work under organizational structures because they work best on their own. Some pioneers will be used by God to start many churches in their lifetime. Once a congregation is established, independent pioneers will move on to begin anew. They are natural catalysts; they are gifted to start churches, but others will keep the churches going.

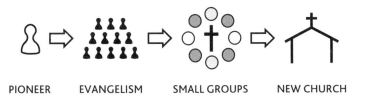

PIONEER   EVANGELISM   SMALL GROUPS   NEW CHURCH

This model has a number of advantages. First, the founder's "pioneer spirit" is often contagious and can provide great impetus for the newly forming group as they face multiple challenges. Second, the people of the new church tend to develop strong personal loyalty to a pioneer planting pastor and enthusiastically share his zeal and sacrifice.

Third, the opportunities for people to participate in ministry and leadership are numerous in this kind of work. Fourth, the pioneer, with no guiding authority, has the freedom to personally make immediate decisions and deal directly with problems, which can stimulate growth in the beginning stages of the new work. Some will be attracted to this model because they do not want to be restricted by denominational dictates, church traditions, or the overruling decisions of other church leaders.

There are, however, many potential weaknesses in the independent pioneer model. First of all, without accountability and the wisdom and experience of others, the independent pioneer can make serious blunders and poor decisions. Scripture repeatedly warns us of the danger of the lack of guidance from other mature believers (Proverbs 11:14; 15:22; 20:18; 24:6). Second, long hours and heavy responsibilities, without much outside assistance, can easily strain the pioneer's marriage and family relationships.

Third, inadequate financing to support their family often requires independent pioneers and/or their spouses to seek outside employment; some pioneers may have to leave the newly launched church to raise more support, thus crippling the new work. Fourth, when an unknown "lone ranger"—an outsider—enters a community to start up a new work without respected organizational backing, this can cause a crippling suspicion or resentment throughout the target community.

Fifth, a pioneer church planting leader is often strong-willed and may be determined to maintain control in the fledgling body. Finally, the planting couple, lacking built-in fellowship and support, can easily become lonely and discouraged, even abandoning the project.

Despite these inherent dangers, many independent pioneers have been greatly used by God to start dynamic growing churches. This model requires that the pioneering couple have even stronger faith and more spiritual toughness than with other approaches. The independent planting couple "must be very creative in developing the fellowship, support, guidance and accountability that this model lacks."[1]

A. The Founding Pastor

The second individual approach comes out of and is quite similar to the first. At times God will direct a person with pastoral gifts to go out and plant a new church. Moved with God-given compassion and vision, the founding pastor not only gathers and builds the initial core group but also stays on as the long-term pastor of the growing church. Founding pastors frequently assemble a team of workers who have the spiritual gifts that the founder lacks.

C. Peter Wagner points out that there are two basic types of founding pastor planters: those with a "lifetime call" to the new church, and those who see themselves as "lead pastors."[2] The one major difference between these two is that the primary gift of many lead pastor planters seems to be evangelism rather than shepherding. Lead pastors will start the new church and effectively build it up to a certain point, but then they voluntarily step aside for another person better equipped to permanently pastor the growing church. They recognize their gifts are better suited for smaller, younger churches.

The advantages and disadvantages of starting a new church with this approach are similar to those discussed under the Independent Pioneer model. Some people will be attracted to this model because their passion is to shepherd a flock, not to lay foundations. And yet they would prefer not to inherit an established church with many long-standing problems.

---

1 Paul Becker, *Dynamic Church Planting: A Complete Handbook.*
2 C. Peter Wagner, *Church Planting for a Greater Harvest*, 71-72.

B. The Bi-Vocational Planter

This is actually another version of the founding pastor approach, but it merits attention because of its own unique challenges and opportunities. Often founding pastors will intentionally seek out secular employment as a "tentmaker," like the apostle Paul, to meet their financial needs. They will serve the new church for years with little or no financial remuneration from the new church. Bi-vocational planting pastors may see their dual role/status as either temporary or permanent. Most plan to work on the side only until the new church grows to the point that it can support them with a full-time salary. Others prefer to keep their dual role. They are convinced God has called and equipped them for this special task.

There are obviously advantages to this approach. The working pastor is very involved in the "real world" and thus has many open doors of witness in the secular marketplace, with numerous contacts among non-Christians. Second, the bi-vocational planter learns to better relate to working people and understand the secular mindset. Pastors who work in the secular arena become more aware of the frustrations and difficulties working people deal with daily; by experiencing the same busy schedule, stresses, and problems, they are better equipped to minister not only to members in their own busy congregations but also to unchurched people in the community. Third, there is less likelihood that these pastors who work outside the ministry will be accused of selfish motivations, such as being in the ministry only for the money. Fourth, bi-vocational planters, realizing they cannot do all the work that needs to be done in a new church, are more apt to encourage their core group and church members to be involved in the ministry and in outreach. Training, empowering, and delegating responsibility for the ministry becomes a top priority.

Fifth, this model allows new churches to be started in rural areas, small towns, inner cities, and other places where sufficient support may be unavailable to fully fund planting pastors. A lack of funding need not stop us from planting churches in needy areas. In fact, growing denominations are increasingly relying on bi-vocational workers in these areas.

Clearly, bi-vocational planters are not to be viewed as second class or mere "part-time" ministers. They can be very effective. A recent study by the Southern Baptist denomination in the United States revealed that churches led by tentmaking pastors actually had a higher ratio of baptisms than those led by fully salaried ministers. Southern Baptist leaders concluded that these churches were more effective in evangelism. Surprisingly, bi-vocational churches also gave a larger percentage of their overall budget to missions.

Nevertheless, those considering this approach in church planting need to be aware of potential challenges. The growth of the newly developing church is often slower or stunted because working pastors have so little time and energy left to give directly to evangelism, discipling, and sermon preparation. Second, a secular occupation tends to put one into a social strata that may be different from the primary social group the church planter needs to be working with and has targeted in the ministry. Third, new churches led by bi-vocational pastors can easily become indifferent to their stewardship responsibilities of providing for those who faithfully preach and teach the Word of God (Gal. 6:6-8; 1 Tim. 5:18).

Churches begun under this model may become so accustomed to letting their pastors provide for themselves that they are slow in providing their salary. Biblically this is their first obligation. Scripture is clear that those who preach the gospel should live from the gospel (1 Cor. 9:13-14).

Fourth, bi-vocational planters can become so secure in their jobs, and dependent upon a set income, that they are reluctant to risk resigning their jobs, trusting God to provide through the giving of his people. Some pastors never do step out by faith—even when their congregation asks them to work full-time in the church. They get used to a comfortable lifestyle guaranteed by a good job. If the leader's faith and vision are small, it is very probable that the congregation's will be meager as well.

Ultimately, bi-vocational pastors must wrestle with a scriptural issue: can a working pastor, often with divided loyalties, serve two masters well? Some pastors are evidently able to fulfill dual roles and not be hindered in their church planting work. The New Testament makes it clear that this was true of the apostle Paul. But Paul was a single man without the added responsibilities of family, unlike most working pioneers today.

In conclusion, there may be situations that require a church planter to earn a living in the marketplace—at least in the beginning. This is a model that facilitates the rapid expansion of the gospel. In some countries, especially in areas of the world that are closed to traditional missionary efforts, such as Islamic countries, it may be the only means of gaining an entrance. There are now Christian organizations that specialize in preparing tentmakers to minister in these "restricted access nations."

Historical Support for the Bi-vocational Model

Read the words of Chrysostom. In the fourth century, he described the life of the rural bishops of Antioch: "These men you may see sometimes yoking the oxen and driving the plough, and again ascending the pulpit and cultivating the souls under their care; now uprooting the thorns from the earth with a hook, and now purging out the sins of the soul by the Word."

— Ralph Moore, *Starting a New Church*, 105.

We now turn to church planting models that are initiated and based out of a local church.

II. MOTHER DAUGHTER MODELS

A. The Daughter Church

Worldwide, the mother-daughter model is probably the most widely used method to plant a new church. In the work of Multiplication Network Ministries (MNM) in many countries on different continents, this model seems to be the single most popular way to start new communities of faith, particularly when a denomination encourages it among the churches. In this model, an established average-size to large-size church decides to multiply itself instead of continuing to grow larger. The existing congregation recruits key leaders and families from its own membership to send out into a needy nearby area. This group forms the nucleus for the fledgling church in the target community. If the seed group is large enough, an immediate daughter congregation can be formed. The new church is usually located within driving distance of the sponsoring church so that nucleus members do not have to move their residences. In this approach, the mother church is providing the workers, financial support, other resources, and basic accountability right from the start. Thus this model offers a far greater likelihood that a healthy, growing church plant will be launched. The success rate of these new churches is very high. In the mother-daughter approach, existing churches are privileged to be directly involved in missionary church planting.

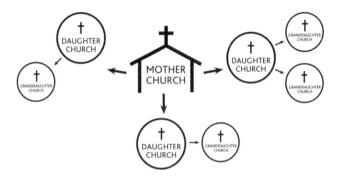

One example of this model is Bethesda Baptist Church in Brownsburg, Indiana, United States. Under the dynamic leadership of Dr. Tyler, this congregation of 1,500 people, over a ten-year period, has intentionally given birth to eight daughter congregations around the Indianapolis metropolitan area.

The mother church provided each daughter church with a fully salaried church planter, up to 50 adult "loaner members," and enough financial assistance to rent a meeting place. Bethesda also provided a full-time staff person to oversee the planting projects. Today the combined attendances of the daughter congregations come to well over 1,000. Amazingly, the mother church still has around 1,500 people in Sunday worship attendance! What a wonderful illustration of the biblical principle that we cannot out-give the Lord! Certainly the cumulative impact upon urban Indianapolis is far greater than if Bethesda had decided instead to focus on being the area's largest church! We know of many smaller congregations, with far fewer resources, that have also given birth to daughter congregations.

There are at least three common situations that can encourage churches to start a daughter church. First, a number of church families may already be living in an area outside of the community the church primarily serves. For some time they have been traveling some distance to get to the mother church, and possibly they have already expressed a desire to see a work started in their own community. This geographic area becomes the target community for the new church, and these families are recruited as members for the new church. The mother church properly recruits those whom God has sovereignly placed as seed families in the target area.

Second, a daughter church may be launched out of a desire to reach groups with other lifestyles, ethnicities, or socioeconomic levels. Even when an established church is growing and effectively reaching new people in its community, it still may be failing to have an impact on certain people groups in the larger region. Some people may not feel comfortable attending worship services in the mother church. The particular needs of these groups (like a different primary language) may call for a new church that can better accommodate their cultural sensitivities and minister to them more effectively.

A third possible scenario might be to launch a daughter church because there is a legitimate need for another style of biblical worship. The mother church may, for example, worship in a very traditional manner, one that the majority prefers and will not easily give up. Yet there are other believers in the church, as well as unchurched people in the community, who would respond better to a more contemporary worship style. If this new style cannot be introduced without causing disunity or disruption, then a daughter congregation may be a better option. The developing church could meet in the mother church's facilities, or they could find a new meeting place with the mother church's blessing and support.

There are significant advantages to mother-daughter church planting. This method is grounded in the biblical principle of spontaneous reproduction. When the core group comes from one established congregation, the people are more likely to have a common philosophy of ministry than if they had not been together previously. With this approach, there are usually ample resources available. The mother church will often provide a fully supported planter, leaders and workers for the new church, prayer support, money for rent and start-up costs, and sometimes basic equipment. All this means the new work should be able to be financially self-sufficient much more quickly than with other approaches. More can be accomplished in a shorter time because of ready resources and expertise.

The baby church is provided immediate visibility and stability in the new community. With faithful families either loaned or permanently given to the new work, the church has an instant membership, mature leadership, regular givers, and a strong doctrinal foundation from the start. It is far less likely that the new group will be "hijacked" by the infusion of a nearby group holding doctrinally heretical views. Also, visitors should be more willing to unite with this new church when they see a well-planned program, led by committed believers.

This approach blesses and benefits the sponsor church in many ways. Mothering normally motivates the parenting church to a greater commitment to evangelism and stewardship. It compels the older church to develop new leaders to replace those who leave for the new church. Participation in a planting project often inspires renewed vision, zeal, and sacrifice to fulfill the Great Commission.

All of this produces a reviving effect and keeps the mother church from spiritual stagnation. Most mother church pastors testify that their churches are not permanently hurt in attendance and giving. God greatly blesses their obedience!

The mother-daughter model provides better support and ongoing supervision for both the church planter and the team. Normally they are accountable for their ministry to either the mother church directly or to a "task force" composed of the planter, the mother church pastor, and key leaders from both the mother church and the core group that has been sent out. Parenting creates a greater sense of responsibility. Mother churches often are more willing to invest substantially to insure their baby church's many needs are being adequately met. Because there is a natural, direct, and close link between the two congregations, normally there are mature workers, and there is solid prayer and financial support available to the younger body. Parenting encourages the careful, well-planned development of the new church. It helps ensure that the characteristics, strengths, and doctrinal focus of the mother church are reproduced.

Another benefit of the mother-daughter model is that the families sent out by the parenting church are usually more culturally similar to the target community. This is because they may already live in the area or may be of similar ethnic or socioeconomic background. With other models, the planting team may be viewed as "outsiders." It is also true that if, sadly, the planting venture were to fail, it is fairly easy to gather the families back into the mother church.

This model builds bridges of unity and belonging for new churches. New believers have others nearby who share their faith and who can encourage them and reinforce what they are being taught from the Word. This spirit of unity can be furthered by holding occasional joint services or combined baptismal services, and by scheduling youth activities, camps, and adult retreats together. For this reason there is great value in mother churches starting a "cluster" of baby churches in nearby communities. This allows all the churches to encourage one another, and the strong can build up the weak. True partnership (*koinonia*) in the gospel is thus realized.

Finally, the mother-daughter model is a tried and proven model, having been used successfully all over the world in diverse cultural contexts, by congregations large and small. Because there is much accumulated experience and wisdom available, those embarking on this approach can obtain lots of solid counsel. It is a far less risky approach than some other models.

Although this model is a strong one, there are some cautions. First of all, the mother church should count the cost before beginning the process. A great deal of planning, preparation, and sacrifice will be needed. It can take months or even years to replace the families, trained leaders, and financial resources that go to the new church. The new work may prove to be more of a financial strain on the sponsoring church than originally expected. The established church will need to make major adjustments after "giving birth." Many established churches struggle to cope with feelings of bereavement after their "loss." The emotional, psychological, and spiritual upheaval of giving birth to a new church may cause serious strain and even "fatigue." Some mother churches may even be damaged in the process. Many churches will not be able to plant daughter churches more than once or twice in a lifetime in certain contexts.

A few members of the mother church may begin to view the new church as competition. If the relationship between the two churches and their pastors is not healthy and clear from the start, it may produce confusion or even conflict over policies and programming in the new church.

There is always the danger of overdependence on the mother church. Providing too much for too long may "smother" the baby and even create a latent hostility. It will take wisdom to discern when to allow the new church to struggle on its own without the mother's help.

It is also possible that some of the "seed" families who left the established church to start the daughter church may become dissatisfied with the new situation and seek to return prematurely to the parenting church. They may feel their family's needs are not being adequately met because the new work offers far fewer ministries than the mother church. Some may bemoan the fact that the new planting pastor's style of ministry is quite different.

Others may get discouraged with the slow growth of the new work. To prevent all this, unrealistic expectations must be dealt with before the seeding families are sent out. Their commitment to the new work should be spelled out up front. Are they going out as "loaners" for one year, or will they be expected to stay? Will they be allowed to continue serving in the mother church, or will they be expected to give all their time, talent, and treasure to the new work? The latter option would be preferable in most cases.

The new church must take great care to ensure that it is truly open to welcome new people. People from the target community who visit the new church may find it difficult to join a fellowship whose members know each other well from their previous church. Perhaps this is a good reason to limit the number of "seed" families sent out from the mother church. This will be particularly true if the group is of a different ethnic or cultural background than those in the new area.

Perhaps the most serious problem to avoid in the mother-daughter model is the danger of cloning rather than planting. The stronger the ties to the mother church and the larger the number of her members who leave to start the baby church, the more likely it will be that cloning will occur. Cloning is the exact duplication of an organism. In our world, cloning is occurring with increasing regularity and is no longer science fiction. In the field of church planting, the term would describe "the process of replicating the structures, style, activities and focus of one congregation in another."[3] In other words,

---

3   Stuart Murray, *Church Planting: Laying Foundations*, 120.

the mother church expects the daughter church to be "made in its image" and allows little or no flexibility or creativity.

Cloning churches is not always wrong, but if the new church is trying to reach another racial, cultural, or generational group, trying to be exactly like the mother church could be detrimental to the daughter's success. When the daughter church will be planted many miles away, or even only a few miles away in an urban community, serious thought should be given regarding the "shape" of the new church. Stuart Murray, a veteran British church planter, reminds us:

> Starting a new church is a glorious opportunity to ask questions and to experiment. The familiar response to new ideas—"we've never done it this way before"—is even less relevant than usual. In a new church, nothing has been "done this way before." Everything is open for discussion. The founding members can make fresh choices and set new priorities. They can dream dreams, take risks, experiment with new patterns, and enjoy the refreshing, but sometimes frightening, liberty of pioneering a new church.[4]

In other words, when we plant a daughter church, we must carefully distinguish what is biblically negotiable and non-negotiable. Mother churches must be careful not to put their offspring into a straitjacket and thus cut off healthy growth.

In conclusion, the mother-daughter church planting model requires a spiritually mature church with a strong pastor, a balanced ministry, and active lay leaders. Giving the process adequate time is essential to avoid a premature birth. Spiritual maturity, not congregational size, is the key. The whole church needs to be united in supporting the project, and must lift up the project in prayer. The church must understand the needs, plans, and problems involved. Leaders must see the project as obedience to the Lord of the harvest, whose plan is that we multiply. Are we prepared to see the process of planting the new church through to the end—that is, until it is capable of being a self-supporting, independent congregation? If so, then both churches, the mother and the daughter, can grow to the glory of God! All in all, the joys of motherhood far outweigh the pains of giving birth.

---

4   Ibid, 121.

Next we present a number of variations of the mother-daughter approach to church planting.

B. Colonization

This model is identical to the more traditional mother-daughter model—with one major exception. In the colonization model, dedicated Christians intentionally move to another city, to a different part of the same city, or even to another state or country for the purpose of founding a new church. The seed families usually relocate at their own expense and find their own employment. They often use their own homes to start up outreach Bible studies in the target community. Because the distance involved is often great, the mother church normally does not send out a large number of its members. Obviously this approach calls for a radical level of commitment to Christ and the Great Commission!

We call this the "Priscilla and Aquila" method of church planting, in honor of the tentmaking lay couple who often accompanied the missionary Paul on his church planting journeys into pioneer areas, helping with the necessary work of evangelism to prepare the soil (see Acts 18:1-3, 18, 26; Rom. 16:3-4; 1 Cor. 16:19).

COLONIZATION MODEL

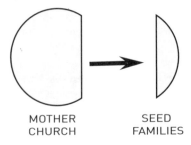

MOTHER   SEED
CHURCH   FAMILIES

C. Adoption

In this parenting variation, a group already in existence seeks assistance from an established church. It could be a Bible study group, prayer group, or cell group that invites an established congregation to supervise the work. Or perhaps the established church takes the initiative when it sees a struggling work—usually of the same or similar doctrinal persuasion—and seeks to come alongside to bring it to maturity. As in human adoption, in church adoption someone else has given birth to the new group, but then the established church makes the new church a part of its family.

ADOPTION "A"

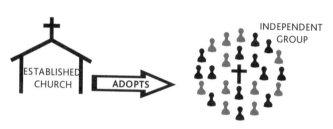

The assistance that the established church gives to the new church may vary. The adopted group often looks to their new mother church to supply leadership, vision, and direction, as well as additional resources of money and/ or people. The adopting church may help by providing a salary for the planting pastor for a short period. Sometimes the adopting church provides one of its own staff members or a pastor-in-training to lead the fledgling work. Pastor John MacArthur and Grace Community Church of Panorama City, California, have revitalized numerous dying churches by supplying them with trained and salaried seminarians from Masters Seminary.

The adoption model is not without potential difficulties. In a normal church plant, visitors are attracted by the new group's excitement; in the adoptive plant, this rarely happens. Furthermore, the two church bodies may be incompatible, or the adopted group may be unwilling to change where needed. It will take more time for the smaller congregation to learn to trust and develop close ties with the larger adopting congregation. Will the adopted church retain its autonomy or surrender it entirely? If they surrender it, will that be temporarily or permanently?

Finally, the very reasons that brought about the young church's decline may persist and thus stymie the desired growth of the new work.

ADOPTION "B"

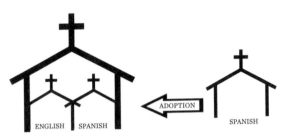

Murray reminds us of a number of reasons why an adopted church may have been declining and now need outside help. These may include unsuitable premises, which may be poorly located, poorly maintained, or inappropriate in size and style for their context. In terms of the congregation, it may suffer problems such as introversion, traditionalism, inflexibility, disunity, cultural distance from the community, or a negative reputation in the community.[5]

D. Accidental Parenthood

This is the opposite of family planning. In this unfortunate situation, a new church forms out of a church split because believers were unable to settle their differences. When congregations fragment over non-biblical issues, the result is often much pain, and this damages the testimony of the church in the community. Even so, the sovereign God is certainly able to bring good out of sinful anger and divisiveness. In a human family, parents naturally love both their planned and unplanned children. Likewise, the Father God loves both the resulting congregations and he is able to make them part of Christ's bride and eternal family.

Church splits over non-essentials, personality conflicts, or procedural issues should always be discouraged. But sometimes a new work arises because believers have been compelled to break away from a church that had seriously compromised the Christian faith.

A church split is justifiable only on biblical grounds—and only after every effort has been made to rectify the situation and maintain the unity of the church. When there is much evidence that God has removed his blessing from

5   Ibid, 249.

a congregation, it may be proper to withdraw from an established church. The evidence might include a tolerance of false doctrine, close cooperation with groups that promote non-biblical positions, or a refusal to deal with long-standing and unrepentant sin in the church.

In some cases, it might even be justifiable to break away and start a new church if the old church has lost its vision and has lapsed into a long-term apathy, like the church in Laodicea (Rev. 3:14-22). When repeated attempts to resolve these and other problems are unsuccessful, then it may be time to leave. To stay in an unbiblical church would be disobedient to the clear teaching of Scripture, even if your intentions are to be a godly influence.

This model unfortunately explains the origin of many churches, often for reasons that are not justified. We are not trying to promote this model but are explaining how some new congregations come into being.

ACCIDENTAL PARENTHOOD

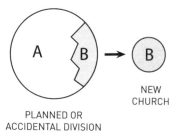

PLANNED OR
ACCIDENTAL DIVISION

NEW
CHURCH

A church planter should be extremely cautious about becoming involved in a church that is the result of a split. You may find strong opposition from the old church. Bitterness and bad attitudes that may be present will hinder the new church's ministry. A poor testimony in the community could hurt the work for years to come. People who could not get along in the former church may cause ongoing problems as well.

Be sure your motives and those of the people are right. There should be a sweet spirit. Have they followed the Matthew 18 pattern for dealing with personal and doctrinal grievances? Have they done everything possible to first make things right with those at the former church (see Matt. 5:23-24)? Make sure that the leadership in the group is saved and baptized—do not assume they are. If the group is composed of committed Christians who have separated from another church for biblical reasons, they can form a strong church to the glory of God. But they must be willing to make the sacrifices necessary to get the new church going and to keep it growing. Bathe the entire situation in prayer. Let the community know that you are motivated by love for people as well as the truth.

A more positive variant of this model arises when two different philosophies of ministry arise in a church. The groups consciously decide to avoid a large conflict, and they use the situation to begin a new church, either in the same building or in another place. This type of adoption requires much wisdom, patience, love, respect, prayer, and discernment of God's will.

E. Multi-Congregational Model

This exciting mothering variation works best in a multiethnic, diverse urban setting. In this model, an established church with a facility located in a changing multiethnic neighborhood intentionally plants several daughter churches. All the language/cultural groups share the same building. They have their services at different times, yet they fellowship together and share as much as they can. Each group normally has its own pastor and leadership. Each contributes equitably to the upkeep of the building. The different ethnic groups may each choose to be totally autonomous or to be subcongregations of one larger, single church.

Several denominations have experimented successfully with this model. One of the earliest and most publicized examples is Temple Baptist Church of Los Angeles. This multi-congregational church has English, Hispanic, Filipino, and Burmese groups, with plans for including several more ethnic groups. An overall church coordinating council, with representatives from each group (to avoid paternalism), meets together regularly to make sure everything is operating smoothly. Once every three months, all the ethnic congregations worship together, with choirs singing in various languages. What a foretaste of the heavenly scene in Revelation 7:9-12!

Even in areas with only one culture, some churches begin a new church with a different ministry philosophy in the same building. For example, a traditional church may decide to start another church for younger people, with different hours, style, music, and organizational structure.

The multi-congregational model commends itself for several reasons. First, it makes financial sense in big cities, where affordable property is often next to impossible to find. Congregations strategically located in historic downtown or urban communities are often tempted to relocate to the suburbs when the neighborhood undergoes transition. They sometimes fail to see that the Lord of the harvest has brought the mission fields of the world to their doorstep.

MULTI-CONGREGATIONAL MODEL

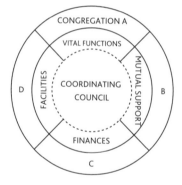

A better option would be to hold on to that valuable property and maximize its use by engaging in cross-cultural church planting and evangelism. By combining the resources of all the subcongregations, a stronger, multiethnic evangelistic witness is maintained in the city.

A second reason this model is worth serious consideration is that it is evangelistically attractive. In the United States, for example, many North Americans are frustrated over the increasing racial division and discord in society. There is much talk and empty rhetoric, even in Christian circles, concerning the need for racial reconciliation. Multiethnic churches provide living demonstrations that the answer to racism is the gospel of Jesus Christ!

The multi-congregational model has other redeeming qualities as well. It offers visitors a choice of language and worship styles. It recognizes the ethnic diversity and autonomy of the various people groups found in our cities. While it preserves homogeneity at the fellowship level to attract nonbelievers, it promotes creative and loving relationships across congregations, and it begins to knock down the walls of racism and discrimination. Thus, this model exhibits and values both the diversity and unity of the body of Christ.

F. Multi-Campus Model

In this mothering variation, a large existing church seeks to expand its ministry impact by starting public services in several scattered sites. The multi-campus model consists of one congregation in more than one location. Normally this church has a united membership, one staff, and one operating budget, but it meets weekly at two or more church properties. Usually a dynamic pastor, with the drive and physical stamina to preach several times on Sunday, pastors this kind of church. At other times, a rotating staff may do the preaching and shepherding.

MULTI-CAMPUS MODEL

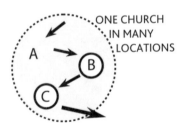

This approach to church planting has seen mixed results. At one time, Scott Memorial Baptist Church in San Diego, where the author's wife grew up, had three locations. After some time, they decided to form three separate autonomous churches. One reason was that the church staff was wearing itself out. In Indianapolis, Pastor Jeffrey Johnson of Eastern Star Baptist Church preaches at three locations each Sunday.

Currently this is the largest and one of the fastest growing congregations in Indianapolis. Two other well-known examples of the multi-campus model are The Church on the Way in Van Nuys, California, pastored by Jack Hayford, and Mount Paran Church of God in Atlanta, pastored by Paul Walker. Only time will tell how effective the multi-campus approach will be. More research will need to be done.

G. Satellite Model

Like the multi-campus church, this model has one church with multiple locations. The difference is that in the satellite model, the new congregations planted are semiautonomous. This is quite similar to a large central bank having numerous branch banks or to a seminary having several extension sites. In each case, the scattered satellites continue to hold a close organic relationship with the mother, while having lots of freedom.

Some church growth enthusiasts feel the satellite model will be the wave of the future. Combining the best features of both larger church and smaller cell group strategies, this approach has potential for reaching our largest cities for Christ by penetrating all the cultural and ethnic mosaics of metropolitan areas.

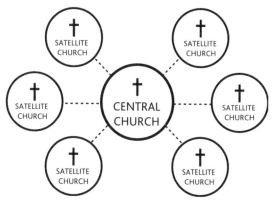

Simply put, new people groups and new urban neighborhoods can be reached by starting new satellites. Most important, each satellite church is expected to reproduce, and all the combined resources of the mother church and the other satellites are made available to help. This is the big advantage of not starting totally independent and disconnected churches.

Some of the largest churches in the world are making an impact on their cities and regions by use of this dynamic model. Researchers Elmer Towns and John Vaughan give numerous examples from Chile, Brazil, Nigeria, and the Philippines. In North American circles, one of the best known examples of the satellite church has been the Highland Park Baptist Church in Chattanooga, Tennessee. Under the leadership of Dr. Lee Roberson, the congregation of 4,000 was at one time reaching an additional 5,000 people in some 60-100 satellite "chapels" and extension Sunday schools. The chapel satellites provided tremendous opportunities for hundreds of pastoral students from Tennessee Temple University to get practical experience preaching and evangelizing. Today several of the larger satellites have been granted autonomy and function as independent churches. The Southern Baptist denomination and others have also experimented with the satellite model.

III. Models Involving Several Churches

In all the church planting models described in the previous section, the agency starting the new congregations was always the local church. In each of the following models, other agencies are also involved in the planting process.

A. Missionary Church Planting

Missionary church planting is probably the best-known method of church planting among North American and European evangelical church groups. A "missionary pastor" goes into a community and starts the church but does not remain as the permanent pastor. This pastor is supported financially by other churches through an established mission agency. Missionary pastors serve as catalysts in the neighborhood, gathering a nucleus from which to found the church. Often called "catalytic church planters," they combine the roles of pastor and evangelist.

Genuine missionary church planters stay with the new congregation no longer than necessary. Their goal is to work themselves out of a job. As soon as the church is grounded in sound doctrine, has trained leadership, and is able to support a pastor fully, they resign and begin the planting cycle all over in a new locale. The time it takes for the church to become self-supporting varies from a number of months to several years.

This traditional method has proven to be reliable through the years. It works well in pioneer situations where there is no nucleus or core group in the target community. Fully supported missionaries can go anywhere to begin a work. They do not have to wait for a nearby church to catch the vision of mothering or assisting the new group.

This method usually relies on strong, experienced leaders to initiate the work, ones gifted in personal evangelism, discipleship, and leadership training. These missionaries are carefully selected and equipped by the sending churches and mission agency. They are called to be church planters. Normally they can be more effective than part-time or untrained lay people who may not have the time or training for the job.

MISSIONARY MODEL

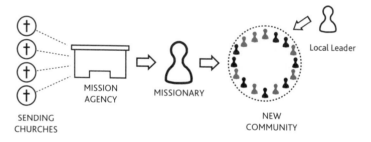

Mission-sponsored church planters are more accountable—they report to both supporting churches and to their agency. A mission administrator can carefully supervise and lovingly counsel in areas of inexperience, weakness, or neglect. Mothering churches often do not have the time or experience to provide this kind of help.

The missionary church planting model provides long-term financial support for the new work. The needs of the missionary's family are met through faithful support from numerous supporting churches, allowing the missionary to work full-time in outreach in the crucial early months. No one in the community can rightly accuse these church planters of coming with suspect motives, since they are not dependent on financial support from the community. Money received in the offerings can go directly into the development of the new church's ministries.

Missionary-planted congregations can almost always build a church building much more quickly. New churches often find it difficult to secure construction loans by themselves, but in this model, the mission agency will often cosign or guarantee the financing for the new church, using its collective resources as collateral. It may even be able to provide a building loan from a mission revolving fund at lower than conventional interest rates.

With this kind of long-term leadership, accountability, and financial backing, we would expect missionary-planted churches to exhibit more stability and strength than others.

There are, however, some potential pitfalls with this method of church planting. First, the promise of long-term outside support can actually become a detriment by eroding a local sense of responsibility for the work. It is tempting for the new church to become too dependent on the missionary's resources. Members and new converts may hold back in their own giving, particularly if they are not adequately challenged by the missionary to give to the ministry. Congregations must be encouraged to assume financial responsibility for the new church as soon as possible, and they should be contributing to their pastor's support from the start. Given the danger of dependence, we recommend that outside support be cut back over a period of time and that the new church be expected to assume an increasingly larger share of the missionary's salary. This motivates all parties to work hard.

Another pitfall of this model is that missionaries must periodically report back to their supporting churches, and their absence from the work for several weeks or months may hurt the church. Some fledgling works never get off the ground because their missionary is constantly away reporting to churches or trying to raise additional support. It is imperative that the missionary not start a church until he has adequate support raised and thus can remain on the field for the first two or three years without having to leave to search for more funding. Likewise, supporters must be patient and understand that the missionary may not be able to report back as often as they would like. The missionary's priority must be given to church planting.

Some have suggested that it takes too long for a missionary-planted church to achieve self-supporting status. This may be true in some cases. There could be several contributing factors. First, if a new church grows to love its missionary pastor, it is only natural that they may not want to turn this pastor lose. Consequently, members may not be as motivated as they should be to evangelize and to grow numerically. Second, even a competent missionary may face resistance in the community because he is viewed as an unwelcome "outsider," slowing the work.

Third, church visitors are sometimes reluctant to join the ministry when they learn that the missionary pastor will not be there permanently. Finally, the missionaries themselves may become too comfortable in the work. Because they are receiving partial support from both the mission and the church, they may fail to encourage the new church to press on toward self-support. For all these reasons, it is very easy for this model to be abused.

Possibly the greatest challenge in this model is to successfully transition to the church's first permanent pastor. When the missionary pastor steps aside, the new pastor will no doubt introduce new ideas or possess a different personality and leadership style. The new person may not be as highly trained or experienced as the founding pastor. For the young church, this could pose a real problem of acceptance. Some new churches show a slower growth rate or even begin declining once a dynamic missionary has moved on. On the other hand, some missionary church planters do not want to pass the baton, and they make themselves "indispensable" in the ministry. They do not foster new leadership, and they end up leaving behind weak churches without a team of leaders prepared for the next phase of ministry.

Even with these potential problems and abuses, we are convinced the missionary model will continue to be blessed by the Lord of the harvest until the end of the church age. It is clearly a scriptural approach, paralleling the Pauline method so prominent in the book of Acts. A number of Bible teachers believe the modern missionary is the counterpart to the first-century apostle or evangelist found in Ephesians 4:11.

These early evangelizers bravely preached the gospel beyond the frontiers where Christ was known, and they enlarged the borders of peoples having faith in Christ. The apostle Paul expressed his missionary strategy this way:

"By the grace God has given me, I laid a foundation as a wise builder, and someone else is building on it" (1 Cor. 3:10). Through the centuries, tens of thousands have been won to Christ and his church through the ministries of these sent ones who lay church foundations so that others can build on them.

B. Missionary Teams

Most mission agencies today prefer that missionary church planters not work alone. They have learned that a team of agency workers laboring together in the gospel can plant new churches much more effectively. A cooperative team is particularly beneficial in urban church planting, where the challenges are many. In recent years, many independent church planters who are not working under a mission agency have also seen the value of recruiting a launch team.

Visionary lead planters, who make it a top priority during the first stage to seek out qualified associates with complementary spiritual gifts, are able to build stronger churches more quickly. This is why well-known and successful church planters like Robert Logan, Paul Becker, and Rick Warren all advocate the team approach. Some proponents even go so far as to state that a team is absolutely essential in order to plant a dynamic church.

The planting team, whether deployed by a mission agency or recruited by an independent planter, has several distinctive features and advantages. The team approach has clear biblical precedent. Jesus our Lord modeled team ministry as he selected and trained the twelve disciples. The Antioch church commissioned a heterogeneous and highly effective missionary team (Acts 13:1-3). The apostle Paul rarely worked alone, using numerous fellow workers—people like Barnabas, John Mark, Silas, Timothy, Luke, Tychicus, Artemas, Priscilla and Aquila, and Epaphroditus.

Because team members often come from and are supported by a variety of local churches, this model does not weaken the sending churches as much as in the mother-daughter method. Often several members of the team are bi-vocational, working to support team leaders and to release them for full-time outreach. As a result, some planting teams may be nearly financially self-supporting, which gives them more flexibility to minister.

Teams provide much mutual support and encouragement. Teammates can be best friends, helping each other in times of loneliness, exhorting each other to persevere in trials and difficulty (see Eccles. 4:8-10). They can protect one another from hostility, false accusation, and even physical attack (Eccles. 4:11-12). One always has a sympathetic prayer partner. A close partner in ministry knows your weaknesses and can give you wise counsel (Prov. 27:6, 9, 17; 11:14; 24:6) and provide accountability (Gal. 6:2; James 5:16).

The team model means the young church begins with a multiple staff and the potential of multiple ministries. The launch team is in one sense a miniature church already. When couples are trained for the ministry and they have complementary spiritual gifts and skills, the baby church is better able to attract and retain new people. One reason is that the team produces synergy, providing for a greater total effect than if they worked individually. There is more productivity and creativity when people work together.

Finally, a mission team produces greater witness in the community and accelerated growth in the church plant. There will be more workers, more resources and finances, and more time given to ministry areas that are frequently neglected by a church planter when working alone. If the team members work together harmoniously and model well the grace and power of God, their impact can be significant. If the team shares a common vision and the same values and works from a common outreach strategy, then the harvest will be greater and the work more enduring. The team approach should significantly increase the efficiency and fruitfulness of each individual on the team. Each person can do what he or she does best and enjoys most.

What are the drawbacks of team church planting? There is always the potential for conflict among teammates or their families. Some teams, arbitrarily placed together, are unable to work together.

They may have differing lifestyles and ministry philosophies. If one member sees more visible results, gets more financial support, is more popular, or takes credit for the work of the group, other members may become jealous (see 1 Sam. 18:7-9). If one member proves incompetent at the assigned responsibilities, others may grow resentful. Sometimes team members resist submission to each other or to the group leader's articulated vision and goals for the plant. All this is to say that the careful selection and unifying of the team members is crucial. Ongoing training, careful mentoring, pastoral support, and team accountability will be essential to ensure the team's ultimate success.

One variation to this model is what some call the Lightning or Blitz Model. In this strategy, a specific zone is chosen, and work teams "invade" the zone, carrying out intensive evangelism and other ministries for a short period of time. The sponsoring group or established church sends musical groups, evangelists, young people's groups, diaconal help, and children's programs to build a nucleus of new believers. The idea is to find a few leaders, give them basic training, and leave them in charge of the newly forming group. This model can be very effective, but there must be careful follow-up and training of persons new to the faith, and special attention needs to be given to the formation of local leaders.

BLITZ MODEL

DIACONAL TEAM
CHILDREN'S TEAM
PRAYER TEAM

YOUTH TEAM
MUSIC TEAM
EVANGELISTIC TEAM

COMMUNITY

EVANGELISM
BIBLE STUDIES
LEADERSHIP FORMATION
NUCLEUS OF THE NEW CHURCH

C. Church - Mission Agency Partnership

This model involves a cooperative effort of one or more churches, aided by a mission agency. A full-time experienced missionary with the agency joins forces with a single local church or group of nearby churches that desire to initiate a new work in a needy area. Each sponsoring church provides financial, moral, and material support as well as "seed" families; this support often makes the formation of an immediate congregation possible in the target community.

The missionary's role is to provide guidance and encouragement. Rather than lead the church plant themselves, missionaries enlist a founding pastor and help that person succeed. In other words, in this model, the missionary's job is to be a trainer/mentor, not a pastor/planter. The missionary is to remain in the background as much as possible. If deemed beneficial, the sponsoring churches might add another entity to the partnership by requesting the assistance of a nearby Bible college or seminary.

The partnership model seems to combine several of the most desirable features of other approaches. It may even multiply the strengths of previous models. Smaller churches, which could not start a daughter church by themselves, can band together to participate in the joys of being mothers or partners. This approach divides the burden among the partner churches, the new church, its pastor, and the missionary. This approach also provides immediate strong leadership and visibility in the target community. This kind of partnership provides on-the-job-training for the founding pastor, who could be a young preacher coming directly out of Bible college or seminary with little experience.

The veteran missionary is readily available to give wise counsel; the pastors from partnering churches can offer their experience as well. The new pastor does not need to apply to a mission agency or spend valuable time raising support. The partnering churches likely cover the pastor's salary. New pastors can enter right into the planting project, growing and maturing with the new church. There is no disruption, nor does the church have to search for a qualified permanent pastor when the missionary leaves. There are many other benefits. The partnering model allows for maximum participation, accountability, and input at the local level. Rapid church growth and self-support are very possible.

There are several potential pitfalls to the partnering model. With several churches and pastors involved, great care will need to be taken to avoid conflict, jealousy, and competition. To get independent congregations to lay aside petty differences and work together may be a challenge! Each sponsoring church should be allowed the privilege of participation without unrealistic expectations and demands of equal financial support or an equal number of families to be given to the project. One church may be able to do more than another. The rule of thumb is that each should contribute according to their ability—not equal gifts, but equal sacrifice. There is also the fuzzy question of accountability: to whom is the new church's founding planter pastor ultimately responsible—to the missionary or the churches (or even to the school, if one is involved)? This must be clarified. It is absolutely essential to form a committee to oversee the church plant, with representatives from each participating church and agency, and including the missionary and the founding pastor.

If the initial core group is composed of individuals coming from several different partnering congregations, it is quite likely that not everyone will share a common vision of what kind of church the new congregation should be. It is thus imperative that a leader be installed and the new church's vision and core values be established early. Finally, roles must be clarified from the very beginning with this model. A missionary could be tempted to dominate or control the new church from behind the scenes, so it is essential that the missionary have a servant's heart. The missionary's role must be carefully defined with both the founding pastor and the sponsoring churches. The founding pastor's role should likewise be carefully protected, lest his leadership be constantly challenged or "second-guessed" by the more experienced pastors. A written agreement that clarifies the responsibilities and privileges of each participating church and project key leader would be beneficial.

D. Associational or Denominational Church Planting

In recent years, many new churches have been started through the visionary initiative and substantial support of an association of churches or a denomination. When many churches covenant together to form a state or national fellowship, they can do much together for God's glory. As churches pool their resources and share their know-how, they can accomplish more than if they are working alone. Associations often carry out careful demographic studies, select strategic areas, and set regional goals for new church planting. With planting sites and strategies already in mind, they go out to carefully recruit suitable planters to fulfill the associational vision.

In Uruguay, the Church of God denomination is repeating in the past five years what it previously took them fifty years to accomplish in church planting. Using the Multiplication Network strategy, the denominational leaders and local pastors agreed to make church planting a national priority. The Assemblies of God in Ecuador is also involved in an aggressive plan to establish hundreds of new communities of faith in the coming years.

Using other strategies, the Southern Baptist Convention starts over 500 churches every year in the United States through its state associations. Other denominations such as the Evangelical Free Church of America, the Conservative Baptists, the Free Methodist Church, the Church of the Nazarene, the Christian and Missionary Alliance, the Presbyterian Church in America, the Church of God, and the Assemblies of God successfully utilize their national mission departments and budgets to provide leadership and finances for church planting.

There are numerous advantages to this approach. The most obvious is the abundant availability of financial resources when compared to the local church. This method provides denominational churches with a joint project that motivates the members to support church planting and missionaries.

Denominational loyalty helps raise large amounts of money, which are often channeled through the cooperative program. The financial load is spread among many churches rather than a few. Denominational or convention missionaries are usually guaranteed an annual salary from headquarters for the initial years.

DENOMINATIONAL MODEL

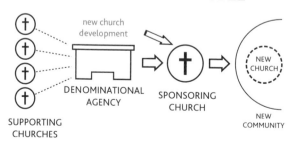

In other cases, associational church planters may have to raise their own support, but at least they can seek support from a network of churches and individuals committed to the association's objectives.

The denominational method often has a well-functioning organizational structure that governs church planting strategy. The duplication of services and ministries is avoided. Administrative efficiency is an obvious plus. State and national leaders can provide the latest surveys, demographic data, and other helps to their planters. Low-interest loans are sometimes available, as are regional church-growth seminars, legal aid, and printed materials.

A final advantage is the network of people and ideas. Denominational or association staff members are normally available to give church planters wise counsel regarding finances, property purchasing, or construction. To oversee the planting projects and to offer encouragement when needed, the association may hire an experienced director of church planting. Pastors and churches, hearing of the new plant, often call with the names of prospects who just moved into the target area. These kinds of referrals help the planter to assemble a core group quickly.

There are a few drawbacks to this method of planting churches. What is gained by administrative efficiency may result in less involvement on the local level. Little room may be left for grass-roots initiative and participation. The zeal of the new church may be weakened when everything is handed to it on a silver platter. Although the rapid construction of church facilities is often possible with the associational model, it can be a drawback if done before there is actually a committed congregation to use it.

Church planters may have less freedom than they would like. Because they are obligated to work with the sponsoring churches, they may feel limited or controlled by the denomination's pre-set program. The planter would be wise to discover upfront what the association's expectations are. In his book *Dynamic Church Planting*, Paul Becker, who has planted churches both under an association and independently, states that the following questions need to be asked:

Does the association require a percentage of the missions budget after the new church is viable? Are there denominational distinctions that the association expects the new church to uphold? Is the financial support on a descending scale? Will the church planter and the church be expected to attend certain meetings of the association?[6] Some associations will have reasonable expectations that benefit both the church planter and the association. Other groups will be quite restrictive. If a church planter cannot in good faith agree to the expectations of the association, then it is ethically wrong for him to accept the association's help in planting the church.

Ultimately, there is the valid question of the new church's autonomy. If an area of disagreement arises, who has the final authority: the local church or the association? These issues must be worked out before beginning the project so that parameters are clear.

Church planters should never assume that all denominational or associational pastors in the region will be enthusiastic about their coming. Some may become fearful of "competition." Leaders of nearby churches that are struggling may view the new plant as entering "their territory." They may be fearful of losing members.

To allay these fears, the church planter would be wise, early in the planning stage of the project, to personally approach area pastors. It is better for them to hear about the new church plant before it begins rather than afterward. Again, Becker gives seasoned counsel: "If they are hurt, frustrated, or combative, hear them out patiently and lovingly. Do not, however, be deflected from the community to which the Lord has called you because of an angry pastor."[7]

The denominational method of church planting sometimes results in "provincialism." This occurs when an association loses sight of the needs in other regions and countries. They may withhold or withdraw support when a church planter moves to another area outside the association's jurisdiction. Associations need to be encouraged to expand their districts so that the administrative structure does not hinder the ongoing church planting ministry.

In spite of these potential problems, this method has great promise. Denominations and associations can be a catalyst for renewed church planting—without sacrificing local church autonomy or key doctrinal distinctives. A

---

6   Becker, *Dynamic Church Planting*.
7   Ibid.

more complex variant of this model is that which Kevin Mannoia calls the Century 21 Church Planting Network.[8] This system has many ingredients that are directed and coordinated by a district of a denomination. It includes ten elements:

1. Network of mother churches: Trains and motivates established congregations.
2. Recruiting network: Establishes a strategy to recruit church planters.
3. Evaluation system: Measures the capacities and abilities of the church planter.
4. New church incubator: Provides pastoral and group support during the first year.
5. Pastor center: Provides pastoral training to lay people to plant churches.
6. Church planters retreat: Designed to orient and prepare church planters.
7. Developing churches group: Provides follow-up for five years.
8. Strategic planning network: Helps with church growth and multiplication.
9. Harvest 1000 plan: A strategy to increase stewardship and finances.
10. Metachurch network: Principles and courses to diagnose the church's health.

E. Regional Church Planting

This model is similar to associational church planting but works on a smaller scale. In fact, the local churches co-sponsoring the new plant may not necessarily be all part of the same association of churches. In this model, churches of like faith, all located in the same region of a state or province, commit themselves to work together for a single church planting project. Normally the number of cooperating congregations is limited to two to five in order to retain maximum local involvement and initiative. The target area for the new church is a nearby town or city. Similar to other sister church models, each partnering church's size, resources, proximity, and desires will determine the extent of sponsor involvement in the planting project.

---

8   Kevin Mannoia, *Church Planting: The Next Generation.*

The major attraction of the regional church planting model is that it permits smaller churches, which may feel that they do not have the resources to single-handedly give birth to a daughter church, to be directly involved in a planting venture. Where there is a great spiritual need nearby, a new church can be launched even when no larger parenting congregation is available in the area.

REGIONAL CHURCH PLANTING

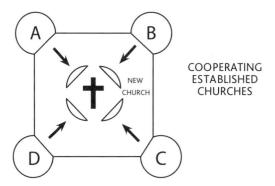

The author, working as a consultant, has seen firsthand the effectiveness of this model. Three churches near to each other came together and sponsored a church plant—Cornerstone Baptist Church of Forest City, Pennsylvania. Two of the three cooperating congregations averaged less than a hundred for Sunday worship. Yet by partnering together, a growing new church was begun in a town that had no evangelical witness. Over 190 people attended Cornerstone's initial celebration service—many of them guests from the three sponsoring churches who came to show support. As a result of its participation in this project, one of the three regional sponsors has determined to start another new church—this one by itself!

IV. OTHER MODELS

There are other variations of these fifteen church planting models, but the ones we have considered are the primary approaches God seems to be using today to successfully raise up dynamic new churches. Our list is certainly not exhaustive.

Some "models" are in reality strategies or methodologies that can be incorporated into the models we have discussed. For example, in the past, Sunday school and crusade strategies have been used, and in some contexts they may function well. The crusade strategy could be used in any of the models.

In addition, we have omitted other newer models that are being proposed today because they are not actually ways to plant new churches as much as they are new kinds of (or "shapes for") churches with which some innovators are experimenting. Three such new "models of church," in particular, have become increasingly popular in recent years: seeker-targeted churches, network churches, and cell churches (also known as house churches or small groups). In China, for example, the house church movement has proven, out of contextual necessity, the incredible multiplicative potential of such a strategy.

Here we present, in graphic form and without much explanation, some additional "models" for your consideration, pointing out that some are better seen as strategies within different models.

A. Cellular Model

This is actually a way to organize a church. Its strength is in the use of the resources of small groups and meetings in homes. The church meets to worship God in a large celebration, but the principal emphases are the cell groups and study groups, as well as worship services in the homes. The small group is the central part of the church and not just another program of a traditional church. A cellular church and a church with cell groups are not the same thing. The key in a cellular church is that the small group is the place of principal focus, and the multiplication of cells is anticipated. In this way, there are a large number of leaders being formed, and these leaders meet with the principal pastors to receive training, to pray, and to plan. The most recent studies show that in general, the cellular churches that grow have been groups in which a very dynamic leadership team begins the work, and in which there are enough leaders (a critical mass) prepared to develop the model.

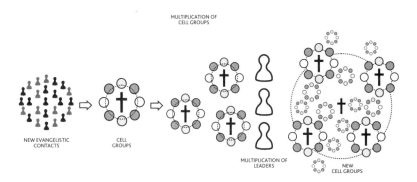

MULTIPLICATION OF
CELL GROUPS

NEW EVANGELISTIC
CONTACTS

CELL
GROUPS

MULTIPLICATION OF
LEADERS

NEW
CELL GROUPS

B. Mass Communication Model

Radio and television can be used for church planting, whether for promotion, preaching, evangelism, or special announcements. An office can be set up in a given location (such as a sponsoring church, a rented space, or even an office in a home) to receive the contacts of people who respond to announcements or programs related to the new church. A follow-up team is prepared under the guidance of the church planter, and these people visit those who have expressed an interest or a need. They do evangelism, disciple new believers, and present the vision for the church to the new flock. This strategy can obviously be used as one more tool in some of the models already presented.

MASS COMMUNICATION MODEL

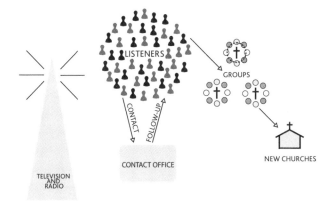

LISTENERS

GROUPS

CONTACT

FOLLOW-UP

CONTACT OFFICE

NEW CHURCHES

TELEVISION
AND
RADIO

C. Crusade Model

This strategy can be used by any model to launch or strengthen church planting. It consists of a year of preparation in places where campaigns or crusades are well received by the community. Preparations include prayer, the organization of a team of volunteers, the mobilization of established churches, the formation of a nuclear group for follow-up, and planning for the new church plant.

CRUSADES MODEL

C. Seminarian Model

Some institutions that prepare Christian leaders, such as Bible institutes and theological seminaries, provide practice opportunities for students in church planting. This process allows professors to model in practice and gives students an opportunity to grow in their ministry abilities. It functions better when a local church or a group of churches can support the work and provide ecclesial coverage to the new work. Part of this strategy includes preparing new leaders within the group to continue developing the new church.

SEMINARIAN MODEL

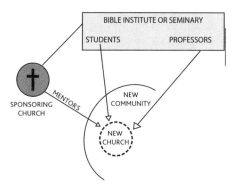

D. Diaconal Model

This strategy can be an integral part of any other model, but it emphasizes social action as a bridge to evangelism and toward establishing a congregation. In Central America, many congregations were born as the result of the outpouring of assistance after a severe hurricane, earthquake, or other natural disasters. This method lets people demonstrate the love of God to the neediest people, and at the same time to share with them the good news of Jesus Christ.

The important thing in this strategy is to maintain a balance in all aspects of the ministry and not become just an agency that provides social assistance without seeking the transformational development of the community—which includes the presence of the body of Christ and the establishment of a church that can continue to be salt and light in a particular context. Murray, in his book *Church Planting: Laying Foundations*, says it is likely that churches begun with this approach may not grow as fast as through other models, but the impact in the long run can be larger.[9]

V. MODELS FOR MULTIETHNIC CONTEXTS

Here we present six successful models of ethnic church planting that churches and agencies may want to consider. Each model has its advantages and disadvantages, and all of these models have been used successfully by evangelical organizations in actual church planting cases. The circumstances

---

9   Murray, *Church Planting*, 246.

of the sponsoring entity and the characteristics of the ethnic group are the most important factors that determine which model to use. This section will be useful for work in countries where there are many ethnic groups.

A. The Mother-Daughter Model

As discussed earlier, this model is used frequently and is normally very effective. For example, in the North American context, if an English-speaking congregation is concerned with reaching its neighborhood with the gospel, and the race and culture of that neighborhood is rapidly changing, the church can begin groups that are targeted to specific ethnic groups. This strategy may be the best method to reach these first generation immigrant groups, who have a strong loyalty to their cultural heritage and maternal language. English-speaking churches normally cannot assimilate groups with different languages into their existing congregations. Where the different language is a challenging factor and where a group's desire to maintain its cultural identity is highly valued, starting a daughter church is frequently the best strategy to reach people of another ethnic group. The mother-daughter arrangement can take three forms. In each case, the sponsoring church will provide the guidance, finances, personnel, and encouragement to the new church.

ETHNIC MOTHER – DAUGHTER MODEL

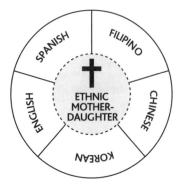

First, the mother church can follow a natural process of giving birth to the church, sponsoring a church planter to begin an ethnically distinct congregation near to or in the same facilities as the mother church. Second, the mother church may adopt an existing congregation of people of the targeted ethnicity that is struggling, and the mother church may provide them with the resources and emotional support they need in order to be a healthy and vibrant church. Third, the mother church can begin a ministry to the targeted ethnic population inside its own walls but having separate contextual worship services. This third approach has all of the advantages of the multi-congregational model discussed below.

B. The Multi-Congregational or Multi-Worship Model

In this model, also described above, a church planting team or a sponsoring church tries to begin and organize a number of churches of differing ethnicities that share the same space. The emphasis is on beginning multiple worship services, each one designed to meet the needs of a specific cultural group. Services can take place at the same time in different parts of the church building, or each congregation can use the same sanctuary at different times. All of the congregations contribute in terms of finances, ministries, and administration. A goal is that the different congregations grow to work together in a spirit of continuous partnership to build unity among themselves. Each congregation has its own pastor and leaders.

MULTI-CONGREGATIONAL MODEL

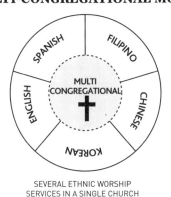

SEVERAL ETHNIC WORSHIP
SERVICES IN A SINGLE CHURCH

The costs associated with the use of the building are shared equitably. In some cases, a coordinating council is formed, with leaders from each of the groups. Periodically, all of the congregations get together for combined worship services and united evangelism efforts. The strengths of this approach include a strong testimony to the community, good stewardship of church properties in expensive urban settings, the option of different languages and worship styles for visitors, and the recognition of cultural differences while still maintaining unity and fellowship. The multi-congregational model is especially useful in large, multicultural cities.

C. The Multiple Sponsorship Model

This model involves several partner churches working together to sponsor a single congregation. This allows smaller churches to combine their resources to plant churches when they lack the finances and personnel to do it individually. Local, regional, and national groups may find this method very useful. One example of this model would involve an agreement between a large established church of the dominant ethnic group and a smaller church of a minority ethnic group, for the purpose of planting another church targeting the minority ethnic group. It may be that the church of the dominant ethnic group has the financial resources, but lacks people who understand the language and the culture of the minority ethnic group. Combining resources, personnel, and a common strategy allow for the formation of an excellent team to plant churches.

D. The House Church Model

In this model, the church is intentionally structured by having numerous groups meet in houses in the community. These cells provide a place for Bible study, fellowship, leadership formation, and worship. All of the cells meet together at regular intervals for a large celebratory worship, but the emphasis of the church is in the weekly meetings of the cell groups in homes. These cellular meetings help to develop a sense of community, lay ministry, pastoral care, leadership development, prayer, and stewardship, and they allow evangelism to happen in a natural way. The church's life is in the cell groups, not in a building. The church is understood as a dynamic, organic, spiritual entity that can only be developed in the life of the believers, regardless of where they are located. Cell groups normally have between 5 and 15 people. It is hoped that the entire network reproduces regularly. The best thing about this model for planting multicultural churches is that cell groups can be designed for different ethnic groups, especially by language; they can also be formed according to age or common interests. Cell churches are very attractive for young adults from a postmodern culture who are disillusioned with "impersonal" traditional churches and who desire more intimate relationships and shared leadership. Given their focus on the harvest, cellular churches normally have a strong emphasis on evangelism, discipleship, and leadership development.

E. The Multilingual Satellite or Multisite Model

Some of the fastest growing churches today sponsor congregations that are located in other parts of the same city and that meet at different times. Worship services can take place in apartments, rented offices, parks, and homes, and they are often led by lay pastors. This is one church in many locations. Normally all of the pastors and leaders from the different satellites are part of a team that meets weekly to pray and plan. All of the offerings go to a central account, and monies are disbursed from that account. All the groups meet a couple times a year for large worship celebrations.

This model has several advantages. A church in many locations can target ministries for the many different cultural and socioeconomic groups around the city. This model motivates young visionary leaders and can be adapted easily for different cultures, allowing a strategy appropriate for the city. A decentralized structure allows for rapid growth. Often, weekly home meetings are organized by common interests, allowing for great evangelistic opportunities. All the people in the church are encouraged to discover and use their spiritual gifts. The expansion of the church is unlimited as the groups in satellite locations grow. Finally, each local body benefits from the help and image of the mother church.

F. The Multiethnic and Multilingual Model

A multiethnic church is an expression of the body of Christ, with diverse cultures and ethnicities, that meets as a congregation. It uses a principal language, but it intentionally designs its services and worship ministries for a variety of cultural groups. The multicultural church adjusts its ministry and administrative structure to represent and adequately involve each group. It intends to develop a worship service that includes a rich diversity of songs, cultural traditions, prayers, and musical instruments. In order to maintain the heritage of each ethnic group, the church encourages the members to celebrate their cultural festivals, to use their national clothing, to share typical foods, and to hold international dinners.

This model works well with second and third generation immigrants, and with families who want their children to learn the language of the church of their new country. Couples from different races often choose this kind of church. This model requires a lot of work, especially if there has been tension or conflict between ethnic groups in the past. In spite of the challenges, the rewards of a positive testimony to the community and the opportunity to disciple previously unreached people makes the multiethnic church worth the effort.

MULTIETHNIC MODEL

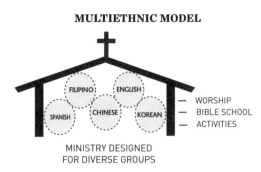

MINISTRY DESIGNED
FOR DIVERSE GROUPS

The multilingual variation of this model takes shape when a congregation is able to provide Sunday school classes and some services in different languages, while the main worship time continues to include everyone. In some cases, translators and interpreters are used during the worship service.

MULTILINGUAL MODEL

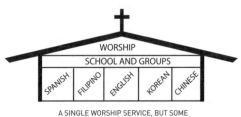

A SINGLE WORSHIP SERVICE, BUT SOME
MINISTRIES IN DIFFERENT LANGUAGES

VI. SELECTING A MODEL

With such a variety of church planting models now available, how do church planters determine which one will work best for their specific target audience? The sheer number of planting approaches—all designed by veteran church planters—may cause some prospective planters to feel overwhelmed. Before quickly selecting the latest publicized model, promoted in evangelical seminars and literature, church planters would be wise to compare and investigate a number of models. As we have seen, each model has its inherent strengths and weaknesses. And each comes packaged with its own core values and basic assumptions. Each has been tested, and some have proven to be more effective among certain socioeconomic or ethnic communities.

Advocates of a particular model may seek to establish biblical precedent or priority for their preferred approach. In our opinion, the New Testament does not provide us with a single scriptural blueprint for how to start new churches. In our opinion, attempts to elevate one model over the rest as if it were more biblical tend to hinder creative thinking. In order to select the best model, we do not need to limit others to one option, but rather we must give each planting team the freedom to engage in biblically discerning interaction with the contemporary culture they are called to reach.

We propose five guidelines to help a planting team select the best model for reaching their particular ministry focus group.

First, select a model that enables you to best reach your immediate ministry goals and aspirations. What kind of church are you seeking to plant? If your objective is to leave a strong, growing, biblically balanced church, capable of reproducing, then select a model that best empowers the young congregation to fulfill that mission. If your goal is to plant a church that can operate independently outside of subsidy and external leadership, then select a model that enables you to gradually turn the ministry over to the local people. Define your goals, and then determine which model—or blend of models—will accomplish them.

Second, select a model that best enables you to fulfill your long-range vision. The vision statement spells out where the team is going, painting in broad strokes what the new church (or churches) should look like in five or ten years or more. It is a statement of faith, declaring what the planters believe God wants to do through this new church in the years to come. Which model will best propel your vision to closure?

Third, select a mode that best fits your particular targeted people group. This is especially crucial in cross-cultural work. Rather than choosing a model that only reflects their own skills, gifts, and cultural background, planters would be wise to craft a model that enables them to sensitively reach their primary target group. This requires an understanding of the community's worldview, beliefs, history, and heritage.

Fourth, select a church planting model that is as comprehensive and yet workable as possible. Tom Steffen suggests a minimum of five components to an effective model: it should be grounded in the Word, exhibit the incarnate character of Christ, be holistic (address both spiritual and physical needs), empower local people to continue the ministry, and facilitate ongoing church reproduction.[10] Ideally all five of these features should be present in your planning model.

Fifth, select a planting model that will be effective in your social context. Some models work best in urban rather than rural settings. Others may be more effective in lower- or middle-class socioeconomic settings. Still other church planting approaches may be more fruitful with a particular ethnic or family group. It may be necessary to consult with other church planting teams that have worked in different social settings to make these final judgments.

---

10   Tom Steffen, "Selecting a Church Planting Model That Works," 369-70.

CONCLUSION

We have stressed that no one method will fit every planting situation. The models presented above can help you have healthy conversations to discover what could work best for you in your particular context. Though each model identified has distinct features, there are common factors in church planting that transcend all the models commonly employed. Interestingly, some new churches that are very similar to each other have been established using very different methods. And some churches that are very different from each other were planted using the same or similar methods and models.

In the end, it is a person or people, and not the method, which the sovereign God uses to start churches. You may select the right method and still fail if you do not experience the power and blessing of God on the planting ministry. It is also true that a Spirit-filled person or team, using the right method with the right motives, can accomplish much for God by his grace and for his glory!

Questions

1.   What must one consider when choosing one of the proposed models?

2.   How does the context affect the choice of models? Give an example.

3.   What are the advantages of the mother-daughter model?

4.   Choose two models and compare them to each other.

5.   Which model best describes the congregation you presently attend? Explain.

6.   What are the disadvantages of the pioneer model?

7.   Which model would work best if you were to start planting a church next month?

8.   List the advantages and disadvantages of the denominational model.

9.   Which was your favorite model? Explain.

10. Which was your least favorite model? Explain.

11 STEPS IN CHURCH PLANTING

Gary Teja and Blayne Waltrip

Introduction

In this chapter, we will look at the steps for planting a church. Each step will be described briefly and then followed by a series of thought-provoking questions for you to answer. We will cover the following steps: (1) doing research, (2) doing evangelism, (3) forming small groups, and (4) making disciples. All of these are essential steps to planting a healthy church in a particular context. We will finish this chapter by talking about the importance of reproduction and multiplication.

I. DOING RESEARCH

Introduction

In order to have a clear mission statement, a church planter needs to understand who the people are that he seeks to reach. Since the mission statement deals with the "target group," the planter needs to know these people "inside and out." In other words, he needs to know their dreams and their needs in order to reflect on how to meet these people in their basic needs and to bring them to the feet of Christ. In the same way that Jesus "became flesh and made his dwelling among us" (John 1:14), the church planter must also become one with the target community. To do so, he must first understand something about that community.

We call this form of research—of getting to know a community—*demographics*. This basically means "the study of people."

What do we want to know?

Some of the data we could gather deal with the following:
- ethnicity and race
- age (adults, children, teens)
- occupation
- employment and unemployment/underemployment rates
- views toward organized religion (or toward Christianity)
- educational levels
- political affiliation
- marital status (married couples, single parents, single adults)
- violence levels in the community (gang presence, types of prevalent crimes)

Why is this information important to the church planter?

Demographic information helps the planter to determine the shape of the ministry. For example, if the community or neighborhood consists mostly of senior retired adults, one will not put a lot of emphasis on "fishing events" focused on reaching young married couples with children. The programs we run as outreach ministries must reflect the needs of the target group. Demographic research informs us of the makeup of the community and of the particular potential needs that the church could address.

Such data gathering also helps us understand the history of the community. Sometimes what happened in the past is not obvious at first, but may be essential in understanding the community today. If you are dealing with a tribal situation, for example, past wars between tribal groups in an area could influence the effectiveness of your outreach.

Demographics even help us to determine the type of worship service we have. Worship styles differ from generation to generation. We need to tailor our worship style to the majority generation in the community, or perhaps a blended style that takes into account different generational worship styles. Will traditional instruments attract people or turn them away? Will this be a highly liturgical (full of rituals) service, or one more free-flowing and spontaneous? Will singing from sheets or hymnals be more appropriate for this community, or will you need to have words projected on a screen with lots of action?

A good church planter who learns to read demographics will also know what preaching style to use. Will it be something that reaches the intellect, or something that reaches the heart, or both? Will it be traditional preaching, or will it be more narrative and life experience storytelling? Will it be a short sermon or a long sermon? What are the expectations of the group? Older generations may prefer a longer sermon, while a young audience will be used to flash bytes.

In summary, demographics help the church planter to know the community in which one lives and ministers. Without demographics, the church planter goes into a new community blind.

How do we do demographics?

There are many ways of doing demographic research. In classes at the seminary, the author used to include this as a group activity. He would ask students to list on the board as many different ways of doing demographics as possible. The class always came up with a list of 35-40 different ways of researching the community. Here are a few you could consider.

- Going to a barbershop
- Reading newspapers
- Frequenting a local store in the neighborhood
- Listening to the radio
- Driving through an area (windshield tour)
- Walking the streets of a neighborhood where you plan to plant a church
- Talking to the police
- Visiting teachers, the mayor, or the village leader
- Consulting other religious leaders

- Analyzing census information, if there is any
- Visiting a city planning board, if one exists
- Talking with real estate agents

Sometimes if a church planter simply goes where the crowds of people are, he can learn a lot about them and their community. For example, going to a local coffee shop as a *participant observer*, a church planter can begin to understand something of the *ethos* of the community. He overhears conversations. He begins to dialogue with people. He asks questions:

- "What are some of the needs in the community?"
- "How has the neighborhood (or community) changed since you came to live here?"
- "What things have been tried to improve the community and have not worked?"
- "If you were looking for a church to attend, what would you like that church to be like?"
- "What kind of church would be a benefit to this neighborhood?"

This type of participant observation can be repeated in other venues, such as a barbershop, a local market, or a corner store.

A windshield tour, in which the church planter drives through a community, provides a quick view of that community. The author drove a local church planter through a small city in the state of Washington called Sunnyside. Together they were able to surmise what percentage of Hispanics were living in that community. They were able to estimate that nearly 85 percent of the businesses in downtown Sunnyside were owned by Hispanics. The signs outside grocery stores also gave a clue to the high presence of Hispanics because of the types of foods that were advertised. The presence of businesses that did cash advances led them to believe that many were probably living from paycheck to paycheck. The prominence of social welfare offices and other community help programs also was a clue to the economic level of many of the inhabitants. In another community the overabundance of corner taverns, pawn shops,[1] and barred windows in one neighborhood said something about the nature of that neighborhood.

---

[1] Pawn shops are where people trade in possessions, such as jewelry or TVs, for cash with the hope of one day being able to redeem them.

Walking around a community gives the church planter an even closer perspective on the community he might not get otherwise. The author took students to the city of Chicago in the United States. They walked around a neighborhood, taking in as much detail as they could. They read the names on mailboxes, giving them an idea of the ethnicity of those who lived in the community. They looked at the names on storefronts, the type of merchandise they carried, and the prices of goods. All of this helped them to understand the nationalities (or countries of origin) of those who shopped in the community. The prices told them something about the economic level of the inhabitants. They observed the flashing blue lights over short-circuit cameras that were connected to the local police station. That told them this was a violent part of town. The graffiti on the sides of buildings told them about gang presence and which gangs claimed the "turf."

Summary

Research, particularly demographic research, is a valuable tool in the church planter's tool box. It helps the church planter to "interpret (exegete)" the community where he hopes to shed God's light. To be able to incarnate in a community, the church planter needs to first identify with that community. Unless he knows the community, he will never be able to identify and therefore never be able to become one with it. As much as possible, the church planter wants to become an "insider" in the community. Without good demographics, he will always remain an "outsider," and everything will seem foreign to him. He will attempt to plant a church by trial and error. Better to begin with even a simple understanding of the community and, by God's grace, minister to the particular needs of that community. As people see the church planter caring for them and their needs, and becoming one with them, the better the possibility that a church will become firmly rooted in the soil of that community.

II. DOING EVANGELISM

Introduction

After we have developed a team, done demographic research, decided on a model and strategy, and arrived in the target context, the hard work of growing the church through conversion begins. Although the Word of God does not specifically charge us to plant churches, the Great Commission does mandate us to go into all the world, preach the good news to all creation, and make disciples of all nations (Matt. 28:19-20; Mark 16:15). There is a clear process of reaching the lost through proclamation wherever we go in the world and of making disciples of converts by baptizing them and teaching them the way of Christ. Since we are to do this among all nations (literally all people groups), we need as many local churches as possible. Making disciples is the task of any church, and the process of discipleship begins with evangelism.

Definitions of Evangelism

There are many definitions of evangelism. The author's definition is that evangelism is both a practice and a lifestyle lived out by the Christian community of witnesses. These witnesses proclaim by word and deed the good news of Jesus Christ to those in the world who do not know him as their personal Lord and Savior. We as followers of Jesus are agents of the kingdom of God, helping others to experience salvation (new birth) provided in Jesus Christ through believing faith. This would be considered "Christian initiation." Conversion is the first step toward becoming a disciple.

Other definitions:
1. Overflow (from the Greek word *plerophoria* (1 Thess. 1:5), referring to a joy that simply overflows.
2. D.T. Niles— "Evangelism is one beggar telling another beggar where to get bread."[2]
3. Archbishop William Temple— "To evangelize is so to present Jesus Christ in the power of the Holy Spirit that men shall come to put their trust in God through him, to accept him as their Savior, and to serve him as their King in the fellowship of his church."
4. C.S. Lewis— "The salvation of a single soul is more important than the production or preservation of all the epics and tragedies in the world."
5. J.I. Packer— "Our business is to present the Christian faith clothed in modern terms, not to propagate modern thought clothed in Christian terms. Confusion here is fatal."

---

2   Exact bibliographic source unknown, although sometimes *That They May Have Life* is given as the source of the citation No page number provided.

6. Paul Little— "The Holy Spirit can't save saints or seats. If we don't know any non-Christians, how can we introduce them to the Savior?"
7. Rebecca M. Pippert— "Being an extrovert isn't essential to evangelism–obedience and love are."
8. Robert Munger— "Evangelism is the spontaneous overflow of a glad and free heart in Jesus Christ."
9. Richard C. Halverson—"Evangelism is not salesmanship It is not urging people, pressing them, coercing them, overwhelming them, or subduing them. Evangelism is telling a message. Evangelism is reporting good news.

Evangelism is not the same as mission. Mission is a greater concept that includes involvement with the social, political, and moral life of the community and nation. Mission is God's redemptive activity in the world as He brings all things under His Lordship. It includes all spheres of life as Christ "makes all things new" and restores, redeems and re-creates. Mission was initiated and is maintained by God, for it is his mission. God's mission is all activity that brings humans back into relationship with him. It is motivated by his love and is the reason why God sent his one and only Son.

Evangelism is but *one* aspect of this mission, though an extremely important one. Evangelism is good news about Jesus:

- It is centered in God the Father—Jesus reveals what the Father is like (John 14:7).
- It depends on the Holy Spirit—the Spirit draws people to Christ, convicts, makes him real, causes them to confess his lordship, baptizes them into his body, and gives assurance of belonging.
- It is a sovereign work of God—no one can come to God unless God draws that person to himself.

The word *evangelism* comes from the Greek word *euangelion,* which is often translated into English as "gospel" (an old English word that means "good news"). Evangelism is an action word describing the activity of telling the good news of God's salvation for us in Christ.

Evangelism as Lifestyle

In light of the contemporary missional church conversation, evangelism is understood as a lifestyle that all Christians live out, not just an activity that certain "called evangelists" do. Evangelism has traditionally been considered an activity by churches, but today's missional movements around the world understand evangelism as an integration of doing and being. Evangelism is what a disciple *is*, not just what one *does*. It is a lifestyle, not a program. We live it out in word and deed. As the famous quote by Francis of Assisi goes, "Preach the gospel at all times, and when necessary use words." As church planters, we manifest the kingdom of God to others. It means to serve and not to be served. The church is a community of "sent-ones" that embodies the good news and expresses it through many means. Because the church is missional, its members live as a community of witnesses.

This lifestyle evangelism is our testimony lived out visibly and through our proclamation. In missional living, evangelism is very relational. We cannot be a witness unless we are in relationship with someone. Therefore, the focus of evangelism is on the person, not on the activity. It is other- and stranger-centered. Being other-centered, we not only speak but also listen to learn how the words and actions are being interpreted. We proclaim the gospel in word, but we also live it out so that people around us will see the kingdom of God lived out.

In the book *The Organic Church*, Neil Cole writes that evangelism must include relationships. He uses the Greek word *oikos* to describe our natural relationships. According to him, *oikos* is the fundamental group of people that one naturally has influence with through relationships. It is "one's family, friends, neighbors, and associates." He adds that "the Lord of the harvest has directed us to the *oikos* to spread the kingdom of God. It appears that the Lord of the harvest has indeed set us up in a particular *oikos* to reach people who do not know him yet."[3] Each person is a door for the kingdom to enter a new *oikos*—i.e., the new church and community of faith. However, the lifestyle of the new church as a community must be a testimony for which people long.

---

3   Neil Cole, *Organic Church: Growing Faith Where Life Happens,* 164.

Connecting

Our natural *oikos* is those people with whom we already have a relationship. By having natural relationships, we already have some influence. However, we must expand our natural *oikos* to include strangers in our city and neighborhood. Our mandate from Christ is to proclaim the gospel to all people, wherever we are sent. However, we must develop new relationships to have the right to be heard. To develop new relationships with the strangers around us, we must live among others in our context and connect with them.

How do we connect?

1. We should connect "naturally," in the context of everyday life. We live and work with people. If a church planter needs to be bi-vocational, it is actually an opportunity to meet people and develop relationships. Of course, there also are neighbors. We must be natural but also deliberate in being relational with neighbors. Depending on the culture, that may not be easy. It may require that the we look for opportunities to know others by inviting people to our home or accepting invitations to theirs. We must practice hospitality by being both hosts and guests. In many cultures, such as in France or Spain, life happens at the table. You cannot truly be a witness if you have not shared a meal, coffee, or tea together—i.e., shared life. We should find ways to connect with neighbors. What are their common problems and sufferings? What are the common family situations (e.g., struggles with parents or siblings or children)? We must be authentic and transparent. Our stories give hope. In addition, what are the common interests? How can we enjoy life together? We will live and share life and that also means having fun together.

2. We can connect with people where they are, in their particular context. In many contexts, the people we are trying to reach—for example, Muslims, Hindus, or secular postmodern Westerners—will not go to a Christian church. We must go where the people go in order to connect with them. If we have a heart to reach surfers, we must go where they surf. If we are in France, we can go to cafés. For our neighbors, we go to their homes. If they have parties, we go to their parties. Of course, we do not have to compromise our values or morals by participating in every activity, especially if we have par-

ticular convictions. In fact, that can be very counterproductive. We are called to live among others, but as a countercultural community. People in society want to see hope in us. The gospel will be offensive for many who live in sin, but they are hungry for life beyond what society offers. We must be countercultural as we share neutral space, living among others.

3. If we cannot go where those we are trying to reach go, we can create what are called "third-space" opportunities. David Fitch talks about the idea of third-space evangelism. He recommends that Christians create third-spaces that are neutral yet conducive to connecting with non-Christians and developing relationships. According to Fitch, third-spaces "can germinate the kind of relationships necessary for postmodern evangelism to take place because strangers can come on their own terms for other purposes (like buying something) and relationships can be formed."[4] This observation is true in any culture. There are missional church plants that are opening their own cafés, art galleries, skate parks, and so on. The goal is to connect with people so that we can develop relationships. We can also have our own parties or use the events already happening, such as "Neighbor Day" in France, Christmas markets, and so on. We can be very innovative and creative in finding neutral space or producing third-spaces for evangelism.

4. Bridge ministries provide another way of reaching out. These are ministries that a church can develop to bridge into their community to connect with people. These creative ministries, or what Eddie Gibbs refers to in his book *In Name Only* as fishing-pond events, can include sports ministries, sporting events, concerts, art displays, recovery programs, and so on.[5] A local church can also offer classes to help people get a job, or to help immigrants learn the language and get settled, or to help marriages and families grow stronger, or to help divorced people heal. If we know our community (because we did your demo-

---

4   David Fitch, *The Great Giveaway: Reclaiming the Mission of the Church from Big Business, Parachurch Organizations, Psychotherapy, Consumer Capitalism, and Other Modern Maladies*, 63-64.

5   Eddie Gibbs, *In Name Only: Tackling the Problem of Nominal Christianity*, 266-68.

graphic research!), a new church will recognize opportunities to bridge into that community with love.

One of the most effective ways of bridging into a community is to serve the community. Of course, benevolence ministries are good. Relieving the pain of others is important, but that may not be enough. If we love our communities, we find ways to empower others and to change the things that cause their suffering or poverty. As a witness to their community, the new church should find ways to serve the people. Social ministry and evangelism should go hand and hand. We call this *holistic ministry* or a *holistic gospel*. But again, to be a true witness, we must be sincere in our love for others.

A warning: In contemporary Western culture, we cannot argue meta-proofs with evangelistic tricks. People know when they are objects of conversion. We are to love others as Christ loves them. As we love others and join the journey of life with others, we introduce Jesus to them. It is true that postmoderns in the West reject absolute truth. However, when we are in relationship with postmoderns, we demonstrate the love and hope of Christ. This is also true for Muslims and others.

What to Know for Evangelism

Being a witness involves being, doing, and saying. However, being a witness also requires knowing. To live out evangelism, we must know the following things.

1. We must know Christ and his message. The gospel is the story of the life, ministry, death, resurrection, and ascension of Jesus. In telling the gospel, we must tell the story of the life of Jesus. He was the Messiah as promised by the Old Testament prophets. Hundreds of years before Jesus' birth, the Old Testament of the Bible recorded the words of the prophets of Israel predicting his coming. The Old Testament, written by many people over a period of 1,500 years, contains more than 300 prophecies describing the Messiah's appearance. All of these details came true, including his miraculous birth, his sinless life, his many miracles, his death, and his resurrection.

The life that Jesus led, the miracles he did, the words he spoke, his death on the cross, his resurrection, and his ascent to heaven all point to the fact that he was not merely human, but more than human. Jesus claimed, "I and the Father are One" (John 10:30), "Anyone who has seen me has seen the Father" (John 14:9), and "I am the way and the truth and the life. No one comes to the Father except through me" (John 14:6).

The life of Jesus changed history like no other personality. He and his message always produce great changes in the lives of people and of nations. Wherever his teachings and influence have gone, the holiness of marriage has been emphasized, women's rights and voices in society have been acknowledged, schools and universities of higher learning have been established, laws to protect children have been made, slavery has been abolished, and a multitude of other changes have been accomplished for the good of humanity.

Jesus of Nazareth was crucified on a cross, was buried in a borrowed grave, and three days later was raised from the dead; Christianity is unique in this regard. Any argument for the validity of Christianity depends on the fact of the resurrection of Jesus of Nazareth.

Note, though, that many who may initially reject Jesus as God's Son, like Muslims, have a deep respect for Him. Talking about Jesus is not offensive to most people. Initially as we talk about Jesus, we do not need to deal with the finer points of doctrine. We want to first introduce Jesus the person and incrementally present his Sonship, his crucifixion, and his death and resurrection. First, we introduce people to Jesus, the compassionate miracle worker, the sinless One who claims to be the only way to true happiness and eternal joy, the one who is making all things new!

2. We must know what Christ did for us personally. Our testimony is crucial for evangelism. We have a story to tell. Our lives become a testimony lived out among others. Our testimony is the message of our story meeting God's story. We overcome by our testimony. Revelations 12:11 explains: "They triumphed over [the devil who leads the world astray] by the blood of the Lamb and by the word of their testi-

mony; they did not love their lives so much as to shrink from death." If we believe in Christ, we have his testimony in us.

1 John 5:10-12 states, "Whoever believes in the Son of God accepts this testimony. Whoever does not believe God has made him out to be a liar, because they have not believed the testimony God has given about his Son. And this is the testimony: God has given us eternal life, and this life is in his Son. Whoever has the Son has life; whoever does not have the Son of God does not have life." Paul says in 1 Corinthians 2:1, "When I came to you, I did not come with eloquence or human wisdom as I proclaimed to you the testimony about God." We testify to whoever will listen, about what God has done in our own lives. When we are a witness of Christ, we tell others about how God found us and changed us. Church planters must tell their story.

Inviting People to Commitment

People are not objects of conversion. Rather they are objects of God's love. It is his passionate desire to bring people into relationship with him. This requires an invitation and commitment. To bring people to commitment, you will have to present the message in a way that the person can receive it.[6] We needs to find those "redemptive analogies" that best reveal the truth of the gospel in a relevant way. We must contextualize the gospel for evangelism. People must make sense of the claims of Jesus as Lord and Savior. Listening to the Holy Spirit is also critical to bring people to commitment. The Holy Spirit works in the hearts of those who are ready to receive Jesus. As a result, we as church planters must pray for those around them. We must also be sensitive and listen to the leading of the Holy Spirit.

As church planters, we seek to bring people to a true commitment. We must pray for those people on a daily basis. We pray that the Holy Spirit will work in their hearts. We pray for guidance and opportunity to share the gospel/our story. As one prays, one should serve and live life with others, and opportunities will present themselves. However, it will require listening and hearing people's stories to find the common ground. One must be there when they are sad and when they are happy, grieving together and celebrating to-

---

6   Redemptive analogies are stories, understandings, or practices in a given culture that demonstrate the gospel.

gether. One must pray for wisdom. Most people just want someone to listen to them and to care.

We think and pray to know how to overcome future objections people may have. How do they think? What would make them object to Christ? What objections did we have in coming to Christ? How did Christ overcome our objections? How did Christ make a difference in our life? How did he give us hope in the midst of our problem?

With some people, we may want to go lightly with sharing the Bible with them. In contemporary Western culture for example, most young postmoderns know nothing of the Bible and do not trust it. The good news (gospel) message of the Bible, nevertheless, is the power of God for salvation (Rom. 1:16). We cannot underestimate how the Bible, through the Holy Spirit's inspiration, can bring about a conversion. Even if they do not believe in the Bible, it will be very powerful once people take the step of faith commitment. The Word will become a new discovery. The Bible is fundamental in discipleship.

At some point, we need to invite the unsaved friend to commit their life to Christ. How we lead them to commitment will depend on the person. Once a person believes and wants to give their life to Christ, there are three kinds of changes that need to take place:

1. *Change of power.* People recognize their own weakness and experience the power of God in their lives through the work of the Holy Spirit, giving them life, breaking the power of sin in their lives, and bringing about the fruit of the Spirit: love, joy, peace, patience, kindness, goodness, faithfulness, gentleness, and self-control (see Gal. 5:22-23).

2. *Change of belief.* People's eyes are opened to accept that Jesus is who the Bible says he is: the resurrected Son of God. People come to see that God speaks through the Scripture and that what he says can be trusted.

3. *Change of will.* People turn their lives over to Jesus[7] and submit to his will in all areas of their lives.

---

7   There is some debate today about whether with nonbelievers initially we should use the

Once a person has committed to him and these changes begin to take place, the work is only beginning.

Follow-up

Follow-up is one of the most important aspects of evangelism. We cannot bring a new child into the world and leave it alone. We must continue our relationship with that person, or if we do not know the person well, continue to develop a relationship. We must help them grow. The new believer must be discipled. A new Christian must become part of a community of faith. This is where the new church is crucial in the life of the new believer. The new church must continue the process and make mature disciples. The Lord's mandate to us is to make disciples, not just converts.

Summary

It is true that there are those Christians who are chosen by the Holy Spirit to have a special call or gift of evangelism. They are natural in apologetics, strategies, and developing relationships. Nevertheless, all believers in Jesus are mandated to be his witnesses. As a result, evangelism should be very natural for all Christians. Because it is done in relationship with God and others, it involves living life with others and sharing the hope that is in us in appropriate, contextualized ways. As our friends come to Jesus, the new churches will grow. The kind of church growth that God seeks is conversion growth. The church planter not only evangelizes but also must equip and train others in the new church to share their faith. As a missional leader, we lead people into mission by showing the way and then training them to do the work of being a witness of Jesus. As a community, the new church participates together in God's mission. What a privilege we have as the people of God to participate in that mission with each other and with God.

---

word *Christ* or simply *Jesus*. The word *Christ* reminds some people, like Muslims, of the Christian Crusades in which Christ-followers showed anything but love and mercy. Even the term "convert to Christ" can be offensive. To become a "Jesus follower" or "to follow Jesus" is more acceptable and less offensive. There is enough in the gospel that is offensive without our adding to it. The word *Christ* itself means "Anointed One" or "Sent One." Once a person has made the choice to follow *Jesus*, he or she will understand better what it means to follow Jesus *Christ* (or Jesus *the Christ*).

III. FORMING SMALL GROUPS

Introduction

The development of small groups is a key step to the success of church planting. Small groups help inquirers get involved in an evangelistic Bible study where they can discover the truths of the gospel. Small groups are also the venue for new believers to deepen their newfound faith in discipleship Bible studies. For both evangelism and discipleship, small groups are a major missiological tool.

What is a small group?

A small group consists of anywhere between 3 and 12 people who meet together around God's Word. If only two people, this constitutes a one-on-one relationship but is not considered a small group. If a group has more than 12 people, it can be difficult to develop the interactivity and dialogue group members need in order to grow in faith.

Normally there is a knowledgeable leader who serves as the facilitator of the group. The leader's role is to keep the discussion going, to ask relevant questions, to maintain a spirit of openness and transparency while also honoring all the input of the group members. Also, in many small groups there is a host in whose home the small group is meeting. This person supplies coffee, tea, or soft drinks and perhaps a light snack of cookies or muffins to provide a friendly, neighborly atmosphere in which to study God's Word.

The focus of the small group is opening up the Bible in order to hear God's voice, whether it is about the need for salvation (evangelism) or the need to continually grow in faith (discipleship). We gather together to deal with things of eternal consequence—salvation and spiritual growth and how all of life is impacted by a Christian worldview.

Ground rules for a small group

In order for dialogue to occur, *there needs to be an atmosphere of trust.* Each person needs to feel confident that what he says will be received in the spirit in which it is spoken. No one is comfortable if what he says is discounted outright or criticized. If a person says something that is obviously wrong, a good facilitator will ask probing questions that may help the speaker to understand the truth.

Besides an atmosphere of trust, *there must also be an air of confidentiality.* Some things spoken in a small group could do harm to a person's reputation if shared outside of the group. Or what is said in a group could be exaggerated as it goes from one person to another. This is gossip and needs to be avoided.

The teacher

In a small group, the Word of God, not the leader or any other member of the group, is the teacher. According to 2 Timothy 3:16, "All Scripture is God-breathed and is useful for teaching, rebuking, correcting and training in righteousness." Likewise, Psalm 119:105 affirms, "Your word is a lamp for my feet, a light on my path."

What does this say, then, about the small group leader? The leader's role is simply to guide the study of God's Word. The Word speaks for itself. The Word can convict us of our sinful nature. The Word can guide us into all truth because the Word is truth. It is through the study of God's Word that we grow in our faith and in our knowledge of spiritual things.

In a small group we are looking for self-discovery. Through the study of God's Word, people begin to discover answers to their questions. Besides self-discovery, there is group discovery. People sharing with each other teach each other. Something someone says may give someone else in the group a new insight or new perspective that he would not have come up with by himself. This interactivity nurtures learning in a way that self-study never would.

A small group leader needs to recognize that he or she is dealing with adults. Adult learners are not like children to be spoon-fed. They are self-directed. Therefore, self-discovery works well with most adults. Consider the traditional way of leading a Bible study, such as in an adult Sunday school class in many parts of the world. The "teacher" stands in front of the "class" and lectures. The teacher presents all the information, forms all the hypotheses, and usually answers all the questions. Only at the very end of the class time will the teacher ask, "Does anyone have something to add?" or "Does anyone have a question?" If the adults are still awake, they are ready to leave and may not take anything of value away with them because they have not participated actively in the group.

Questions

A good small group leader will, instead, ask questions. This leader/facilitator is interested in helping the adults in the Bible study—whether evangelistic or discipleship-oriented—to think for themselves. The leader will also make certain there is time for people to ask questions, questions that generally should *not* be answered by the group facilitator.

The leader/facilitator asks questions such as . . .
"What did the passage say?"
"What did the author mean by this?"
"What does this mean to you?"
"How do you apply this passage to your own life?"

These create opportunities for sharing and reflecting.

The leader can ask questions *for clarification* when someone says something that is not understood or may be wrong:
"Could you rephrase that statement for us?"
"What do you think is the implication of what you just said?"

The group leader also tries *to involve everyone* in the group discussion:
"Joseph, what do you think about this passage?"
"Joanne, what do you think about Jack's statement?"
"Ahmed, do you have a different interpretation of this passage? Would you please share it with the group?"

There are, therefore, different kinds of questions the group leader can ask:
- questions that deal with the content of the passage being studied
- questions for clarification, as we saw above
- application questions

How does one ask a question? For example, the leader can also "field" questions rather than answering them. Remember, the role is to facilitate, not dominate the conversation. If a small group member asks a question of the group leader, rather than responding personally, the leader has several options. He or she can bounce the question back to the person who asked: "Tell me what *you* think." This is important to do at times when we think the person knows the answer and only needs to think through the question a bit more. The leader can also pass the question to a third person, "José, do you have an answer for Felipe?" Questions directed to specific people also can be used when someone appears to be daydreaming and is not fully focused on the Bible study or has not yet contributed to the discussion.

Inductive Bible study

What we have described above is what is called an *inductive* Bible study. Rather than giving answers to the group, the small group leader guides the study by asking questions. The adult members of the group discover for themselves the answers as they interact with the questions and with each other. The Bible study is much more interactive, dynamic, and rich if the inductive method is used. The inductive Bible study method lends itself as a major tool for planting a church. Forming people into small groups to study God's Word and to reflect on the passage and to ask their own questions helps the inquirer come to terms with the truth of Scripture and, for the new believer, as a means of growing in his or her newfound faith.

Also, as small group members become accustomed to this methodology, they in turn will be able to lead their own inductive Bible studies, allowing the Bible to speak for itself. Small groups are the basis of the new church as the number of people involved in a small group Bible study grows exponentially, forming the critical mass needed for the formation of a new church.

Note: Because the small group focuses on the Bible and reflects on questions based on the passage, little or no preparation is required on the part of the small group members. They simply come with open minds, led by the Spirit, ready to read the passage and discuss it. Considering the busy lives that we all live, the less "homework" we have will help make us more apt to continue coming week after week, discovering something new that God has for us.

How to study the Bible in a small group

There are different ways in which we can study the Bible together in a small group. One way is called the *topical approach*. We look at specific topics or themes in Scripture. For example, we could look at what the Bible has to say about sin by reading passages that deal with the word "sin." Or, for other examples, we could look at what the Bible says about lepers and leprosy, or about prayer, or marriage, or about miracles.

We can also take a *verse-by-verse approach* to studying the Bible. Choose a passage of Scripture like the Beatitudes (Matt. 5:3-12) and study each statement verse-by-verse in its setting. This way we read Scripture in its context.

Likewise we can approach Bible study with a specific *focus* in mind. It can be evangelistically focused, or discipleship focused, or focused on the spiritual habits we need to develop, or for inspiration, or for learning doctrine.

We can look at the stories of people who have been called "heroes of the faith." Bible stories about Daniel, or David, or Paul are examples of this approach. In all of these examples, though, we do not want to moralize, saying we need to be like these people. Rather, we ought to approach Scripture as *redemptive history* in which the focus is on the God behind these people and their acts. For example, as faithful as Daniel was to God in standing against the unjust laws of Babylon, we want to emphasize even more so God's faithfulness in protecting Daniel from the mouths of lions and guiding him to be a reputable leader appointed by the king even though he was a Jewish captive in exile.

Small group personalities

When we engage in a small group Bible study, either evangelistic or for discipleship training, we are dealing with different personalities in the group. Not everyone has the same personality. That is what makes a small group interesting!

- Some appear disinterested. Try to ask them questions in which they have an interest to get them involved. "So you see, Yusuph, that Jesus knew how to fish. I know you are a fisherman. How would you have reacted if Jesus had been your fishing partner? How difficult is it to catch fish?"

- Others are know-it-alls. They like to dominate the conversation. Simply say, "Let's see if anyone else has something to say."
- There are also those who ask all kinds of questions, relevant or not to the topic. You can always say, "That's a good question. Let's discuss it after our session."
- There are oftentimes people too shy or timid to speak up. Involve them in the discussion by saying, "What do *you* think the passage is saying?"

Other personalities can be found in the group as well. Try to think of some and how you personally would handle them.

Summary

Volumes have been written on the subject of small groups. One excellent resource was written by Rev. Alfredo Vallellanes titled *Healthy Small Groups.* It can be found in the Tool Box at www.multiplicationnetwork.org. We encourage you to read this book, since, as we said at the beginning, small groups are a valuable step in the planting of a new and healthy church.

IV. MAKING DISCIPLES

Introduction

In previous sections of this chapter, we saw the importance of evangelism and doing this by means of small groups. In the small groups section, we also saw that some groups could be discipleship groups. The Great Commission is to "Go and make disciples." Evangelism is only the initiation of becoming a follower of Jesus.[8] Discipleship is the method of taking a new believer and equipping him with the knowledge and skills to be a truly committed follower of Jesus. The new disciple must eventually become part of the community of faith. In the same way in which a bonfire can only survive as twigs and branches are thrown on it, a new believer can only truly be a disciple of Jesus and survive if he or she is involved in a local body of believers. A single stick will quickly lose its flame, while several sticks together will continue to burn

---

8   Evangelism leads to discipleship.

brightly. In Matthew's version of the Great Commission (Matt. 28:19-20), Jesus expounds on how to make disciples: "baptizing them in the name of the Father and of the Son and of the Holy Spirit, and teaching them to obey everything I have commanded you." In addition to baptism, the new church must teach the new disciples to obey Christ's commandments. The greatest of God's commandments is to love God and to love others. The new healthy church helps people of all ages to know Christ and his will so that they follow him in all areas and aspects of their daily life. As we teach disciples, they mature to know Christ and his will better and learn to depend on the Holy Spirit. They become more like Christ. The challenge for the new church is to teach new disciples in ways that are culturally effective and age appropriate. Discipleship must be contextualized.

Definitions and Rationale

By definition, a disciple is a follower, one who accepts and assists in spreading the doctrines of another. In Greek, the word disciple means "a learner." According to *Dictionary.com*, a disciple is defined as follows:

1. A person who is a pupil or adherent of the doctrines of another.
2. One who embraces and assists in spreading the teaching of another.
3. Any follower of another person.[9]

Technically, a disciple is a student of the teachings of someone else. Christian discipleship is the process by which disciples follow the teachings of Jesus Christ. They grow in the Lord Jesus Christ and are equipped by the Holy Spirit. The goal of the disciple is to be more like Christ. The disciple becomes more like Christ in the following:

1. Conduct/behavior. The behavior of the disciple becomes more and more like Jesus (Phil. 1:27; Eph. 5:1-2). Jesus is our role model.
2. Thinking. Disciples are transformed by the renewing of their minds to discern God's will (Rom. 12:2). As the mind of the disciple is renewed, the disciple will have the mind (and attitude) of Christ (Phil. 2:5; 4:8).
3. Character. The disciple will reflect the fruit of the Spirit (Gal. 5:22-23; Col. 3:12-17).

---

9 "Disciple."

4. Commitment. The disciple commits himself/herself to God's will, no matter the cost (Matt. 26:39; John 6:38).

This process requires believers to respond to the Holy Spirit's prompting to examine their thoughts, words, and actions and to compare them with the Word of God. In a real sense, the Word of God is the plumb line for life. Discipleship requires learning from others and studying the Word daily. It also means obeying the Word—to be doers of the Word. As disciples are transformed, they will be ready to testify of the reason for the hope that is within them (1 Pet. 3:15).

In addition to personal growth, every disciple must become a disciple maker by teaching others to be more like Christ. A mature disciple will be missional and have a passion from the love of God to spread the gospel to the people around them (their *oikos*) and to assist others in that missional task.

Discipleship requires the church to teach the ways of Christ. Traditionally, preaching has focused on adults. However, teaching has the potential of reaching every age level, as well as various stages of spiritual development. From the Word and early church history, teaching was a method used to keep the church alive for the next generation. It is the method for passing along the faith and heritage to each generation.

The Master Teacher

Some believe that the teaching expertise of Jesus was a divine gift from God (see Luke 2:52; 4:18). Obviously Jesus was anointed to teach, as many teachers of the Word still are. However, Jesus also acquired skills. If these skills were acquired, where did Jesus learn them?

Jesus was born into a devout Jewish home. Joseph and Mary made available the best education for Jesus that their circumstances would allow. Young Jesus was exposed in his home to the rituals and feasts required by the scriptural Law. Luke 2:21-39 tells of Jesus' circumcision and consecration. Luke tells of Jesus' going at the age of 12 with his parents to the Passover celebration in Jerusalem. There, as we learn in Luke 2:46-48, though his parents were unaware he had stayed behind when they left for home, Jesus remained "in the temple courts, sitting among the teachers, listening to them and asking them questions. Everyone who heard him was amazed at his understanding and his answers." And "when his parents saw him, they were astonished."

The young Jesus received the basic synagogue education. In the synagogue school and at home, he was taught to read and write. He learned of Moses, the prophets, and the other great leaders of Israel. He learned Hebrew poetry and proverbs. He was taught the history of the Jewish people during what we know today as the intertestamental period. Many scholars are certain that his adoptive father Joseph taught Jesus the family trade of carpentry (see Mark 6:3). Scripture shows that Jesus had particular teaching roles during his ministry. Jesus was the master teacher. Of all the many titles used for Jesus in the Gospels, the one most frequently used was Teacher. This title occurs 43 times in the NIV, and the particular title *Rabbi* occurs 14 times:

1. "Teacher" = 43 times in the NIV
   Matthew = 10 times
   Mark = 12 times
   Luke = 14 times
   John = 7 times

2. "*Rabbi*" = 14 times
   Matthew = 2 times
   Mark = 4 times
   Luke = none
   John = 8 times

   Jesus most likely did not receive the formal schooling expected of a rabbi. Nevertheless, Jesus taught in the synagogues: "On the Sabbath day he went into the synagogue, as was his custom" (Luke 4:16). He was found asking and answering questions regarding the Law (Matt. 15:1-9). Jesus gathered disciples to himself just like other rabbis (Matt. 4:18; Mark 1:16-20; 3:13-19; John 1:35-51; 1 Cor. 15:5).

3. "*Prophet*"—In this role as a moral messenger, Jesus sometimes illustrated his message with an object lesson:
   - Matthew 21:11: "The crowds answered, 'This is Jesus, the prophet from Nazareth in Galilee.'"
   - Mark 11:15-18: "On reaching Jerusalem, Jesus entered the

temple courts and began driving out those who were buying and selling there. He overturned the tables of the money changers and the benches of those selling doves, and would not allow anyone to carry merchandise through the temple courts. And as he taught them, he said, 'Is it not written: "My house will be called a house of prayer for all nations"? But you have made it a den of robbers.' The chief priests and the teachers of the law heard this and began looking for a way to kill him, for they feared him, because the whole crowd was amazed at his teaching."

- Luke 19:45-47: "When Jesus entered the temple courts, he began to drive out those who were selling. 'It is written,' he said to them, "'My house will be a house of prayer"; but you have made it "a den of robbers."' Every day he was teaching at the temple. But the chief priests, the teachers of the law and the leaders among the people were trying to kill him. Yet they could not find any way to do it, because all the people hung on his words."

- Mark 6:4: Jesus referred to himself as a prophet when he said, "A prophet is not without honor except in his own town, among his relatives and in his own home."[10]

4. "*Sage*"—a wise man. References: Luke 11:31; Matthew 12:38-42. Ordinary rabbis merely repeated what they had been taught. Jesus taught as "one who had authority." Robert Stain expounds: "The parallel between Jesus and Solomon is best understood as follows: Jesus is greater than Solomon because even as the wisdom of Solomon was renowned throughout the world, so the wisdom of Jesus is greater still. Something greater than Solomon is present because the kingdom of God has come and its bearer possesses greater wisdom than Solomon. Jesus is thus the ultimate wise man and his wisdom excels all others."[11]

When Jesus taught, his school was unstructured. He taught wherever people were willing to listen and learn: (1) on a mountainside (Matt. 5:1), (2) sitting in a boat along the seaside (Matt. 13:1), (3) in the countryside (Luke 9:10-12), and (4) in Jerusalem (Mark 11:17). Jesus had many disciples, not

---

10   See also Mark 8:27-30; Luke 7:16, 39.
11   Robert Stain, *The Method and Message of Jesus' Teachings*, 3.

only the Twelve. Jesus taught anyone who wanted to learn. He taught people from all walks of life and levels of society:

- He taught Nicodemus, a member of the Jewish ruling council (John 3).
- He taught a Samaritan woman, who was a social outcast (John 4).
- Jesus encouraged women to learn; for example, Mary and Martha, the sisters of Lazarus (Luke 10:38-42).
- He taught individuals like Zacchaeus, the tax collector (Luke 19).
- He taught crowds of thousands (Matt. 5).

Luke tells us that Jesus' traveling school was composed of all types of people and included both men and women (Luke 8:1-3): "Jesus traveled about from one town and village to another, proclaiming the good news of the kingdom of God. The Twelve were with Him, and also some women who had been cured of evil spirits and diseases: Mary (called Magdalene) from whom seven demons had come out; Joanna the wife of Chuza, the manager of Herod's household; Susanna; and many others. These women were helping to support them out of their own means."

Contextualization for Culture

Jesus is the perfect role model as the Master Teacher. To make disciples of the people in the new church's context, church planters will have to contextualize their teaching methods and ministries for the various cultures, ages, and individual learning styles. The new church will be in a specific culture and society. The people of that culture have been enculturated to learn in a specific way. As a result, to make mature disciples, the church planter cannot simply teach as in the planter's home culture, unless the planter is from the same culture. As a result, the church planter will have to contextualize discipleship so that the new disciples grow to be like Christ in their culture. Although there are some foundational methods, one cannot teach people in Africa exactly the same as in the United States, Germany, or Japan. Again, the church planter will teach the people through incarnational living. The church planter will have to learn before being able to teach in another culture. By learning about the people of the culture, the church planter will learn to adapt to teach in culturally appropriate ways. The best way to learn is first to sit under other teachers in that culture.

Contextualization for Ages

In order to contextualize discipleship to the people we teach, the church planter should be aware of each age level. Each level has specific needs, desires, and hopes, and each level is at a different stage of development. Every local church must seriously consider each age group and minister to them. The discipleship ministries, also known as Christian education in many churches, must consider three major divisions in people's lives:

1. Childhood: Birth to age 11
2. Adolescence: ages 12-17[12]
3. Adulthood: age 18 and up

Discipleship of children is essential for any new church. According to George Barna in his book *Transforming Children into Spiritual Champions,*[13]

1. A person's moral foundations are generally in place by the time they reach age nine. Their fundamental perspectives on truth, integrity, meaning, justice, morality, and ethics are formed early in life. After age nine, most people simply refine their views as they age without large changes in what they learned.

2. A person's response to the meaning and personal value of Jesus Christ's life, death, and resurrection is usually determined before a person reaches age eighteen. In the U.S., the majority of people make a lasting determination about the personal significance of Christ's death and resurrection by age twelve.

3. A person's spiritual beliefs, in most cases, are irrevocably formed when they are pre-teens. An identical survey was given to adults and to thirteen year olds, which had identical belief perceptions of the nature of God, the existence of Satan, the reliability of the Bible, perceptions regarding the after-life, the holiness of Jesus Christ, the means of gaining God's favor, and the influence of spiritual forces in a person's life.

---

12   Not every culture has what Westerners refer to as "adolescence" or the teenage years. Oftentimes children begin to learn to do adult tasks at a very early age, guided by older siblings or parents or grandparents.

13   George Barna, *Transforming Children into Spiritual Champions: Why Children Should Be Your Church's #1 Priority.*

In essence, what you believe by the time you are thirteen is what you will die believing, unless you go through a life-changing experience, such as salvation. Most people's minds are made up, and they believe they know what they need to know spiritually by age thirteen.

4. More than four out of five church leaders had consistently been involved in the ministry to children for an extended period of years. Such leaders are pastors, church staff, and lay leaders. Therefore, the church leaders of the future are probably active in church discipleship today.

Statistics indicate that 85 percent of all people who are still not a Christian by the age of eighteen years never will be. Barna says 85 percent of Christians accept Christ by an age of fifteen years and under.[14] In light of the statistics, children and youth should be the heart of both evangelism and discipleship. This is an important age level, and the most influential in their developmental stage.

Church planting teams must develop a strategy to teach children and youth. There are basic steps to consider:

1. Pray.
2. Know the children: learning styles, stages of development, family situation, etc. Children will not care what you teach until they know how much you care.
3. Organize facilities to be age appropriate.
4. Acquire supplies: tools like toys, games, puppets, videos, clay, blocks, etc.
5. Develop a team of volunteers to teach according to the age group for which they are gifted.
6. Find training for yourself and for your volunteers.
7. Be open to change. The culture of youth is changing. Be creative, such as using puppets, clowns, drama, etc.
8. Get the children involved.

For youth ministry, it is best to divide youth into two categories: ages 13-15 and ages 16-19 (20- to 25-year-olds are usually considered young adults).

---

14 Ibid.

This may vary according to culture. Some youth workers feel very strongly that these age groups should remain separated, and others include all ages in their ministry. Teenagers need guidance to help them balance what they are learning with what they already know or accept to be true. Teenagers begin to reject the advice of their parents and other adults, and begin to accept the advice of other teenagers, even if that advice is not correct. Teenagers need guidance, which will help them develop reality from a Christian perspective.

The major task of the teenager is the formation of the secure ego identity that includes all of one's perceptions and feelings about self. Specific needs arise during this developmental period:

1. *Need to accept oneself as God's special creation.*
    Many young people are struggling with their physical bodies and appearance. They look in the mirror and worry that they do not measure up to the cultural norm. They are too small or too large; too tall or too short; their hair is too curly or not curly enough. The list could go on forever. Youth need to be affirmed that their worth as a person is not related to their physical capabilities or appearance.

2. *Need for balance in self-esteem.*
    Teenagers need to know that they individually have worth to God and that they are unique persons.

3. *Need for clear gender role definition.*
    Society works hard to distort legitimate biblical views regarding the roles of men and women. Many have falsely taught that the Bible strictly limits the roles of women. Teenagers have a right and a need for accurate teaching in this matter. Women were active in ministry in Bible times, and teenage girls need to be active in ministry today.

4. *Need for biblical guidance and human sexuality.*
    Teenagers need to be taught the biblical model for human sexuality and how abstinence before marriage protects them from the emotional trauma of sexual promiscuity, pain related to disease and death, and the heartache of unwanted pregnancy.

5. *Need to make appropriate and responsible decisions in the face of peer pressure.*
    Many Christian teenagers have a great deal of difficulty going against the flow of their peers when they make decisions. They need support to make the right decisions. They need Christian community.

6. *Need for an outlet to contribute to the life of the church.*
    Teenagers in church today are not interested in sitting and being entertained. They seek involvement in ministry. This may be found through teaching children, outdoor camps, worship, counseling with children, short-term mission trips, etc. The church should help teenagers discover their spiritual gifts and release them for ministry.

7. *Teenagers need to be affirmed in areas where their development is matching biblical patterns.*
    Teenagers need to be encouraged when they have proper attitudes and behaviors. They need to be positively reinforced when they display proper biblical patterns of living. There is a need for spiritual parents and mentors. Many teens come from dysfunctional families, and many parents, especially in the world, do not take the time with them or help them develop in godly ways.

When developing discipleship for youth, pray for guidance from the Holy Spirit for three things: people, resources, and facilities.

1. *People:* You cannot just hire a youth pastor and expect that person to answer all of your needs for youth. Many people need to get involved in youth ministry. The pastor must be willing to support the activities of the youth.
2. *Resources:* A successful youth program in any local church will have some costs. Children need craft materials to make things and be creative. Teenagers need pizza and soft drinks and fun trips from time to time to help establish relationships. They are worth the investment!
3. *Facilities:* It would be wonderful if every youth ministry had a building, but that is not always possible for a church plant. It is also very positive to hold youth meetings in your home or another locale to develop a more relaxed atmosphere, which can help teenagers feel more comfortable. The youth need their own space for certain gather-

ings.[15] It is also important to note that the church plant does not need all these things for dynamic ministry to take place. It is about love and passion for the youth. Further, the youth should also be with the adults as often as possible and be part of the church life.

It is the adults in the church who make decisions, such as what kind of a church it will be, whom to call as pastor, what to do with funds, which strategies to implement, what resources are needed and how to use them, how to minister to the community and reach out to the world. That reality is fairly universal among cultures.

The following are eight significant needs of most adults for discipleship:

1. *A personal relationship with Christ.* Never assume that someone is saved just because they attend church and are listening to what you are saying. Become actively involved in conversation and listen to them talk. Have a relationship with them.

2. *Fellowship.* An important aspect of ministry to adults is the development of new relationships with God's people. Again, the church plant needs to develop community.

3. *Healing.* Sin causes pain, and it cannot always be cured with one simple prayer. Sometimes this process will take years. We must be willing to commit ourselves to adults who need healing.

4. *Discipleship.* This is a lifelong process and involves all that a Christian does to grow in his or her faith. Adults need to learn and be trained to disciple others.

5. *Service.* Jesus taught his disciples for a three-year period, then sent them out to do ministry. We need to follow his example. Some of the adults will actually leave the church and start new ministries. This is healthy and should be encouraged. Unfortunately, some pastors fear this.

---

15   Again, this is not necessarily the case in all cultures. In some cultures, youth are expected to meet at the church building and their parents may even attend the youth meetings. Compartmentalizing is typically a Western church concept.

6. *Learning laboratory.* Adults need to be exposed to preaching, teaching, and spiritual concepts. During this phase, God's Word is taken from the head to the heart and applied to life in the real world.

7. *Worship.* Adults need to participate, not just become spectators. Worship needs to be a way of walking with God. We must learn to worship through music, through the Word, through testimony, through tithes and offerings, through raising our families, throughout our entire lives.

8. *Evangelism.* Adults need to tell other adults about Christ. The church planter cannot expect new disciples to know how to be a witness. They have to be equipped, empowered, and released. The new church is an equipping center for life and ministry.

Regarding discipleship of senior adults, one of the Ten Commandments (Ex. 20:12, the fifth commandment) says, "Honor your father and your mother, so that you may live long in the land the LORD your God is giving you." In many cultures, especially in Eastern cultures, it is important to show great respect to older people. That respect has diminished in the West. For example, thousands of senior citizens died in France during the heat wave of the summer of 2003 because nobody cared enough to check on them. The "golden years" of senior citizens should be spent enjoying their lives, perhaps traveling and visiting family and friends. Unfortunately, too many people did not put away enough money to travel and do the things they dreamed about all their lives. Many senior citizens stay at home and wait to die.

The church planter must consider discipleship of senior adults. However, senior adults also have much wisdom to share in a church plant. It is important to listen and release senior adults for ministry. Because many senior adults are retired, they have time and wisdom to benefit the new church. However, the church planter must also be aware of their concerns. Concerns of senior adults may include disease, physical ailments, caregiving (e.g., will someone have to take care of them in their old age?), abuse, nursing homes, losing a spouse or a child, family, death, crisis, grief, and loneliness. Ways to help senior citizens are to visit them, help them connect with their families and friends, and help them remember to celebrate life.

Learning Styles

Regardless of the culture and age, every individual has a particular learning style. Not all people learn in the same way. Therefore, the church planter must be aware of basic learning styles and adjust their teaching to include each one. According to Marlene LeFever, there are four basic learning styles:[16]

1. *Imaginative Learner*

    Imaginative learners are feeling people who get involved with others and learn best in settings that allow interpersonal relationships to develop. These curious, questioning learners learn by listening and sharing ideas. They see the broad overview or big picture much more easily than the small details. They learn by sensing, feeling, and watching. They can see all sides of the issues presented. Imaginative learners easily share from their past experience, providing a context for learning.

2. *Analytic Learner*

    Analytic learners learn by watching and listening. They expect a teacher to be the primary information giver, while they sit and carefully assess the value of the information presented. These are the students who learn in the way most teachers have traditionally taught, and so they are often considered the best learners. They are strategic planners, and they aim for perfection—the right answers, the "A" grades in school and in life. These learners want all the data before they make a decision.

    Analytic learners are often defined as the best students since they fit the teaching/learning methods traditionally used in Western education. They grow uncomfortable when a teacher veers from these methods. Exact and accurate in their thinking, they are mainly interested in "just the facts, nothing but the facts." Analytic learners do not like being divided into groups. Rather, they want the teacher to teach them in a lecture in class. Analytic learners need to learn something new in each lesson.

---

16   Marlene LeFever, *Learning Styles: Reaching Everyone God Gave You to Teach,* 20-21.

3. *Common Sense Learner*
    Common sense learners like to play with ideas to see if they are rational and workable. These students want to test theory in the real world, to apply what has been learned. They love to get the job done. They are hands-on people who, using their own ideas, can analyze problems and solve or fix them. Common sense learners, as the name suggests, excel when dealing with what is practical and of immediate importance to them. They learn best when learning is combined with doing. Common sense learners need to see if what they learned makes sense now.

4. *Dynamic Learner*
    Dynamic learners also enjoy action as part of the learning process. Rather than thinking projects through to their rational conclusion, dynamic learners excel in following hunches and sensing new directions and possibilities. These risk takers thrive on situations that call for flexibility and change and find real joy in starting something new, or putting their personal stamp of originality on an idea. Dynamic learners like to come up with an amazing array of ideas for fanning the flame of ministry in the church. Dynamic learners find creative ways to use what they have learned.

Everyone has a learning style. In fact, you may have a combination of styles. However, most people are strongest in a particular style. It can change with age and experience. By knowing your style, you can grow in other styles and not stay locked into one. If church planters know the learning styles of their disciples, it will help them not miss any learning style when teaching or leading.

There are other names for learning styles as well. Here are a few examples:

*   Visual Learners: they learn through seeing.
*   Auditory Learners: they learn through listening.
*   Tactile/Kinesthetic Learners: they learn through moving, doing, and touching.

Methods of Teaching

In all cultures, ages, and learning styles, effective teaching should encourage student participation and the sharing of knowledge and experience. There are many types of discipleship ministries that a church can establish to teach:

1. Small groups and home Bible studies
2. Sunday school
3. Children's church
4. Christian camps
5. Adult Bible class
6. Classes for singles or other specific groups

The method must make sense for the context. However, churches that rely on a Sunday message alone are not truly making disciples. The new church must also establish other methods and ministries to teach disciples. For children and youth, there are several methods to teach. For adults, small groups are especially effective when used appropriately for discipleship. In the next section, we will go deeper with small groups. Another method that was used by Jesus was mentoring, but it has been lost in contemporary culture. Disciples need mentors. Mentors help disciples learn from life examples, especially mistakes. The mentor works as a sage to teach the disciple from his/her own experiences. Of course, the church planter as pastor cannot possibly be a mentor to all the disciples in the church. Every disciple should be a mentor to another disciple, especially to younger disciples. The most effective mentors are the ones who have led the person to Christ. The relationship between mentor and disciple is critical. There must be trust, which may take time to develop.

Summary

There are many methods to teach new disciples, such as small groups, classes, and mentoring. There are so many that it is beyond the scope of this section and chapter to describe them all. Teaching methods must be contextualized for the culture, age, and learning style. However, discipleship is more than cognitive learning about biblical principles or religious tenets. Discipleship and equipping involve knowing, doing, and being (head, hands and heart). Like evangelism, discipleship must be a lifestyle. Discipleship happens as life happens in the new church. People are dynamic and become more like

Christ in many ways. Disciples are formed, informed and transformed. The church planter and his/her team have the responsibility to make sure that discipleship happens as Christ mandated us in the Great Commission. If the new church makes disciples in holistic ways, integrating knowing, doing, and being, the church will not only grow; it will be a community of mature, empowered, trained, wise, and passionate Christ followers ready to do their part in the life of the church and the mission of God.

V. MAKING LEADERS

Our work as church planters is not done when we have made disciples. We also want to make leaders for the church. Every new believer needs to become a disciple, or committed follower of Jesus Christ. Some of these disciples will eventually take on leadership roles in the emerging church. It is our role to help prepare these leaders.

We call this process of making leaders, mentoring. We will discuss this in depth in the next chapter. Suffice it to say in this chapter that we *disciple* new believers and we *mentor* emerging leaders.

Paul was mentored by Barnabas. Paul mentored Timothy and Silas. Barnabas mentored John Mark. Paul, Timothy, Silas and John Mark were already disciples of Christ with different degrees of maturity. Each needed to be mentored into a leader.

Paul speaks of the importance of making leaders in Ephesians 4. Some become apostolic missionaries, while others speak with a prophetic voice, and still others are pastors, evangelists and teachers. In 1 Cornthians 12, Paul speaks of the diversity of gifts among members/leaders for the edification of the church body. Paul points out that not everyone can be a head or a foot. A body would be incomplete if we each tried to be a single body part. Put all the body parts together and we have a completely functioning body. This is how the church should be as well. With gifted leaders, the church has the makings of everything it needs to be the church.

How do we help disciples to become leaders? One way is to do a gift assessment. There are many different assessments available. One which MNM has and promotes is "Discover Your Gifts." We have people fill out the questionnaire and it helps leaders to discover what their strong gifts and waiting gifts are so they can nurture these for the building up of the local body of Christ, the church.

As church planters, we can help them, then, to develop these gifts and to use these as they lead the church as elders, deacons, teachers, and so forth. Some of the characteristics of healthy leaders have been described in the chapter on the key commitments of a healthy church.

But our work is still not done. There is a sixth step for us to look at before we can say we have done our job in planting the church.

VI. REPRODUCTION AND MULTIPLICATION

When we plant a seed, it gives birth to a plant that in turn produces more seeds for birthing more plants. Human beings produce offspring who in turn produce their own sons and daughters. We call this reproduction.

Reproduction in the natural world is something we see also in the spiritual world. We are to reproduce ourselves in those who follow us. Paul, in his second letter to his disciple Timothy, wrote, "The things you have heard me say in the presence of many witnesses entrust to reliable men who will also be qualified to teach others" (2 Tim. 2:2). Paul taught Timothy, who in turn was to teach the same things to others.

In the same way in which individual disciples are expected to reproduce themselves in other disciples, churches are expected to reproduce themselves. A church that does not reproduce itself at least once is a *sterile church*. Sterility in the Old Testament was considered a curse.

Plants have a way of mutating because of the context in which they are planted. Depending on the composition of the soil—if it is acidic or alkaline—a flower may take on a different color from what it was expected to have. Plants become hardier if they grow under harsh conditions. Churches, likewise, should reflect the context in which they are being planted. This means that a daughter church may not look exactly like its parent. Its reproduction will give it a different "face" because of the people it is trying to reach.

The result is still reproduction, but that does not mean the daughter will look exactly like the parent.

With most plants, reproduction often includes multiplication, the reproduction of several plants at the same time. Take a dry dandelion. If you blow on the white, feathery seeds that take flight, these disperse and in turn will reproduce into many more dandelions. Ask anyone who has tried to eliminate dandelions from their yard! This is a prime example of the principle of multiplication.

We can also talk about churches multiplying. Churches should multiply and not just reproduce. If we were to plant a single church that planted a daughter church, which in turn planted another church, it can be encouraging to see churches being planted. Nevertheless, the process is slow. We would like to see a single church parent several churches over its lifetime. No two church plants may look the same, but they are still products of that parent church.

Church multiplication takes a concerted effort. We need to establish a multiplication DNA in the mother church. How can we do this? The pastor must constantly preach about the making of disciples and the forming of new churches. Potential church planters must be identified and trained and then released to plant a new church. A church's finances should take church planting seriously as an item in the budget. Members should be encouraged to become part of a new church plant. As Daniel Sánchez has pointed out, no church has ever closed due to "giving away" members to a church plant.[17] On the contrary, new people have come into that church as members catch the vision, become enthusiastic about church planting, and even begin witnessing to their neighbors.

---

17   Daniel Sánchez, *Starting Reproducing Congregations: A Guidebook for Contextual New Church Development.*

CONCLUSION

As we have noted, to plant a church strategically requires many steps, from doing demographic research to evangelizing the lost, to forming small groups, to making disciples who will contextually impact their community. But church planting does not end when we have seeded a new church. Reproduction and multiplication must occur so that the church of God continues from one generation to the next and exponentially across the nations.

Questions

1. Why it is important for a church planter to do a demographic study of the proposed community?

2. What would be some traditional gathering places for people where a church planter could observe and begin to develop relationships?

3. What is an *oikos*? Who are these people in your life?

4. How can you connect with unbelievers?

5. What is third-space evangelism? What would you do for third-space evangelism?

6. What are the two ground rules that must exist in a small group in order for it to be successful?

7. What are several kinds of questions the leader can ask?

8. For us, a small group does inductive Bible study. What does it mean to do an inductive study?

9. Name several different personalities we might find in a small group. Add your own examples if you can think of more.

10. What is a disciple? What is Christian discipleship?

11. Why is it important to contextualize to the culture?

12. How can we help emerging leaders to discover their gift or gifts?

13. What do you think are your gifts? Have these been confirmed by others in the church?

14. What is the difference between *reproduction* and *multiplication*?

15. How can a church develop a multiplication mentality?

12 MENTORING THE CHURCH PLANTER

Gary Teja

Introduction

Mentoring has been, and continues to be, a primary vehicle for the development of men and women by contact with more experienced practitioners, through the transmission of knowledge, the passing on of needed skills, and the sharing of moral and ethical codes. But what about mentoring in the church planting context?

In this chapter, we will attempt to put flesh on the skeleton of what we call mentoring. We will explain what mentoring is *not*. We will move on to defining the church planter as an adult learner. We will also look at the mentoring relationship. We will conclude this chapter with the nuts and bolts of mentoring a church planter.[1]

---

1 The contents of this chapter are adapted from the book *Masterful Mentoring* by James Osterhouse and Gary Teja, available in digital format from Multiplication Network Ministries (www.multiplicationnetwork.com). Additional help can be found in this ebook, such as questions to ask a church planter and a sample mentor's log.

Definitions

We first need to define words such as *mentoring, mentor, mentee, mentoring relationships,* and *spiritual mentoring.* This will then allow us to discuss what mentoring is not about.

Mentoring

As simple as we may think it is to define these terms, experts in the field of mentoring have stated that there is actually a lack of preciseness when talking about the activity we call mentoring. "Mentoring appears to mean one thing to development psychologists, another thing to business people, and a third thing in academic settings."[2] Another expert in the field, Breda Bova, cites ten different examples of definitions for mentoring![3]

For all intents and purposes, we will define or describe mentoring as the activity of helping another person to grow in their skills, character, and knowledge in any given area of life. This usually implies that one of the two persons is more experienced, more knowledgeable, and therefore has something worth transmitting to the (often younger) less experienced, less knowledgeable person. The delivery system for such "transmission" is what we are calling mentoring.

Since this is the hardest term in our list to define, we will leave it at that. The term will take on more solidity as we describe it in actual practice and as we define and describe the mentor.

Mentor

Entire books have been written about this one word. A beginning point is a definition given by Gordon Shea in 1999: "One who offers knowledge, insight, perspective, or wisdom that is helpful to another person in a relationship that goes beyond doing one's duty or fulfilling one's obligations."[4]

Mentors are also described as midwives "who assist other people in giving birth to new ideas, new skills, new metaphors, and new ways of being and

---

2   Sharan Merriam, "Mentors and Protégés: A Critical Review of the Literature," 161-73.
3   Breda Bova, "Mentoring as a Learning Experience for Adults."
4   Gordon Shea, *Making the Most of Being Mentored: Mentors Help. Mentees Do,* 3.

doing. They assist learners in giving birth to their own ideas, visions, and goals."[5]

Lest we always think, though, of a mentor as the expert with nothing to learn, we are brought back to reality by others who see the mentor as a co-learner, someone who also learns along the way. If you have ever tried your hand at mentoring, I am sure you have realized that you learned as much in the process as did the person you were mentoring. The mentor is not a master but a fellow traveler, fine-tuning his or her own skills and knowledge as he or she mentors the other person.[6]

The mentor has often been described also as a trailblazer, presenting several paths open to the person in any given situation. Life is full of choices, and several of them may be equally good. The mentor provides a life map and can therefore be called a guide or a scout. He or she may be a coach, allowing the other person to develop his or her skills at their own pace. A mentor has also been described as a lifeguard who throws out a lifeline, always available to listen when needed, acknowledging the feelings of the other person in his or her development. In line with this nautical theme, Sharon Parks says, "Good mentors help to anchor the promise of the future."[7]

Some have described the mentor as not only a map provider but also one who enables the other person to develop his or her own maps.[8] I can especially identify with Tim Elmore's definition of the mentor as "a people grower."[9] Far from treating another person as someone with a clean slate in which to pour one's knowledge and skills and experiences, the mentor sees the other person as an emerging plant to be watered and nurtured along the way, to take advantage of the nutrients around it, to soak up the warmth of the sun, and to turn that sun into life-giving chlorophyll.

A mentor inspires. One educator sums it up with these words: "We need to be around people who believe in us so that we can more fully believe in

---

5   Linda Vogel, "Reckoning with the Spiritual Lives of Adult Learners," 24.
6   Kathleen Taylor, et al., *Developing Adult Learners: Strategies for Teachers and Trainers*, 330.
7   Sharon Parks, *Big Questions, Worthy Dreams: Mentoring Young Adults in their Search for Meaning, Purpose, and Faith*, 128.
8   Laurent Daloz, *Effective Teaching and Mentoring: Realizing the Transformational Power of Adult Learning Experiences*, 226.
9   Tim Elmore, *Mentoring: How to Invest Your Life in Others*.

ourselves. This enduring belief in our own capabilities, more than anything else, is the gift that mentors give."[10]

What might the church of Jesus Christ look like if its pastors and leaders were mentors to those who felt called to plant new churches? What kind of a mentoring culture would emerge if leaders had the attitudes and qualities of a masterful mentor?

Mentee

The emphasis so far has been on the mentor of the church planter. Just as "it takes two to tango," it also takes two to make a mentoring relationship: a mentor and a mentee. We have chosen to be consistent in the use of the term *mentee*. The church planter is the mentee. What is a mentee? Unlike *mentor*, the word *mentee* does not have a long and prestigious history of usage. The term was not developed until 1978 when Daniel J. Levinson wrote a book ti-tled *The Seasons of a Man's Life.*[11] Levinson looked at life transitions, recogniz-ing that we go through stages in our adult development, and the importance of having someone there at the critical moments of transition. In our context, a mentee is the church planter who needs to be assisted as he develops the new church.

The church planter as a mentee is "someone who makes an effort to assess, internalize and use effectively the knowledge, skills, insights, perspectives, or wisdom offered . . . who seeks out such help and uses it appropriately for developmental purposes wherever needed."[12] The mentee is not a clone of someone else; rather, he or she is an individual who is helped along the way in order to develop his or her own uniqueness as a church planter.

Mentoring relationships

What occurs between a mentor and a mentee is a mentoring relationship. Shea defines a mentoring relationship as "a developmental, caring, sharing, and helping relationship where one person invests time, know-how, and effort in enhancing another person's growth, knowledge, and skills."[13]

---

10   Lou Tice, *Personal Coaching for Results: How to Mentor and Inspire Others to Amazing Growth,* 145.
11   Daniel Levinson, *The Seasons of a Man's Life.*
12   Shea, *Making the Most of Being Mentored,* 3.
13   Ibid.

Those who mentor church planters need to invest in them. It cannot be an infrequent relationship. Mentors need to be consistent in spending time with their church planter mentee if they are to help him or her develop their skills and know-how in church planting.

Spiritual mentoring—some biblical examples

In 1 and 2 Kings, the prophet Elijah spiritually mentored Elisha. Elisha became Elijah's servant, observing all that he did. Eventually Elisha succeeded Elijah as God's messenger (2 Kings 2:11-15). This passing of the office of prophet was symbolized through Elisha putting on the cloak of the old prophet. We can also see a mentoring relationship between Moses and his father-in-law Jethro. Likewise, Moses takes on Joshua as his mentee and prepares him to lead the people of Israel after his demise.

Jan McCormack, professor of mentoring at Denver Seminary, presents several other Old Testament examples of mentoring relationships: Jehosheba and Jehoiada with King Joash in 2 Kings 11:1-12:2; Eli to Samuel in 1 Samuel 3; Hilkiah to King Josiah in 2 Kings 22-23; as well as the well-known story of Naomi and Ruth in the book of Ruth.[14]

In the New Testament, we have the example of Paul of Tarsus who, upon his encounter with Christ, was mentored by Barnabas the Encourager. Acts 9:26-27 says, "When he came to Jerusalem, he tried to join the disciples, but they were all afraid of him, not believing that he really was a disciple. But *Barnabas took him and brought him to the apostles*. He told them how Saul on his journey had seen the Lord. . . ." This act of taking him and bringing him to the apostles was a mentoring action, a sponsoring of Paul, as mentors often do. Robert Clinton and Laura Raab, in their study of Barnabas, consider his mentoring role of both Paul and John Mark to have been of vital importance in the future expansion of Christianity in the early church.[15] As a good mentor, Barnabas knew when to disappear into the shadows. Fourteen years after Barnabas began mentoring Paul, Paul took over the leadership role (Gal. 2:1). Having learned well, Paul even criticized his former mentor's failings (Gal. 2:3-3:1).

---

14   Jan McCormack, *Building Institutional Mentoring Programs.*
15   Robert J. Clinton and Laura Raab, *Barnabas: Encouraging Exhorter: A Study in Mentoring*, 6-7.

The mentoring cycle did not end there, though. Paul now took on the task of mentoring young Timothy. In 1 Corinthians 4:17, Paul refers to Timothy as "my son;" in 2 Corinthians 1:1 as "our brother," in 1 Timothy 1:2 as "my true son," and in 2 Timothy 1:2 as "my dear son." In this mentoring relationship, Paul treated Timothy like a son in the flesh, and by the time he wrote Philippians 2:22, the mentor (Paul) was able to say of his mentee, "Timothy has proved himself." Part of Timothy's mentoring was to observe and to do what his mentor did. In 2 Timothy 2:2, Paul counsels Timothy, saying, "And the things you have heard me say in the presence of many witnesses entrust to reliable people who will also be qualified to teach others."

Some see Priscilla and Aquila's relationship with Apollos as a mentoring relationship also (see Acts 18:24-26). These serve as examples for a mentoring relationship for church planting.

What makes for a good mentor?

First, a good mentor is a good listener. Mentors have the temptation of sharing all of their learned wisdom with their mentee, much to the chagrin of that mentee. "Why would they ask me to be their mentor in the first place if they did not want my advice?" we might ask out loud. Nevertheless, it behooves us to listen more than we speak. An old Spanish proverb says that the Creator has given us two ears, two eyes, and one mouth. We should deduce from this that we ought to listen and observe twice as much as we speak. Someone once called this "assertive listening." Tice calls it "active listening." He explains, "Its primary purpose is to understand the meaning of the message from the speaker's point of view."[16] The mentor needs to be an empathetic listener, "to understand, not to critique, analyze, advise, or argue."[17] Laurent Daloz describes active listening as "actively engaging with the student's world and attempting to experience it from the inside."[18] In other words, we want to get into the mentee's head. We want to understand the situation from the mentee's point of view.

Also, listening is more than simply hearing words being spoken. Non-verbal communication—either by gestures or nods or actions—is just as im-

---

16 Tice, *Personal Coaching for Results.*
17 Ibid, 192.
18 Daloz, *Effective Teaching and Mentoring,* 215.

portant as the words being spoken. As a mentor, I need to be able to pick up on those nonverbal cues. What I'm hearing being spoken may not be what is really being said. What's below the surface may help me to understand the needs of the mentee much more than what he or she verbalizes to me.

Shea points out that a side effect of being a good listener is that the mentee takes ownership and becomes his or her own problem solver.[19] This is especially necessary for the church planter. They need someone to listen as they mentally and verbally work through a problem they are facing in church planting.

Second, a good mentor deals with the "just-in-time" moments in church planting. We are there to help a church planter in his or her development. We provide them with just-in-time mentoring. Further in the church planting process, they will one day outgrow us or their need for us. Until then, we have a role to play.

Third, good mentors are midwives. A midwife assists in giving birth to new life. A mentor/midwife does just that, assisting "other people in giving birth to new ideas, new skills, new metaphors, and new ways of being and doing. They assist learners in giving birth to their own ideas, visions, and goals."[20] A church plant is a new life, a birth. Mentors help the church planter to give birth to the new church.

Fourth, a good mentor helps a church planter see the options. Especially in problem solving, church planters sometimes need another person to help them see the options open to them. Shea sees the mentor as one who explores options, in which mentor and mentee brainstorm to see more choices, to be more creative in solving problems.[21] Church planters can be so close to an issue that they find themselves going down a dead-end street. They only see one option, if that. The synergy of speaking to another person is enough to help them begin to identify other options or alternatives.

Fifth, a good mentor is an inspirer. "We need to be around people who believe in us so that we can more fully believe in ourselves. This enduring belief in our own capabilities, more than anything else, is the gift that mentors

---

19   Shea, *Mentoring: Helping Employees Reach Their Potential*, 46-49.
20   Vogel, "Reckoning with the Spiritual Lives of Adult Learners," 24.
21   Shea, *Mentoring*.

give."[22] Church planters need those who believe in them, someone who can come alongside, especially in difficult moments, and say, "You're doing great! You are in God's will. God will see you through." Church planters receive enough criticism without the mentor adding to it.

Sixth, a good mentor is a critical thinker. Mentors need to model critical thinking for the mentees. This idea is reinforced by other specialists in the field of mentoring. The mentor facilitates critical thinking even, as we have seen, in the making of decisions by looking at the options. Part of critical thinking even involves the establishing of clear expectations in the mentoring relationship, modeling appropriate behavior, developing mutual respect, and knowing when to influence actions.[23]

Part of critical thinking may even be to challenge the church planter, especially when it appears he or she is going off in the wrong direction. This is not done by a simple negative statement; rather, it is accomplished by asking questions so that the church planter "discovers" for himself or herself that things are going awry.

Mentor behaviors to avoid

Shea, who has written volumes on the mentor and mentee in the business world, gives us a list of seven things to avoid.[24]

1. *Giving advice too freely.* This makes sense in light of the positive behavior of being an active listener. We can quickly shut down the lines of communication if we fail to listen and are quick to give advice.

2. *Criticizing.* Who likes criticism, especially when you have just shared a problem or a quandary you find yourself in? Criticism only adds fuel to the fire. Again, the best advice is to listen.

3. *Rescuing.* A church planter may want to be rescued, but will rescuing really solve the problem or help him or her in the long run? Again, a good mentor will not be quick to rescue. When Jesus' disciples found

---

22 Tice, *Personal Coaching for Results*, 145.
23 Kevin Johnston, "Why Mentoring Graduate Students Matters," 14.
24 Shea, *Mentoring*.

themselves in a situation where they were unable to cast out demons, they did not come back to Jesus expecting him to go cast out the demons. They came to him expecting him to give them some just-in-time teaching so that they in turn could go back out and accomplish the task.

4. *Sponsoring inappropriately.* Do we sometime put forth a mentee before he or she is ready? Do we sometimes try to move our mentees into positions of influence for which they do not have the training or the skills? We may need to ask ourselves what our motivation for doing this is. Is it self-inflating to sponsor even when it is inappropriate?

5. *Building barriers unnecessarily.* Sometimes we place barriers or stumbling blocks in the way of our mentees. I know of a pastor who delegates but then makes it impossible for the mentee to succeed. Unconsciously the pastor is afraid that the mentee will do a better job than he himself is doing. We make excuses why the mentee cannot possibly accomplish a task, and we go about doing everything possible to set him or her up for failure. Sometimes this is the result of jealousy, or even the consequence of our not wanting the mentoring relationship to end. If our mentee is not ready and able to function on his or her own, we will be able to continue getting our thrills from mentoring that person. Those who mentor church planters are not exempt from this failing.

6. *Ignoring the "why."* Much of what is said in a mentoring session has a "why" behind it. Why did you just say what you did? Why did you do what you did? To ignore the why is to miss the very essence of the moment.

7. *Discounting.* We discount what our mentee is able to do on his own. We make light of it, when we should really be applauding him or her for their accomplishments. Or we don't take seriously a problem that a church planter presents to us. We may have dealt with a similar problem ourselves at one time. It becomes easy for us, then, to minimize what the church planter is experiencing.

Elmore discusses "how to spot a toxic mentor."[25] These seven behaviors will certainly be found in a toxic mentor, and they will curtail the learning that could occur in the mentoring relationship before it even gets started.

What makes for a good mentee?

One might think that of the two people in a mentoring relationship, the mentor is the more important. In some ways the mentor is. But in other ways, both are equally important. There are behaviors that will make the church planter either a good mentee or a bad one.

The church planters themselves have a responsibility when it comes to the mentoring relationship. As Daloz has phrased it, "The trip belongs, after all, to the traveler, not the guide."[26] The church planter as an adult learner is "someone who makes an effort to assess, internalize and use effectively the knowledge, skills, insights, perspectives, or wisdom offered . . . who seeks out such help and uses it appropriately for developmental purposes wherever needed."[27] The first characteristic, then, of a good mentee is one who takes responsibility for his own learning. In my mentoring relationships, I usually leave it up to the mentee to contact me. In some cases, we set the next mentoring session when we are ready to conclude our meeting. In other cases, I leave it open-ended and ask the mentee to contact me when he is ready to meet again. In both cases, we work around the mentee's availability first. The church planter needs to schedule time with me. The mentoring session needs to be important enough to the church planter that he actually opens his calendar and looks for a time when we can meet. This makes sense when we think of the church planter as an adult learner. One of the characteristics of an adult learner is self-direction. He/she knows when and where to go for help. A good mentee determines in some respects his or her own needs or wants.

Second, a good church planter mentee is an active listener. I previously mentioned how this was important for the mentor. Shea calls the mentee to be an "assertive listener."[28] The church planter needs to hear what his or her mentor is saying, and then determine what to do with it.

---

25 Elmore, *Mentoring*, 59-61.
26 Daloz, *Effective Teaching and Mentoring*, 3.
27 Shea, *Making the Most of Being Mentored*, 3.
28 Ibid, 32.

Third, a good mentee is a proactive learner. Shea says that mentees need to choose "to develop and change themselves."[29] Humans are intrinsically motivated. There really is no such thing as extrinsic motivation. Try as we might, we cannot change anyone. "You can lead a horse to water, but you can't make him drink" is a true enough adage. With our church planters, we pray that they, under the influence of the Holy Spirit, will indeed change. We cannot change them. They must be proactive in wanting to change. In a survey conducted at Michigan State University, the proactive mentee/learner is described as one who must . . .

> Seek helpful feedback and demonstrate appreciation for the same.
> Not be afraid to ask for whatever one needs to grow.
> Never be afraid of asking questions.
> Actively participate in the relationship.
> Take advantage of the mentor's expertise and experience.[30]

Fourth, a good mentee is a lifelong learner. The church planter will not always have a mentor at his or her beck and call. Nevertheless, the planter needs to learn where to go when help is needed. This could be to a person, to a printed resource, to a website, and so on.

Fifth, a good mentee is transparent. Church planters will be open and frank with their mentors. They will not withhold vital information. A doctor can misdiagnose if a patient withholds vital information. A planter must be honest about deficiencies and needs and must communicate problems clearly. A mentor, like a doctor, can only help based on what information the mentor has at hand.

Let these five characteristics of a good mentee suffice for now. If a church planter as a mentee is responsible for his or her own learning, is an active listener, is a proactive learner, is a lifelong learner, and is transparent, then the mentoring relationship has a strong probability of being successful. He or she will gain the knowledge and skills and heart necessary to carry out his or her tasks in the church plant, empowered by the Holy Spirit.

---

29   Shea, *Mentoring*, 60.
30   Johnston, "Why Mentoring Graduate Students Matters," 15.

The mentoring relationship

"The things you have heard me say in the presence of many witnesses entrust to reliable men who will also be qualified to teach others" (2 Tim. 2:2). With these words, the apostle Paul, thinking about the future of the church after he was gone, instructs—even pleads?—with his mentee Timothy to share with other mentees the good news of the gospel in all of its dimensions. Paul realized his own mortality and his inability to share the gospel and the "full counsel of God" with future generations. He also realized that in order for this gospel to be proclaimed throughout the then-known world, this message had to be entrusted to others who, exponentially, would multiply those who hear. This was a lesson I wish I had learned early on in ministry.

What is the mentoring relationship like? It is being defined now as a transformational journey, with the mentor being described as a "trusted guide." "Like guides, we walk at times ahead of our students, at times beside them; at times, we follow their lead."[31] In this relationship both mentor and mentee benefit from the process. Both develop and grow. It is a relationship that is both transactional and transformational—both actively participate, and both are changed in the process. A person who agrees to mentor a church planter must recognize that even he can learn something in the process.

What makes for a healthy mentoring relationship? One mentor describes a healthy relationship as one that is "intentional, mutually demanding, and meaningful."[32] Bob Devries, retired professor at Calvin Theological Seminary, writes,

> Each party assigned to or entering the relationship must have a *commitment* both to the relationship and to the other person involved in this relationship. This commitment is evident by the amount of *intentionality* the person brings to the relationship, the intensity of *involvement*, and the level of *care* for the person or interest in the relationship that the party evidences. A healthy mentoring relationship has been described as a 'passionate and fertile relationship.[33]

---

31 Daloz, *Effective Teaching and Mentoring*, 244.
32 Parks, *Big Questions, Worthy Dreams*, 127.
33 Daloz, et al., *Common Fire: Lives of Commitment in a Complex World*, xxiv.

Another sees this relationship as a "developmental, caring, sharing, and helping relationship" in which the mentor "invests time, know-how, and effort in enhancing another person's growth, knowledge, and skills, and responds to critical needs in the life of that person."[34] We see repeatedly the idea of caring, of intentionality, of responding. Developing a mentoring relationship doesn't happen overnight, nor can it be sustained without commitment. A mentoring relationship ought not to be entered into lightly, if it is to be sustainable and healthy.

Father-and-son mentoring specialists Howard and William Hendricks, in *As Iron Sharpens Iron: Building Character in a Mentoring Relationship*, describe what amounts to a healthy mentoring relationship. Here are nine ways in which a mentor helps a mentee:[35]

1. by serving as a source of information
2. by providing wisdom
3. by promoting skills development and appropriate behaviors
4. by providing feedback
5. by coaching, preparing the mentee to succeed in life
6. by serving as a sounding board
7. by being available in times of personal need
8. by helping the mentee plan for his or her own growth
9. by "nurturing curiosity," showing possibilities, opening new doors, presenting options

Can you see yourself doing this in the life of another person? If so, you be may a candidate for a mentoring relationship.

Benefits of a mentoring relationship

As altruistic as we would want to be in going into a mentoring relationship, there must be some benefits to the mentor if he or she is to make the time commitment needed for a meaningful mentoring relationship to develop. One writer describes three benefits for both mentor and mentee: learning, growth, and development. When we mentor, we learn new skills and ideas.

---

34   Shea, *Mentoring*, 13.
35   Howard Hendricks and William Hendricks, *As Iron Sharpens Iron: Building Character in a Mentoring Relationship*, 158-60.

Our ability to mentor gets fine-tuned every time we do it. We begin to think more critically before responding, and we begin to analyze our techniques for teaching and sharing ideas. We grow personally from the relationship. We also grow professionally. We may even be forced to reexamine some of our past decisions in light of what is transpiring in the mentoring sessions. Given our ages, we are moving into Erikson's stage of generativity, in which we begin reproducing ourselves in others. Our self-worth is enhanced, and we have a positive feeling of passing something on to the next generation of leaders.

Tice writes, "In a vital, active, ongoing mentoring relationship, you may find your assumptions and beliefs challenged, your energy renewed, your mind doing fresh work with old ideas."[36]

Likewise, church planters being mentored learn new skills that will help them in planting a new church. They may learn the unwritten rules of the organization. They grow in self-confidence, in self-identity, in taking ownership for tasks that need to be performed. They may become aware of their own decision making skills. From a developmental standpoint, church planters eventually move on to autonomy or to another mentoring relationship. They begin to work independently or interdependently. They learn what a mentoring relationship is all about and one day—sooner or later—find themselves mentoring others. A mentoring culture begins to develop as mentees take up the cloak and repeat the process in others. Mentoring emerging leaders is crucial in a church plant.

Dynamics of a mentoring relationship

No two people enter into a relationship without being changed. What is at play here is the dynamics of a relationship. Lois Zachary gives a list of assumptions about the dynamics of a mentoring relationship.[37] For her, mentoring is a powerful growth experience for both. She calls it a process of engagement for both mentor and mentee. It requires reflection, preparation, and dedication. At its best, it focuses on the learner, the learning process, and the learning that occurs. At the same time, mentor and mentee are co-learners who both benefit and grow from the relationship.

---

36 Tice, *Personal Coaching for Results*, 149.
37 Lois Zachary, *The Mentor's Guide: Facilitating Effective Learning Relationships*.

There is a dynamic of facilitation in the mentoring relationship. The mentor is not a teacher in the traditional sense; he or she is more of a facilitator. If we want our church planters to become responsible for their own lives, and self-directed in their ministry, then we need to facilitate rather than dictate. Facilitation requires the mentor not to say, "This is what you have to do." Instead, the mentor asks, "So, what do you see as your next steps?" Facilitation is called "listening, empowering, coaching, challenging, teaching, collaborating, aiding, assisting, supporting, expediting, easing, simplifying, advancing, and encouraging."[38] "Listening . . . is a powerful intervention, perhaps the most powerful we have as mentors."[39] Both the mentor and the church planter must be good listeners.

What we find here, then, is a description of two people coming together in a relationship that can benefit both. The success of a mentoring relationship is very much dependent on both the mentor and the church planter. Coming to agreement regarding what the mentoring entails, when the two shall meet, what can be covered, how to maintain confidentiality, and listing exit points in the mentoring—all will stand the mentoring relationship in good stead.

A mentoring theoretical framework

A mentoring theoretical framework basically asks, "What makes for good mentoring?" This has changed over time. The best explanation of those changes is found in "Elements in the Learner-Centered Mentoring Paradigm" developed by Zachary.[40] The paradigm demonstrates that the mentee moves from being a passive person to an active participant. At the same time, the mentor moves from being an authoritative figure to a facilitator. The mentor works hard to create an environment that will promote learning. In the learning process, the relationship moves from being mentor-directed to having the mentee show greater responsibility for what happens in the relationship. No longer determined by specific time frames, the relationship is determined by set goals, a condition most adults appreciate. Rather than living through a single mentoring relationship, the mentee may experience several over the course of their lifetime. There are multiple settings for mentoring; not all of it has to be face-to-face. Mentoring is process-oriented, allowing for critical reflection, an ability that will last a lifetime.

---

38 Ibid, 23.
39 Daloz, *Effective Teaching and Mentoring*, 205.
40 Zachary, *The Mentor's Guide*.

Elements in the Learner-Centered Mentoring Paradigm[41]

Mentoring Element	Changing paradigm	Adult learning principle
Mentee role	From: Passive To: Active partner	Adults learn best when they are involved in diagnosing, planning, implementing, and evaluating their own learning
Mentor role	From: Authority To: Facilitator	The role of the facilitator is to create and maintain a supportive climate that promotes the conditions necessary for learning to take place.
Learning process	From: Mentor-directed, with mentor responsibile for mentee's learning To: Self-directed, with mentee responsible for own learning	Adult learners have a need to be self-directing.
Length of relationship	From: Calendar-focused To: Goal-determined	Readiness for learning increases when there is a specific need to know.
Mentoring relationship	From: One Life = one mentor = one mentee To: Multiple mentors over a lifetime and multiple models for mentoring: individual, group, peer models	Adult learners have an inherent need for immediacy of application
Setting	From: Face-to-face To: Multiple and varied venues and opportunities	Adult learners have an inherent need for immediacy of application.
Focus	From: Product oriented: knowledge transfer and acquisition To: Process oriented: Critical reflection and application	Adults respond best to learning when they are internally motivated to learn.

41   Ibid.

This paradigm relies heavily on the theory of adult learning, which will help any mentor in a church planting context to relate to the church planter and establish the climate for mentoring to occur.

Do's and Don't's of mentoring

Good mentoring does not "just happen," at least not good *formal* mentoring. It requires some training on the part of the mentor. It also requires understanding on the part of the church planter mentee as to his or her role. In fact, Gailbraith and Cohen write, "If adult . . . educators are going to be effective mentors and if adult learners are going to be effective mentees, then a *deliberate* effort must be made to acquire appropriate training."[42]

The mentor

We will discuss our list under two headings, (1) relational do's and don't's and (2) skill-related do's and don't's. Relational do's and don't's will cover the following action words: respect, value, trust, model, affirm, encourage, inspire, and pray. Skill-related do's and don't's will encompass these actions: listen, ask, clarify, draw out, have an agenda, give time, guide, review, resource, and provide perspective.

Relational do's and don't's
- Respect: Don't belittle.
  A mentor needs to respect his or her church planter, allowing that person to be honest and transparent without fear of being belittled. If you cannot respect your mentee for being honest with you, the mentoring relationship will be short-lived. Your attitude has a lot to do with this. If you consider yourself superior to your mentee or feel you have more to offer your mentee than he or she has to offer you in the relationship, you will have problems. Go into this relationship with a positive outlook regarding your church planter.

- Value: Don't devalue.
  We all like to be valued as persons. Being in a mentoring relationship does not mean that a mentor should lord it over the church planter, or that the mentor should point a finger at the mentee regarding all

---

42 Michael Galbraith and N. Cohen, "Issues and Challenges Confronting Mentoring," 91. Italics mine.

the possible areas of improvement. Rather, the mentor needs to value the mentee. Perhaps Paul's words to the Galatians are applicable here: "Serve one another humbly in love" (Gal. 5:13). The mentoring relationship ought to reflect a Christ-like love. Also, there is mutuality at play in a mentoring relationship. "Submit to one another out of reverence for Christ" (Eph. 5:21). Value each other. In fact, Paul exhorts the Roman believers, "Honor one another above yourselves" (Rom. 12:10).

- Trust.
"Trust God's ability, wisdom, and strength."[43] Jeanette Gray, in her book *Unleashing Women in the Church*, says, "Building and maintaining trusting relationships is hard work that never ends. It takes time and cannot be hurried. Building trust is a little like waiting for bamboo to sprout. You carefully tend it for years before it does. Over and over you prove you are an honest, faithful friend, a safe person. A person who truly rejoices and praises growth in others."[44]

- Model: Don't meddle.
Modeling for a mentee is paramount. If the mentee sees us modeling who we are as a servant of the Lord, this will speak volumes. At the same time, we need to avoid meddling into the mentee's affairs in areas where we have not been invited. When necessary, the mentee will eventually invite us if we are modeling Christ to them.

- Affirm: Don't condemn.
It is so easy for us to become judgmental. Paul says to the church, "Stop passing judgment on one another" (Rom. 14:13), rather, "accept one another . . . just as Christ accepted you" (Rom. 15:7). We can help our mentee more by affirming him or her than by being judgmental. When it is necessary to confront, we can do so still without a judgmental attitude. Affirm your church planter, then point out "in love" what needs to change. Or, better yet, ask him or her what needs to change. Paul says to the church in Ephesus, "Be kind and compassionate to one another, forgiving each other, just as in Christ God forgave you" (Eph. 4:32). Part of affirming is being empathetic.

---

43 Ibid.
44 Jeanette Finley Gray, *Unleashing Women in the Church*, 180.

We need to understand what the church planter is going through. We affirm their situation; we don't ignore it or downplay it.

- Encourage: Don't discourage.
  "Encourage one another and build each other up" (1 Thess. 5:11). All Christians are called to do this in order to establish community. It is vitally important in a mentoring relationship. Encourage this emerging leader, or he or she will soon become discouraged and become stunted in his or her spiritual and professional growth as a church planter.

- Inspire: Don't deflate.
  Closely linked with the need to encourage is the need to inspire and not to deflate. Help your church planters see a brighter future, a greater vision, a reachable goal. Tell them, "You can do it!" more often than you tell them, "Hmm, seems like an impossible task on your part." Children accomplish the seemingly impossible when someone urges them on. The same holds true for adults. Be your planter's inspirer. Pat them on the back as you give them a gentle nudge ahead. We all need people who believe in us. Be that person in someone's life.

- Pray: Don't patronize.
  Paul says to the Philippian Christians, "Value others above yourselves" (Phil. 2:3). Patronizing includes the tendency of considering ourselves better than others. When we are patronizing, we tend to be condescending or to treat another person in a condescending manner. If we pray, we are less apt to be patronizing. We seek the other person's good. We take his or her cares to the throne of grace. We demonstrate the love that Christ had for the church when he prayed the high priestly prayer in John 17. If anyone had reason to be patronizing, it was Jesus, yet his approach to his weak, oftentimes disappointing followers was to *pray for* them.

Skill-related do's and don't's
- Listen: Don't talk.
  We need to listen more than we talk. Most of us learn this the hard way over time. We have discussed this previously, calling it "active lis-

tening." Says Tice, "Its primary task [active listening] is to understand the meaning of the message from the speaker's point of view."[45] Daloz also says, "Listening . . . is a powerful intervention, perhaps the most powerful we have as mentors."[46] Listen to your church planter. He or she has something to say to you.

- Ask: Don't tell.

  How can we discern what a planter needs if we are only listening to ourselves talk? The truth is that you can usually better influence the direction a person takes by asking the right questions than by telling them what you think they should do. Self-discovery is part of the secret of good question asking. As a mentee discovers for himself or herself through a well-phrased question, the answer oftentimes becomes quite obvious.

- Clarify: Don't claim.

  By asking questions, you can clarify what it is the mentee needs. Otherwise, you may give a ready-made answer for the wrong situation, claiming wisdom that the mentee doesn't have. Likewise, be clear on what you want to say.

- Draw out: Don't pour in.

  This "do/don't" combo is similar to "Ask/Don't tell." Draw out from your mentee the information you need in order to help. Don't simply pour into your mentee. I am reminded of a drawing that shows a professor pouring all of his knowledge through a funnel into the supposedly empty skull of a student. Although it may seem the right thing to do, avoid it. Take the time necessary to draw the church planter out. Ask clarifying questions. Ask questions that challenge the mentee to think even more deeply and to respond again in different ways. Coax the church planter, in other words. Remember, the mentees are full of their own rich experiences. Make use of those experiences for further learning. Remember the words of Galbraith and Cohen: this is a journey of "self-discovery."[47]

---

45   Tice, *Personal Coaching for Results*, 189.
46   Daloz, *Mentor: Guiding the Journey of Adult Learners*, 205.
47   Galbraith and Cohen, "Issues and Challenges Confronting Mentoring," 6.

- Have an agenda.
  Agendas keep you on track. At the top of your mentoring session should be the concerns expressed by the church planter. You can also have items you feel are essential to cover. Flexibility is important in the session, since expressed concerns may take you down a path you had not intended to go as you thought about this meeting prior to sitting down with Planter Joe. The items you wanted to follow-up on from the previous session and the new ideas you wanted to share may not be as important to Joe as something that happened to him since you last met. An agenda, nonetheless, will give some structure to your meeting, even if you need to put it aside for an emergency teaching.

- Give time: Don't shortcut.
  A mentoring relationship takes time. We have emphasized that often in this book. Give the time necessary. Don't try to take shortcuts. For example, take the time to build a relationship. There can be no trust factor between mentor and mentee without a previously established relationship. Take time to establish the ground rules for the mentoring. This will avoid many problems in the future. Some issues the planter faces will not be resolved in a single mentoring session. Take the number of sessions necessary for resolution to occur. Some issues will recur over and over until the lesson is learned.

- Guide: Don't goad.
  Mentors are guides. We're not goading our mentees with a stick. We're not using a cattle prod charged with electricity. We're guiding, pointing a way, pulling back a curtain, opening a door. It is the mentee who needs to walk through, voluntarily and freely, responsible for his or her own decisions. "Assist other people in giving birth to new ideas, new skills, new metaphors, and new ways of being and doing."[48]

- Review: Don't fail to reinforce.
  Each time you get together with your planter, review past learning/growth. Reinforcement is a standard teaching tool that helps the mentee to develop a pattern, or to remember a concept, or to put something learned into practice. Review also adds continuity from

---

48   Vogel, "Reckoning with the Spiritual Lives of Adult Learners," 24.

one session to another. It demonstrates the value of previous meetings and previous discussions.

- Resource: Don't research.

  Let us not do our mentee's work. We should serve as a resource and point them to other resources, but we ought not to do the research for them. They are adult learners and capable of self-direction. What one researches on his or her own is much more valuable (and remembered over time) than what is handed to one on a platter. Remember what Daloz had to say? "The trip belongs, after all, to the traveler, not the guide."[49]

- Provide perspective: Don't give pat answers.

  Hendricks and Hendricks talk about "nurturing curiosity," showing possibilities, opening new doors, giving the mentee a peek at different perspectives and opportunities.[50] We can be helpful to our planters by opening to them other ways of seeing into an issue. This does not mean, though, that we provide pat answers. Far from it. We want our mentees to find the solution for themselves if at all possible. Pat answers are nothing more than trite or glib answers that serve no useful purpose. Most questions cannot be answered quickly and easily. Providing perspective, on the other hand, may clarify the issue, problem, or situation so that the mentee can discover a solution. Mentors usually come with years of experience. They can offer perspective and put a situation *into* perspective. There really is nothing new under the sun, so what may seem to a mentee to be an earth-shattering situation beyond resolution, many people have already faced before. Also, a mentor can keep the planter moving ahead when the mentee begins to go down a rabbit trail. The mentor keeps the mentee on track and helps the mentee to see what is important at the moment and what is not.

---

49 Daloz, *Mentor*, 33.
50 Hendricks and Hendricks, *As Iron Sharpens Iron*, 160.

The mentee

The mentee also has responsibilities in this mentoring relationship that must be fulfilled if the mentoring is to be successful. As the mentor, be sure to help the mentee understand their role in the mentoring relationship. This list of do's and don't's from the perspective of the mentee should help. This list will also be divided into relational and skill-related do's and don't's.

Relational do's and don't's

- Be transparent: Don't be opaque.
  Ask for help. Don't expect your mentor to guess what you need. The more transparent you are, the more your mentor can help. Your mentor will also be able to "customize" that help.
- Be open to suggestions: Don't be closed-minded.
  If you had all the answers, you would not be seeking the assistance of a mentor. Be open to suggestions, recommendations, looking at resources your mentor provides you. You may not agree with what your mentor suggests; at least follow through and then reflect critically.
- Be realistic: Don't expect miracles.
  Mentoring will not solve all your problems in planting a church, or make you into a star leader. Recognize the limitations of mentoring. Understand what your mentor can do for you. Be realistic when it comes to your expectations of your mentor. He or she is not a miracle worker. Your mentor is a guide at your side, not a wizard.
- Be your own person: Don't try to become a clone.
  You may feel that the greatest compliment you can pay your mentor is to become just like him or her. On the contrary, your mentor wants you to be/become your own person. You have your own personality, your own gift mix, your own strengths and weaknesses, your own knowledge base. Your mentor wants you to become all that *you* can be.
- Listen to the Spirit's leading: Don't ignore the message.
  Recognize that this is a spiritual experience. It is a mentoring relationship between you, your mentor, and God. Be open to what the Spirit of God may be saying to you through the interactions, through the readings, and through the applications from your sessions.

Skill-related do's and don'ts

- Listen assertively: Don't fail to hear what your mentor says.

  As an adult learner, you need to be an "assertive listener."[51] This is more than listening with a half-cocked ear; it is active listening, which requires concentration and effort, combined with critical reflection.

- Complete assignments: Don't be a procrastinator.

  Any tasks assigned to you by your mentor or initiated by you should be completed in a timely fashion and will serve as fodder for the next session. In order for your mentoring sessions to be productive, it is important for you to complete these tasks prior to the next meeting. This will also demonstrate to your mentor your commitment to the mentoring relationship.

- Do research: Don't expect handouts.

  As a mentee, expect to put some hard work into this relationship. Your mentor does not have to hand you everything on a platter. Your mentor may suggest that you read a book, listen to a tape, do some original searching of the web. Do it. This is part of self-discovery and demonstrates a proactive, self-direction on your part as an adult learner. Shea reminds us that in the mentoring relationship "Mentors help—mentees do!"[52]

- Be self-directed: Don't be dependent.

  Self-direction is an attribute of a successful adult learner. Gerald Grow says that an adult learner goes through four stages of self-direction: (1) dependent, not self-directed; (2) moderately self-directed, (3) intermediate level of self-direction, and (4) self-directed.[53] As a mentee, you will find yourself somewhere along this continuum. You will want to move from dependency to self-direction. You become responsible for your own learning, thriving in what Grow calls "an atmosphere of autonomy."[54]

- Take advantage of your mentor's gifts: Don't hold back.

  You have asked someone to be your mentor because of something you see in him or her. Take advantage of what this person can teach you. There may be things you will ignore, but you will also find a rich resource in this person. Enjoy your mentoring relationship to its fullest!

---

51   Shea, *Making the Most of Being Mentored*, 32.
52   Ibid, 11.
53   Gerald Grow, "Teaching Learners to be Self-Directed," 134-35.
54   Ibid.

CONCLUSION

Church planting can be a lonely enterprise. The church planter may be sent off with lots of prayer and best wishes, but when it comes to the actual church plant, he is often alone in the process of sowing the seed. Mentoring provides the church planter with a sounding board, someone who can walk alongside him, asking him strategic questions to keep him on target when it comes to his personal walk with God, the care of his family, and the ongoing busy-ness of ministry. Often a neglected element in church planting, mentoring may be the one factor between an effective church planter and a disillusioned one.

Questions

1. Describe in a short paragraph what mentoring is.

2. Define the word "mentor."

3. List at least 4 characteristics of a good mentor and explain why each is important.

4. Enumerate at least 3 characteristics of a toxic or bad mentor.

5. Define the word "mentee."

6. List at least 4 characteristics of a good mentee and explain why each is important.

7. List at least 3 things that make for a bad mentee.

8. Explain why the author says that mentoring needs to be relational.

9. List at least4 do's and don't's in mentoring and explain each one in a short sentence.

10. On a scale of 1 to 10 (10 being perfect), determine where you see yourself as a mentor .

MORE CHURCHES

A STRATEGY FOR THE PLANTING OF HEALTHY CHURCHES

Leaders are challenged to plant new churches with this proven strategy. Practical skills, biblical training, mentoring and follow-up form part of this intensive action/reflection model.

1	2	3	4	5
INTRODUCTION TO CHURCH PLANTING VISIONIZING WORKSHOP	**CHURCH PLANTER RETREAT**	**MENTOR TRAINING** SELECTION PROCESS	**CHURCH PLANTER MODULES** 12 REPORTS	**CELEBRATION** BIRTH CERTIFICATE OF THE NEW CHURCH

STRONGER CHURCHES

A PROCESS TO STRENGTHEN THE LOCAL CHURCH

Evaluative tools help assess the church's health and vitality, leading to strategic planning to enter into a preferred future. Then, the church is encouraged to plant a daughter congregation.

1	2	3	4	5
INTRODUCTION TO STRENGTHENING YOUR CHURCH WORKSHOP	**TAKE YOUR CHURCH'S PULSE**	**STRATEGIC PLANNING PROCESS**	**SMALL GROUP MINISTRY**	**REVITALIZATION** CHURCHES READY TO MULTIPLY
				TOOL BOX

Bibliography

Chapter 1— What Is Church Planting? Definition, Justification, And Objections

Garrison, David. *Church Planting Movements: How God is Redeeming a Lost World.* Monument, CO: WIGTake Resources, 2004.

Schaller, Lyle E. *44 Questions for Church Planters.* Nashville: Abingdon Press, 1991.

Wagner, Peter. *Church Planting for a Greater Harvest.* Ventura, CA: Regal Books, 1990.

Bibliography

Chapter 2— Why Multiply Healthy Churches? Biblical and Missiological Foundations

Bakke, Ray. *Misión Integral en la Ciudad.* Buenos Aires: Kairós, 2002.

Barth, Karl. "An Exegetical Study of Matt. 28:16-20" in *The Theology of Christian Mission* by G. H. Anderson. Nashville: Abingdon, 1961.

Barth, Karl. *Church Dogmatics.* Vol. 4.3.2. Edinburgh: T & T Clark, 1958.

Barth, Karl. *Credo: A Presentation of the Chief Problems of Dogmatics with Reference to the Apostles' Creed.* J. S. McNab, tr. New York: Scribners, 1936.

Bavinck, John H. *An Introduction to the Science of Missions.* Phillipsburg, NJ: Presbyterian and Reformed Publishing, 1960.

Berger, Peter. "Foreword" in *Tongues of Fire: The Explosion of Protestantism in Latin America* by David Martin. Oxford: Blackwell Publishers, 1990.

Berkhof, Hendrikus. *Christian Faith.* Grand Rapids: Eerdmans, 1979.

Blauw, Johannes. *The Missionary Nature of the Church: A Survey of the Biblical Theology of Mission.* Grand Rapids: Eerdmans, 1974.

Bosch, David. *Witness to the World: The Christian Mission in Theological Perspective.* Atlanta: John Knox, 1980.

Conn, Harvie. *Evangelism: Doing Justice and Preaching Grace.* Grand Rapids: Zondervan, 1982.

Costas, Orlando. *Christ Outside the Gate.* Maryknoll, NY: Orbis Books, 1982.

Costas, Orlando. *El Protestantismo en América Latina Hoy.* San Jose: IDEF, 1975.

Costas, Orlando. *The Church and Its Mission: A Shattering Critique from the Third World.* Chicago: Tyndale, 1974.

Costas, Orlando. *The Integrity of Mission: The Inner Life and Outreach of the Church.* New York: Harper & Row, 1979.

de Ridder, Richard. *Discipling the Nations.* Grand Rapids: Baker Books, 1975.

Driver, Juan. *Imágenes de una Iglesia en Misión: Hacia una Eclesiología Transformadora.* Guatemala: Clara Semilla, 1998.

Fernando, Ajith. "Grounding Our Reflections in Scripture: Biblical Trinitarianism and Mission," in *Global Missiology for the 21st Century: The Iguassu Dialogue* by William Taylor, ed. Grand Rapids: Baker Books, 2000.

Fuellenback, John. *The Kingdom of God: The Message of Jesus Today.*: Maryknoll, NY: Orbis Books, 1995.

Glasser, Arthur with Charles Van Engen, Dean S. Gilliland, and Shawn B. Redford. *Announcing the Kingdom.* Grand Rapids: Baker Books, 2003.

Gnanakan, Ken R. *Kingdom Concerns: A Biblical Exploration Towards a Theology of Mission.* Bangalore: Theological Book Trust, 1993.

Guder, Darrell L. *Ser Testigos de Jesucristo: La Misión de la Iglesia, Su Mensaje y Sus Mensajeros.* Buenos Aires: Kairós, 2000. Published in English as *Be My Witnesses.* Grand Rapids: Eerdmans, 1985.

Guder, Darrell L. *The Continuing Conversion of the Church.* Grand Rapids: Eerdmans, 2000.

Hedlund, Roger. *The Mission of the Church in the World: A Biblical Theology.* Grand Rapids: Baker Books, 1985.

Herron, Fred. *Expanding God's Kingdom Through Church Multiplying.* New York: Writer's Showcase, 2003.

Kaiser, Walter C., Jr. *Mission in the Old Testament: Israel as a Light to the Nations.* Grand Rapids: Baker Books, 2000.

Kittel, Gerhard and Gerhard Friedrich, eds. *Theological Dictionary of the New Testament: Abridged in One Volume.* Grand Rapids: Eerdmans, 1985.

Küng, Hans. *The Church.* London: Search Press, 1971.

Ladd, George E. *The Gospel of the Kingdom.* Grand Rapids: Eerdmans, 1959.

Ladd, George E. *The Presence of the Future.* Grand Rapids: Eerdmans, 1974.

Logan, Robert. *Beyond Church Growth: Action Plans for Developing Dynamic Church.* Grand Rapids: Baker Books, 1989.

Logan, Robert. "Church Reproduction: New Congregations Beyond Church Walls" in *Seeing Beyond Church Walls: Action Plans for Touching Your Community* by Steve Sjogren, ed. Loveland, CO: Group Publishing, 2002.

Malphurs, Aubrey. *Planting Growing Churches for the 21ˢᵗ Century: A Comprehensive Guide for New Churches and Those Desiring Renewal.* Grand Rapids: Baker Books, 2004.

McGavran, Donald, ed. *Understanding Church Growth.* Grand Rapids: Eerdmans, 1970.

Moltmann, Jürgen. *The Church in the Power of the Spirit.* New York: Harper and Row, 1977.

Montgomery, Helen Barrett. *The Bible and Mission.* Brattleboro, Vermont: The Central Committee on the Study of Foreign Missions, 1920. Edited and republished in 2002 in Pasadena by Shawn Redford.

Mora C., Fernando A. *Manual de Líderes de Células.* Los Teques, Caracas, Venezuela: self-published, 2000.

Murray, Stuart. *Church Multiplying: Laying Foundations.* London: Paternoster Press, 1998.

Nelson, Marlin. *Principles of Church Growth.* Bangalore: Theological Book Trust, 2001.

Nissen, Johannes. *New Testament and Mission.* New York: Peter Lang, 1999.

Nuñez, Emilio A. *Hacia una Misionlogía Evangélica Latinoamericana.* Miami: UNILIT, 1997.

Padilla, C. René, ed. *Bases Bíblicas de la Misión.* Grand Rapids: Eerdmans, 1998.

Padilla, C. René. *Mission Between the Times.* Grand Rapids: Eerdmans, 1985.

Padilla, C. René and Tetsunao Yamamori, eds. *La Iglesia Local Como Agente de Transformación: Una Eclesiología para la Misión Integral.* Buenos Aires: Kairós, 2003.

Ridderbos, Herman N. *The Coming of the Kingdom.* Phillipsburg, NJ: Presbyterian and Reformed Publishing, 1962.

Sánchez, Daniel R. with Ebbie C. Smith and Curtis E. Watke. *Starting Reproducing Congregations: A Guidebook for Contextual New Church Development.* Cumming, GA: Church Starting Network, 2001.

Schaff, Philip. *History of the Christian Church Vol. 1.* Grand Rapids: Eerdmans, 1950.

Senior, Donald and Carroll Stuhlmueller. *The Biblical Foundations for Mission*. Maryknoll, NY: Orbis Books, 1983.

Snaith, Norman. *The Distinctive Ideas of the Old Testament*. London: Epworth Press, 1944.

Snyder, Howard A. with Daniel V. Runyon. *Decoding the Church: Mapping the DNA of Christ's Body*. Grand Rapids: Baker Books, 2002.

Steuernagel, Valdir R. *Al Servicio del Reino en América Latina*. Monrovia, Liberia: Visión Mundial, 1991.

Steuernagel, Valdir R. *Obediencia Misionera y Práctica Histórica*. Grand Rapids: Eerdmans – Nueva Creación, 1996.

Stott, John. "The Living God is a Missionary God" in *Perspectives on the World Christian Movement: A Reader* by Ralph D. Winter and Steve Hawthorne, eds. So. Pasadena: WCL, 1981.

Strom, Mark. *The Symphony of the Scripture: Making Sense of the Bible's Many Themes*. Downers Grove, IL: InterVarsity Press, 1990.

Towns, Elmer and Douglas Porter. *Churches That Multiply: A Bible Study on Church Multiplying*. Kansas City: Beacon Hill Press, 2003.

Van Engen, Charles. *God's Missionary People: Rethinking the Purpose of the Local Congregation*. Grand Rapids: Baker, 1991. Translated into Spanish: *Pueblo Misionero de Dios*. Grand Rapids: Libros Desafío, 2004.

Van Engen, Charles. *Mission on the Way: Issues in Mission Theology*. Grand Rapids: Baker Books, 1996.

Van Engen, Charles. *The Growth of the True Church: An Analysis of the Ecclesiology of Church Growth Theory*. Amsterdam: Rodopi, 1981.

Van Engen, Charles, Dean Gilliland and Paul Pierson, eds. *The Good News of the Kingdom.* Maryknoll, NY: Orbis Books, 1993.

Van Rheenen, Gailyn. *Biblical Anchored Missions.* Austin: Firm Foundation, 1983.

Verkuyl, Johannes. *Contemporary Missiology.* Grand Rapids: Eerdmans, 1978.

von Rad, Gerhard. *Old Testament Theology Vol. 1.* New York: Harper, 1962.

Wagenveld, John. *Sembremos Iglesias Saludables: Un Acercamiento Bíblico y Práctico al Estudio de la Plantación de Iglesia.* Miami: FLET, 2005.

Wagner, C. Peter. *Your Church Can Grow.* Glendale, CA: Regal Books, 1980.

Wagner, C. Peter. *Church Multiplying for a Greater Harvest: A Comprehensive Guide.* Ventura, CA: Regal Books, 1990.

Wright, George Ernest. *The Old Testament Against Its Environment.* Chicago: Alec Allenson, 1955.

Bibliography

Chapter 3— Church Planting in the New Testament

Allen, Roland. *Missionary Methods, St. Paul's or Ours: A Study of the Church in the Four Provinces.* New York: Fleming H. Revell, 1913.

BAGD: Walter Bauer, William F. Arndt, Felix W. Gingrich, and Frederick W. Danker. *Greek-English Lexicon of the New Testament and Other Early Christian Literature.* 2nd ed. Chicago: University of Chicago Press, 1979.

Barrett, C.K. *A Commentary on the First Epistle to the Corinthians: Black's New Testament Commentary.* New York: Harper & Row, 1968.

Barrett, C.K. *Acts of the Apostles,* ICC. Edinburgh: T&T Clark, 1994.

BDAG: Walter Bauer, Frederick W. Danker, William F. Arndt, and Felix W. Gingrich. *Greek-English Lexicon of the New Testament and Other Early Christian Literature.* 3rd ed. Chicago: University of Chicago Press, 2000.

Blauw, Johannes. *The Missionary Nature of the Church: A Survey of the Biblical Theology of Mission.* London: Lutterworth, 1962.

Bock, Darrell L. *Acts: Baker Exegetical Commentary on the New Testament.* Grand Rapids: Baker Academic, 2007.

Bosch, David J. "The Scope of Mission." *International Review Mission* 73:289. 1984.

Bosch, David J. *Transforming Mission: Paradigm Shifts in Theology of Mission.* Maryknoll, NY: Orbis Books, 1991.

Bowers, W. Paul. "Fulfilling the Gospel: The Scope of the Pauline Mission." JETS 30. 1987.

Bowers, W. Paul. "Paul and Mission." EDWM. Ed. A Scott Moreau. Grand Rapids: Baker Books, 2000.

Clark, Andrew C. *Parallel Lives: The Relation of Paul to the Apostles in the Lucan Perspective.* Paternoster Biblical Monographs Vol. 4. Waynesboro, GA: Paternoster, 2001.

Coenen, Lothar and Allison A Trites. "Testimony, Witness." *The New International Dictionary of New Testament Theology.* Ed. Colin Brown. Grand Rapids: Regency Reference Library, 1986.

Conzelman, Hans. *1 Corinthians: A Commentary on the First Epistle to the Corinthians: Hermeneia: a Critical and Historical Commentary on the Bible.* Philadelphia: Fortress Press, 1975.

Craddock, Frank B. *Luke: Interpretation: A Bible Commentary for Teaching and Preaching.* Louisville: John Knox Press, 1990.

Cranfield, C.E.B. *A Critical and Exegetical Commentary on the Epistle to the Romans,* ICC. Edinburgh: T&T Clark, 1975-1979.

Cullmann, Oscar. *Peter: Disciple, Apostle, Martyr.* Trans. Floyd V. Filson. New York: Living Age Books, 1958.

Davies, W.D. and Dale C. Allison Jr. *A Critical and Exegetical Commentary on the Gospel According to Saint Matthew, ICC.* Edinburgh: T&T Clark, 1988.

Detwiler, David F. "Paul's Approach to the Great Commission in Acts 14:21-23." *BibSac* 152. 1995.

Hagner, Donald A. *World Biblical Commentary Volume 33A: Matthew1-13.* Dallas: World Books, 1993.

Hagner, Donald A *World Biblical Commentary Volume 33B: Matthew14-28.* Dallas: World Books, 1995.

Hahn, Ferdinand. *Mission in the New Testament: Studies in Biblical Theology, First*. Vol. 47. Napervile, IL: Alec R. Allenson, 1965.

Hesselgrave, David J. *Planting Churches Cross-Culturally: A Guide for Home and Foreign Missions*. Grand Rapids: Baker Book House, 1980.

Fitzmyer, Joseph A. *The Acts of the Apostles: A New Translation with Introduction and Commentary*. The Anchor Yale Bible Commentaries. New Haven, Conn: Yale University Press, 1998.

Fitzmyer, Joseph A. *The Gospel According to Luke I-IX Volume 28*. New York: Doubleday, 1970.

France, R.T. *The Gospel of Matthew*, NIGTC. Grand Rapids: Eerdmans, 2007.

Garrett, Robert. "The Gospels and Acts: Jesus the Missionary and His Missionary Followers." *Missiology*. Eds. John Mark Terry, Ebbie Smith, and Justice Anderson. Nashville: Broadman & Holman, 1998.

Gilliland, Dean. *Pauline Theology and Mission Practice*. Jos, Plateau State, Nigeria: Albishir Bookshops, 1983.

Grassi, Joseph A. *A World to Win: The Missionary Methods of Paul the Apostle*. Maryknoll, NY: Maryknoll Publications, 1965.

Green, Michael. *Evangelism in the Early Church*. Grand Rapids: Eerdmans, 1970.

Green, Michael. *Thirty Years That Changed the World: The Book of Acts for Today*. Grand Rapids: Eerdmans, 2002.

Gundry, Robert H. *Matthew: A Commentary on His Literary and Theological Art*. Grand Rapids: Eerdmans, 1982.

Kane, J. Herbert. *Christian Missions in Biblical Perspective*. Grand Rapids: Baker Book House, 1976.

Köstenberger, Andreas J., and Peter T. O'Brien. *Salvation to the Ends of the Earth: A Biblical Theology of Mission. New Studies in Biblical Theology, Vol. 11.* Downers Grove, IL: InterVarsity Press, 2001.

Köstenberger, Andreas J. *The Missions of Jesus and the Disciples According to the Fourth Gospel.* Grand Rapids: Eerdmans, 1998.

Machen, J. Gresham. *The Origin of Paul's Religion.* Grand Rapids: Eerdmans, 1947.

Marshall, Howard. "Luke's Portrait of the Pauline Mission." *The Gospel to the Nations: Perspectives on Paul's Mission.* Eds. Peter Bolt and Mark Thomspon. Downers Grove, IL: InterVarsity Press, 2000.

Marshall, Howard. *The Acts of the Apostles: An Introduction and Commentary,* TNTC. Grand Rapids: Eerdmans, 1980.

McGavran, Donald, ed. *Understanding Church Growth.* Grand Rapids: Eerdmans, 1970.

Moo, Douglas J. *The Epistle to the Romans,* NICNT. Grand Rapids: Eerdmans, 1996.

Morris, Leon. *The Gospel According to Matthew,* PNTC. Grand Rapids: Eerdmans, 1992.

Nolland, John. *The Gospel of Matthew,* NIGTC. Grand Rapids: Eerdmans, 2005.

Nolland, John. *World Biblical Commentary Volume 35B: Luke 9:21-18:34.* Dallas: Word Books, 1993.

Ott, Craig. "Churches Planted by the Apostle Paul in the Book of Acts." Course handout for "Global Church Planting" at Trinity Evangelical Divinity School.

Peters, George W. *A Biblical Theology of Missions.* Chicago: Moody Press, 1972.

Polhill, John B. *An Exegetical and Theological Exposition of Holy Scripture: Acts: The New American Commentary,* Vol. 26. Nashville: Broadman Press, 1992.

Rogers, Cleon L. "The Great Commission." *BibSac* 130. 1973.

Schnabel, Eckhard J. *Early Christian Mission.* Two volumes. Downers Grove, IL: InterVarsity Press, 2004.

Schreiner, Thomas R. *Paul, Apostle of God's Glory in Christ: A Pauline Theology.* Downers Grove, IL: InterVarsity Press, 2001.

Schreiner, Thomas R. *Romans,* BECNT. Grand Rapids: Baker Books, 1998.

Senior, Donald and Carroll Stuhlmueller. *The Biblical Foundations for Mission.* Maryknoll, NY: Orbis Books, 1983.

Squires, John T. *The Plan of God in Luke-Acts.* Society for New Testament Studies Monograph Series, Book 76. Cambridge: Cambridge University Press, 1993.

Stetzer, Ed. *Planting New Churches in a Postmodern Age.* Nashville: Broadman & Holman, 2003.

Wallace, Daniel B. *Greek Grammar Beyond the Basics.* Grand Rapids: Zondervan, 1996.

Wilkins, Michael J. *Discipleship in the Ancient World and Matthew's Gospel,* 2nd ed. Grand Rapids: Baker Books, 1995.

Bibliography

Chapter 4— Historical Highlights of Church Planting: Instruction & Information for Today

Aikman, David. *Jesus in Beijing: How Christianity Is Transforming China and Changing the Global Balance of Power.* Washington: Regnery Publishing, 2003.

Bjork, David. "The Future of Christianity in Western Europe." *Missiology: An International Review* XXXIV. 3. July 2006.

Chidester, David. *Christianity: A Global History.* New York: HarperCollins Publishers, 2000.

Clouse, Robert G., Richard V. Pierard, and Edwin M. Yamaugh, *The Story of the Church.* Singapore: Moody Press, 2002.

Collins, Michael and Matthew A. Price. *The Story of Christianity: 2,000 Years of Faith.* London: Dorling Kindersley, 1999.

Deddens, K. "Reformation and Mission." *Clarion.* Vol. 35, No. 13-16 and 22. 1987.

Dowley, Tim, ed. *Eerdmans Handbook to the History of Christianity.* Grand Rapids: Eerdmans, 1977.

Hirsch, Alan. *The Forgotten Ways: Reactivating the Missional Church.* Grand Rapids: Brazos Press, 2006.

Hulse, Erroll. "John Calvin and his Missionary Enterprise." *Reformation Today.* 1998. http://reformed-theology.org/html/issue04/calvin.htm

Jenkins, Philip. *The Lost History of Christianity: The Thousand-Year Golden Age of the Church in the Middle East, Africa and Asia—and How It Died.* New York: Harper-Collins Publishers, 2008.

Jenkins, Philip. *The Next Christendom: The Coming of Global Christianity*. New York: Oxford University Press, 2002.

Laurent, Bob. *Watchman Nee: Sufferer for China*. Uhrichsville, OH: Barbour Publishing, 1998.

Martin, David. *Tongues of Fire: The Explosion of Protestantism in Latin America*. Oxford: Blackwell Publishers, 1990.

McClung, Grant, ed. *Azusa Street and Beyond: 100 Years of Commentary on the Global Pentecostal, Charismatic Movement*. 2nd Ed. Gainesville, FL: Bridge-Logos, 2006.

Neill, Stephen. *A History of Christian Missions*. London: Penguin Books, 1991.

Ott, Craig. "Church Planting in the 21st Century: Seven Developments." *Extending God's Kingdom: Church Planting Yesterday, Today, Tomorrow*. Epilogue 2 in the EMQ monograph. Laurie Fortunak Nichols, A. Scott Moreau, and Gary R. Corwin, eds. Wheaton, IL: EMIS, 2011.

Payne, J. D. *Discovering Church Planting: An Introduction to the Whats, Whys, and Hows of Global Church Planting*. Downers Grove, IL: InterVarsity Press Books, 2009.

Rooy, Sidney H. *Lutero y La Misión: Teología y Práctica de la Misión en Martín Lutero*. St. Louis: Editorial Concordia, 2005.

Sundkler, Bengt and Christopher Steed. *A History of the Church in Africa*. Cambridge: University Press, 2000.

Synan, Vinson. *The Century of the Holy Spirit: 100 Years of Pentecostal and Charismatic Renewal*. Nashville: Thomas Nelson Publishers, 2001.

Tertullian. *Apologeticum*.

Tong, John. "The Church from 1949 to 1990." *The Catholic Church in Modern China: Perspectives.* Edmond Tan and Jean-Paul Wiest, eds. Maryknoll, NY: Orbis Books, 1993.

Wagner, C. Peter. *Third Wave of the Holy Spirit: Encountering the Power of Signs and Wonders Today.* Ann Arbor, MI: Servant Publications, 1988.

Bibliography

Chapter 5— Planting the Church: Historical Models

Adeleye, Gabriel with Kofi Acquah-Dadzie. *World Dictionary of Foreign Expressions: A Resource for Readers and Writers.* Wauconda, IL: Bolchazy-Carducci Publishers, Inc., 1999.

Anderson, Gerald. *Biographical Dictionary of Christian Missions.* Grand Rapids: Eerdmans, 1998.

Aquinas, Thomas. *Summa Theologica, First Part, Question 47.* 1947.

Benge, Janet and Geoff. *Sundar Singh: Footprints over the Mountains.* New York: YWAM Publishing, 2005.

Bosch, David. *Transforming Mission: Paradigm Shifts in Theology of Mission.* Maryknoll, NY: Orbis Books, 1993.

Brunner, Emil. *The Word and the World.* London: Student Christian Movement Press, 1931.

Escobar, Samuel. *The New Global Mission: The Gospel from Everywhere to Everyone.* Downers Grove, IL: InterVarsity Press, 2003.

Kingdon, Robert. *Geneva and the Coming Wars of Religion in France, 1555- 1563.* Geneva: Librairie Droz, 1956. Republished 2005.

Irvin, Dale and Scott W. Sunquist. *History of the World Christian Movement: Vol. II: Earliest Christianity to 1453,* Maryknoll, NY: Orbis Books, 2001.

Latourette, Kenneth Scott. *A History of the Expansion of Christianity.* Volumes I-VII. Grand Rapids: Zondervan, 1970.

Neill, Stephen. *History of Christian Missions.* New York: Penguin Books, 1964.

Newbigin, Lesslie. *The Gospel in a Pluralistic Society*. Grand Rapids: Eerdmans, 1989.

Rooy, Sidney H. *Lutero y La Misión: Teología y Práctica de la Misión en Martín Lutero*. St. Louis: Editorial Concordia, 2005.

Rooy, Sidney H. "La Pastoral de los Refugiados Franceses en Ginebra: 1546 – 1565." *Vox Evangelii, segunda serie, I.* Buenos Aires: ISEDET, 1984.

Singh, Sadhu. *Wisdom of the Sadhu: Teachings of Sundar Singh.* New York: Walden, 2014.

Winter, Ralph and Stephen Hawthorne, eds. *Perspectives on the World Christian Movement: A Reader, Third Edition.* Pasadena: William Carey Library Publishers, 1999.

Bibliography

Chapter 6— Who Should Plant Churches? Leadership in Church Planting

Descubriendo Mis Dones, based on *Descubra Sus Dones*. Grand Rapids: Libros Desafío, 1996.

Greenway, Roger. *¡Vayan! Y Hagan Discípulos*. San José, Costa Rica: IINEF, 2002.

Havighurst, Robert. *Development Tasks and Education*. Second edition. New York: David McKay, 1972.

Hunter, George. *Radical Outreach: Recovery of Apostolic Ministry and Evangelism*. Nashville: Abingdon Press, 2003.

Knowles, Malcolm. *The Adult Learner: A Neglected Species*. Houston: Gulf Publishing Company, 1984.

Malphurs, Aubrey. *Planting Growing Churches in the 21st Century: A Comprehensive Guide for New Churches and Those Desiring Renewal*. Grand Rapids: Baker Books, 2004.

McIntosh, Gary. *Biblical Church Growth: How You Can Work with God to Build a Faithful Church*. Grand Rapids: Baker Books, 2003.

Mims, Gene and Ramón Martínez. *Principios para el Crecimiento de la Iglesia*. Nashville: Convention Press, 1995.

Ogne, Steven and Thomas Nebel. *Capacitando a Líderes*. Grand Rapids: Libros Desafío, 1998.

Ridley, Charles and Robert Logan. *Training for Selection Interviewing*. Ft. Wayne, IN: ChurchSmart Resources, 1999.

Sánchez, Daniel, Ebbie C. Smith, and Curtis E. Watke. *Cómo Sembrar Iglesias en el Siglo XXI*. El Paso, TX: Casa Bautista de Publicaciones, 2001.

Stetzer, Ed. *Planting New Churches in a Postmodern Age*. Nashville: Broadman and Holman, 2003.

Thompson, J. Allen and Timothy Keller. *Redeemer Church Planting Manual*. Redeemer Presbyterian Church. New York: Redeemer City to City, 2002.

Wagner, C. Peter. *Church Planting for a Greater Harvest: A Comprehensive Guide*. Ventura, CA: Regal Books, 1990.

Wood, H. Stanley. "New Church Development for the 21st Century: Sharing Initial Research Finds and Survey Data Insights." A press communication by email from Dr. Wood. NCD@CTSnet.edu.

Bibliography

Chapter 7— Five Commitments of a Healthy Church

Blackaby, Henry, Richard Blackaby, and Claude King. *Experiencing God.* Nashville, Tennessee: Broadman & Holman Publishers, 1994.

Hall, John. *Urban Ministry Factors in Latin America.* Ann Arbor, MI: UMI Dissertation Information Service, 1992.

Hesselgrave, David J. *Planting Churches Cross-Culturally: North America and Beyond.* 2nd ed. Grand Rapids, MI: Baker Books, 2000.

Koster, Tim and John Wagenveld. *Take Your Church's Pulse.* Sauk Village, IL: Multiplication Network Ministries, 2014.

Shenk, David W. and Ervin R. Stutzman. *Creating Communities of the Kingdom: New Testament Models of Church Planting.* Scottdale, PA: Herald Press, 1988.

Van Gelder, Craig. *The Essence of the Church: A Community Created by the Spirit.* Grand Rapids: Baker Book House, 2000.

Bibliography

Chapter 8— Five Functions of a Healthy Church

Choung, James. "Big Story." *James Choung.* Accessed December 16, 2003. http://www.jameschoung.net/resources/big-story/

Easum, William M. *The Church Growth Handbook.* Nashville: Abingdon Press, 1990.

Hewett, James S. *Illustrations Unlimited.* Wheaton: Tyndale House Publishers, Inc, 1988.

Koster, Tim and John Wagenveld. *Take Your Church's Pulse.* Sauk Village, IL: Multiplication Network Ministries, 2014.

Moore, Ralph. *Starting a New Church: The Church Planter's Guide to Success.* Ventura, CA: Regal Books, 2002.

"Nairobi Statement on Worship and Culture." *Calvin Institute of Christian Worship.* Accessed December 4, 2014. http://worship.calvin.edu/resources/resource-library/nairobi-statement-on-worship-and-culture-full-text/

Scherer, James and Stephen Bevans. *New Directions in Mission and Evangelization.* Maryknoll, NY: Orbis Books, 1992.

Shaw, R. Daniel and Charles Van Engen. *Communicating God's Word in a Complex World.* Lanham, MD: Rowman & Littlefield Publishers, Inc., 2003.

Wagenveld, John. *Sembremos Iglesias Saludables: Un Acercamiento Bíblico y Práctico al Estudio de la Plantación de Iglesia.* Miami: FLET, 2005.

Bibliography

Chapter 9— Contextualization Issues

Allen, Roland. *Spontaneous Expansion of the Church*. Eugene, OR: Wipf & Stock Publishers, 1997.

Brislin, Richard. *Cross-Cultural Encounters: Face-to-Face Interactions*. New York: Pergamon Press, 1981.

Cole, Neil. *Organic Church: Growing Faith Where Life Happens*. San Francisco: Jossey-Bass, 2005.

Dietterich, Inagrace T. *Cultivating Missional Communities*. Eugene, OR: Wipf & Stock Publishers, 2006.

Guder, Darrell L. *The Continuing Conversion of the Church*. Grand Rapids: Eerdmans, 2000.

Guder, Darrell L. *The Incarnation and the Church's Witness*. Eugene, OR: Wipf & Stock Publishers, 1999.

Hall, Edward T. *Beyond Culture*. Garden City, NY: Anchor/Doubleday, 1976.

Hesselgrave, David J. and Edward Rommen. *Contextualization: Meanings, Methods, and Models*. Pasadena: William Carey Library, 1989.

Hesselgrave, David J. *Planting Churches Cross-Culturally: A Guide for Home and Foreign Missions*. 2nd ed. Grand Rapids: Baker Books, 1991.

Hiebert, Paul G. "Critical Contextualization." *Anthropological Insights for Missionaries*. Grand Rapids: Baker Book House, 1985.

Hodges, Nelvin. *The Indigenous Church*. Springfield, MO: Gospel Publishing House, 2002.

Hunsberger, George R. and Craig Van Gelder, eds. *Church Between Gospel & Culture: The Emerging Mission in North America.* Grand Rapids: Eerdmans, 1996.

Flanders, Christopher. "Fixing the Problem of Face." *Evangelical Missions Quarterly,* Vol. 45, No. 1. Jan. 2009.

Fujino, Gary. "Toward a Cross-Cultural Identity of Forgiveness." *Evangelical Missions Quarterly,* Vol. 45, No. 1. Jan. 2009.

Johns, Cheryl Bridges. *Pentecostal Formation: A Pedagogy Among the Oppressed.* Sheffield: Sheffield Academic Press, 1993.

Kraft, Charles H. with Marguerite Kraft. *Christianity in Culture: A Study in Biblical Theologizing in Cross-Cultural Perspective.* Maryknoll, NY: Orbis Books, 1979.

Lane, Patty. *A Beginner's Guide to Crossing Cultures.* Downers Grove, IL: InterVarsity Press, 2002.

Lanier, Sarah. *Foreign to Familiar: A Guide to Understanding Hot- and Cold-Climate Cultures.* Hagerstown, MD: McDougal Publishing, 2000.

Moreau, A. Scott, ed. "Syncretism." *Evangelical Dictionary of World Missions.* Grand Rapids: Baker Books, 2000.

Muller, Roland. *Honor and Shame: Unlocking the Door.* Bloomington, IN: Xlibris Corporation, 2000.

Nevius, John Livingston. *The Planting and Development of Missionary Churches.* Charleston, SC: Nabu Press, 2011.

Payne, J.D. *Discovering Church Planting: An Introduction to the Whats, Whys, and Hows of Global Church Planting.* Downers Grove, IL: InterVarsity Press, 2009.

Richardson, Don. *Peace Child.* Norwood, MA: Regal Press, 2005.

Stetzer, Ed. *Planting New Churches in a Postmodern Age.* Nashville: Broadman & Holman Publishers, 2003.

Sweet, Leonard. *Post-Modern Pilgrims: First Century Passion for the 21st Century World.* Nashville: B&H Publishing Group, 2000.

Tokunaga, Paul. "Introduction: Learning Our Names." *Following Jesus Without Dishonoring Your Parents.* Jeanette Yep, coordinator. Downers Grove, IL: InterVarsity Press, 1998.

Van Rheenen, Gailyn. *Communicating Christ in Animistic Contexts,* Pasadena, CA: William Carey Library, 1991.

Van Rheenen, Gailyn. "MR #17: Transplanted and Contextualized Churches." *Missiology.org.* http://www.missiology.org/?p=239. Accessed April 11, 2002.

Wurzel, Jaime S. and Nancy K. Fischman. *A Different Place: The Intercultural Classroom.* Newtonville, MA: Intercultural Resource Corporation, 1994.

Yep, Jeanette, coordinator. *Following Jesus Without Dishonoring Your Parents..* Downers Grove, IL: InterVarsity Press, 1998.

Bibliography

Chapter 10— Is There Another Way to Plant a Church? Alternative Models for Church Planting

Becker, Paul. *Dynamic Church Planting: A Complete Handbook*. Vista, CA: Multiplication Ministries, 1992.

Mannoia, Kevin. *Church Planting: The Next Generation*. Indianapolis: Light and Life Press, 1994.

Moore, Ralph. *Starting a New Church: The Church Planter's Guide to Success*. Ventura, CA: Regal Books, 2002.

Murray, Stuart, *Church Planting: Laying Foundations*, Scottsdale, AZ: Herald Press, 2001.

Steffen, Tom A. "Selecting a Church Planting Model That Works." *Missiology* 22.3. July 1994.

Wagner, C. Peter. *Church Planting for a Greater Harvest*. Ventura, CA: Regal Books, 1990.

Bibliography

Chapter 11— Steps in Church Planting

Barna, George. *Transforming Children into Spiritual Champions: Why Children Should Be Your Church's #1 Priority*. Ventura, CA: Regal Books, 2003.

Cole, Neil. *Organic Church: Growing Faith Where Life Happens*. San Francisco: Jossey-Bass, 2005.

"Disciple." *Dictionary.com*. www.dictionary.reference.com/browse/disciple?s=t

Fitch, David E. *The Great Giveaway: Reclaiming the Mission of the Church from Big Business, Parachurch Organizations, Psychotherapy, Consumer Capitalism, and Other Modern Maladies*. Grand Rapids: Baker Books, 2005.

Gibbs, Eddie. *In Name Only: Tackling the Problem of Nominal Christianity*. Pasadena, CA: Fuller Theological Seminary, 1994.

LeFever, Marlene. *Learning Styles: Reaching Everyone God Gave You to Teach*. Colorado Springs: David C. Cook Publishing, 1995.

Sánchez, Daniel R. with Ebbie C. Smith and Curtis E. Watke. *Starting Reproducing Congregations: A Guidebook for Contextual New Church Development*. Cumming, GA: Church Starting Network, 2001.

Stain, Robert. *The Method and Message of Jesus' Teachings*, revised edition. Louisville: Westminster John Knox Press, 1994.

Bibliography

Chapter 12— Mentoring the Church Planter

Bova, Breda Murphy. "Mentoring as a Learning Experience for Adults." *Journal of Teacher Education,* 35.3. May-June 1984.

Clinton, Robert J. and Laura Raab. *Barnabas: Encouraging Exhorter: A Study in Mentoring.* Altadena, CA: Barnabas Resources, 1985.

Daloz, Laurent. *Effective Teaching and Mentoring: Realizing the Transformational Power of Adult Learning Experiences.* San Francisco: Jossey-Bass Publishers, 1986.

Daloz, Laurent. *Mentor: Guiding the Journey of Adult Learners.* San Francisco: Jossey-Bass Inc., 1999.

Daloz, Laurent Parks, Sharon Daloz Parks, Cheryl H. Keen, and James P. Keen. *Common Fire: Lives of Commitment in a Complex World.* Boston: Beacon Press, 1996.

Elmore, Tim. *Mentoring: How to Invest Your Life in Others.* Indianapolis: Kingdom Building Ministries, 1995.

Galbraith, Michael and N. Cohen. "Issues and Challenges Confronting Mentoring." *New Directions for Adult and Continuing Education,* 66. Summer 1995.

Gray, Jeanette Finley. *Unleashing Women in the Church.* St. Charles, IL: ChurchSmart Resources, 2007.

Grow, Gerald. "Teaching Learners to be Self-Directed." *Adult Education Quarterly.* 41.3. 1999.

Hendricks, Howard and William Hendricks. *As Iron Sharpens Iron: Building Character in a Mentoring Relationship.* Chicago: Moody Press, 1999.

Johnston, Kevin. "Why Mentoring Graduate Students Matters." *The Graduate Post.* Spring 2002.

Levinson, Daniel. *The Seasons of a Man's Life.* New York: Random House Publishing, 1978.

McCormack, Jan. *Building Institutional Mentoring Programs.* Paper presented at the National Conference on Mentoring: Mentoring— Shaping People Who will Shape the World. Denver Seminary, Englewood, CO, 2002.

Merriam, Sharan. "Mentors and Protégés: A Critical Review of the Literature." *Adult Education Quarterly*, 33.3. Spring 1983.

Oosterhouse, James and Gary Teja. *Masterful Mentoring: The Role of Mentoring in the Local Church.* Sauk Village, IL: Multiplication Network Ministries, 2014.

Parks, Sharon Daloz. *Big Questions, Worthy Dreams: Mentoring Young Adults in their Search for Meaning, Purpose, and Faith.* First edition. San Francisco: Jossey-Bass Inc., 2000.

Shea, Gordon. *Making the Most of Being Mentored: Mentors Help. Mentees Do.* Menlo Park, CA: Crisp Publications, Inc., 1999.

Shea, Gordon. *Mentoring: Helping Employees Reach Their Potential.* New York: Amercan Management Association, 1994.

Taylor, Kathleen, Catherine Marienau, and Morris Fiddler. *Developing Adult Learners: Strategies for Teachers and Trainers.* San Francisco: Jossey-Bass Publishers, 2000.

Tice, Lou. *Personal Coaching for Results: How to Mentor and Inspire Others to Amazing Growth.* Nashville: Thomas Nelson Publishers, 1997.

Vogel, Linda. "Reckoning with the Spiritual Lives of Adult Learners." *New Directions for Adult and Continuing Education,* 85. Spring 2000.

Zachary, Lois. *The Mentor's Guide: Facilitating Effective Learning Relationships*. First edition. San Francisco, CA: Jossey-Bass Publishers, 2000.

CONTRIBUTORS TO THIS WRITING PROJECT

Todd Benkert

Todd A. Benkert is a church planter and pastor and has ministered in Indiana and Kentucky, USA. He currently serves as pastor of Harvest Baptist Fellowship in Indiana where he lives with his wife and five children. He is Assistant Professor of Global Studies for Liberty University Online.

His educational background includes a BM from Belmont University and an MDiv and PhD in Christian Missions from the Southern Baptist Theological Seminary. He has served in various denominational roles on the state and local level as an advocate for North American church planting and for local church participation in global missions. Todd is actively involved in the orphan care movement and is an adoptive and foster parent. He also works toward racial reconciliation and multi-ethnic ministry in northwest Indiana. He has been involved in several church plants in Indiana and has served in short term missions, training pastors in Asia and doing evangelistic work in North America.

Ken Davis

Ken Davis has more than 25 years of experience in planting cross-cultural churches. He presently serves as the director of church planting at Baptist Biblical Seminary in Clarks Summit, Pennsylvania. From there he directs Project Jerusalem, training church planters in theory and supervised practice. Ken is also co-founder of The School of Church Planting for Mid-Missions, a Baptist organization training over 300 church planters from different parts of the world. He is the son of missionaries in Guyana and for this reason has an interest in seeing cross-cultural churches planted. He holds a D. Min. in missiology from Trinity Evangelical Divinity School. He also co-authored a church planting textbook recently published. Ken has been married to his wife Sharon for over 35 years. Together they have four children.

Tim Koster

With over 25 years of experience as a pastor in the Christian Reformed denomination, Tim Koster brings a wealth of wisdom and knowledge as he serves as Multiplication Network Ministries' (MNM) Chairman of the Board at the time of this writing. He holds an MDiv from Calvin Theological Seminary and is co-author of *Take Your Church's Pulse,* a book that helps churches diagnose the health of their congregational life and mission. His tangible experience as a theologian and pastor has combined well with his gift of writing to contribute to this work. In addition to serving on MNM's Board since its beginning, Koster served on Chicago Christian Counseling Center's board for six years. He has pastored Emmanuel CRC in Sauk Village, Illinois, for the past twelve years. When not working, Koster enjoys fishing and spending time with his wife and four grown children.

Sidney Rooy

Sid Rooy served as a missionary of Christian Reformed World Missions on loan to the Reformed Church of Argentina as a pastor and also as professor of History and Missions at the Instituto Superior Evangélico de Estudios Teológicos (ISEDET) in Buenos Aires. He also collaborated with the Fraternidad Teológica Latinoamericana with a special interest in higher education and the training of leaders throughout the Latin American continent. Rooy holds a doctorate in Church History from the Free University of Amsterdam. Dr. Rooy, although retired from active ministry, is still widely respected as a church historian and author, as well as a coveted professor and lecturer.

Daniel Sánchez

Daniel R. Sánchez is Professor of Missions at Southwestern Baptist Theological Seminary, Director of the Scarborough Institute of Church Planting and Growth, Associate Dean in the Roy Fish School of Evangelism and Missions and President and CEO of Church Starting Network. Sánchez and his wife Carmen have three children. His educational experience includes a BA from Howard Payne University, an MDiv from Southwestern Baptist Theological Seminary, a DMin from Fuller Theological Seminary and a PhD from the Oxford Centre for Mission Studies, Oxford, England.

His ministry experience includes starting two churches in Texas, serving as a missionary in the Republic of Panama; Academic Dean, Panama Baptist Theological Seminary; Assistant Director, Home Mission Board; Evangelism Director, Baptist Convention of New York; State Missions Director, Baptist

Convention of New York; and Professor of Missions, Southwestern Seminary. Among his publications are: *Starting Reproducing Congregations*, 2001; *Sharing The Good News With Roman Catholic Friends*, 2003; *Gospel in the Rosary*, 2003; *Hispanic Realities Impacting America*, 2006; *Church Planting Movements in North America*, ed., 2006; *Bible Storying for Church Planting, 2008; Lifestory Conversations*, 2010; and *Worldview: Implications for Missionary Work, 2012*. Sánchez has taught in over 50 countries in Africa, Asia, Europe, Latin America and the Islands of the Pacific.

Gary Teja

Dr. Gary Teja is the main editor for this writing project. He has been in ministry for the past 46 years. He studied missions at Reformed Bible Institute (today Kuyper College). He earned a B.A. degree from Western Michigan University in Spanish with a minor in Latin American Studies, holds an M.A. degree from Wheaton College Graduate School in Missions and Intercultural Studies, and earned a PhD in adult learning and distance education from Michigan State University.

Dr. Teja worked with church plants in Western Michigan, ministered among Mexican migrants in Minnesota, and served in Nicaragua and Costa Rica as a church planting missionary for Christian Reformed World Missions. During that time, Dr. Teja also worked in Theological Education by Extension (TEE) in training new pastors, elders, and deacons for the emerging churches. He was also director of distance education for the Missiological Institute of the Americas in San Jose, Costa Rica. Back in the United States, Dr. Teja worked in curriculum development at CRC Publications, later served as the director of Hispanic ministry, and participated as a member of the team giving oversight for all new church plants in the U.S. and Canada for the denomination. Dr. Teja served as director of an online M.A. in church planting at Calvin Theological Seminary and as associate professor and academic dean of distance education at Kuyper College.

More recently, Dr. Teja served in various capacities at Bible League International: director of Eastern Europe, director of the Americas, and director of Muslim ministry development. In 2012, Dr. Teja joined Multiplication Network Ministries (MNM) as its first International Ministry Director.

Dr. Teja has written more than 10 autodidactic TEE textbooks, published a book on spiritual formation published by CLIE in Spain, and co-authored *Masterful Mentoring,* a book on mentoring that is available through MNM in ebook format. Dr. Teja's specialization has been in mentoring pastors and church planters over the course of his years in active ministry.

Charles Van Engen

Charles (Chuck) E. Van Engen is the Arthur F. Glasser Professor of Biblical Theology of Mission in the School of Intercultural Studies at Fuller Theological Seminary in Pasadena, California. As the son of Reformed Church in America (RCA) missionaries, he was born and grew up in Mexico. He and his wife Jean later returned to Chiapas as RCA missionaries to administer a theological education program in cooperation with the National Presbyterian Church of Mexico. Chuck and Jean founded a seminary and were involved in extension theological education, leadership formation, and training evangelists for the National Presbyterian Church of Mexico from 1973 to 1985. Both Chuck and Jean are graduates of Hope College in Holland, Michigan. Chuck holds a master of divinity degree from Fuller Theological Seminary and a doctoral degree from the Free University of Amsterdam.

He is the founding President and CEO of Latin American Christian Ministries that seeks to form a new generation of scholars, writers, and seminary professors for the churches and mission agencies of Latin America through the Latin American Doctoral Program in Theology, known in Latin America as PRODOLA. Among his publications are *The Growth of the True Church,* 1981; *God's Missionary People,*1991; *Mission on the Way,*1996; *God So Loves the City* with Jude Tiersma, 1994; *Evangelical Dictionary of World Missions,* edited with A. Scott Moreau and Harold Netland, 2000; *Announcing the Kingdom: The Story of God's Mission in the Bible* with Arthur Glasser, Dean Gilliland, and Shawn Redford, 2003; *Paradigm Shifts in Christian Witness* edited with Darrell Whiteman and Dudley Woodberry, 2008; and *You are My Witnesses,* 2009. He has offered lectures and taught at seminaries in many countries around the world.

John Wagenveld

John Wagenveld is the founder and Executive Director of Multiplication Network Ministries (MNM), an organization that provides modular training to thousands of church planters around the world. John co-edited this book with his mentor, Dr. Gary Teja. John grew up in Argentina, the son of missionary parents. He studied theology at Dordt College, Missions and Church Growth at Calvin Theological Seminary, and holds a Doctor of Ministry degree from Trinity Evangelical Divinity School.

John served for seven years as a church planter and professor in Puerto Rico for Christian Reformed World Missions. He authored a Spanish book on church development and edited another on church planting upon which this one is based. The Church Multiplication Training Center invited him to lead Church Planter Bootcamps as a volunteer. John then served in several positions at Bible League International. After serving as Executive Director of International Ministry where he led regional leaders with over 700 staff in Africa, Asia, Latin America, and Eastern Europe, John transitioned to give full-time leadership to MNM in 2010. The vision is to see a sustained and systematic church planter training ministry with low cost and high impact serving ten thousand church planters worldwide each year. John speaks Spanish and French and has traveled to over 90 countries. He lives in Chicago and in his free time plays soccer, rides bike with his wife Angela and spends time with his four children.

Blayne Waltrip

Dr. Blayne Waltrip is Assistant Professor of Global Mission and Church Development at the Pentecostal Theological Seminary (PTS) and is director of the Center for Global Education and Mission (cGEM). A native of California, he earned a Bachelor of Arts degree in International Business from California State University at Fullerton. After working several years in international business, Dr. Waltrip left his career to study at the Church of God Theological Seminary (now PTS) and graduated in 1999 with a Master of Arts degree in Discipleship and Christian Formation. He has been a missionary for several years in Europe. In France, he worked in youth ministry, evangelism, church planting and ministerial training. Dr. Waltrip and his wife taught four years at the European Theological Seminary in Kniebis, Germany.

Dr. Waltrip graduated in 2011 from Fuller Theological Seminary with a Ph.D. in Intercultural Studies. As Church of God missionaries, the Waltrips' global ministry is to teach and direct cGEM, which is a collaborative effort between PTS and Church of God World Missions. The mission of cGEM is the mobilization of leaders, missional pastors and church planters to multiply churches through global collaboration. In addition to teaching at PTS and Lee, the Waltrips teach adjunct at several COG schools around the world, including SEMISUD (South American Seminary) in Ecuador, ASCM (Asian Seminary of Christian Ministries) in the Philippines, ETS (European Theological Seminary) in Germany, and Discipleship College in Kenya. They also partner with the Global Coaching Network and Multiplication Network Ministries to mobilize pastors and church planters around the world. Dr. Waltrip speaks French, German, Spanish, Italian, and Portuguese.

Multiplication Network Ministries (MNM) envisions a healthy church representing the kingdom of God in every community. To do this, Christian leaders are trained and equipped to strengthen and multiply healthy churches.

multiplication network

more churches, stronger churches

If you would like to contact the authors, please write
www.multiplicationnetwork.org
or call 708-414-1050.
